AF773605

In this admirable collection, contributors probe the governance challenges and opportunities that are presented by the transition from Web2 to Web3, offering readers important insights about not only the governance of Web3 artefacts – NFTs, smart contracts, DAOs, and the like – but also about the interface between, on the one side, law and policy and, on the other, the latest online technologies that support decentralisation, co-production, and user-centricity.

Roger Brownsword, *Professor of Law, King's College London and Bournemouth University*

This remarkably informative and insightful volume offers lawyers and policymakers a thorough roadmap into the possible futures in which we will likely find ourselves in the age of Web3. As the learned contributors demonstrate, the existing knowledge in the field remains highly relevant for understanding and responding to novel issues. The sources of creativity and innovation, however, are nowadays increasingly more diversified and widely distributed across actors and places in the world.

Xin Dai, *Associate Professor and Vice Dean, Peking University Law School*

Web3 law and policy has evolved as quickly and diversely as the technological environment it seeks to govern. Featuring examples from multiple jurisdictions, this timely and comprehensive volume tackles a wide range of topics that are important to understanding this new environment. Whether you are into cryptoassets, cybersecurity, data regulation, the platform economy, online disputes or jurisdictional questions, this book will provide a one-stop reference for the changing legal landscape surrounding Web 3.0. Highly recommended!

Peter K. Yu, *University Distinguished Professor, Texas A&M University*

Web3 Governance

Focusing on four key aspects of Web3, the book explores metaverses, data governance, public and private law interfaces, and access to justice, presenting new research on the impact of data analytics on transactions within law, on regulatory activities, and on the practice of law.

Artificial intelligence (AI) and data analytics have played a key role in the development of Web3, transforming the governance of existing digital platforms and enabling the formation of new platforms. Web3 is increasingly used for commercial and social interactions and is predicted to be the future of the internet. As a blockchain-based web, Web3 provides a platform for cryptocurrencies, non-fungible tokens (NFTs), decentralised autonomous organisations, and decentralised finance. Web3 users can read, write, and even own their own version of the web, which has transformed the space for commerce and social interaction, but brings inherent risks. This book identifies the principles in law and policy which can be used as the basis for the development of Web3 activities and their regulation with a focus on security, scalability, and sustainability. Though digital platforms and underlying technologies have reshaped our daily lives and business practices, they have also caused numerous legal problems. The book considers the interaction of data analytics with well-established fields of study such as financial law, tax law, intellectual property, data protection, private international law, and internet law.

Addressing the current knowledge gap in the legal literature on Web3, including blockchain, AI, and data governance in commercial and social activities, it develops new baseline frameworks which will form the foundation for new research into data governance, FinTech, and RegTech, as well as social and market infrastructure, and will be essential reading for scholars in law, business studies, economics, public administration, and regulation.

Joseph Lee is a reader in corporate and financial law at the University of Manchester School of Law. He is founding programme director of Manchester Online LLM Master of Laws in International Commercial and Technology Law. He is author of the book *Crypto-Finance, Law and Regulation: Governing an Emerging Ecosystem* and editor of the book *Data Governance in AI, FinTech and RegTech*. He is a member of the LawTech Advisory Council of the Astana International Financial Centre and of the Manchester LawTech Initiative. Dr Lee has been principal investigator of research projects funded by the UKRI, British Academy, and British Council. He has held a number of visiting positions, including at KU Leuven and Tokyo University. He is also an attorney-at-law of New York State.

Jyh-An Lee is a Professor and the Executive Director of the Centre for Legal Innovation and Digital Society at the Chinese University of Hong Kong Faculty of Law. He has been featured on ABC News, BBC News, Bloomberg News, *Financial Times*, and *Fortune* as an expert on intellectual property and internet law. His works have been cited by the US Court of Appeals for the Fifth Circuit, the UK High Court of Justice, and the European Union (in a WTO dispute-settlement case).

Routledge Research in the Law of Emerging Technologies

Cryptocurrencies and Regulatory Challenge
Allan C. Hutchinson

Regulating Artificial Intelligence in Industry
Edited by Damian M. Bielicki

The Law of Global Digitality
Edited by Matthias C. Kettemann, Alexander Peukert and Indra Spiecker gen. Döhmann

Internet of Things and the Law
Legal Strategies for Consumer-Centric Smart Technologies
Guido Noto La Diega

Regulating the Metaverse
A Critical Assessment
Ignas Kalpokas and Julija Kalpokienė

The Regulation of Digital Technologies in the EU
Act-ification, GDPR Mimesis and EU Law Brutality at Play
Vagelis Papakonstantinou and Paul de Hert

Privacy, Data Protection and Data-driven Technologies
Edited by Martin Ebers and Karin Sein

Social Media, Criminal Law and Legality
Laura Higson-Bliss

Web3 Governance
Law and Policy
Edited by Joseph Lee and Jyh-An Lee

For more information about this series, please visit: https://www.routledge.com/Routledge-Research-in-the-Law-of-Emerging-Technologies/book-series/LAWTECHNOLOGY

Web3 Governance

Law and Policy

**Edited by Joseph Lee
and Jyh-An Lee**

Routledge
Taylor & Francis Group
LONDON AND NEW YORK

First published 2025
by Routledge
4 Park Square, Milton Park, Abingdon, Oxon OX14 4RN

and by Routledge
605 Third Avenue, New York, NY 10158

Routledge is an imprint of the Taylor & Francis Group, an informa business

© 2025 selection and editorial matter, Joseph Lee and Jyh-An Lee; individual chapters, the contributors

The right of Joseph Lee and Jyh-An Lee to be identified as the authors of the editorial material, and of the authors for their individual chapters, has been asserted in accordance with sections 77 and 78 of the Copyright, Designs and Patents Act 1988.

All rights reserved. No part of this book may be reprinted or reproduced or utilised in any form or by any electronic, mechanical, or other means, now known or hereafter invented, including photocopying and recording, or in any information storage or retrieval system, without permission in writing from the publishers.

Trademark notice: Product or corporate names may be trademarks or registered trademarks, and are used only for identification and explanation without intent to infringe.

British Library Cataloguing-in-Publication Data
A catalogue record for this book is available from the British Library

ISBN: 978-1-032-57191-1 (hbk)
ISBN: 978-1-032-61896-8 (pbk)
ISBN: 978-1-032-61897-5 (ebk)

DOI: 10.4324/9781032618975

Typeset in Times New Roman
by Apex CoVantage, LLC

Contents

Contributors

Songyin Bo earned her Ph.D. in laws from the Chinese University of Hong Kong (CUHK), specialising in intellectual property and dispute resolution studies in China. Dr. Bo received the Young Asian IP Scholar Award in January 2020 and actively presents in academic conferences worldwide. She holds attorney licenses in both the U.S. and China, and she practiced law in both countries before pursuing her doctoral studies, focusing on civil litigation, M&A, and IPOs.

Luke D. Graham is a lecturer in Public Law and Human Rights at the University of Manchester, U.K. He focuses, in particular, on economic, social, and cultural rights. He has published on the relationship between law, human rights, and poverty/destitution. This work engages the right to an adequate standard of living more broadly, and at the same time he has published more focused work on the right to continuous improvement of living conditions and the right to adequate clothing.

Rougang Li is a Ph.D. researcher at the University of Manchester, specialising in company law, with a focus on the application of blockchain in corporate governance and governance of blockchain-based organizations. He obtained his LLM from the University of Leeds and his LLB from Shanghai Jiao Tong University. He has passed the Bar exam in China and has prior experience working in a Chinese law firm on commercial law.

Jingwen Liu is a Ph.D. candidate at the CUHK Faculty of Law and a legal journalist at JURIST. She has been listed as a WIPO ADR Young Member since 2023. She is interested in intellectual property law, competition policy, data governance, and comparative legal study, with publications appearing in various academic journals. Prior to commencing her Ph.D. study, she was a practicing lawyer in the People's Republic of China specialising in trademark and brand protection.

Eliza Mik has joined the CUHK Faculty of Law in January 2021. Before joining academia, she worked in-house for a number of software and telecommunications companies in Australia, Poland, Malaysia, and the United Arab Emirates. She advised on software licensing, technology procurement, digital signatures, and e-commerce regulation. Her Ph.D. focused on the private law aspects of e-commerce and on general problems of transaction automation. From 2014, Eliza's research has centered on smart contracts and the use of artificial intelligence in transaction automation. Eliza has advised the World Bank, the Monetary Authority of Singapore, and the Hong Kong Applied Science and Technology Research Institute. At present, she is a member of the UNCITRAL Expert Group for the Digital Economy, a member of the Inclusive Global Legal Innovation Platform on ODR (iGLIP, Hong Kong), a Research Associate at the Tilburg Institute for Law, Society and Technology (TILT, Netherlands), and an Affiliate Researcher with the Centre for AI and Digital Ethics at the University of Melbourne (CAIDE, Australia).

Rachael Ntongho is a lecturer in Law at the University of Manchester. She specialises in corporate governance and commercial law. Her research is interdisciplinary combining law, economics, politics, and social theories in addressing regulatory challenges of corporate governance and the financial market. She is particularly interested in regulatory developments of corporate law of emerging markets.

Pinar Oruc is a lecturer in Commercial Law at the University of Manchester. Pinar has completed her Ph.D. on copyright law in Queen Mary University of London. She worked as a postdoctoral researcher in the University of Glasgow, UK Copyright and Creative Economy Centre (CREATe) on Horizon 2020 project 'ReCreating Europe: Rethinking digital copyright law for a culturally diverse, accessible, creative Europe'. She is a member of the Istanbul Bar Association.

Jianzhong Shi is a professor and PhD supervisor, Vice President of China University of Political Science and Law (CUPL). He is also the Director of the CUPL Data Law Lab, the Dean of the Institute for Data Law of CUPL, and the Director of CUPL Center for Competition Law. His research interests include Competition Law, Data Law, and Economic Law. In addition, Professor SHI Jianzhong serves as a member of the Expert Advisory Group of the Anti-monopoly and Unfair Competition Commission of the State Council.

Neerav Srivastava is a lecturer at Deakin Law School, Australia, specialising in law and technology, in particular digital platforms and artificial intelligence. He has published in reputable journals and been cited in court.

Dicky King Fung Tsang is an associate professor in the Faculty of Law at CUHK. His primary research interests include private international law and company law. He has published extensively in leading international journals and his works have been cited by several courts. Dr. Tsang completed his LL.B. and Postgraduate Certificate in Laws at the University of Hong Kong. Additionally, he holds degrees from Georgetown University (S.J.D.), Columbia University (LL.M., J.D.), and University College London (LL.M.).

Jingyi Wang is an assistant professor at the Faculty of Law, CUHK. She holds a Ph.D. from King's College London. Jingyi's research and teaching interests focus on comparative tax law and fiscal policy. Her recent work examines the taxation of cryptocurrency, taxation of the digitalised economy, and Chinese tax law reform. Her academic work has appeared in publications such as the *Singapore Journal of Legal Studies*, *British Tax Review*, *Australian Tax Forum*, *Hong Kong Law Journal*, and *Tax Notes International*.

Runhua Wang is an associate professor of law at the University of Science and Technology Beijing. Her research interests are in the areas of intellectual property, innovation policy and management, and law and technology. Her research employs empirical methods, law and economics theories, and comparative analyses. She has published in *Minnesota Law Review*, *American Business Law Journal*, *Technological Forecasting & Social Change*, etc. She received an LL.M. and J.S.D. from the University of Illinois College of Law.

Normann Witzleb is an associate professor of Law at CUHK, where he leads the Obligations Lab Asia of the Faculty of Law. He is also an adjunct associate professor of Law at Monash University, Australia. He has published widely on data protection and privacy law, the law of torts and remedies, as well as comparative law.

Abubakri Yekini is a Law lecturer at the University of Manchester, U.K. He earned his Ph.D. from the Centre for Private International Law, University of Aberdeen. Dr. Yekini was a visiting scholar at the Max Planck Institute Luxembourg for International, European, and Regulatory Procedural Law in 2019. He was also recently awarded the Schumann Fellowship for Young Scholars by the University of Munster, Germany, for 2021–2022. He is the author of *The Hague Judgments Convention and Commonwealth Model Law: A Pragmatic Perspective* (Hart Publishing, 2021).

Roadmap to Legal Implications of Web3

An Introduction

Joseph Lee and Jyh-An Lee

The Broader Picture and Structure of the Book

The internet has undergone significant transformations over the past three decades, progressing from the early 'read-only' Web1 to the interactive 'read-and-write' Web2, and is now entering the era of Web3 marked by decentralisation, user-centricity, and transparency. In Web3, users transition from passive consumers to active participants, contributors, and owners of the digital landscape. Essentially, in this Web3 space, participants enjoy greater autonomy to create their own 'society' and engage in transactions.

The transformative essence of Web3 lies in its principles of 'decentralisation' and 'disintermediation' that enable users to circumvent the centralised structure of the internet, typified by large tech companies controlling servers, data centres, and platforms. This paradigm shift extends beyond a mere technological progression rooted in blockchain, smart contracts, and artificial intelligence (AI). It signifies a wide-ranging movement with profound economic, social, and cultural implications spanning various industries, including but not limited to banking, finance, manufacturing, retail, and healthcare.

Amidst the continuous evolution of internet technologies, numerous legal and policy controversies persist, with Web3 introducing a host of new challenges for policymakers, courts, lawyers, and legal academics. Some of these challenges echo those experienced in the eras of Web1 and Web2, while others stand as unique in the history of the internet. The extent and form of Web3 remain uncertain. However, it is evident that efficient governance will need to be in place to address significant policy challenges. In a Web3 era, law can play an important role in mediating competing interests and values in the policy area while mitigating risks and addressing harms.

This book is dedicated to offering an extensive understanding of the legal and policy issues surrounding Web3. We adopt an approach that integrates lessons from past experiences with existing digital platforms, while also projecting potential challenges that may emerge with Web3, aiming to anticipate future governance issues. Leveraging existing knowledge in the field of internet laws and policies, our objective is to assess their relevance within the unique context of Web3.

DOI: 10.4324/9781032618975-1

Furthermore, we explore legal innovations and challenges that correspond to the advancements in Web3 technologies.

We examine the existing tools and regulations that are already in place to address policy issues, risks, and harms, as well as anticipate new issues that could arise from the emergence of Web3. By using the 'horizon scanning' approach, we seek to identify any discrepancies between our projections for the future and the current governance framework established for Web2. Taking a cross-disciplinary approach within the field of law, we identify these gaps with the aim of assisting policymakers, technology developers, and lawyers in forming a holistic view of the governance challenges presented by Web3. We envisage that with more robust legal frameworks and oversight, Web3 can more effectively contribute to the betterment of our society.

This book is structured into five interconnected parts. In Part A, non-fungible tokens (NFTs) and smart contracts are presented to highlight the challenges that Web3 introduces to two fundamental institutions: property and contract. These challenges spark new policy debates also in the domain of taxation within the Web3 environment. This part highlights the emergence of NFTs as a core element of Web3, reshaping digital ownership, creativity, and the notion of value. Additionally, blockchain stands out as the groundbreaking technology facilitating secure and transparent token transactions, alongside the automated execution of smart contracts.

Part B investigates the adaptive responses of business organisational structures to the Web3 landscape, addressing two key issues. The first paper explores the rise of decentralised autonomous organisations (DAOs) as a novel form of business organisation. The second one examines the adjustments made to corporate governance structure in response to the new risks associated with digital technologies and cybersecurity.

In Part C, the focus shifts onto the governance of data – the driving force behind the global economy and the foundation of Web3. It begins by using recent reforms in China's data-related laws to illustrate the unique legal nature of data and the resulting regulatory challenges. Additionally, international and comparative copyright law is employed as a lens to comprehend the legal risks associated with employing big data in AI technologies.

While Web3 is often described as trustless and permissionless, this does not eliminate disputes or legal liabilities. Moreover, despite reducing the need for intermediaries, various existing and emerging platforms, such as decentralised finance (DeFi) and decentralised exchanges (DEXs) platforms, play a crucial role in facilitating the Web3 economy. Part D addresses legal issues related to online disputes and legal responsibilities arising from the platform economy. This part analyses how liabilities are determined and disputes are resolved within the platform economy. It explores whether and to what extent platforms should be liable for harm resulting from increased user interactions. Using major Chinese platforms as examples, it illustrates how to incorporate the essence of Web3, particularly decentralised and user-centric decision-making, into online dispute resolution (ODR).

The increasing decentralisation brought about by Web3 is often in tension with the international order based on state sovereignty, leading to a series of transnational legal issues. Part E provides international and transnational views on Web3. Following the public international law perspective on access to the internet, it discusses private international law issues regarding cryptocurrency and online defamation.

Individual Chapters

The extensive adoption of NFTs across financial, gaming, and creative sectors has showcased the unparalleled potential of Web3. Runhua Wang, Jyh-An Lee, and Jingwen Liu shed light on the property and contractual attributes of NFTs. Through the analysis of a Chinese court decision concerning copyright and NFTs, they elucidate how misconceptions about these characteristics can result in undesirable application of the law. The authors contend that the legal classification of NFTs hinges on their technological features and the interoperability of the platform where they are stored.

The creations and transactions of NFTs and other cryptoassets on the blockchain introduce novel challenges related to taxation. Acknowledging the technical and economic characteristics of cryptocurrencies, tokens, and the metaverse, Jingyi Wang offers a comprehensive and forward-looking tax policy perspective within the context of Web3. The chapter also explores the tax considerations associated with DeFi, a significant subsector of Web3. Furthermore, it provides a comparative law outlook on major taxation approaches to Web3.

Smart contracts constitute a pivotal infrastructure for Web3, composed in code and stored on the blockchain to automate transactions. Despite the growing recognition of the advantages they bring to Web3, certain aspects are either exaggerated or misunderstood. Eliza Mik dispels several myths associated with smart contracts, clarifying that they are not contracts in a legal sense, and their presumed certainties and transparency are often overstated. Additionally, she highlights unresolved issues inherent in smart contracts, such as challenges related to immutability and the inadvertent execution of untrusted code.

DAOs function through rules encoded as computer programmes on a blockchain, embodying a fundamental aspect of Web3 due to their decentralised decision-making structure devoid of a central authority. Utilising a novel typology of DAOs, Joseph Lee and Rougang Li employ transaction cost, agency cost, and collective action theories to analyse the economic nature of DAOs. This chapter not only delineates the significant distinctions between DAOs and traditional business organisational forms but also investigates into the emerging legal issues surrounding DAOs, proposing potential solutions.

In addition to the establishment of new organisational forms through legislation, companies can manage risks associated with emerging technologies by addressing them within their internal governance structures. Many Web3 technologies, such as blockchain, are still relatively nascent and face various vulnerabilities like protocol hacks. Drawing from Resource Dependency Theory, Joseph Lee and Rachael Ntongho examine diverse governance mechanisms to tackle cybersecurity risks. These include setting expertise requirements for board members, acquiring insurance, designing the role of a chief cybersecurity officer, and having an audit committee. The chapter also considers the involvement of regulators in mitigating these risks.

Data plays a crucial role in economic growth, empowering organisations to make informed decisions and develop new products and services. In today's digital economy and Web3 ecosystem, the collection, analysis, and diverse applications of data offer significant profit opportunities. Jianzhong Shi elucidates the unique attributes of data and the resulting regulatory challenges. Drawing insights from recent Chinese data legislation and case law, especially the Anti-Unfair Competition Law and Anti-Monopoly Law, he advocates for a balanced policy approach to unleash the value of data while ensuring fair market competition.

Although data holds immense value, its unauthorised use can result in undesirable legal consequences. Pinar Oruc employs computer vision as an example to illustrate the legal risks faced by AI developers using unauthorised training data. The risk is particularly evident when the training data comprises copyrighted works owned by another party. This chapter explores possibilities for AI developers to be exempt from copyright infringement liability in both the United Kingdom and the European Union. It also provides a comparative perspective on the American and Japanese approaches to copyright limitations and exceptions for using unauthorised training data.

Web3 evolves in tandem with the platform economy, enabling extensive interactions among users. While these interactions present numerous opportunities and advantages, they also pose potential harm to users. In instances where users suffer harm due to these interactions, platforms, often perceived as gatekeepers, become the natural focus of legal claims. Neerav Srivastava and Normann Witzleb delve into the liability of digital platforms under tort and consumer law within common law jurisdictions, specifically addressing user-to-user harm in situations where the platform facilitates physical interactions. While general tort principles may offer users more viable claims against platforms compared to vicarious liability, this chapter emphasises the need for legislative intervention to effectively provide redress to injured users.

Platforms play a vital role in Web3, connecting users and offering robust dispute resolution mechanisms. Online dispute resolution (ODR), a concept existing for decades alongside the internet, has evolved to encompass the ethos of Web3. In China, the world's fastest-growing electronic commerce market, sophisticated and responsive ODR mechanisms have been increasingly developed. Through an examination of IP-related dispute resolution on prominent Chinese online platforms, Songyin Bo illustrates how Web3 principles, emphasising user-centric decision-making, participation, and transparency, have been woven into the fabric of ODR design.

The internet has eroded the boundaries between sovereign states, and Web3's decentralised nature intensifies this blur. Consequently, courts must articulate distinct principles governing jurisdiction and choice of law when adjudicating cases involving Web3 elements. Employing cross-border cryptocurrency disputes as illustrations, Abubakri Yekini initially highlights the tension between Web3's decentralisation feature and the bedrock of private international law, rooted in connecting activities to territory. Following an examination of key approaches to crypto jurisdiction along with their advantages and drawbacks, he presents both legal and technical solutions to address this challenge.

Dicky King Fung Tsang's chapter covers another important jurisdiction issue: online defamation, a growing concern in the metaverse. He criticises the European Court of Justice's mosaic approach, allowing a claimant to seek damages in each member state where the defamatory content is accessible. This chapter argues that the mosaic approach inadvertently encourages forum shopping, parallel litigations, and poses a potential threat to free speech. In conclusion, the chapter advocates for the adoption of the U.S. jurisdiction rule, which mandates that the defendant must have purposefully directed their conduct toward the forum. This approach is deemed more advantageous for addressing online defamation, striking a balance between protecting individuals' reputations and safeguarding free speech.

As we increasingly reap the benefits of Web3 and the new generation is considered digital natives, it is crucial not to take internet access for granted. The reality that a significant portion of the global population lacks stable internet access, coupled with the growing interconnectedness of every resource to the internet, highlights the digital divide as a fundamental human right concern. Lukc D. Graham delves into the legal foundation of internet access from an international human rights perspective. He contends that the right to internet access should find its grounding in Article 11 of the International Covenant on Economic, Social, and Cultural Rights.

Conceptualising Web3 Law and Policy

Web3 is an evolving concept and space, and its future trajectory will be shaped by various factors, including vision, technology, the policy, and the law. Law and policy will play a crucial role in determining the development of Web3. While many policymakers are adopting a technology-neutral approach, it is important to note that this does not mean that technologies will not be regulated or will be beyond the pale of law. Throughout our research project, we have found that the existing frameworks are crucial in showing the legal and non-legal risks for business operators and users of Web3 activities as Web3 becomes an increasingly regulated space. Web3 does not necessarily demand a complete overhaul of legal concepts and norms to ensure safety, scalability, and sustainability. Yet choosing the appropriate legal tools for governance will be challenging.

Runhua Wang, Jyh-An Lee, and Jingwen Liu demonstrate how technology influences the treatment of an object in intellectual property law. Similarly, Jingyi Wang explores the suitability of property law for categorising digital assets for tax purposes. Eliza Mik examines whether and to what extent contract law should govern 'smart contracts'. Joseph Lee and Rougang Li investigate whether new digital enterprises such as DAO should be regulated by company law. Joseph Lee and Rachael Ntongho discuss whether increasing cybersecurity risks can be effectively addressed through minor adjustments to existing corporate governance designs. Neerav Srivastava and Normann Witzleb analyse whether tort law alone, as a principles-based and judges-developed legal framework, is adequate for defining platform liability pertaining to users' physical interaction. While these issues may seem disparate in terms of relevant legal principles and fields of law, they all stem from a fundamental question: whether and to what extent existing law and policy are applicable to Web3.

The comparative law aspect and jurisdiction-specific studies presented in this book offer insights into various possibilities for policymaking, legislation, and business practices. Jianzhong Shi sheds light on competition policy concerns related to data law in China, while Songyin Bo explores innovations in ODR within the country's private sector. Pinar Oruc examines different approaches taken by the European Union (EU), Japan, United Kingdom, and the United States regarding the unauthorised use of copyrighted data. King Fung Tseng outlines the different jurisdictional approaches to defamation cases in the EU and US. These policy variances may be reconciled through international legal instruments as discussed by Abubakri Yekini on the use of the Hague Convention to mitigate the risk of conflict of laws. In particular, Luke D. Graham elucidates the inherent challenges associated with employing public international law as a tool to achieve policy objectives such as bridging the poverty gap in the digital age.

This book will be relevant to policymakers, tech developers, legal practitioners, researchers, and students by offering a holistic view of how law and policy will shape the development of Web3. The cross-disciplinary approach demonstrates the potential for complementary treatment but also for conflict across the law disciplines. While the scientific exploration of Web3 continues, this book illustrates how traditional subjects continue to provide a framework for analysis – identifying risk, pinpointing gaps between law and practice, formulating policy, and borrowing legal concepts and principles to address challenges. It is also crucial to acknowledge that technology may offer solutions to issues that law cannot resolve – the so-called lawtech and regtech. We are likely to witness more of these applications in Web3 to tackle problems arising from physical operations, such as agency cost in corporations and transaction costs in cross-border operations. Given that the book covers private law, public law, international law, and transactional law, it contributes to the broader discussion of digital constitutionalism.

This book is the outcome of an international collaboration between the University of Manchester (UoM) Department of Law and the Centre for Legal Innovation and Digital Society (CLINDS) at the Chinese University of Hong Kong (CUHK) Faculty of Law. It evolved from two conferences 'Digital Platform Governance: Security, Scalability and Sustainability' in Hong Kong and 'Web3 Governance: Law and Policy' in Manchester, organised by the editors with support from the UoM-CUHK Research Fund and the British Council Going Global Partnerships.

Part A

Property and Contract

1 Deciphering the Legal Enigma of NFTs

Runhua Wang, Jyh-An Lee, Jingwen Liu

I. Introduction

Despite the assertion by Bill Gates that non-fungible tokens (NFTs) are '100% based on the greater fool theory' and have limited potential to improve the world,[1] the NFT market persists and thrives.[2] With thousands of daily NFT sales,[3] the most expensive NFT reached a staggering 91.8 million U.S. dollars as of April 2023.[4] Yet, the NFT market is not without its challenges, as some artists exploit the system by torching their physical artworks and simultaneously minting digital versions as NFTs for sale.[5] Prior to significant market fluctuations on April 15, 2022,[6] a majority of NFTs (53.6%) sold for below 200 U.S. dollars, while only a small portion (17.9%) fetched prices exceeding 700 U.S. dollars.[7]

1 See, e.g., Mark Bergen, 'Bill Gates Blasts Crypto, NFTs as Based on "Greater-Fool" Theory' *Bloomberg News* (15 June 2022) <www.bloomberg.com/news/articles/2022-06-15/bill-gates-blasts-crypto-nfts-as-based-on-greater-fool-theory#xj4y7vzkg> accessed 23 June 2023; Ryan Browne, 'Bill Gates Says Crypto and NFTs Are 100% Based on Greater Fool Theory' *CNBC* News (15 June 2022) <www.cnbc.com/2022/06/15/bill-gates-says-crypto-and-nfts-are-based-on-greater-fool-theory.html> accessed 23 June 2023.

2 Statista Research Department, 'Market Cap of Art Blocks NFT Projects Worldwide November 2020–June 2022' (*Statista*, 1 July 2022) <www.statista.com/statistics/1291885/art-blocks-nft-market-cap/> accessed 23 June 2023 ('As of 30 June 2022, the market cap of Art Blocks NFT projects available on the Ethereum blockchain and listed on OpenSea was worth roughly 840 million U.S. dollars.').

3 Thomas McGovern, 'How Many NFTs Are Sold Per Day in 2022?' (*Earth Web*, 5 August 2022) <https://earthweb.com/how-many-nfts-are-sold-per-day/> accessed 23 June 2023 ('The most recent data shows that on average, in March 2022, 3,200 NFTs are sold per day. In contrast to January where the per day average was 26,000.').

4 Fang Block, 'PAK's NFT Artwork "The Merge" Sells for $91.8 Million' (*Penta*, 7 December 2021) <www.barrons.com/articles/paks-nft-artwork-the-merge-sells-for-91-8-million-01638918205> accessed 23 June 2023.

5 Adam Iscoe, 'Burnt Banksy's Inflammatory N.F.T. Not-Art' *The New Yorker* (10 May 2021) <www.newyorker.com/magazine/2021/05/17/burnt-banksys-inflammatory-nft-not-art> accessed 23 June 2023.

6 Statista Research Department, 'NFT Sales Value in the Art Segment Worldwide in the Last 30 Days July 2022' (*Statista*, 27 July 2022) <www.statista.com/statistics/1235263/nft-art-monthly-sales-value/> accessed 23 June 2023.

7 Kimberly Parker, 'Most Artists Are Not Making Money off NFTs and Here Are Some Graphs to Prove It' (*Medium*, 19 April 2021) <https://thatkimparker.medium.com/most-artists-are-not-making-money-off-nfts-and-here-are-some-graphs-to-prove-it-c65718d4a1b8> accessed 1 July 2023.

DOI: 10.4324/9781032618975-3

NFTs are integral to Web 3.0, enhancing its decentralized applications by securing and upgrading communications, and various transactions.[8] They foster community building, allowing Web 3.0 users to recognize each other's identities and encouraging active participation in governance.[9] Beyond these technological and managerial contributions, the most impactful aspect of NFTs in the context of Web 3.0 is their introduction of business models and financial transactions related to virtual art,[10] significantly boosting the sustainability of Web 3.0. However, recent profit contractions in the secondary market, experiencing a more than 80% decline in 2022,[11] pose a threat to the sustainability of Web 3.0. Many NFT buyers struggle to recoup their investments,[12] exacerbating the challenges faced by the NFT market, including legal uncertainties related to fraud, money laundering, intellectual property (IP) infringement, and unfair competition.[13]

These legal uncertainties present substantial risks and emerging challenges to NFT governance, leading to a surge in legal disputes involving various stakeholders. Stakeholders, regulators, and courts are yet to reach a consensus on the legal nature of NFTs and how interests should be balanced among different parties to maximize their value. Similar debates persist in academia, with some arguing for NFTs as personal property due to their property interests,[14] while others assert

8 Iman Bashir, 'The Metaverse, NFTs and the Inevitability of Web3' *Forbes* (15 April 2022) <https://www.forbes.com/sites/forbestechcouncil/2022/04/15/the-metaverse-nfts-and-the-inevitability-of-web3/?sh=7d361ca428d0> ('Built on top of the blockchain, Web3 applications, augmented by decentralized products and NFTs, are ushering in a new era of how we all connect, interact, work and play – all within a transparent, open ecosystem.').

9 See Pooja Lekhi and Guneet Kaur, *Concepts, Technologies, Challenges, and the Future of Web 3* (IGI Global 2023) 231.

10 Some consumers purchase NFTs for digital collections. Alex Silverman, 'Millennials, Not Gen Zers, Are Driving the Recent Physical and Digital Collectibles Boom' (*Morning Consult*, 5 April 2021) <https://morningconsult.com/2021/04/05/millennials-nfts-collectibles/> accessed 1 July 2023; see Lekhi and Guneet Kaur (n 9) 12–13 ('[NFTs] enable the ownership and trade of in-game assets, such as characters, weapons, skins, or virtual real estate.'); see Runhua Wang, Jyh-An Lee and Jingwen Liu, 'Unwinding NFTs in the Shadow of IP Law' (2024) 61 Am Bus LJ 31, 38 (introducing the business models involving NFTs, which have been broadly adopted by the fashion industry).

11 UPYO.com, 'NFT Market Collapse: Reasons, Effects, and Future' (*UPYOBlog*, 19 February 2023) <https://upyo.com/en/post/nft-market-collapse> accessed 24 June 2023 ('An 88% drop in the trading volume on non-fungible token platforms; An 80% drop in the value of the non-fungible tokens.').

12 Hannah Murphy and Joshua Oliver, 'How NFTs Became a $40bn Market in 2021' *Financial Times* (31 December 2021) <www.ft.com/content/e95f5ac2-0476-41f4-abd4-8a99faa7737d>.

13 Andrea Kramer and others, 'Applying Anti-Money Laundering Practices to NFT Market' *Law 360* (15 August 2022) <www.law360.com/articles/1521137/applying-anti-money-laundering-practices-to-nft-market> accessed 23 June 2023; see also, Felicia J Boyd and others, 'Hermès' Challenge of "MetaBirkin" NFTs Foretells Future Trademark Litigation Trends' (*IPWatchdog*, 30 June 2022) <www.ipwatchdog.com/2022/06/30/hermes-challenge-metabirkin-nfts-foretells-future-trademark-litigation-trends/id=149916/> accessed 24 June 2023.

14 Joshua A Fairfield, 'Tokenized: The Law of Non-Fungible Tokens and Unique Digital Property' (2022) 97 Ind LJ 1261, 1290–300.

that the legal relationship between NFT sellers and buyers is governed by smart contracts.

This chapter contends that the legal nature of NFTs depends on their technological features and the interoperability of the hosting platform. It dissects the technological features, illustrating how they can generate misunderstandings and conflicts among market participants using a recent legal dispute as an example. The analysis extends to the property and contractual characteristics of NFTs, complemented by considerations of their economic features, emphasizing the illusory nature of uniqueness and scarcity. These characteristics challenge the adequacy of defining NFTs as traditional property. The chapter concludes by demonstrating how misunderstandings about the technological and economic characteristics of NFTs have led to problematic applications of law, particularly within IP law. Clearing these issues is essential for fully unlocking and sustaining the economic value of NFTs in the evolving landscape of Web 3.0.

II. Understanding NFTs

In 2021, the NFT market surged to prominence, particularly following Christie's notable auction of Beeple's 'Everydays: The First 5,000 Days' for a staggering 69 million U.S. dollars.[15] This marked the emergence of NFTs as one of the most lucrative sectors in the digital landscape of Web 3.0.[16] Recognizing the strategic importance of NFTs in the Web 3.0 era, IP holders actively embraced them, utilizing

15 Taylor Locke, 'Mark Cuban Is Bullish on NFTs, and Now They're Mainstream After a $69 Million Auction at Christie's' *CNBC* (18 February 2021) <www.cnbc.com/2021/02/18/christies-to-auction-beeple-nft-art-and-will-accept-ether-as-payment.html> accessed 23 June 2023.

16 See, e.g., Brian L Frye, 'How to Sell NFTs Without Really Trying' (2022) 13 Harv J Sports & Ent L 113, 113 ('Suddenly last summer, the internet went nuts for 'non-fungible tokens' or 'NFTs.' In a matter of months, NFT sales swelled from a sleepy slough of the blockchain to a thundering cataract that shows no sign of slaking.'); Carol R Goforth, 'How Nifty! But Are NFTs Securities, Commodities, or Something Else?' (2022) 90 UMKC L Rev 775, 775 ('Suddenly, NFTs seemed to be on everyone's mind.'); Mark Conrad, 'Non-Fungible Tokens, Sports, and Intellectual Property Law Issues: A Case Study Applying Copyright, Trademark, and Right of Publicity Law to a Non-Traditional Ownership Vehicle' (2022) 32 J Legal Aspects Sport 132, 132 ('NFTs have become a hot commodity among collectors and investors, in some cases selling for millions of dollars.'); Daniel S Cohen and others, 'The Coming Blockchain Revolution in Consumption of Digital Art and Music: The Thinking Lawyer's Guide to Non-Fungible Tokens (NFTs)' (2021) 26(6) Cyberspace Lawyer NL 1, 1 ('[W]hen Beeple's digital art piece "Everydays: The First 5000 Days" sold at Christie's for US$69 million, the NFT mania truly began.'); An P Doan and others, 'NFTs: Key U.S. Legal Considerations for an Emerging Asset Class' (2021) 24 Fintech L Rep NL 1, 1 ('Although the technology that makes NFTs possible has been around for several years, NFTs have very much emerged into public consciousness in 2021'); Jonathan Emmanuel and others, 'Non-Fungible Tokens: What's All the Fuss?' (2021) 39 Westlaw J Computer & Internet 4, 4 ('Non-fungible tokens (NFTs) have been around for many years but have recently gained huge traction.'); Anthony J Dreyer and David M Lamb, 'Can I Mint an NFT with That? Avoiding Right of Publicity and Trademark Litigation Risks in the Brave New World of NFTs' (2021) 28 Westlaw J Intell Prop 3, 3 ('Almost overnight, non-fungible tokens (NFTs) have become a sensation.').

NFT launches to extend their business reach and influence within this digital realm.[17] Prominent examples include Nike's introduction of NFT sneakers through RTFKT Studios,[18] Lamborghini's inaugural NFT project, 'Space Time Memory,'[19] and JPMorgan's foray into the Decentraland Metaverse with the launch of its virtual branch.[20] The pervasive enthusiasm for digital market expansion within Web 3.0 was unmistakable, evident in both self-revelation and rapid dissemination of this 'buzz.'[21] As the NFT market expands and stakeholders engage in competitive acquisitions, the primary governance questions revolve around the nature of NFTs and their potential societal impacts, be they harmful or contributory.

A. *How Do NFTs Function?*

Technically, an NFT is a data unit stored on a digital ledger known as a 'blockchain,'[22] serving to indicate ownership and authenticate a specific asset.[23] This definition encompasses two key aspects: firstly, an NFT comprises a unique dataset featuring a tokenID and a blockchain address, [24] and, secondly, it signifies ownership of a distinct digital (and crypto) asset.[25] While sharing characteristics

17 See Wang, Lee and Liu (n 10) 38.

18 Jyh-An Lee, Liang Yang and Pan Hui, 'Legal Implications of Self-Presence in the Metaverse' (2023) 25 Media & Arts Law Review 267, 273; Khristopher J Brooks, 'Nike's New NFT Sneakers Selling for More Than $100,000' *CBS News* (28 April 2022) <www.cbsnews.com/news/nike-cryptokicks-nft-blockchain-metaverse-rtfkt> accessed 29 June 2023. Reportedly, Nike has also filed a patent for tokenized shoes branded "CryptoKicks"; see Oscar Holland, 'How NFTs Are Fueling a Digital Art Boom' *CNN* (10 March 2022) <https://edition.cnn.com/style/article/nft-digital-art-boom/index.html> accessed 29 June 2023.

19 'The NFT Space Time Memory' (*Lamborghini*) <https://nft.lamborghini.com> accessed 21 May 2022.

20 'Opportunities in the Metaverse' (*JPMorgan*) <www.jpmorgan.com/content/dam/jpm/treasury-services/documents/opportunities-in-the-metaverse.pdf> accessed 21 May 2022.

21 Dreyer and Lamb (n 16) 4.

22 Frye (n 16) 113 ('An NFT is just an encrypted unit of data stored on a digital ledger.'); Conrad (n 16) 133 ('An NFT is a data unit stored on a digital ledger (or digital wallet), known as a blockchain.'); Emmanuel and others (n 16) ('An NFT is a one-of-a-kind digital token created (or "minted") and recorded on a digital ledger, called a blockchain.'); Cohen and others (n 16) ('NFTs are non-fungible tokens issued on a distributed ledger such as a blockchain.').

23 Dreyer and Lamb (n 16) ('At a high level, an NFT is a unique digital certificate stored on a blockchain that conveys certain limited ownership rights to an asset, typically a digital one.'); Doan and others (n 16) ('In general terms, an NFT is a digital asset, based on computer code and recorded on a blockchain ledger to prove ownership and authenticity of a unique asset.').

24 Andres Guadamuz, 'The Treachery of Images: Non-Fungible Tokens and Copyright' (2021) 16 J Intell Prop L & Practice 1370 ('The first core element to the NFT is a number known as the tokenID, which is generated upon the creation of the token; the second is the contract address, this is a blockchain address that can be viewed everywhere in the world using a blockchain scanner. The combination of elements contained in the token makes it unique: there can only be one token in the world with the combination of tokenID and contract address.').

25 See, e.g., Goforth, 'How Nifty! But Are NFTs Securities, Commodities, or Something Else?' (n 16) 777 ('NFTs are cryptoassets,. . .'); L Lewis and others, 'Non-Fungible Tokens and Copyright Law' (2021) 33 Intell Prop & Tech LJ 18, 18 ('An NFT is a cryptographic tool using a suitable blockchain,

such as immutability, authenticity, and scarcity with other cryptoassets such as Bitcoin and Ether,[26] the inherent qualities of indivisibility and uniqueness set NFTs apart.[27] Unlike interchangeable assets, each NFT is distinct and irreplaceable, hence embodying its 'non-fungible' nature.[28] Each NFT is designed to provide a unique authentication of ownership for the associated asset.[29]

NFT transactions are executed through smart contracts, which are computer codes stored and executed on blockchains.[30] Smart contracts ensure that subsequent NFT buyers receive rights neither narrower nor broader in scope than the initial rights issued by minters and encoded within the smart contracts.[31] Beyond the technological role fulfilled by smart contracts, the utilization of digital assets linked to NFTs in metaverses is governed by contractual provisions outlined by the hosting platforms. In alignment with these terms, platforms may restrict NFT owners' access to and use of the assets, and in some cases, unilaterally remove or disassociate assets according to the contractual provisions.[32]

---

most commonly Ethereum, to create a unique, non-fungible digital asset.'). The categorisation of NFTs as digital 'assets' have recently been recognised by courts in different jurisdictions including the United Kingdom, Singapore, and China. See *Osbourne v Ozone* [2022] EWHC 1021 (U.K.) (hereinafter '*Osbounre*'); *Janesh S/O Rajkumar v Unknown Person* HC/OC 41/2022 (Singapore); Shenzhen Qice Diechu Wenhua Chuangyi Youxian Gongsi Su Hangzhou Yuan Yuzhou Keji Youxian Gongsi (深圳奇策迭出文化创意有限公司诉杭州原与宙科技有限公司) [*Shenzhen Qice Diechu Cultural Creativity Co, Ltd v Hangzhou Yuanyuzhou Technology Co Ltd*] (Hangzhou Internet Ct 2022) (China) (hereinafter '*Panghu*').

26 See, e.g., Cohen and others (n 16) ('[NFTs are] similar to cryptocurrencies like bitcoin in that they can be identified individually and are authenticated through a decentralized system of nodes via a consensus protocol.').

27 Lewis and others (n 25) at 18 ('[T]hey differ from cryptocurrencies in that they are each unique, indivisible, and "non-fungible".'); Doan and others (n 16) (noting that the non-fungible nature 'distinguishes an NFT from other digital assets.').

28 To put it more specifically, 'the holder of one NFT cannot necessarily obtain equal value by exchanging a token for another NFT within the same ecosystem.' See JE Bedar and others, 'Tokenization: The Revolution Is Now' (2021) 27 Westlaw J Derivatives 11, 11; see also, Emmanuel and others (n 16) (noting that NFTs are 'non-fungible', which means unique and not interchangeable because each token comprises the unique data of code and other metadata to be distinguished from other tokens running based on blockchains); Goforth, 'How Nifty! But Are NFTs Securities, Commodities, or Something Else?' (n 16) 777 ('"Non-fungible" means that each NFT is unique, encoded onto the underlying blockchain with certain metadata that makes it different from every other token, even if the underlying work of art or other asset is the same.').

29 Bedar and others (n 28) ('NFTs have been used to transform collectibles – for example, a digital work of art – into one-of-a-kind, verifiable assets that can be traced, authenticated, and sold/traded on-chain.').

30 See, e.g., Rebecca Carroll, 'NFTs: The Latest Technology Challenging Copyright's Law's Relevance Within a Decentralized System' (2022) 32 Fordham Intell Prop Media & Ent LJ 979, 988.

31 'DAO-Enabled NFT Platform' (*LeewayHei*) <www.leewayhertz.com/dao-enabled-nft-platform/> accessed 21 August 2022.

32 João Marinotti, 'Can You Truly Own Anything in the Metaverse? A Law Professor Explains How Blockchain and NFTs Don't Protect Virtual Property' (*The Conversation*, 21 April 2022) <https://theconversation.com/can-you-truly-own-anything-in-the-metaverse-a-law-professor-explains-how-blockchains-and-nfts-dont-protect-virtual-property-179067> (using the terms of Sandbox,

Therefore, owning NFTs does not equate to owning the digital assets associated with them.[33] An NFT represents ownership or authenticity of a digital asset, rather than being the asset itself.[34] When acquiring an NFT for a piece of digital art, for example, the NFT does not contain the image file; rather, it operates as a blockchain-based record verifying ownership or the art's authenticity.[35] Obtaining an NFT typically does not confer ownership or possession of the underlying asset,[36] and it does not involve the transfer of any IP associated with that asset.[37] Consequently, some observers view an NFT transaction as a limited non-exclusive license to showcase and use the underlying artwork.[38] While this explanation provides clarity, it offers only a partial perspective on the legal nature of NFTs, as the complexities of their potential classification as securities and the regulations surrounding their creation and transfer extend beyond those applicable to other digital assets or the tokenization of tangible or intangible assets.[39]

B. The Case of 'Quantum' NFT

The dispute between Free Holdings Inc. and artist Kevin McCoy highlights challenges related to the ownership of NFTs.[40,41] McCoy, credited with minting the world's first NFT, 'Quantum,' on the Namecoin blockchain in May 2014, encountered issues due to Namecoin's provisions requiring periodic renewal. Failure to renew results in the potential re-registration and claim of ownership by others over expired NFTs.[42]

---

an NFT and metaverse platform, as an example); see also, Carroll (n 30) 986 (explaining that '[w]hether a buyer holds any ownership or rights to the underlying artwork depends on individual transaction and the market place used for the transaction').

33 Marinotti (n 32); Carroll (n 30) 986.

34 Rob Nightingale, 'What Do You Actually Own if You Buy an NFT?' (*MUO*, 29 March 2021) <www.makeuseof.com/what-do-you-actually-own-if-you-buy-an-nft/> accessed 29 June 2023.

35 ibid.

36 Unless the parties agree otherwise. For example, buyers of StockX Vault NFTs, according to the Vault NFT Terms, gains title to both the purchased Vault NFT (i.e., the digital collectible) and the Stored Item (i.e., the physical goods) to which the NFT corresponds. See *Nike, Inc v StockX*, No 1:22-CV-00983 (S D N Y 2022 Feb. 3, 2022). Goforth, 'How Nifty! But Are NFTs Securities, Commodities, or Something Else?' (n 16) 779.

37 ibid.

38 Carol Goforth, 'What You Should Know Before Buying or Selling an NFT in the US' *Cointelegraph* (3 April 2021) <https://cointelegraph.com/news/what-you-should-know-before-buying-or-selling-an-nft-in-the-us> accessed 29 June 2023.

39 Goforth, 'How Nifty! But Are NFTs Securities, Commodities, or Something Else?' (n 16) 787; see the U.S. Securities and Exchange Commission, 'SEC Charges Creator of Stoner Cats Web Series for Unregistered Offering of NFTs' (*SEC Press Release*, 13 September 2023) <https://www.sec.gov/news/press-release/2023-178> accessed 16 September 2023.

40 *Memorandum of Law in Opposition to Motion, Amended Complaint, Free Holdings Inc v McCoy*, No 1:22CV00881, 2022 US Dist CT Motions Lexis 246347 (SDNY, 1 February 2022).

41 Kevin McCoy, 'Quantum' (*McCoySpace*) <https://mccoyspace.com/project/125/> accessed 30 May 2022.

42 The reasons for such requirements include: first, it incentivizes owners of names who no longer intend to use them to either let them expire or sell them, thereby decreasing squatting; and second,

McCoy did not update the record for Quantum in time, leading to its expiration in January 2015.[43]

Free Holdings re-registered the Namecoin-based Quantum NFT and claimed ownership in April 2021. Meanwhile, McCoy re-minted it on the Ethereum blockchain in May 2022,[44] asserting to have 'moved' and 'preserved' the Quantum NFT across different blockchains, with traceable provenance and ownership.[45] The Ethereum-based Quantum NFT linked to the Namecoin-based Quantum NFT was auctioned at Sotheby's for 1.472 million U.S. dollars in June 2021.[46] Subsequently, Free Holdings sued McCoy for slander of title, deceptive and unlawful trade practices, and commercial disparagement for the misrepresentation of the ownership and status of the Quantum NFT.[47]

Free Holdings contended that it acquired the title to the Namecoin-based Quantum NFT, and the re-minted Ethereum-based Quantum NFT was simply an 'authorized print of the original NFT.'[48] Its core argument relied on McCoy's metadata description of Namecoin during the creation of the Namecoin-based Quantum NFT, as follows:

> I assert title to the file at the URL http://static.mccoyspace.com/gifs/quantum.gif with the creator's public announcement of [its] publishing at the URL https://twitter.com/mccoyspace/status/462320426719641600. The file whose SHA256 hash is d41b8540cbacdf1467cdc5d17316dcb672c8b43235-fa16cde98e79825b68709a is taken to be the file in question. Title transfers to whoever controls this blockchain entry.[49]

The court, however, did not sustain this argument. Judge Cott ultimately granted a motion to dismiss the case, reasoning that Free Holdings had failed to establish standing to sue by not alleging sufficient injuries.[50]

---

it ensures that if a name owner loses their private keys, the name will eventually be returned to the pool of available names instead of permanently being stuck in limbo. See Namecoin, 'FAQ' <www.namecoin.org/docs/faq/#why-do-names-have-to-be-renewed-regularly> accessed 1 June 2022.

43 *Free Holdings* (n 40).

44 'Sotheby's Sued Over Quantum NFT Auction' *Ledger Insights* (4 February 2022) <www.ledgerinsights.com/sothebys-sued-over-quantum-nft-auction/> accessed 1 July 2023 ('Nowadays, if you're selling an NFT, ideally, it should be on one of the better-known blockchains to make it easily transferable.').

45 'Kevin McCoy Quantum' (*Sothby's*) <www.sothebys.com/en/buy/auction/2021/natively-digital-a-curated-nft-sale-2/quantum> accessed 2 June 2022.

46 ibid.

47 *Free Holdings* (n 40). Free Holdings sued McCoy, Sotheby's, and the successful bidder at the auction.

48 ibid.

49 ibid 1–2.

50 *Free Holdings* (n 40) (ruling that Free Holdings had 'failed to allege a proprietary interest in Quantum', and that the alleged statements on Namecoin were 'insufficient to give rise to a legally-protected interest in Quantum').

C. *The Property and Contract Attributes of NFTs*

The challenges surrounding the ownership of NFTs stem from the ambiguous legal nature of these tokens, particularly when the market is thriving. Many participants assume NFTs are property based on transactional characteristics, with some platforms allowing the transfer of ownership and even empowering new owners to potentially destroy underlying assets.

One notable theory supporting NFTs as property is advanced by Joshua Fairfield and Lawrence Trautman.[51] They argue that NFTs should be legally treated as digital personal property, as they embody strong property interests that enable parties to buy, sell, or own digital assets similar to personal property. Fairfield argued that to sustain the prosperity of NFT markets, NFTs should be delinked from IP rights protecting the underlying works, and NFT transactions should not be treated as IP licensing agreements.[52] The U.K. High Court of Justice recently also ruled that NFTs should be recognized as property, placing them in alignment with various other forms of cryptoassets.[53] In line with this approach, several European scholars, including Zoi Krokida, argue for the classification of NFTs as goods, proposing their regulation under Article 2 of the Unfair Commercial Practices Directive.[54]

However, critics, including Edward Lee, caution against severing the connection between NFTs and their underlying artworks,[55] emphasizing that the value of NFTs is intrinsically linked to the associated property, but purchasers do not necessarily gain the ownership of the property itself. Additional skepticism is voiced by Juliet Moringiello and Christopher Odinet, who challenge the claim treating NFTs as properties.[56] They compared the characteristics of NFTs with those of negotiable instruments, securities, deeds of real property, bills of lading, and other legal tokens, finding that it was groundless to claim property rights in NFTs.[57] They emphasize the absence of a tethering effect and argue that without substantive control over the underlying assets, deeming NFTs as property becomes inconsequential.[58]

51 Lawrence J Trautman, 'Virtual Art and Non-Fungible Tokens' (2022) 50 Hofstra L Rev 361, 412–18; Fairfield (n 14) 1268, 1292–93.

52 Fairfield (n 14) 1290.

53 *Osbourne* (n 25) para. 15 ('[I]t has been consistently held that crypto assets, are to be treated as located at the place where the owner of them is domiciled. There is no reason at any rate at this stage to treat non fungible tokens in any other way, assuming for present purposes as I do that they are to be treated as property as a matter of English law.').

54 Zoi Krokida, 'Address at the European Policy for Intellectual Property: Non-Fungible Tokens and Liability of Online Marketplaces: A European Perspective' (13 September 2023) <https://epip2023.confer.uj.edu.pl/documents/152401432/153462333/EPIP_plenaries_sessions/776db15b-8698-47e6-9a43-b9527d5846d1>.

55 Edward Lee, 'Episode 3 NFT Myth Busting Buying an NFT Is NOT Buying the Art' (*YouTube*, 19 October 2021) <www.youtube.com/watch?v=Fy6uh_QRks&ab_channel=nounft> accessed 29 June 2023.

56 See, generally, Juliet M Moringiello and Christopher K Odinet, 'The Property Law of Tokens' (2022) 74 Fla L Rev 607.

57 ibid 615–27.

58 ibid 641–43.

Debates also centre around the role of smart contracts in governing NFT transactions.[59] While some argue that smart contracts define the legal relations between NFT sellers and buyers, others reject this perspective, viewing smart contracts more as a technological tool rather than as a legally binding contract.[60]

Beyond the technological role played by smart contracts in NFTs, the contractual nature of NFTs is more evident in the terms and conditions of NFT platforms. The platforms centrally design their terms of service, governing the so-called ownership of the NFTs or of the platforms.[61] Depending on these terms, the U.S. Securities and Exchange Commission may classify certain NFTs as investment contracts, falling under the category of securities.[62] This classification often arises when investors expect profits based on managerial and entrepreneurial efforts from NFT platforms.[63]

In this chapter, we propose a compromise based on the technological features of NFTs. We argue that these features determine whether an NFT resembles property or a contract. The features are crucial to clarifying the ownership of a digital asset when it is 'hashed' to a blockchain.[64] An NFT may include a pointer to the art, a hash of art, or both. The storage location of digital assets, whether on-chain or off-chain, plays a crucial role in defining the legal nature of an NFT. If the digital asset is stored in a centralized server, this off-chain stored asset ceases to exist if the company operating the server ceases to exist.[65] The legal interests underlying this NFT are then subject to contractual or non-contractual restrictions imposed by the server host.[66] Therefore, the off-chain storage of digital assets may entail a greater number of contract characteristics in an NFT. In contrast, if digital assets are hashed into the token, which means that they are stored on-chain,[67] then the assets are retained on blockchains regardless of the existence of the original company

59 See, e.g., Carroll (n 30) 1001 ('NFTs and the blockchain on which it is recorded allow artists to program a set of contracts with the buyer governing the use of the work. This allows the artist to contract directly with the buyer . . . and define what rights, if any, are transferred with the purchase').

60 Eliza Mik, Chapter 2 in this volume.

61 Marinotti (n 32); see also, Carroll (n 30) 988 (indicating that '[t]he creation and sale of an NFT is . . . governed by the terms of services in the various marketplaces. Depending on which market place is chosen, different terms will apply to the NFT'), 1001 ('NFTs are . . . bought and sold through third-party marketplaces with their own terms and conditions for the buyers and sellers to follow'); Genevieve Bellarchive, 'The Metaverse Is a New Word for an Old Idea' *MIT Technology Review* (2 February 2022) <www.technologyreview.com/2022/02/08/1044732/metaverse-history-snow-crash/> accessed 29 June 2023 (defining a metaverse as 'an immersive, rich digital world combining aspects of social media, online gaming, and augmented and virtual reality').

62 See Respondent for Stoner Cats 2, Admin Proc File No 3-21655 (Sec. Exchange Commission 13 September 2023) at 2.

63 ibid.

64 Fairfield (n 14) 1274; Trautman (n 51) 365, 371 (indicating that NFT is 'a digital proof of purchase that is recorded on a digital ledger known as a blockchain').

65 Fairfield (n 14) 1283.

66 ibid.

67 See, e.g., Carroll (n 30) 986.

that hosts servers to store digital contents.[68] On-chain storage provides a tethering effect, thereby overcoming the concerns raised by Moringiello and Odinet.[69] The sustainability of on-chain storage makes the connected NFTs more like property.[70] However, since it is quite costly to store a large amount of data in tokens, only a few digital assets can be stored on-chain.[71]

Additionally, the interoperability of a platform influences the legal nature of NFTs, with cross-platform transactions leaning towards property characteristics, while platform-tied transactions align more with contracts. If an NFT can be performed in cross-platform transactions, indicating that platforms have limited control over the NFT and its underlying digital assets, then the NFT would resemble a property. However, if the NFT is tied on a single platform and cannot be transacted across platforms, it aligns better with a contract than with property because the transferability of the token depends on the contractual relations between the platform and the owner. Currently, many NFT and metaverse platforms are not interoperable, and the asset ownership represented is not portable.[72] Therefore, the ownership of these assets is subject to the terms of service provided by the platform companies that host the assets.

III. The Uniqueness and Scarcity of NFTs

The debates surrounding the legal nature of NFTs extend beyond isolated discussions, intertwining with certain technological and economic aspects. These features, notably uniqueness and scarcity, remain inadequately explored and settled, potentially leading to misunderstandings within the market and legal system.

Many scholars have presumed NFTs to be rivalrous and unique, attributing scarcity to the underlying digital assets.[73] Fairfield, based on NFT market performance, contends that NFTs are scarce, attracting a substantial consumer base willing to pay royalties both in the short and long term.[74] This argument relies on the assumption that NFTs possess inherent scarcity value.[75] Additionally, from a technical perspective, each NFT is distinct, contrasting with other cryptoassets.[76] The rivalry

68 Fairfield (n 14) 1283.

69 See Moringiello and Odinet (n 56) at 641–43.

70 *Cf* Guadamuz (n 24) 1371 ('on-chain works . . . can only be exchanged and transferred with other people on the blockchain, so the NFT acts more like true ownership of the work').

71 Fairfield (n 14) 1283; see also, ibid 1371 ('[t]here are not many projects that upload the full work to the blockchain . . . [because] . . . the cost of writing data into blockchain is prohibitively expensive and this is so by design').

72 See, e.g., Marinotti (n 32).

73 See, e.g., ibid 1263–64, 1304; Tonya M Evans, 'Blockchain and the Genesis of Creative Justice to Disintermediate Creativity' (2022) 26 Lewis & Clark L Rev 219, 223–24; Guadamuz (n 24) 1370; Trautman (n 51) 364, 392; see also, Carroll (n 30) 981 (arguing that NFTs introduces 'scarcity to the internet for the first time').

74 See Fairfield (n 14) 1300.

75 ibid 1264.

76 ibid 1272.

attribute implies that NFTs resemble tangible property rather than conventional intangible IP. Consequently, NFT buyers can confidently assert sole ownership of the transacted assets pointed by the NFTs.[77] Tokenizing and linking a digital asset to an NFT inherently limits its quantity,[78] elucidating how NFTs generate scarcity in digital assets.[79] The uniqueness facilitated by NFTs significantly enhances the value of underlying digital assets, a quality not adequately addressed by current laws, including IP laws.[80]

Built on the premise that NFTs are both unique and scarce, many scholars perceive NFTs as technical solutions operating independently of existing regulations.[81] They consequently believe that NFTs offer a novel mechanism for generating information, fostering innovation and creativity. However, the rising number of reported NFT-related frauds and complaints regarding IP infringement cast doubt on the assumed uniqueness and scarcity of NFTs.

To dispel the doubts, a reassessment of the characteristics of information, a fundamental component of NFTs, is imperative. Information exhibits robust traits akin to public goods, notably non-rivalry and non-excludability.[82] Firstly, information is non-rivalrous, as its consumption does not deplete its quantity;[83] multiple parties can concurrently access the same piece of information without diminishing its availability to others.[84] Secondly, information is non-excludable, as preventing its dissemination proves challenging.[85]

However, the non-exclusiveness of information is not immutable. IP, a legal monopoly, has made IP-protected information exclusive to counteract under-production of public goods and address the free-riding problem.[86] In essence, IP-protected information retains its non-rivalrous nature but becomes excludable. Despite this transformation, IP holders encounter various challenges in enforcing their rights due to the inherent non-rivalrous nature of information.

In the realm of NFTs, the technological underpinnings of blockchains, while safeguarding the authenticity of NFT ownership and transactions, do not inherently validate the concepts of uniqueness or scarcity associated with NFTs. Despite

77 ibid 1264; see also, Evans (n 73) 222 (describing NFTs as 'a means for providing verifiable and immutable proof of ownership of an asset').

78 Fairfield (n 14) 1274.

79 Trautman (n 51) 410–11.

80 See, e.g., Guadamuz (n 24) 1383; Fairfield (n 14) 1265, but see Carroll (n 30) 988–89 ('[W]hile the NFT satisfies the scarcity, it does not create the demand.').

81 See, e.g., Guadamuz (n 24) 1368.

82 See Christopher S Yoo, 'Copyright and Product Differentiation' (2004) 79 NYU L Rev 212, 214–15 (introducing the public goods' economic feature of nonrivalry to copyrights); see also, Jyh-An Lee, 'Tripartite Perspective on the Copyright-Sharing Economy in China' (2019) 35 Comp L & Security Rev 434–35.

83 Fairfield (n 14) 1296. But still, the value of the information can be exhausted from the perspective of trade secrets.

84 ibid.

85 ibid.

86 ibid.

blockchain technologies ensuring the security of NFT-related activities, they do not prevent the unauthorized creation of multiple NFTs for the same artwork, as anyone can mint identical NFTs without approval from IP holders or the initial minters, even when NFTs are ostensibly unique.[87] This loophole allows potential IP infringers to sell NFTs linked to identical digital assets across various platforms,[88] as exemplified by the 'Quantum' dispute, which, while not addressing IP concerns, highlighted the issue of cross-blockchain double minting,[89] exposing a flaw in the presumed uniqueness of NFTs. Furthermore, the ownership of an artwork represented by an NFT does not act as a deterrent against technical or legal replication of the artwork.[90] Scholars like Moringiello and Odinet have directly challenged the foundational notion of the scarcity of NFTs by disputing the scarcity of digital artworks and the rivalry of NFTs – two premises underlying the assumption that NFTs are scarce.[91] Conversely, scholars like Guadamuz argue that the scarcity is not intrinsic to NFTs but is rather derived from the copyrights associated with them.[92]

Both perspectives critical of the scarcity of NFTs highlight that the technological features of NFTs do not empower market participants to sidestep the governance of IP laws. In essence, rather than directly involving property or contract law, issues related to IP law become a crucial consideration based on the economic features of NFTs. Therefore, overlooking IP laws in the context of NFT activities is groundless.[93]

IV. The Misunderstanding of NFTs in Legal Practice

The limited comprehension of NFT characteristics is evident in recent judicial practices. In July 2023, a court in China rendered a decision in *Wang v. iBox Science & Technology Co.*, which involved an NFT platform's unauthorized minting and offering of a visual artist's copyrighted work.[94] The court had rightfully recognized that the minting and initial offering of the work as an NFT was indeed an infringement of the author's right to dissemination. However, the major source of dispute came from the court's characterization of the subsequent resales of the NFT via the platform.

Notably, after being minted by the defendant and subsequently sold to the initial purchaser for RMB 17,970 (approximately 2,462 U.S. dollars), the NFT

87 Guadamuz (n 24) 1370.

88 ibid 1000.

89 Amended Complaint, *Free Holdings Inc v McCoy*, No 1:22CV00881 (SDNY, 15 August 2022).

90 ibid 1384.

91 Moringiello and Odinet (n 56) 644–47.

92 Guadamuz (n 24) 1383–84 (following Jake Linford and believing that scarcity is a part of copyright); see also Jake Linford, 'Copyright and Attention Scarcity' (2020) 42 Cardozo L Rev 143, 146.

93 But see Fairfield (n 14) 1268, 1298–300.

94 Wang Chengyu Su Hainan Lianhe Keji Youxian Gongsi (王程玉诉海南链盒科技有限公司) [*Wang Chengyu v Hainan iBox Science and Technology Co, Ltd*] (Sichuan High People's Ct 2023) (China).

underwent multiple transactions, culminating in a final sale at a price of RMB 578,495 (around 79,262 U.S. dollars).[95] Despite these subsequent resales, the court dismissed the plaintiff's claim that these actions constituted copyright infringement. Instead, the court computed damages exclusively based on the initial transaction price (reflecting the plaintiff's actual loss) plus the gas fees charged by the defendant for each resale (representing the defendant's illicit gains). Consequently, the court awarded compensatory damages totaling RMB 58,342 (approximately 8,004 U.S. dollars).[96]

In justifying the decision that the resale of an NFT does not amount to copyright infringement, the court provided the following rationale. Firstly, NFT transactions do not entail copying or transacting the underlying copyrighted work. This is because the initial buyer does not need to download a copy of the copyrighted work to his or her computer or upload another copy to complete the transaction; instead, the transaction is executed through a smart contract. Secondly, aligning with the approach of the U.K. High Court, NFT artworks are characterized as property, and each purchase bestows a credit over that property. Subsequent resales of the NFT are considered transfers of creditor rights, granting each buyer the right to transfer their interests without infringement, even if the initial minting of the NFT breached others' copyrights. Thirdly, an NFT platform lacks the ability to predict or control user-initiated resales, and any royalties generated from these sales are collected by users rather than by the platform. Therefore, the platform should not be held liable for copyright infringement in connection with these subsequent resales.[97]

The analysis conducted by the Chinese court lacks persuasiveness when compared to our prior analysis due to its failure to fully grasp the technological and economic characteristics of NFTs. Firstly, as previously argued, under our proposed characterization, an NFT would exhibit more attributes of property only when stored on-chain and capable of an inter-platform transfer. In contrast, when stored and transacted off-chain, with no transferability among platforms, the NFT would lean more towards a contractual nature.[98] In the case at hand, the NFT was stored in a centralized server, necessitating a third-party payment processor for each transaction.[99] Additionally, the defendant's user agreement explicitly stated that the purchased asset could not be transferred to another platform.[100] Consequently, ownership and rights associated with the asset heavily relied on the contractual relationship between the platform and participants. Characterizing it as property, as done by the court in *iBox*, overlooks the strong control retained by the platform over the NFTs sold.

95 ibid.
96 ibid.
97 ibid.
98 See Section II.C.
99 See, e.g., Terms of Services of Lianpay (*Lianpay*, 5 January 2022) <https://lianpay.ibox.art/lian/agreement/?type=agreement> accessed 17 August 2023.
100 iBox User Agreement (*iBox*, 28 June 2023) <https://ibpublic.ibox.art/static/web/html/userAgreement.html?1692266753017> accessed 17 August 2023.

Secondly, the court's assertion that each resale of the NFT constituted a transfer of a creditor's interest contradicts the understanding that an NFT transaction does not necessarily involve the transfer of ownership or IP in the underlying asset it represents. The technological features of NFTs dictate that acquiring an NFT guarantees neither ownership of the underlying asset nor any associated IP.[101] The court in *iBox* held that after the artwork had been minted and sold by the defendant, any subsequent purchaser would essentially be acquiring a credit against the minter (i.e., the defendant) by paying the resale price. This right, according to the court, would not be affected by whether the NFT was copyright-infringing initially.[102] However, this holding signifies a significant misinterpretation of the technological features of NFTs and NFT transactions, as an NFT differs from the digital asset it represents. An NFT transaction confers no right to the underlying asset but only to the NFT itself, to the acquirer.

Thirdly, the court's ruling that resales did not constitute copyright infringement undermined the copyright holder's ability to continually benefit from their creation. An integral aspect of an NFT's economic value lies in its capacity to enable authors to capture the appreciation in the value of their creations by collecting royalties from each resale.[103] This concept originates from *droit de suite* provisions, initially established in France[104] and subsequently adopted in around 30 jurisdictions.[105] Despite opposition to this legal right due to enforcement challenges,[106] smart contracts can mitigate transaction costs for enforcing *droit de suite*. The technological features of smart contracts facilitate the automatic collection of royalties from resales, enhancing the economic value of NFTs by advancing the interests of IP holders and encouraging innovation and creativity.[107] This exemplifies Law 3.0,

101 Goforth, 'How Nifty! But Are NFTs Securities, Commodities, or Something Else?' (n 16) 779; Tianxiang He and Huan Zhang, 'Copyright, Platform and NFT Digital Collections: Exploring the Proper Regulatory Mode in China' (2024) 19 J Intellet Prop Law 18, 23.

102 *Wang v iBox* (n 94).

103 Fairfield (n 14) 1280–81; Carroll (n 30) 990.

104 Katreina Eden, 'Fine Artists' Resale Royalty Right Should Be Enacted in the United States' (2005) 18 NY Int'l L Rev 121, 123–25; Michael B Reddy, 'The Droit de Suite: Why American Fine Artists Should Have a Right to a Resale Royalty' (1995) 15 Loy LA Ent L Rev 509, 509–10; David E Shipley, 'Droit De Suite, Copyright's First Sale Doctrine and Preemption of State Law' (2017) 39 Hastings Comm & Ent LJ 1, 5.

105 Reddy (n 104) 510.

106 Alexander Bussey, 'The Incompatibility of Droit de Suite with Common Law Theories of Copyright' (2013) 23 Fordham Intell Prop Media & Ent LJ 1063, 1080; Michelle Janevicius, 'Droit de Suite and Conflicting Priorities: The Unlikely Case for Visual Artists' Resale Royalty Rights in the United States' (2015) 25 DePaul J Art, Tech & Intell Prop L 383, 427; Lara Mastrangelo, 'Droit De Suite – Why the United States Can No Longer Ignore the Global Trend' (2018) 18 Chi-Kent J Int'l & Comp L 1, 3–4 (noting that the enforcement of *droit de suite* is not effective in some European countries).

107 Michael D Murray, 'NFTs Rescue Resale Royalties? The Wonderfully Complicated Ability of NFT Smart Contracts to Allow Resale Royalty Rights' (2023) 14 (2) Case W Res JL Tech & Internet 206, 214.

a concept introduced by Roger Brownsword, which describes a situation where technologies replace the regulations and the human entities responsible for creating, implementing, and enforcing them.[108] In the *iBox* case, the defendant's unauthorized minting of the plaintiff's copyrighted work as an NFT essentially deprived the plaintiff of the right to collect resale royalties. Allowing the plaintiff to mint the NFT herself would provide an opportunity to set a royalty percentage for each resale after the initial transaction, making it more reasonable to include the amount of resale royalties in the plaintiff's actual loss for damage calculation.

Fourthly, the court's decision contradicts a prior ruling by the Hangzhou Internet Court in *Panghu*,[109] the first NFT case in China, concerning platform liabilities for NFT marketplaces. The decision was subsequently upheld by the Hangzhou Intermediate Court.[110] In *Panghu*, the court emphasized that NFT marketplaces have a higher duty of care compared to normal internet service providers (ISPs), subject to a simpler notice-and-take-down rule.[111] This created a due diligence standard for NFT platforms, considering factors such as the platform's capacity to review and control posted content without incurring extra costs, direct profits from NFTs through commissions and gas fees, and failure to implement any prevention measures.[112] The defendant, an NFT marketplace, in *Panghu* was held vicariously liable for copyright infringement due to its user's unauthorized minting of others' copyrighted work. The inconsistency between *Panghu* and *iBo*x raises questions about the application of due diligence standards and liabilities for NFT platforms in China.

Applying the factors established by the Hangzhou Internet Court to *iBo*x reveals an unreasonably lenient consequence for the defendant iBox based on its business model and activities. Notably, there appears to be no discernible difference between the business model and nature of the two NFT platforms involved in *Panghu* and *iBox*. Compounding the issue, in *iBox*, the infringing NFT was minted by the platform itself rather than by its users, rendering it directly liable rather than merely a vicarious infringer. Moreover, considering that iBox also collects a 4.5% gas fee for each subsequent transaction of the infringing NFTs, excluding these resales from the scope of infringement would equate NFT platforms like iBox to regular ISPs in terms of their duty of care. This stance is inconsistent with the rationale established in *Panghu*. Over time, such inconsistencies may negatively impact the application of IP rules in the burgeoning NFT market.

108 Roger Brownsword, 'Law's Imperfect Governance: Is the Metaverse the Solution?' (2023) 25 Media & Arts L Rev 241, 249.

109 *Panghu* (n 25).

110 Shenzhen Qice Diechu Wenhua Chuangyi Youxian Gongsi Su Hangzhou Yuan Yuzhou Keji Youxian Gongsi (深圳奇策迭出文化创意有限公司诉杭州原与宙科技有限公司) [*Shenzhen Qice Diechu Cultural Creativity Co, Ltd v Hangzhou Yuanyuzhou Technology Co, Ltd*] (Hangzhou Interm People's Ct 2022) (China).

111 ibid.

112 ibid.

V. Conclusion

Artists, investors, and consumers have increasingly immersed themselves in the rapidly expanding realm of NFTs. However, a myriad of biases and misunderstandings envelop the understanding of NFTs and their intricate relationship with property, contracts, and IP. These misconceptions have ignited disputes and led to legal misapplications, ultimately diminishing the economic value of NFTs.

It is vital to recognize that acquiring an NFT does not equate to obtaining ownership of the underlying artwork or any associated IP rights. NFTs exist independently from the underlying assets they represent. Failing to grasp this fundamental concept has triggered legal disputes globally, particularly regarding IP infringement. The absence of a comprehensive understanding of the technological, economic, and legal nature of NFTs has planted seeds of uncertainty in the NFT market.

Addressing these uncertainties, this chapter asserts that an NFT truly resembles property when stored on-chain and when it can be transferred across various platforms. However, applying traditional property rules to NFTs without considering IP neglects the evolution of private law that underpins information transactions. Such an approach not only fails to enhance the NFT market but also impedes its potential to complement the IP regime in fostering creativity in the long run.

2 Taxation of Cryptoassets and Web 3.0

*Jingyi Wang**

1. Introduction

The world is entering yet another new digital era, Web 3.0. 'If Web 1.0 was the read-only iteration, Web 2.0 could be seen as the read/write upgrade, or what we know as the internet today.'[1] Web 2.0 is dominated by monopolistic and centralized companies such as Google, Facebook, and Amazon, whereas Web 3.0 is designed to be decentralized and reliant on a new technology, blockchain. Many new concepts based on the blockchain have emerged, such as cryptocurrencies, the metaverse, non-fungible tokens (NFTs),[2] and decentralized autonomous organizations.[3] An even more striking development over the past decade is the cryptoassets market, which has created enormous wealth. According to simulations conducted by the European Commission, the potential revenue from taxing capital gains on bitcoin[4] in the European Union (EU) in 2020 was estimated at around EUR 900 million, which is equivalent to 0.3% of the total tax revenue from property taxation in the EU.[5] Due to 'their lack of centralized control, (pseudo-)anonymity, valuation difficulties, hybrid characteristics (including both aspects of financial instruments and intangible assets)',[6] the proliferation of blockchain-based/enabled cryptoassets and transactions creates significant challenges for tax administration.

* The author would like to thank Jyh-An Lee and Joseph Lee for their great comments and help with the chapter.

1 Dan Ashmore, 'A Brief History of Web 3.0' (24 April 2023) <https://www.forbes.com/advisor/investing/cryptocurrency/what-is-web-3-0/> accessed 17 May 2023.

2 Runhua Wang, Jyh-An Lee, and Jingwen Liu, Chapter 1 in this volume.

3 Joseph Lee and Rougang Li, Chapter 4 in this volume.

4 In this chapter, capitalized 'Bitcoin' refers to the blockchain network, while bitcoin in lowercase or BTC refers to the native coin issued in the Bitcoin network.

5 Andreas Thiemann, 'Cryptocurrencies: An Empirical View from a Tax Perspective' (2021) JRC Working Papers on Taxation and Structural Reforms 12/2021 <https://joint-research-centre.ec.europa.eu/system/files/2021-08/jrc126109.pdf> accessed 4 May 2023.

6 OECD, *Taxing Virtual Currencies: An Overview Of Tax Treatments And Emerging Tax Policy Issues* (OECD 2020) 54 <www.oecd.org/tax/tax-policy/taxing-virtual-currencies-an-overview-of-tax-treatments-and-emerging-tax-policy-issues.htm>

DOI: 10.4324/9781032618975-4

There is no universally adopted approach to taxing cryptoassets. How jurisdictions deal with cryptoassets is determined by how they characterize the relevant cryptoassets and transactions.[7] In many OECD countries, for example, exchanging one type of cryptocurrency for another can result in a taxable event. However, this is not true in France, where only transactions involving the exchange of cryptocurrency for fiat currency would lead to a tax obligation.[8] In Italy, the Netherlands, and Portugal, no tax is levied on the realization of capital gains from cryptocurrencies unless the transactions are considered speculative.[9]

Investors in cryptoassets need to consider the potential tax liability and reporting obligations of their transactions. Governments need to review their cryptoassets tax regimes frequently if they are to keep pace with this rapidly evolving market. Governments also need to consider the effect of taxation on the attractiveness and competitiveness of their domestic cryptoassets markets; this is especially important for countries seeking to be hubs for the digital assets industry.

When taxability of cryptoassets is considered, the following questions are relevant: is there a taxable event? Who is the taxpayer? How much is the taxable income/gain? Where should the tax be collected and when? In recent years, many jurisdictions have issued tax regulations or guidance to help investors find answers to these questions. Nevertheless, due to the rapid development of new kinds of blockchain-based cryptoassets and economic activities, state governments are lagging behind when it comes to taxing specific kinds of cryptoasset transactions. Tax authorities should consider whether their existing tax regimes can be stretched to cover these new assets and business models, or whether further legislation is needed to keep pace with the new digital ecosystem. Even when no special tax regime is provided for cryptoassets, they could be taxed according to basic tax principles.[10] This means individuals earning income from a cryptocurrency business, such as mining or staking, can be taxed as though they are self-employed.[11] Individuals could also be subject to capital gains tax on gains they earn on the disposal of cryptoassets. If a company gains from investment in cryptoassets, it would be subject to corporation tax. Any losses from investing in cryptoassets cannot be claimed until the losses are realized after the disposal of the cryptoassets.[12]

This chapter, divided into five sections, examines the emergence of Web 3.0 and its tax implementations. After the introduction, the chapter discusses the taxability of cryptocurrencies in section 2 and of the metaverse in section 3. Section 4 examines the tax implications of decentralized finance, and section 5 reviews the latest developments in information reporting in relation to cryptoassets.

7 Abubakri Yekini, Chapter 4 in this volume.
8 Thiemann (n 5) 4.
9 ibid.
10 Sofia Thomas, 'Cryptocurrency and Taxation' (21 February 2023) <https://financialremediesjournal.com/content/cryptocurrency-and-taxation.3a598bdecae74c20b6bff2502156980b.htm> accessed 5 May 2023.
11 ibid.
12 ibid.

2. Cryptocurrencies

The initial reason for developing blockchain technology was to deal with the transaction costs and risks associated with traditional financial institutions. As outlined in a white paper by the pseudonymous Satoshi Nakamoto, financial institutions have functioned as trusted third parties in processing electronic payments.[13] However, reliance on this trust-based model made it difficult for transactions to be completely non-reversible; in other words, payment cannot be made in a non-reversible way.[14] Nakamoto advocated the adoption of a peer-to-peer cash system using cryptographic proof to enable direct payment between seller and buyer, thus reducing transaction costs.[15] Bitcoin, as the first blockchain to implement this peer-to-peer regime, uses a two-key encryption technique known as asymmetric encryption.[16] Asymmetric encryption uses a dual public and private key distribution technique to enable mathematical authentication of a document by the public key-holder and decoding only by the private key-holder.[17] Low and Mik define blockchains as 'a species of distributed databases that are maintained by a network of geographically dispersed computers, or "nodes".'[18]

Blockchains can be either permissioned or permissionless. As these names suggest, permissionless blockchains are open and anonymous, allowing anyone to join the network without disclosing their identity or agreeing to any system rules or terms of use,[19] whereas permissioned blockchains only grant access to permitted participants who subscribe to system rules.[20] Permissionless blockchains are public blockchains and permissioned chains are private.[21] Cryptocurrencies, like bitcoin (BTC), ether (ETH), and Dogecoin (DOGE),[22] known as their respective blockchains' native cryptoassets, are distributed to participants as 'an economic incentive to produce blocks and hence maintain the integrity of the entire system.'[23] Permissioned or private blockchains are used for 'data storage, digital ID systems,

13 Satoshi Nakamoto, 'Bitcoin: A Peer-to-Peer Electronic Cash System' (31 October 2008) 1 <https://www.ussc.gov/sites/default/files/pdf/training/annual-national-training-seminar/2018/Emerging_Tech_Bitcoin_Crypto.pdf> accessed 27 April 2023.

14 ibid.

15 ibid.

16 Ben Fearnley, 'Cryptoassets – Still an Enigma?' (13 October 2022) <https://financialremedies-journal.com/content/cryptoassets-still-an-enigma.609696782b244f358ea233512a1eba97.htm> accessed 27 April 2023.

17 ibid.

18 Kelvin FK Low and Eliza Mik, 'Pause the Blockchain Legal Revolution' (2020) 69 Int'l & Comp LQ 135–36.

19 ibid 3.

20 ibid 5.

21 Matthew Beedham, 'Here's the Difference Between "Permissioned" and "Permissionless" Blockchains' (5 November 2018) <https://thenextweb.com/news/permissioned-permissionless-blockchains> accessed 27 May 2023.

22 Cryptopedia Staff, 'What Does Permissionless Mean?' (1 July 2022) <https://www.gemini.com/cryptopedia/what-is-permissionless-crypto-permissionlessness-blockchain> accessed 27 May 2023.

23 Low and Mik (n 18) 3.

and inventory and supply-chain management. Popular permissioned blockchains include Quorum, R3 Corda, and Hyperledger Fabric.'[24] CoinMarketCap reports that there are 22,932 cryptocurrencies.[25] Most major cryptocurrencies, such as bitcoin, run on permissionless blockchain networks.[26]

The bitcoin market has experienced extreme volatility over the years. In April 2023, one bitcoin costs USD 29,064, whereas its all-time high was USD 68,789.63. The value of bitcoin has appreciated by 9,033.58% since its advent. The bitcoin market cap reached USD 1.15 trillion in October 2021, and the cryptocurrency market is predicted to experience a compound annual growth rate of 56.4% between 2019 and 2025.[27] According to Chainalysis's calculation, in 2020 the total estimated capital gains from bitcoin in the EU amounted to EUR 12.7 billion, including EUR 3.6 billion of realized gains.[28] Using Chainalysis's data, Thiemann calculated that the realization ratio (dividing realized capital gains by total gains) of bitcoin ranged between 24% in Spain and 32% in Slovenia.[29] This means that in the near future, there could be huge capital gains to be realized.

In 2023, it was estimated that global crypto-ownership rates were at an average of 4.2% of the worldwide population, with over 420 million crypto users worldwide.[30] There have been several large exchanges of cryptocurrencies, including Binance, Kraken, Gate.io, Coinbase. and Bitstamp.[31] Given the volume of trading in these exchanges (for example, Binance's trading volume was USD 287 billion in April 2023),[32] jurisdictions have attempted a number of different approaches to tax-related gains and income.

Blockchain's original design relies on transparency: although the identity of payers and recipients is kept anonymous, information recorded in the blockchain is visible to the public.[33] What is interesting is that neither of the two main features of the blockchain envisaged by Nakamoto, anonymity and decentralization, has been fully achieved; transactions thought to be anonymous actually leave a

24 Cryptopedia Staff (n 22).

25 Coryanne Hicks, 'Different Types of Cryptocurrencies' (15 March 2023) <https://www.forbes.com/advisor/investing/cryptocurrency/different-types-of-cryptocurrencies/#:~:text=How%20Many%20Cryptocurrencies%20Are%20There,market%20capitalization%20of%20%241.1%20trillion.> accessed 18 May 2023.

26 Cointelegraph.com, 'Permissioned Blockchain vs. Permissionless Blockchain: Key Differences' <https://cointelegraph.com/learn/permissioned-blockchain-vs-permissionless-blockchain-key-differences#:~:text=Most%20of%20the%20major%20cryptocurrencies,no%20gatekeepers%20and%20no%20censorship.> accessed 29 May 2023.

27 TripleA, 'Cryptocurrency Ownership Data: Cryptocurrency across the World' (2023) <https://triple-a.io/crypto-ownership-data/> accessed 5 May 2023.

28 Thiemann (n 5) 2, citing data released by Chainalysis.com.

29 ibid 16.

30 TripleA (n 27).

31 Fearnley (n 16).

32 Lyllah Ledesma, 'Crypto Exchange Binance Trading Volume Fell Almost 50% in April' (10 May 2023) <https://www.coindesk.com/markets/2023/05/10/crypto-exchange-binance-trading-volume-fell-almost-50-in-april/> accessed 20 June 2023.

33 ibid.

permanent record that can be traced, and many people who own cryptocurrency depend on intermediaries, which goes against the original intention of decentralized finance.[34] After years of development, many blockchains are 'not open-source, publicly accessible, or decentralized.'[35] For example, in El Salvador, where bitcoin has been adopted as legal currency, payments need to be made through a digital wallet that is centrally managed.[36] This traceability, along with the involvement of intermediaries, makes regulation of cryptoassets possible. Bitcoin, the first cryptoasset, is based on distributed ledger technology (DLT), whereas many later distributed ledger technology applications are often not fully distributed or decentralized, which makes it possible to regulate and supervise the operation of these applications.[37]

2.1 The Character of Cryptocurrency

Although there is no unified definition of cryptoassets, different definitions emphasize certain common features, such as representation of value, distributed ledger technology, and cryptography. For example, the Financial Action Task Force defines virtual assets (cryptoassets) as 'any digital representation of value that can be digitally traded, transferred or used for payment. It does not include digital representation of fiat currencies.'[38] The final report of the UK's Cryptoassets Taskforce defines a cryptoasset as 'a cryptographically secured digital representation of value or contractual rights that uses some type of DLT and can be transferred, stored or traded electronically.'[39] The report classifies cryptoassets as payment tokens, utility tokens, and security tokens.[40] These different categories of token may be classified differently for purposes of accounting and taxation.[41] Payment tokens, such as bitcoin and ether, also known as exchange tokens, can be used as a method of payment.[42] Utility tokens are issued for accessing the product or service offered by the token issuer, such as a ride-hailing token for paying for a taxi journey but not anything else.[43] Security tokens, which provide the owner with a contractual right to cash or another financial asset, can be regarded as tokenized equity or debt

34 Thiemann (n 5).
35 ibid 136.
36 ibid.
37 HM Treasury, Financial Conduct Authority and Blank of England, *Cryptoassets Taskforce: Final Report* (HM Treasury 2018) 8.
38 Financial Action Task Force, 'Virtual Assets' <https://www.fatf-gafi.org/en/topics/virtual-assets.html>
39 HM Treasury, Financial Conduct Authority and Bank of England (n 37) 11.
40 Thiemann (n 5) 3.
41 OECD, *Taxing Virtual Currencies* (n 4) 15.
42 Joseph Lee, 'Law and Regulation for a Crypto-Market: Perpetuation or Innovation?' (11 July 2020) 6 <https://ssrn.com/abstract=3648701>
43 Ian Bradley, 'How Taxes on Cryptocurrencies and Digital Assets Will Soon Take Shape' (23 March 2022) <https://www.ey.com/en_lu/tax/how-taxes-on-cryptocurrencies-and-digital-assets-will-soon-take-shape> accessed 28 May 2023.

and would be taxed according to tax rules of securities.[44] Transactions involving payment tokens are the most common. These transactions have received major attention from investors and tax authorities, but most jurisdictions have not issued guidance on the tax treatment of utility tokens or security tokens.[45] This section will therefore focus on the taxability of payment tokens. When cryptocurrencies are discussed in this section, 'cryptoassets' mainly refers to payment tokens.

Thiemann notes that there are four main ways of using cryptocurrencies: as a means of payment, as a form of investment, for illicit activities, and as a tax haven.[46] Although cryptoassets are often labelled as currency or coin, and more and more retailers are willing to accept cryptocurrencies, cryptocurrency as a means of payment is still limited due to its severe price volatility.[47] Most cryptocurrencies are held for investment purposes,[48] which makes taxation on related gains or losses a relevant factor to be considered by investors. Illicit activities or tax evasion justify information reporting requirements over and above the need to collect information for tax purposes.

There is a lack of consensus regarding the characterization of cryptocurrency.[49] The purpose and function of a specific cryptocurrency could affect its classification, which will in turn determine the tax consequences of a related transaction.[50] In particular, 'the significance of classification for tax purposes relates to whether a tax system defines income in a global or schedular way.'[51] Classification matters more for a schedular tax system than a global income tax regime, because a schedular tax system treats income from different sources differently. Individual circumstances also need to be taken into account: cryptocurrency miners treat their currency as stock-in-trade, occasional sellers transact in virtual currency as a hobby, and professional entrepreneurs accept virtual currency as a means of payment.[52] Both the classification of the cryptocurrency and the specific use made of the cryptoasset will affect the tax consequences.

Although cryptoassets have features that differentiate them from traditional currencies or property, the taxation of cryptoassets also needs to reflect the principle of neutrality, which means that 'neutrality between investment alternatives' and commercial considerations, rather than tax consequences, should determine whether

44 PwC, 'PwC Annual Global Crypto Tax Report 2020' 12 <https://www.pwc.ch/en/publications/2021/pwc-annual-global-crypto-tax-report-2020.pdf> accessed 15 May 2023.

45 Bradley (n 43).

46 Thiemann (n 5) 8–10.

47 ibid 8.

48 ibid 9.

49 Robert Armstrong, 'Unhedged: Bitcoin Is Equity, Not Money' (21 May 2021) <https://www.ft.com/unhedged?spoor-id=cks91341c00005j6zbfr3x3gt&page=15> accessed 5 May 2023.

50 Louise Fjord Kjærsgaard and Autilia Arfwidsson, 'Taxation of Cryptocurrencies from the Danish and Swedish Perspectives' (2019) 47 Intertax 620, 620.

51 ibid 623.

52 Aleksandra Bal, 'Developing a Regulatory Framework for the Taxation of Virtual Currencies' (2019) 47 Intertax 219–20.

to invest in an asset.[53] Tax policies adopted by a jurisdiction in relation to cryptoassets should reflect the principle of neutrality both horizontally and vertically. Horizontal neutrality means neutral treatment of cryptoasset transactions by different persons or organizations, while vertical neutrality requires neutral treatment of cryptoassets compared with other kinds of asset. Neutrality does not mean identical tax treatment but rather tax treatment appropriate to the specific circumstances.

2.2 Taxability of Cryptocurrency

From a taxpayer's perspective, the relevant tax questions in relation to cryptocurrencies include:

> What is the status of a virtual currency for tax purposes? Does it qualify as property, currency or something else? Is it possible to treat all virtual currency types in a one-size-fits-all manner? When do disposals of virtual currency result in income and when in a capital gain? Is the mere possession of virtual currency subject to income tax? Does currency mining result in taxable income? When may a person mining or selling virtual currency be considered an entrepreneur for tax purposes? Under which circumstances does trade in virtual currency trigger a VAT registration obligation? Which transactions in virtual currency may benefit from a VAT exemption? What are the compliance obligations of persons mining and transacting in virtual currencies? What is the most optimal method of regulation for virtual currencies?[54]

These questions reveal the complexities of taxing cryptocurrencies, including the technicalities of tax rules and the uncertain nature of cryptoassets per se. The complexity may also explain why national governments are taking a long time to put forward their tax policies in relation to cryptoassets. Bal suggests that in order to answer these questions, at least three factors should be investigated: income classification, income determination and compliance obligations (record keeping and reporting).[55]

According to the PwC annual crypto tax reports, which were launched in 2020, in recent years, more and more jurisdictions have legislated or provided guidance on the taxability of cryptoassets.[56] PwC's 2020 report expressed concern that the taxation of cryptoassets may hinder the development of the crypto industry, especially when cryptocurrencies are treated differently from fiat currency. For example, taxation on crypto funds cannot benefit from the tax exemption policies enjoyed by investment funds, and crypto lending cannot be taxed in a similar way

53 Kjærsgaard and Arfwidsson (n 50) 633.
54 Bal (n 52) 220.
55 ibid 220.
56 PwC, 'PwC Annual Global Crypto Tax Report 2020' (n 44).

to the lending and repaying of money.[57] The PwC's crypto tax report notes that 'triggering a tax charge every time an individual spends using digital assets could be problematic. . . . This represents an immense barrier to mass adoption of cryptocurrencies as a means of exchange.'[58] Although this comment sounds reasonable, whether taxation on cryptocurrencies would be a barrier really depends on the tax policies and characterization of cryptocurrencies adopted by a state, in particular, to what extent that state wishes to accept cryptocurrencies as a means of exchange and how the state characterizes cryptocurrencies.

On 9 June 2021, El Salvador became the first country to make bitcoin legal tender, requiring all businesses to accept the cryptocurrency.[59] Because the Salvadoran Bitcoin Law established only bitcoin as legal tender not subject to capital gains tax, all other cryptocurrencies could be treated as intangible assets liable to capital gains tax.[60] While the international community is closely monitoring the bitcoin experiment in El Salvador,[61] there is currently no specific statement in Salvadoran tax law regarding the taxability of other cryptocurrencies.[62]

Although it is mandated by law in El Salvador that all businesses must accept bitcoin, only 20% of firms have received bitcoin as a way of payment.[63] Only around 5% of total sales are settled through the official digital wallet, Chivo Wallet, in bitcoin. Most Chivo users choose cash holdings over bitcoin, and 88% of firms convert their bitcoin earnings into dollars.[64] According to a survey released by the Chamber of Commerce and Industry of El Salvador in March 2022, a significant majority (86%) of businesses have never conducted a transaction using bitcoin, and only 20% of businesses comply with the legal requirement to accept the cryptocurrency.[65]

To date, no other jurisdiction has accorded cryptocurrencies the status of legal tender. Most jurisdictions categorize cryptoassets as property or intangible property, while some treat cryptoassets as 'other' without specification of their character.[66] For instance, the International Financial Reporting Interpretations Committee

57 ibid 8.
58 ibid 9.
59 Laurent Belsie, 'El Salvador's Experiment with Bitcoin as Legal Tender' (July 2022) <https://www.nber.org/digest/202207/el-salvadors-experiment-bitcoin-legal-tender> accessed 18 May 2023.
60 PwC, 'PwC Annual Global Crypto Tax Report 2022' 33 <https://www.pwc.com/gx/en/financial-services/pdf/global-crypto-tax-report-2022.pdf> accessed 17 May 2023.
61 MacKenzie Sigalos and Arjun Kharpal, 'El Salvador's Bitcoin Experiment: $60 Million Lost, $375 Million Spent, Little to Show so Far' (13 October 2022) <https://www.cnbc.com/2022/10/13/el-salvadors-bitcoin-holdings-down-60percent-to-60-million-one-year-later.html> accessed 28 May 2023; PwC, 'EI Salvador's Law: A Meaningful Test for Bitcoin' (2021) <https://www.pwc.com/gx/en/financial-services/pdf/el-salvadors-law-a-meaningful-test-for-bitcoin.pdf> accessed 28 May 2023.
62 PwC, 'PwC Annual Global Crypto Tax Report 2022' (n 60) 33.
63 Belsie (n 59).
64 ibid.
65 Sigalos and Kharpal (n 61). EI Salvador's tourism industry benefits from the Bitcoin experiment. According to official government estimates, the tourism industry is up 30% since the Bitcoin Law took effect. The country's tourism minister also notes that 60% of tourists now come from the U.S.
66 PwC, 'PwC Annual Global Crypto Tax Report 2020' (n 44) 9.

indicated that cryptocurrencies meet the definition of an intangible asset under IFRS 38, which defines an intangible asset as 'an identifiable non-monetary asset without physical substance.'[67] In the UK, several cases (e.g., *AA v Persons Unknown*)[68] hold that bitcoins are property, rather than a choice in action or a choice in possession.[69] In a recent case involving the now-defunct crypto exchange Gatecoin, the Hong Kong High Court recognized that cryptocurrency is property.[70]

Because the blockchain ecosystem is evolving quickly, and it takes time for governments to react to new developments, most jurisdictions try to tax cryptoassets according to their existing tax regime by providing updated guidance and explanations rather than by making special tax rules. The US Internal Revenue Service (IRS) guidance treats digital assets as property for federal tax purposes and suggests that general tax principles for property transactions apply to transactions using digital assets.[71]

The IRS suggests that taxable gain or loss may result from transactions of digital assets, including but not limited to:

> Sale of a digital asset for fiat; exchange of a digital asset for property, goods, or services; exchange or trade of one digital asset for another digital asset; receipt of a digital asset as payment for goods or services; receipt of a new digital asset as a result of a hard fork; receipt of a new digital asset as a result of mining or staking activities; receipt of a digital asset as a result of an airdrop; any other disposition of a financial interest in a digital asset; and receipt or transfer of a digital asset for free (without providing any consideration) that does not qualify as a bona fide gift.[72]

The Australian tax authority, the Australian Tax Office (ATO), provides regularly updated guidance on taxation of cryptoassets. This guidance sets up a useful analysis framework for understanding the important factors when taxing cryptoassets. When considering the tax consequences of cryptoassets, the ATO asks taxpayers to think about two questions: 'Has there been a change of ownership? And has there been a capital gains tax event, like transfer, swapping and selling?'[73]

67 OECD, *Taxing Virtual Currencies* (n 4) 16.

68 [2019] EWHC 3556 (Comm).

69 Fearnley (n 16).

70 Xinmei Shen, 'Cryptocurrency Is Property in Hong Kong, Court Rules for the First Time, Bolstering City's Efforts to Promote Industry' (20 April 2023) <https://www.scmp.com/tech/tech-trends/article/3217747/cryptocurrency-property-hong-kong-court-rules-first-time-bolstering-citys-efforts-promote-industry> accessed 28 May 2023; Sebastian Sinclair, 'Hong Kong Court Recognizes Crypto as Property' (19 April 2023) <https://blockworks.co/news/crypto-property-hong-kong> accessed 28 May 2023.

71 IRS, 'Digital Assets' (25 May 2023) <https://www.irs.gov/businesses/small-businesses-self-employed/digital-assets> accessed 28 May 2023.

72 ibid.

73 Australian Tax Office, 'Crypto and Your Taxes' (28 March 2023) <https://community.ato.gov.au/s/article/a079s0000009GmxAAE/crypto-and-your-taxes> accessed 9 May 2023.

The ATO provides detailed guidance on the tax treatment of cryptoassets.[74] Cryptoassets are defined as

> a digital representation of value that you can transfer, store, or trade electronically. This also includes non-fungible tokens (NFTs). . . . Crypto-assets are a subset of digital assets that use cryptography to protect digital data and distributed ledger technology to record transactions.[75]

The ATO holds that cryptoassets are not a form of money.[76] No special tax rules are provided for cryptoassets, and the tax treatment is based on existing tax rules, which examine how a taxpayer acquires, holds, and disposes of the assets.[77]

The ATO categorizes trading in cryptoassets according to whether the trade is for business, investment, or personal use.[78] For investors, cryptoassets are taxed as capital gains tax (CGT) assets, while rewards for staking crypto are treated as ordinary income for tax purposes.[79] Businesses transacting in cryptoassets as trading stock rather than investment need to count the proceeds of selling the cryptoassets as ordinary income and the cost of acquisition of the cryptoassets as deductible expenses.[80] When cryptoassets are held for purely personal use, they will not be subject to CGT.[81] Here, the key question is to define the boundary between making an investment (which means the investor is taxed for CGT) and trading in cryptoassets (which means the trader is taxed for ordinary income). A trader is defined for this purpose as 'active in crypto as a means to generate an income and is operating from a business setup.'[82] Typical examples include running a crypto trading, forging, or mining business, regularly buying and selling for short-term gain, or running a crypto exchange.[83] Compared with the regular and frequent trading activities of a crypto business, an investor usually 'buys and sells crypto as personal investment "stock" with the goal of gradually building wealth over an extended period of time with their profit made from long-term capital gains.'[84] Investors can access a 50% CGT discount for long-term gains, which is not available for traders.[85]

74 Australian Tax Office, 'Crypto Asset Investments' (29 June 2022) <https://www.ato.gov.au/Individuals/Investments-and-assets/Crypto-asset-investments/> accessed 9 May 2023.

75 Australian Tax Office, 'What Are Crypto Assets?' (19 August 2022) <https://www.ato.gov.au/individuals/Investments-and-assets/crypto-asset-investments/what-are-crypto-assets-/> accessed 9 May 2023.

76 ibid.

77 ibid.

78 Australian Tax Office, 'Crypto and Your Taxes' (n 73).

79 Australian Tax Office, 'What Are Crypto Assets?' (n 75).

80 ibid.

81 ibid.

82 Michelle Legge, 'Crypto Tax Australia: Here's How Much You'll Pay in 2023' (3 May 2023) <https://koinly.io/guides/crypto-tax-australia/> accessed 9 May 2023.

83 ibid.

84 ibid.

85 ibid.

Australia was the first country to provide a legal definition of virtual currency for tax purposes, and the ATO makes it clear that sales and purchases of virtual currency are not subject to Goods and Services Tax after 1 July 2017.[86]

In the Australian approach, the character of cryptoassets and the ownership or intended use of cryptocurrencies are determinative factors for the taxability of cryptoassets. It is important to point out that different jurisdictions treat these factors differently, and there is no universally adopted approach to taxing cryptoassets; the same cryptoasset or transaction could be taxed differently in different jurisdictions.

The way in which cryptocurrency transactions are characterized will affect the taxability of related assets and trading activities. For example, the first taxable event for mined virtual currencies is treated differently by different states. Finland treats the receipt of newly mined tokens as income other than income from capital; direct costs incurred in earning this income, such as the cost of electricity and equipment used in mining, are deductible.[87] New virtual currencies generated by forging are treated as a return on existing assets in Finland, and the income is treated as capital income at the time the holder acquires control of the new token.[88] Some other jurisdictions do not tax the receipt of cryptocurrencies, treating only the disposal of cryptocurrencies as a taxable event.[89] And some, such as Switzerland and Singapore, will only tax the disposal of cryptocurrencies if this disposal is regarded as trading and do not tax private mining activity.[90]

3. Taxation and the Metaverse

Since Bitcoin's advent in 2009, the pace of disruptive innovation in the blockchain industry has not slowed, and many new business models and activities have emerged. A prominent example is the metaverse, which may represent the next iteration of the internet.[91] Author Neal Stephenson first introduced the term 'metaverse' in his 1992 sci-fi novel *Snow Crash*, in which he depicted a virtual realm where individuals could engage with each other and virtual entities in real time.[92] The popularity of the metaverse is believed to have the potential to affect everything, 'from employee engagement to the customer experience, omnichannel sales and marketing, product innovation, and community building.'[93]

86 Bal (n 52) 221.

87 OECD, *Taxing Virtual Currencies* (n 4) 24.

88 ibid 24.

89 ibid 25.

90 ibid 26.

91 Norelle Ng and Forbes Technology Council, 'Is the Metaverse the Next Iteration of the Internet?' (25 January 2023) <https://www.forbes.com/sites/forbestechcouncil/2023/01/25/is-the-metaverse-the-next-iteration-of-the-internet/?sh=29dbfb5f2d42> accessed 28 May 2023.

92 ibid.

93 McKinsey & Company, 'Value Creation in the Metaverse' (20 June 2022) 5 <https://www.mckinsey.com/capabilities/growth-marketing-and-sales/our-insights/value-creation-in-the-metaverse>

The metaverse ecosystem presents a new immersive digital experience for users by combining elements such as online multiplayer gaming, cryptocurrency, NFTs, and virtual reality.[94] The annual revenue that could be created by this market opportunity has been estimated at over 1 trillion US dollars.[95] Although the metaverse is a virtual world, the value created and gains earned in it are associated with real-world natural persons or legal entities, which may need to bear related tax liability.[96] The tax residency of the real-world parties to such virtual/hypothetical transactions is the key factor when attempting to identify the taxpayer and their tax liability.[97]

NFTs are probably the most popular items in the metaverse, but there is no consensus on the definition of NFTs. From a technical perspective, an NFT is 'not the underlying asset itself, but an electronic record proving ownership of the asset that is separate from other legal ownership risks.'[98] Currently, the majority of tax experts concur that NFTs can be viewed as a form of art, specifically digital art.[99] If a person selling art in the real world is subject to CGT, then a person earning a gain from selling NFTs should be taxed in a similar way.[100]

Sales made by retail companies and fashion brands of both digital and physical goods in the metaverse could incur liability for both direct and indirect taxes.[101] Major transactions that can happen in the metaverse include:[102]

1. Sale of digital goods, such as NFTs, skins, and avatar accessories
2. Sale of second-hand digital goods
3. Sale or rental of virtual real estate

The key question is: what has been traded? That is, what is the characterization of the underlying object being transacted? Due to the virtuality of the assets presented in the metaverse, characterizing these items is not straightforward. For example, when discussing the complex tax issues arising from the metaverse, a PwC commentary raises the following questions:

94 Roger van de Berg and Henrik Stipdonk, 'Taxes Become More Complex When Entering the Metaverse' (5 October 2022) <https://www.bakermckenzie.com/en/insight/publications/2022/10/taxes-complex-metaverse> accessed 28 May 2023.

95 David Grider, 'The Metaverse: Web 3.0 Virtual Cloud Economies' (*Grayscale Research*, November 2021) 8 <https://grayscale.com/wp-content/uploads/2021/11/Grayscale_Metaverse_Report_Nov2021.pdf> accessed 29 April 2023.

96 Julia Cockroft, 'Taxation in the Metaverse' (11 October 2022) <https://www.lexology.com/library/detail.aspx?g=f45df7d2-d819-4578-864b-26df0893204f> accessed 29 April 2023.

97 ibid.

98 PwC, 'PwC Annual Global Crypto Tax Report 2021' 13 <https://www.pwc.com/gx/en/insights/pwc-annual-global-crypto-tax-report-2021.pdf> accessed 16 May 2023.

99 Global Business Outlook, 'Tax on Metaverse: How Does It Work?' (15 November 2022) <https://www.globalbusinessoutlook.com/tax-on-metaverse-how-does-it-work/> accessed 28 May 2023.

100 ibid.

101 Berg and Stipdonk (n 94).

102 ibid.

> If you sell digital real estate in the metaverse, is it a digital product? If it requires ongoing support, is it a digital service? Is it both? . . . NFTs generally grant the right to consume, sell or license a digital product, such as a song or artwork. NFTs may also grant the right to receive (and perhaps resell) digital services, or the right to lease or receive physical products – *or* a combination of all of the above.[103]

To a great extent, the metaverse is a virtual representation of the real world. Assets available now and items to be created in the near future, such as real estate, vehicles, clothes, and artwork, are likely to find physical counterparts in the real world. Most items traded in the metaverse are digital goods, which can be purchased outright or licensed for the right to use over a certain period of time on payment of royalties. If, after the transaction, ongoing support is required, that means part of the remuneration is for services. It will be necessary to apportion the payment between the sale of the digital item and the services provided if these two kinds of income are subject to different taxes.

3.1 Taxability and Timing

After determining the taxability of transactions taking place in the metaverse, the next question to consider is when the gains should become taxable.[104] Different characterization of cryptocurrencies will affect the tax liability of transactions of NFTs. When cryptocurrencies are regarded as property, and a customer uses bitcoin to purchase an NFT from a metaverse store, then a tax liability can arise for both buyer and seller. Transactions in the metaverse are usually settled in cryptocurrency.[105] There are at least two relevant junctures in taxation: the moment when the virtual transaction happens and the moment when the cryptocurrency is converted into fiat currency.[106] An increase in the value of a cryptocurrency may also be taxable if a country collects wealth tax. The place of real residence of a business operating in the metaverse is therefore important, as the tax resident will be taxed according to their home state's tax rules.[107] If the home state charges exit tax, the business may need to reconsider the location of its business.[108] Apart from being taxed by the home state, the business may also be taxed where its employees

103 PwC, 'What Are the Sales and Use Tax Implications of the Metaverse?' <https://www.pwc.com/us/en/tech-effect/emerging-tech/metaverse-tax-implications.html> accessed 16 May 2023.

104 ibid.

105 Bernard Marr, 'How The Metaverse Will Change Cryptocurrency' (25 April 2022) <https://www.forbes.com/sites/bernardmarr/2022/04/25/how-the-metaverse-will-change-cryptocurrency/?sh=45454f434fe4> accessed 28 May 2023.

106 Berg and Stipdonk (n 94).

107 ibid.

108 ibid.

conduct their activities, which might give rise to a permanent establishment in the host state.[109]

The UK approach to taxing the exchange of one virtual asset for another is as follows:

1. CGT is levied on an individual on the disposal of their cryptocurrency when buying the NFT, assuming the value of the cryptocurrency has increased since they acquired it and the individual has no CGT reliefs available.
2. Corporation tax is levied on a UK company on the profit generated from the sale of the NFT.
3. CGT is levied on an individual on any future sale of the NFT, assuming the value of the NFT has increased since its acquisition and the individual has no CGT reliefs available.[110]

Identifying the tax residency of a company that is well-known in the real world is relatively easy, but identifying the tax residency of an individual may be very challenging given the anonymity of the person holding cryptocurrencies.[111] The situation will become even more complex when a metaverse sale is conducted by a decentralized autonomous organization.[112]

Transactions in the metaverse also raise issues of indirect taxation; for instance, should the purchase of a plot of NFT real estate in the metaverse using cryptocurrencies be subject to value-added tax (VAT), or is it a bartering transaction that results in income-based (capital gains) taxation?[113] In New Zealand, an NFT is defined as 'a crypto-asset that contains unique distinguishing identification codes or metadata.'[114] NFTs are excluded from the definition of cryptocurrency in New Zealand's Goods and Services Tax Act, and sales of NFTs are taxed as supplies of electronically supplied services or remote services.[115]

4. Decentralized Finance (DeFi)

Apart from outright transactions of cryptoassets, various derivative transactions have been created, such as lending and borrowing cryptocurrency, derivatives, and insurance contracts.[116] New methods of finance based on blockchain technology create a decentralized finance market, known as DeFi. It is estimated that more than 80 billion US dollars are locked up in various DeFi protocols.[117]

109 ibid.
110 Cockroft (n 96).
111 ibid.
112 ibid.
113 Global Business Outlook (n 99).
114 PwC, 'PwC Annual Global Crypto Tax Report 2022' (n 60) 16.
115 ibid 17.
116 ibid 9.
117 Miles Brooks, 'The Comprehensive Guide to DeFi Taxes (2023)' (2023) <https://coinledger.io/blog/defi-crypto-tax-guide> accessed 28 May 2023.

In contrast to centralized finance (CeFi), which relies on intermediaries like banks and financial institutions,[118] DeFi offers an alternative approach to financial services such as trading, borrowing, and lending. DeFi leverages blockchain technology to build decentralized financial applications that operate on a peer-to-peer basis, which eliminates the need for traditional intermediaries and the associated delays and fees.[119]

The UK tax authority, His Majesty's Revenue and Customs (HMRC), notes that DeFi is

> an umbrella term used to provide products akin to traditional financial services through distributed ledger technology. DeFi platforms can provide services such as decentralized exchanges (DEXs), saving, lending and derivatives. Most services are currently built on Ethereum utilizing smart contracts and can be used by anyone.[120]

Without the involvement of traditional financial institutions, DeFi would be more cost- and time-efficient for its users.[121]

DeFi is complicated because there are many different kinds of crypto-finance involving different companies and different kinds of cryptoassets. This section will examine DeFi lending and liquidity mining.

DeFi lending uses cryptocurrency as collateral to obtain a loan. McClure recommends that taxable events related to DeFi lending may consist of actions such as depositing collateral for a loan, experiencing forced liquidation, receiving a different cryptocurrency as collateral, and obtaining self-repaying loans.[122] The tax implications of these events are contingent upon subsequent alterations in the initial value of the cryptoassets, as well as the receipt of any return or tokens that represent an increase in value.[123]

By providing liquidity or acting as a lender, an individual can potentially earn a profit from participating in DeFi loans. The tax treatment of the income received by the lender or liquidity provider is dependent on whether their activities qualify as trading. HMRC expects that individuals involved in making DeFi loans will only be held to be carrying out a trade in rare circumstances.[124] If an individual is not

118 Mr Big Whale, 'The Key Difference between DeFi and CeFi' (15 February 2023) <https://www.binance.com/en/feed/post/219866> accessed 28 May 2023.

119 Zac McClure, 'The Essential DeFi Tax Guide for 2023' (12 April 2023) <https://tokentax.co/blog/defi-tax-guide> accessed 28 May 2023.

120 HM Revenue & Customs, 'CRYPTO61110 – Decentralised Finance: Lending and Staking' (30 March 2021) <https://www.gov.uk/hmrc-internal-manuals/cryptoassets-manual/crypto61110> accessed 28 May 2023.

121 Brooks (n 117).

122 McClure (n 119).

123 ibid.

124 HM Revenue & Customs, 'CRYPTO61211 – Decentralised Finance: Lending and Staking: Income Tax: Making a DeFi loan' (30 March 2021) <https://www.gov.uk/hmrc-internal-manuals/cryptoassets-manual/crypto61211> accessed 28 May 2023. The relevant factors to consider when

carrying out a trade, or if the activity generating the income falls outside the scope of any trade, then the act of making a DeFi loan or staking may be seen as disposal of a chargeable asset, which would be subject to CGT.[125] If a lender charges the borrower an agreed rate of return for the duration of the loan, this income may be subject to income tax rather than CGT.[126]

Individuals or companies participating in DeFi lending transactions may refer to the return received by the lender as 'interest', but HMRC does not recognize it as such for tax purposes.[127] This is because interest is typically associated with returns on money. As cryptocurrencies are usually not considered to be the same as money, the return on cryptocurrencies is not equivalent to interest for tax purposes. When the lender or liquidity provider receives a return in exchange for lending tokens to the borrower or staking tokens with a DeFi lending platform, this return may be considered taxable income for the lender or liquidity provider and be subject to income tax or corporation tax.[128] The reward structure for the lender and how the return is calculated will depend on the transaction's operating model, which in turn will determine whether the return should be treated as taxable income or a chargeable gain.[129] As there is no standard operating model for DeFi lending platforms, the tax treatment of the return will vary depending on the specific circumstances of the transaction.

Liquidity mining, also known as 'yield farming', is 'an investment strategy through which crypto holders lend assets to a DeFi exchange and receive rewards in return, typically resulting in a share of trading fees on tokens swapped.'[130] Yield farming is 'a method of earning interest on a person's cryptocurrency holdings by lending them out or staking them in decentralized finance protocols.'[131] Relevant events for tax purposes in respect of liquidity mining could include entering or exiting a liquidity pool.[132]

Entering a liquidity pool means investors deposit a cryptocurrency that is compatible with DeFi protocols, such as Ethereum or Binance Smart Chain, into a DeFi

determining whether an individual has a trade involving the making of DeFi loans would be similar to those applied to transactions in shares, securities, and other financial products.

125 ibid.

126 ibid.

127 HM Revenue & Customs (n 117).

128 HM Revenue & Customs, 'CRYPTO61214 – Decentralised Finance: Lending and Staking: Income Tax: Making A DeFi Loan: Nature of the Return' (30 March 2021) <https://www.gov.uk/hmrc-internal-manuals/cryptoassets-manual/crypto61214> accessed 28 May 2023.

129 HM Revenue & Customs, 'CRYPTO61130 – Decentralised Finance: Lending and Staking: Making a DeFi Loan' (30 March 2021) <https://www.gov.uk/hmrc-internal-manuals/cryptoassets-manual/crypto61130> accessed 28 May 2023.

130 McClure (n 119).

131 Avinandan Banerjee, 'Staking vs Yield Farming vs Liquidity Mining: What's the Difference?' (20 March 2023) <https://www.blockchain-council.org/defi/staking-vs-yield-farming-vs-liquidity-mining/> accessed 28 May 2023.

132 McClure (n 119).

protocol (e.g., a liquidity pool).[133] The investors become yield farmers and receive a liquidity pool token in return, representing their share of the pool.[134] Yield farmers use their liquidity pool tokens to take part in various DeFi activities, including lending, borrowing, or trading.[135] By providing liquidity to the pool, yield farmers can earn additional cryptocurrency or interest payments. One reason for the popularity of yield farming is high returns; some DeFi protocols offer annual percentage yields as high as 400%.[136] When investors exit the liquidity pool, the yield farmers will realize capital gains or losses, which might trigger CGT or income tax.[137]

However, in some situations, the lender or liquidity provider still retains economic ownership of the cryptoassets after depositing the cryptocurrency. If this disposal triggers CGT, then HMRC acknowledges that 'this can lead to tax outcomes that do not reflect the underlying economic substance, and to a tax liability from a transaction where no gain has been realized in a form which can be used to meet the liability.'[138] The UK government is therefore seeking input from the public on the possible implementation of a taxation scheme for DeFi lending and staking.[139] The goal of this scheme is to exclude from CGT any disposal of beneficial ownership that may occur when cryptoassets are staked or lent. Instead, a CGT charge will only apply when the cryptoassets are economically disposed of, such as in an outright sale or when they are exchanged for goods and services.[140]

5. Reporting

Given the anonymity of blockchains and cryptoassets, it is necessary to have a mechanism to help tax authorities identify taxable events and tax liability. For example, individuals can maintain multiple accounts in different exchanges located in different tax jurisdictions.[141] If the taxpayer does not declare capital gains or income earned from trading cryptocurrencies honestly, then it is very difficult for a single tax authority to assess the accuracy of the information reported by the taxpayer.[142] A coordinated and automated exchange of information among different countries on cryptocurrency-related capital gains will help national tax authorities cross-check the accuracy of reported information.

133 Banerjee (n 131).
134 McClure (n 119).
135 Banerjee (n 131).
136 ibid.
137 McClure (n 119).
138 HM Revenue & Customs, 'The Taxation of Decentralised Finance (DeFi) Involving the Lending and Staking of Cryptoassets' (27 April 2023) <https://www.gov.uk/government/consultations/the-taxation-of-decentralised-finance-involving-the-lending-and-staking-of-cryptoassets/the-taxation-of-decentralised-finance-defi-involving-the-lending-and-staking-of-cryptoassets-2> accessed 28 May 2023.
139 ibid.
140 ibid.
141 Thiemann (n 5) 12.
142 ibid 12.

To tackle the issue of information asymmetry, the OECD has been working on a framework for the automatic exchange of information on cryptoassets.[143] In August 2022, the OECD approved the Crypto-Asset Reporting Framework (CARF), which provides for the reporting of tax information on transactions in cryptoassets in a standardized manner, with a view to automatically exchanging such information.[144]

The rules and commentary of the CARF have been designed around four key elements: (i) the scope of cryptoassets to be covered; (ii) the entities and individuals subject to data collection and reporting requirements; (iii) the transactions subject to reporting as well as the information to be reported in respect of such transactions; and (iv) due diligence procedures to identify cryptoasset users and the relevant tax jurisdictions for reporting and exchange purposes.[145]

The Common Reporting Standard (CRS) is the existing international automatic information exchange framework sponsored by the OECD. It mainly applies to traditional financial institutions and financial account information, which means that new forms of virtual assets that have arisen with Web 3.0 are usually not covered. The CARF has been developed to update the current information exchange mechanism in line with the development of the virtual world.

The CARF mainly targets cryptoassets enabled by cryptographically secured distributed ledger technology, including stablecoins, derivatives issued in the form of cryptoassets, and certain NFTs.[146] These cryptoassets are known as 'relevant cryptoassets' and exchange transactions in relevant cryptoasset will give rise to reporting on the targeted transactions.[147] Three categories of cryptoasset are excluded from the reporting obligation: (i) cryptoassets that cannot be used for payment or investment purposes; (ii) central bank digital currencies; and (iii) specified electronic money products that function as a single fiat currency.[148] The last two kinds of asset are reportable under the CRS.[149]

Cryptoasset service providers that need to comply with CARF requirements will target entities or individuals who provide services effectuating exchange transactions in relevant cryptoassets for or on behalf of their customers.[150] These service providers will need to comply with reporting requirements once their domestic law adopts the CARF rules. The reporting nexus will be established when the reporting

143 Cockroft (n 96).

144 OECD, 'Crypto-Asset Reporting Framework and Amendments to the Common Reporting Standard' (10 October 2022) <https://www.oecd.org/tax/exchange-of-tax-information/crypto-asset-reporting-framework-and-amendments-to-the-common-reporting-standard.htm#:~:text=In%20August%202022%2C%20the%20OECD,to%20automatically%20exchanging%20such%20information.> accessed 1 May 2023

145 ibid 11.

146 ibid.

147 ibid.

148 ibid.

149 ibid 13.

150 ibid 11.

cryptoasset service providers either are tax resident or establish sufficient legal or economic connection in a jurisdiction adopting the reporting rules.[151]

Transactions of cryptoassets that are reportable under the CARF are of three types: (i) exchanges between relevant cryptoassets and fiat currencies; (ii) exchanges between one or more forms of relevant cryptoasset; and (iii) transfers (including reportable retail payment transactions) of relevant cryptoassets.[152]

What is particularly useful for tax assessment is the value of the cryptoassets for reporting. For cryptoasset-to-fiat currency transactions, the reporting amount is the fiat amount paid or received at the time of acquisition as the acquisition amount or gross proceeds. For cryptoasset-to-cryptoasset transactions, the CARF proposes to divide the transactions into two separate elements. The first element is the disposal of cryptoasset A, and the reporting amount equals the market value of asset A at the time of disposal. The second element is the acquisition of cryptoasset B, and the reportable value is based on the market value at the time of acquisition.[153]

In order to identify these reportable assets and transactions, reporting cryptoasset service providers are required to carry out due diligence procedures to identify their cryptoasset users, the relevant tax jurisdictions for reporting purposes, and the required information for reporting.[154]

The OECD suggests that the due diligence procedures are based on the CRS's current self-certification process as well as existing anti-money laundering or Know Your Customer obligations.[155] When a customer opens a new account with a cryptoasset exchange, identity verification is required as part of the Know Your Customer procedure.[156]

In order to facilitate the adoption of the CARF within the CRS framework, the OECD states that if certain assets can be reportable under both CRS and CARF, the CRS provides the option to cancel gross proceeds reporting if this information is reported under the CARF.[157] The OECD also extends the CRS to cover indirect investment in reportable cryptoassets through traditional financial products, such as derivatives or interests in investment vehicles.[158]

151 ibid 12. The reporting nexus will be established when the reporting crypto-asset service providers satisfy one of the following conditions: (i) tax resident in, (ii) both incorporated in, or organized under the laws of, and have legal personality or are subject to tax reporting requirements in, (iii) managed from, (iv) having a regular place of business in, or (v) effectuating relevant transactions through a branch based in a jurisdiction adopting the rules.

152 ibid 12.

153 ibid.

154 ibid 13.

155 ibid.

156 Binance, 'How to Complete Identity Verification' (23 April 2019) <https://www.binance.com/en/support/faq/how-to-complete-identity-verification-360027287111> accessed 4 May 2023.

157 OECD, 'Crypto-Asset Reporting Framework and Amendments to the Common Reporting Standard' (n 144) 13.

158 ibid.

The EU and the US are also developing cryptoasset reporting standards. The EU proposes to amend the Directive on Administrative Cooperation (DAC) to include the exchange of information related to cryptoassets (the resulting amended directive being DAC8).[159] The DAC8 proposal is the Commission's initiative to integrate both the CARF and the latest iteration of the CRS into the EU's legal framework.[160]

The US introduced new legal reporting requirements in the Infrastructure and Investment Jobs Act, which became law in November 2021 and effective in January 2023.[161] The new requirements for reporting cryptocurrency transactions have been expanded beyond cash transactions exceeding USD 10,000 to include a new category of transactions involving digital assets.[162] The US government expects these new reporting requirements to generate additional tax revenue of around USD 28 billion over the next decade.[163]

6. Conclusion

After years of rapid development, the blockchain industry has evolved into a dynamic and sophisticated market. The enormous value and wealth associated with cryptoassets and their derivative transactions is attracting increasing attention from investors and governments, and tax authorities are putting forward tax guidance to clarify the potential taxability of cryptoassets. Most governments tax cryptoasset-related income or gains through their existing tax regime and usually treat cryptoassets as a form of property rather than as fiat currency. This chapter finds that there is no unified approach to taxing cryptoassets and their related trading activities, which means that investors in cryptoassets need to keep an eye on tax rules and potential tax liability. The sophistication and anonymity associated with cryptoassets create significant challenges for tax administrations, so both international organizations and national governments are developing cryptoasset reporting frameworks. With more information available from digital market participants, national tax authorities can gather important details about cryptocurrency

159 PwC, 'PwC Annual Global Crypto Tax Report 2022' (n 60) 5.

160 Pieter Baert, 'Tax Transparency Rules for Crypto-Asset Transactions (DAC8)' (January 2023) <https://www.europarl.europa.eu/RegData/etudes/BRIE/2023/739310/EPRS_BRI(2023)739310_EN.pdf> accessed 28 May 2023.

161 PwC, 'PwC Annual Global Crypto Tax Report 2022' (n 60) 5.

162 Thomson Reuters Tax & Accounting, 'Refresher: Infrastructure and Investment Jobs Act's Crypto Reporting Requirements' (6 December 2022) <https://tax.thomsonreuters.com/news/refresher-infrastructure-and-investment-jobs-acts-crypto-reporting-requirements/#:~:text=The%20Act%20extends%20reporting%20requirements,in%20regards%20to%20crypto%20transactions> accessed 28 May 2023.

163 ibid. In the US, digital currency brokers will be required to file Form 1099-B, Proceeds from Broker/Exchange, which summarizes customers' annual gains and losses subject to taxation. Typically used by brokerages, Form 1099-B provides an annual summary of a customer's gains and losses that may be subject to taxes.

transactions, allowing them to better understand the market and determine whether regulatory measures are necessary. Nevertheless, the regulatory framework is far from being settled due to the rapid development of the market and the complicated character of cryptoassets. Tax policies will need to be reviewed and updated regularly to keep pace with the industry and provide greater certainty to investors and tax administrations.

3 The Sense and Nonsense of Smart Contracts

*Eliza Mik**

1. Introduction

Smart contracts feature in many stories. Written in future tense, these stories abound in promises of fairness, democratization, and personal empowerment. This better future is inextricably tied to the gradual transition to Web3 and to the crypto-economy, an economy based on decentralized and programmable money as well as on peer-to-peer transactions, which eliminate the need for evil bankers, expensive lawyers, or other devious intermediaries. In this better future, Web3 will enable a decentralized community of peers, cryptocurrencies will provide financial liberation, and smart contracts will ensure unprecedented transparency and certainty. We cannot help but believe. After all, stories resonate with us on an emotional level and are more accessible than complex technical papers. Facts are dry and impersonal, lacking the emotional impact that stories can offer. We have a natural inclination towards narrative comprehension, as stories simplify complex information. Facts are, however, indispensable for rational decision-making – not to mention regulation and disciplined legal analyses. The latter cannot rely on stories concocted by crypto-enthusiasts that conveniently hide the fact that the technology supposed to provide all of those benefits is inherently insecure and that the crypto-driven Web3 economy replaces one group of intermediaries, bankers and lawyers, with another – coders. After all, both the creation and the safe use of smart contracts require deep technological expertise that is beyond the reach of the average person.

In principle, smart contracts are supposed to reduce – or even eliminate – commercial uncertainty by technically ensuring that certain rules are followed. Translated into the sphere of contract law, smart contracts are supposed to preclude the possibility of breach and ensure perfect performance. By expressing contractual obligations in code, smart contracts are supposed to reduce opportunistic behavior and guarantee the achievement of the agreed outcomes.[1] The problem with these claims is that smart contracts are computer programs and computer programs are,

* Research on this chapter has been supported by the CUHK Direct Research Grant No. 4059058, titled "Legal and Regulatory approaches to Smart Contracts and Smart Legal Contracts."

1 H Halaburda, N Levina and S Min, 'Digitization of Transaction Terms as a Shift Parameter Within TCE: Strong Smart Contract as a New Mode of Transaction Governance' (2024) 48 MIS Quarterly,

DOI: 10.4324/9781032618975-5

by definition, unpredictable and unreliable. Moreover, being computer programs, smart contracts cannot be discussed by means of an analytical framework reserved for contracts or, to be more precise, by means of tools that aim to establish whether the parties have reached agreement and whether such agreement is legally enforceable. Legal scholars and regulators must abandon their blind belief in nonsensical "crypto-newspeak" and focus on the facts.

This chapter makes three simple points. Smart contracts cannot be analyzed *as if* they were contracts. Instead, assuming a more technical approach, they should be analyzed as computer programs that can *in some circumstances* assist in automating the performance of specific contractual obligations. Moreover, contrary to popular claims, smart contracts cannot ensure commercial certainty. Their common attributes, such as immutability and transparency, offer few benefits and may, in many instances, prove detrimental. To set solid foundations for future regulatory efforts and legal analyses, legal scholars and legal practitioners must refrain from proliferating misconceptions and adopt a more fact-based, technical perspective as to the attributes and operation of smart contracts. They must not skip over the question of whether smart contracts create any legal problems and whether they provide any benefits at all.[2]

Outline

Before regulating or analyzing smart contracts, we must first achieve terminological and conceptual clarity. The wide adoption of this unfortunate nomenclature has led to a hodgepodge of inconsistent approaches, as illustrated by the recent publications of the UK Law Commission,[3] as well as a number of regulations and regulatory proposals in the European Union and the United States.[4] The chapter commences with a discussion of the various definitions and descriptions of smart contracts, emphasizing the absence of a consistent understanding of the term. As an example of the resulting confusion, it briefly discusses three recent attempts to regulate and analyze smart contracts. The chapter proceeds with some broader observations regarding the need for a standardized approach and the dangers of creating new terminology without a clear purpose. The terms we use shape our thinking and determine the analytical approach to a particular problem. Before regulating or

825; Aaron Wright and Primavera De Filippi, *Blockchain and the Law: The Rule of Code* (Harvard UP 2018) 80–81.

2 Inioluwa D Raji and others, 'The Fallacy of Functionality' (ACM Conference on Fairness, Accountability, and Transparency (FAccT 22), Republic of Korea, Seoul, ACM, New York, NY, 21–24 June 2022).

3 UK Law Commission, *Smart Legal Contracts Advice to Government* (Law Com 401, 2021).

4 For a description of such efforts, see: Thiebault Schrepel, 'Smart Contracts and the Digital Single Market Through the Lens of a "Law + Technology" Approach' (European Commission Report 2021); for regulatory attempts in the United States, see, for example: Ariz Rev Stat 44-7061 (2017); Nev S B 398 (2017); Cal A B 2658 (2018); Ill H B 2257 (2018); NY S B 8858 (2018); NY A B A8780 (2017) and Ohio S B 300 (2018).

analyzing "something," we should know what this "something" is. To clarify the potential role of smart contracts in the contracting practices, the discussion revisits the basic stages in the life cycle of a contract, highlighting the technology-neutral character of contract law and the lack of legal obstacles to the automation of contract formation and contract performance by means of computer programs. Next, to demonstrate the futility of approaching smart contracts *as if* they were contracts in the legal sense, the chapter attempts to analyze them with the tools traditionally used to evaluate the existence of legally enforceable agreements. Readers must be forewarned of many awkward sentences. It is, after all, difficult to fit square pegs into round holes, that is, fit computer programs into the conceptual framework reserved for contracts. Lastly, to demonstrate the nonsensical nature of the popular crypto-narrative that largely drives the promotion of Web3, the chapter investigates the popular claim that smart contracts can provide commercial certainty by guaranteeing perfect performance.

2. Defining Smart Contracts: A State of Confusion

Legal analyses of smart contracts are difficult given the absence of a universally accepted definition of the term.[5] Smart contracts have been described as "systems which automatically move digital assets according to arbitrary pre-specified rules,"[6] "transactional scripts,"[7] "low-level code stored and running on a blockchain,"[8] or the embedding of legal terms in hardware and software to prevent breach.[9] The US National Institute of Standards and Technology, a leading and internationally recognized standards body, defines a smart contract as a "collection of code and data (sometimes referred to as functions and state) that is deployed using cryptographically signed transactions on the blockchain network."[10] The main book on Ethereum, the second-most-popular blockchain after Bitcoin, states that smart contracts are the back-end of so-called distributed applications: programs running on multiple computers within a geographically dispersed network.[11] The book acknowledges that "in the context of Ethereum, the term is actually a bit of

5 For a general review, see Eliza Mik, 'Smart Contracts: Terminology, Technical Limitations and Real-World Complexity' (2017) 9 LIT 269; A Walch, 'The Path of the Blockchain Lexicon (and the Law)' (2016) 36 Rev Banking & Fin L 713.

6 Vitalik Buterin, 'Ethereum White Paper: A Next Generation Smart Contract and Decentralized Application Platform' (2015) <https://github.com/ethereum/wiki/wiki/White-Paper> accessed 30 December 2022.

7 Shaanan Cohney and David A Hoffman, 'Transactional Scripts in Contract Stacks' (2020) 105 Minn L Rev 319, 323.

8 Alessandro Brighente, Mauro Conti and Satish Kumar, 'Extortionware: Exploiting Smart Contracts Vulnerabilities for Fun and Profit' (2022) *ArXiv* abs/2203.09843.

9 Nick Szabo, 'Smart Contracts: Formalizing and Securing Relationships on Public Networks' (1997) 2(9) First Monday.

10 DJ Yaga and others, 'Blockchain Technology Overview' National Institute of Standards and Technology Internal/Interagency Report 8202 (2018) 54.

11 Andreas Antonopoulos and Gavin Wood, *Mastering Ethereum* (2nd edn, O'Reilly 2020) 269.

a misnomer, given that Ethereum smart contracts are neither smart nor legal contracts, but the term has stuck."[12] In many technical papers, the term *smart contract* is also used interchangeably with various blockchain applications, such as games, escrow services, lotteries, wallets, stable coins, or crowdfunding systems.[13] For example, we read that the Ethereum standard for NFTs, called ERC-271, "allows for the implementation of a standard API for NFTs within smart contracts. This standard provides basic functionality to track and transfer NFTs."[14] The same document states that "we provide for simple ERC-721 smart contracts as well as contracts that track an arbitrarily large number of NFTs." Seemingly then, smart contracts can denote NFTs or mechanisms that transfer NFTs.[15] There seems to be a purely technical approach to the term, as illustrated by the preceding statements, and a "hybrid approach" that implies their *quasi*-contractual character. Although technical literature generally speaks of smart contracts being *created*, *deployed*, *called*, or *used* rather than formed or performed,[16] it often discusses them with a combination of technical and legal jargon, implying their revolutionary potential in changing traditional contracting practices. In other words, smart contracts are not necessarily seen as a purely technical phenomenon, and their significance stretches beyond simply moving assets on blockchains. The IBM website, for example, states that

> smart contracts are simply programs stored on a blockchain that run when predetermined conditions are met. They typically are used to automate the execution of an agreement so that all participants can be immediately certain of the outcome, without any intermediary's involvement or time loss.[17]

The company also provides a tutorial to "get hands-on experience configuring, developing, and deploying smart contracts (in chaincode) on IBM Blockchain networks." There, developers and system architects can learn "how to create and package a smart contract."[18] These statements illustrate a common problem: smart contracts are supposed to be computer programs automating the execution of agreements by being "configured, developed and deployed." There is little benefit, however, in automating the *execution* of an agreement. It is unclear how automated execution would provide "immediate outcomes" unless the writers referred to the

12 ibid 270.

13 Massimo Bartoletti and Livio Pompianu, 'An Empirical Analysis of Smart Contracts: Platforms, Applications, and Design Patterns' in Michael Brenner and others (eds), *Financial Cryptography and Data Security Proceedings 2017* (Springer 2017).

14 William Entriken and others, 'ERC-721: Non-Fungible Token Standard' Ethereum Improvement Proposals No 721 (January 2018) <https://eips.ethereum.org/EIPS/eip-721>

15 Runhua Wang, Jyh-An Lee, and Jingwen Liu, Chapter 1 in this volume.

16 See, for example: Zibin Zheng and others, An Overview on Smart Contracts: Challenges, Advances and Platforms (2020) 105 FGCS 475.

17 <https://www.ibm.com/topics/smart-contracts>

18 <https://www.ibm.com/docs/en/blockchain-platform/2.5.4?topic=contracts-deploy-smart-fabric-v2x> accessed 23 March 2023.

quick preparation of contractual documents or simply conflated execution with performance. Needless to say, the execution of a contract need not involve intermediaries or significant time loss.

It can be suspected that technical writings often use legal terms in an uninformed manner and that crypto-enthusiasts often misunderstand the role and practical functioning of "traditional" contracts.[19] As observed by Reyes, lawyers and technologists often use the same terms of art within their own fields without regard for the stark difference between their actual and presumed meaning.[20] To recall, the original paper on smart contracts was written by a computer scientist who was unfamiliar with the fundamental legal concepts.[21] Vending machines were, for example, described as "contracts with bearer," and it was claimed that "most contractual dispute (sic) involves an unforeseen or unspecified eventuality.[22] Although the latter statements are nonsensical and demonstrate the flimsy theoretical underpinnings of smart contracts, the basic idea that smart contracts can improve upon or replace traditional contracts has become firmly embedded in many technical papers. Regrettably, this idea has also percolated into legal scholarship (and regulations!), mainly due to a number of early papers on the subject.[23] The unfortunate *status quo* can be attributed to the legal community latching onto buzzwords without investigating their actual meaning or provenance.[24] The resulting confusion can be illustrated by a number of recent legal and regulatory approaches in the UK and in the EU.

UK Law Commission

The UK Law Commission defines smart contracts as "computer code that, upon the occurrence of a specified condition or conditions, is capable of running automatically according to pre-specified functions."[25] The Commission elaborates that smart contracts can perform transactions on decentralized cryptocurrency

19 For an example of such common misunderstandings, see: Kiran Bohyer and Thaier Hayajneh, 'Modernizing Contracts Across Industries: A Review of Smart Contract Applications and the Evolving Legal Landscape' (2023) 10 ICST Transactions on Scalable Information Systems. The paper assumes that contract formation and performance require multiple intermediaries: "contracts can be costly to create and expensive to enforce. Creating them often requires many parties including the contracting parties, legal advisors, subject matter experts, or third-party service providers to ensure the proper development and execution of a contract." [at 1]

20 Carla Reyes, 'Emerging Technology's Language Wars: Smart Contracts' (2023) Wisconsin Law Rev 85–89.

21 Szabo (n 9) above.

22 see: ibid.

23 Aaron Wright and Primavera De Filippi, 'Decentralized Blockchain Technology and the Rise of Lex Cryptographia' (2015) <;>http://papers.ssrn.com/sol3/papers.cfm?abstract_id=2580664>; Joshua AT Fairfield, 'Smart Contracts, Bitcoin Bots and Consumer Protection' (2014) 71 Wash Lee Law Rev Online 35, 37–38; Marco Dell'Erba, 'Demystifying Technology: Do Smart Contracts Require a New Legal Framework? Regulatory Fragmentation, Self-Regulation, Public Regulation' (2018) < accessed>https://ssrn.com/abstract=3228445> accessed 10 July 2023.

24 Reyes (n 20) 110.

25 UK Law Commission (n 3) vii.

exchanges, facilitate games and the exchange of collectibles on a distributed ledger, as well as run online gambling programs.[26] These statements seem to reflect a technical approach to smart contracts, equating them with blockchain applications or computer programs in general. The Commission states, however, that "smart contracts can also be used to define and perform the obligations of a legally binding contract."[27] This type of smart contract is referred to as a "smart legal contract" and described as legally binding contracts "in which some or all of the contractual obligations are defined in and/or performed automatically by a computer program."[28] As described following, this approach is nonsensical. Although computer programs – including smart contracts – can be used to automate the performance of certain contractual obligations, it is illogical to claim that computer programs can define and perform obligations. Only the parties to a contract can define and perform their obligations. The parties can express their obligations in various forms, including computer code. It is unclear, however, why such expression would warrant a separate legal category. Similarly, while the parties can perform their obligations *by means* of various technologies, such technologies are tools of performance – not contracts. The Commission's approach effectively states that computer programs used to perform contractual obligations are legally binding contracts. It is also unclear why the Commission chose to introduce three forms of smart legal contracts. Depending on the role played by the code, there are: natural language contracts with automated performance, hybrid contracts, or solely code contracts.[29] Regarding the first form, it is necessary to observe that this type of "smart legal contract" has pervaded commerce for more than 40 years. There is nothing novel or revolutionary in automating contractual performance, as exemplified by every e-commerce website providing online content or services. Notably, every set of terms accompanying e-commerce transactions, especially those that involve the provision of digital content, can be regarded as a smart legal contract of the first type. Regarding the second form, one that combines natural language and code, the purpose of such "combination" is unclear given that contract law is neutral as to the manner in which the parties express their agreement. The latter, as explained following, derives from the parties' intentions, and its expression is only important to prove what was agreed. In other words, why would parties want to express some of their obligations in code if they have to agree on them first? Why would they express them in code instead of putting them in writing? The benefit of expressing parts of a contract in code is unclear given that the available programming languages cannot, in principle, handle more complex contractual language and that the expression of obligations in a programming language need not guarantee their performance. The risks of breach would, effectively, be replaced with the risk of computer error. Lastly, the Commission seems oblivious to the fact

26 ibid 1.
27 ibid.
28 ibid 8, 23.
29 ibid 11.

that "solely code" contracts are technically impossible and practically unnecessary. None of the existing programming languages is sufficiently rich and expressive to embody the entirety of legal terms.[30] A contract "solely in code" would have to be extremely simple, limited to the most basic provisions that could be accommodated by any of the programming languages.[31] Moreover, it is not immediately apparent why provisions that do not describe primary obligations, such as jurisdiction clauses or limitations of liability, should be expressed in code. Such provisions are, after all, addressed to the courts and are therefore impossible to automate. In sum, the introduction of the term smart *legal* contract, as well as its division into separate categories, creates additional confusion as to the legal nature of smart contracts (if any!).

Two Additional Legal Approaches Require Mention

First, the EU Data Act defines a smart contract as a "computer program used for the automated execution of an agreement or part thereof, using a sequence of electronic data records and ensuring their integrity and the accuracy of their chronological ordering."[32] The Data Act aims to allow users to access data they generated when using connected devices and to share such data with third parties to enable a range of data-driven services.[33] To this end, it promotes the use of smart contracts for executing data-sharing agreements and prescribes certain requirements for developers who create or integrate such smart contracts.[34] Interestingly, while the Data Act declares that it is technology neutral, it seems to mandate the use of smart contracts as a special type of computer program. Given the context and the wording of the relevant sections, the term "execution" must be associated with the performance of an agreement, not with its more traditional meaning, that of making a legal instrument valid by signature. As, by definition, the automation of data-sharing agreements must involve computer programs, it remains unclear why the legislator focused on smart contracts in the first place – the more so that later sections introduce the requirement that smart contracts have internal functions that can reset or stop their further operation.[35] The idea of interrupting a smart contract, however, contradicts their very nature and purpose![36] The reason that such functionality is required is obvious: it should be possible to stop data sharing or abort a planned data transfer if, for example, it eventuates that the required consent was

30 For a detailed explanation, see: Eliza Mik, 'Contracts in Code?' (2021) 13 LIT 1.

31 ibid 29.

32 Art 2 (39) Regulation of the European Parliament and of the Council on harmonised rules on fair access to and use of data and amending Regulation (EU) 2017/2394 and Directive (EU) 2020/1828 (Data Act).

33 Data Act art 1.

34 ibid art 36 & Recital 80.

35 ibid art 36 (1) b.

36 F Casolari and others, 'How to Improve Smart Contracts in the European Union Data Act' (2023) 2 Digital Society 9.

not obtained or the data was inaccurate. It is, however, pointless to introduce the concept of smart contracts that lack the core characteristics of smart contracts! Moreover, as the Data Act does not associate smart contracts with blockchains,[37] one can wonder why they were included in the instrument in the first place. The same outcomes could be accomplished with computer programs, albeit with much less controversy and uncertainty. A more apt term would be "automated data sharing agreement."

Second, the EU Blockchain Observatory and Forum regards smart contracts as the backbone of the Web3 ecosystem as they provide a "more efficient and enhanced mechanism of agreement, transacting, and transferring value."[38] Despite associating them with "mechanisms of agreement," the Observatory defines a smart contract as "an event-driven programme that runs on a decentralized, distributed shared and replicated ledger, which can take custody over and instruct the transfer of assets on that ledger."[39] Smart contracts are, however, also described as "self-executing contracts in which the buyer and seller agreements are documented and embedded directly into lines of code," and their adoption "serves to make transactions traceable, transparent, and irreversible."[40] This inconsistent approach may be a product of the pervasive terminological confusion: while smart contracts are regarded as blockchain-based computer programs, they are also seen as a special type of contract that, in line with the crypto-narrative, can execute itself. As described as follows, such claims are nonsensical.

3. An Unfortunate Nomenclature

The confusion surrounding smart contracts is largely attributable to the general inability to disregard the unfortunate terminology (smart *contract*) and to the failure to investigate what smart contracts actually are.[41] As I have observed elsewhere,[42] there is no prohibition to call a computer program a contract and proclaim its superiority over conventional contracts. There is also no prohibition to purchase a cat, call it a horse, and treat it *as if* it were a horse. This linguistic gimmick will cause no difficulties until the owner of the cat puts it in front of a cart, uses the cat in horse races, or feeds it hay. When the sick cat is taken to the veterinarian, the vet

37 Data Act art 2 (39).

38 EU Blockchain Observatory and Forum, *Smart Contracts* (2022) 29 <https://blockchain-observatory.ec.europa.eu/document/download/53a0aeb4-d144-4054-841e-dc169b44f94d_en?filename=Smart ContractsReport_Final.pdf&prefLang=cs>

39 ibid 2.

40 ibid.

41 For a broader overview of the failure of legal scholarship to verify popular claims, see Kelvin FK Low and Eliza Mik, 'Pause the Blockchain Legal Revolution' (2020) 69 ICLQ 135; see also: Mike Orcutt, 'States That Are Passing Laws to Govern "Smart Contracts" Have No Idea What They're Doing' MIT Tech Rev (29 March 2018) <https://www.technologyreview.com/2018/03/29/144200/states-that-are-passing- laws-to-govern-smart-contracts-have-no-idea-what-theyre-doing/>

42 Eliza Mik, 'Deconstructing Smart Contracts' in N Kim and S Elvy (eds), *Emerging Issues at the Intersection of Commercial Law and Technology* (CUP in production, 2023).

will not treat the cat as if it were a horse. In a time of crisis, the owner will have to face reality. Irrespective of the peculiar "labelling," the vet will follow the rules pertaining to cats, not those pertaining to horses. Labels cannot trump the actual characteristics of the animal. The actual characteristics of "something" become important – and undeniable – when things go wrong. In the event of a dispute, courts will have to investigate whether a type of computer program referred to as a smart contract is in fact a contract.

The problem does not, however, lie in the unfortunate nomenclature alone but in the fact that many scholars and regulators take the term 'smart contract' at face value. Consequently, something that is a purely technological phenomenon – a computer program – is being examined by means of an unsuitable analytical framework. If something is a computer program, then analyzing it *as if* it were a contract results in a category mistake, a semantic or ontological error where things from one category are presented as if they belonged to a different category. False categorizations lead to false analyses, and false analyses result in legal and regulatory disasters. Legal certainty cannot be achieved without certainty of terminology. Meaningful discussions are impossible if everybody is talking about a different thing and using the incorrect analytical framework. The need for a correct categorization of smart contracts is particularly important given the amount of regulatory activity in this area. Such categorization is, however, only possible if it is acknowledged what smart contracts are. Guadamuz rightly observes that smart contracts should be understood strictly from a technical perspective and that any legal response is entirely dependent on their technical capabilities.[43] Without a consistent approach as to the nature and purposes of smart contracts, legal analyses as well as regulatory efforts are unlikely to succeed.[44]

4. Clarifying the Basics

Paradoxically, although the technical concept of a smart contract seems unrelated to the legal meaning of the term "contract," the technology itself is often portrayed as being able to ensure the performance of a contract or the achievement of some contractually agreed-upon results. Given the state of confusion, it is worth revisiting the basics. In particular, to understand the potential role of smart contracts in contracting practices, it is necessary to clarify the difference between the formation and the performance of a contract.

The parties enter into agreements to achieve specified results, to obtain some benefit from their exchange. The first step is contract formation. The common law of contract is technology neutral and generally oblivious to the manner in which the parties manifest their intentions and reach agreement.[45] A contract can be formed

43 Andres Guadamuz, 'All Watched Over by Machines of Loving Grace: A Critical Look at Smart Contracts' (2019) 35 CLSR 1–2.

44 Reyes (n 20) 102.

45 Hugh Beale, *Chitty on Contract* (31st edn, Sweet & Maxwell 2013) at para 2–163.

by conduct, by the exchange of written documents, or by a series of clicks on a website. In principle, no formalities are required when forming a contract. In most circumstances, contracts are put into writing for evidentiary reasons not due to statutory requirements. Moreover, the source of the parties' obligations is the parties' agreement in the abstract sense, not the physical document.[46] In the event the contract is formed orally or by conduct, a document may not even exist. It is also worth emphasizing that if the parties decide to formalize their agreement and put it into writing, then it is common to speak of execution. To execute a contract means to enter into a contract by signing or otherwise acknowledging a contractual document. Execution is thus inextricably tied to the formation of a contract. Most importantly, there are no legal obstacles to automate the contract formation process, as illustrated by the millions of contracts entered into by means of vending machines, on e-commerce websites, or on the stock market. Consequently, there are also no obstacles to using computer programs to form contracts.

Once the contract is formed, the parties are obliged to perform their respective side of the bargain. To discharge their obligations, each of the parties must undertake or refrain from undertaking specific actions. While agreements and the obligations are abstract concepts, the actions undertaken to discharge these obligations are concrete and, depending on the contractual subject matter and method of payment, involve physical or digital objects. In a contract for the sale of goods, for example, one party is obliged to transfer ownership in such goods, and, in return, the other party is obliged to transfer money as payment. The required actions will usually take the form of a physical transfer of an object or the transfer of the document giving rights to such objects. Payment can be made in cash, by means of a credit card, or via a bank transfer. Logically, whenever such actions concern digital (or: *digitized*?) objects, be it goods or documents, their transfer will require a computer program. In other words, some obligations can only be performed by means of computer programs. This does not raise any doctrinal problems as the common law of contract is technology neutral and generally oblivious to the manner in which obligations are performed. The parties are free to use whatever technology they choose to automate their respective performances or certain aspects thereof. Of course, some actions can be automated while others require human performance. It is, for example, impossible to automate the preparation of a restaurant meal or the building of a house, whereas it is easy to automate payment obligations, as exemplified by standing orders or credit card transactions. For example, banks perform many of their obligations, such as money transfers and the dispensing of banknotes (money!), by means of computer programs. Such programs operate via internet banking websites, mobile apps, or ATMs. The latter are *tools* enabling the automated performance of the banks' obligations that result from their contracts with consumers. Similarly, providers like Netflix or Spotify automatically stream the selected content to their authorized subscribers. What is interesting in these

46 Adam J Kolber, 'Not-So-Smart Blockchain Contracts and Artificial Responsibility' (2018) Stan Tech L Rev 198, at 219.

examples is that customers are oblivious to the type of computer program used by the bank or the streaming service. What matters is the performance of the obligation, the achievement of the contractually promised result. The point is simple: we rarely, if ever, care about the technology underpinning those services. And rightly so. As long as the service is provided in accordance with the terms of the contract, the technology used to provide it is irrelevant. In light of the foregoing, the use of smart contracts to form or to perform contracts is legally unobjectionable.[47] The parties can choose whatever technology they want to automate their respective obligations. Such technology does not require discrete legal categories and need not be analyzed as if it were a contract just because 40 years ago, somebody decided to include the word "contract" in its name.

At present, smart contracts control and manage the transfer of various blockchain-based cryptoassets. Consequently, their use is limited to the automation of those obligations, which involve the transfer of such assets. A typical example would be the purchase of an NFT for a certain amount of Ether or the purchase of goods or services for a certain amount of Bitcoin. In sum, as their current capabilities are confined to controlling cryptoassets, such as Bitcoin or Ether when certain conditions are met,[48] smart contracts can be used to automate those actions that involve the transfer of such cryptoassets. Theoretically, smart contracts could also control physical objects, such as cars or doors. In such instances, objects such as immobilizers or locks[49] would have to be equipped with the relevant software that would control their operation and hence enable the smart contract to control its operation. Again, from a purely legal perspective, the deployment of such "smart objects" poses no problem. The discussion could end here were it not for the fact that a large part of legal scholarship – and some regulators – persist in treating smart contracts as a type of contract.

5. Computer Programs as Contracts?

Irrespective of the number of times one refers to technical definitions or describes the actual functioning of smart contracts, many scholars and regulators continue to inquire whether they are contracts. The question of whether smart contracts are contracts has been addressed on multiple occasions.[50] Unfortunately, the majority of analyses are based on factual misunderstandings of their technical characteristics and, somewhat surprisingly, considerable confusion concerning the principles

47 J Cieplak and S Leefatt, 'Smart Contracts: A Smart Way to Automate Performance' (2017) 1 Georgia L & Tech Rev 417.

48 See generally: Low and Mik (n 41) 135.

49 M Raskin, 'The Law and Legality of Smart Contracts' (2017) 1 Geo LJ Tech Rev 304, 339.

50 Helen Eenmaa-Dimitrieva and Maria Jose Schmidt-Kessen, 'Creating Markets in No-Trust Environments: The Law and Economics of Smart Contracts' (2019) 35 CLSR 69; Mark Verstraete, 'The Stakes of Smart Contracts' (2019) 50 Loyola U Chic LJ 743.

of contract law.[51] In principle, when asking whether smart contracts can be contracts, we are asking whether they can be enforceable agreements. This requires the application of the analytical framework used to evaluate the parties' intentions as to what are, effectively, computer programs. In common law, for an agreement to be enforceable, it must fulfill two prerequisites: intention and consideration. Contracts involve two (or more) parties *agreeing* to do something or to achieve a particular result. There can be no agreement without reciprocity, where one party acts (or promises to act) *in return* for the other party's act (or promise to act). It is unnecessary to delve into theoretical details if the basic principle is clear: there can be no contract without agreement. Consequently, before asking whether an agreement is enforceable, we must establish that there is, in fact, an agreement. This is when the smart contract analysis hits a wall: how can computer programs be agreements? When speaking of contracts and computer programs, we are dealing with two unrelated concepts that cannot be approached with the same analytical tools. Once we consider how smart contracts work in practice, we quickly realize that they cannot be evaluated in terms of enforceability.

In practice, smart contracts are *mechanisms* of transferring or controlling cryptoassets. Their operation, or execution, results in the change of the state of a database – the blockchain.[52] For example, in the context of token-based fundraising, popularly referred to as initial coin offerings (ICOs), smart contracts are software that governs the characteristics and distribution of tokens or coins.[53] In the context of decentralized finance (DeFi),[54] smart contracts are referred to as the "backbone of all DeFi protocols and applications" because they "lock in" or control funds.[55] They can also create and manage stable coins.[56] In the context of non-fungible tokens (NFTs),[57] smart contracts constitute the mechanism of creating and transferring NFTs.[58] In the context of decentralized autonomous organizations (DAOs), smart contracts control and distribute funds in various voting and governance processes.[59] We also read that DAOs rely on smart contracts to define their governance

51 See generally: Fairfield (n 23) 35; J Sklaroff, 'Smart Contracts and the Cost of Inflexibility' (2017) 166 U Penn L Rev 263; Alexander Savelyev, 'Contract Law 2.0 "Smart Contracts" as the Beginning of the End of Classic Contract Law' (2017) 26 Inf Comm Tech L 2.

52 Yaga and others (n 10)

53 Shaanan Cohney and others, 'Coin-Operated Capitalism' (2019) 3 Colum L Rev 591, 594, 623.

54 Fabian Schär, 'Decentralized Finance: On Blockchain- and Smart Contract-Based Financial Markets' (2021) 103 FRB St Louis Rev 153.

55 ibid 154, 158, 164.

56 Kara J Bruce, 'The Private Law of Stablecoins' (16 August 2022) <https://ssrn.com/abstract=4191646 or http://dx.doi.org/10.2139/ssrn.4191646>

57 Dan Chirtoaca and others, 'A Framework for Creating Deployable Smart Contracts for Non-Fungible Tokens on the Ethereum Blockchain' (IEEE International Conference on Decentralized Applications and Infrastructures (DAPPS) 2020) 100.

58 Kelvin FK Low, 'The Emperor's New Art: Cryptomania, Art & Property' (2022) 86 Conveyancer and Property Lawyer, 378.

59 Robbie Morrison, Natasha Mazey and Stephen Wingreen, 'The DAO Controversy: The Case for a New Species of Corporate Governance? (2020) 3 Front Blockchain 25; Interestingly, the Unidroit Principles on Digital Assets and Private Law associate smart contracts with Digital Autonomous

structures, such as how many tokens must be held to create a proposal or how many tokens are required for such a proposal to pass.[60] In sum, smart contracts are mechanisms of transmitting and controlling various cryptoassets on blockchains.[61] While nothing stands in the way of smart contracts being tools of performance, there is no point in enquiring about their enforceability.

Anticipating heated objections to the claim that smart contracts are nothing but mechanisms of controlling cryptoassets, it is worth demonstrating the futility of analyzing them in the same manner that courts and lawyers analyze the interactions of the parties to determine whether they have reached agreement. Admittedly, smart contracts could be analyzed as acts that manifest the parties' intention that could lead to the formation of a contract. As indicated, contractual intention can be manifested in any manner – including conduct or the placement of computer code on a blockchain. One party could, for example, write a smart contract and deploy it on the blockchain.[62] Such a smart contract could represent the party's intention to contract on the terms embodied in its code. It could then be "accepted" by another party by sending value to it.[63] This analysis turns out to be artificial, however, once we examine how smart contracts actually work. The problem does not lie in the manner of expressing intention but in the fact that, in practice, *a* smart contract is written by someone (a developer) and deployed[64] on the blockchain *for others to use*. To recall, in the context of Ethereum, anyone can create smart contracts, and anyone can use such smart contracts. The operative word in the previous sentences is "use." Smart contracts are created and used – not formed or performed. Much depends on the type of smart contract. If, for example, the smart contract forms part of a casino or a game, then its execution will enable its users to gamble or to play a game, just like the execution of traditional computer programs enables them to play online games or gamble in online casinos. If the smart contract forms part of a DeFi platform, then it enables platform users to borrow or stake cryptocurrencies. In both scenarios, smart contracts cannot be seen as manifestations of intention to contract but simply as computer programs running blockchain-based applications. More importantly, a developer writes a smart contract *for others to use* – not to

---

Organizations and with the code that controls digital assets on blockchains, see: Draft Unidroit Principles on Digital Assets and Private Law, Unidroit 2023 Study LXXXII – PC, January 2023, p 38.

60 Ian Appel and Jillian Grennan, 'Control of Decentralized Autonomous Organizations' (2023) 113 AEA Papers Proc 182–85, 182; see also: Complaint, *CFTC v Ooki DAO*, 3:22-cv-5416 (ND Cal 2022) alleging a DAO is formed by smart contracts.

61 Cohney and others (n 53) 591, 604, 620; Reyes (n 20) 91.

62 For an attempt to analyze smart contracts in terms of offer and acceptance, see: Mateja Durovic and Andre Jenssen, 'The Formation of Blockchain-Based Smart Contracts in the Light of Contract Law' in Larry A diMatteo, Michael Cannarsa and Cristina Poncibo (eds) *Cambridge Handbook of Smart Contracts, Blockchain Technology and Digital Platforms* (CUP 2019) 61.

63 For a description of a smart contract life-cycle, see: H Zhou and others, 'The State of Ethereum Smart Contracts Security: Vulnerabilities, Countermeasures, and Tool Support' (2022) 2 J Cybersecur Priv 358, 360–61.

64 The term "deploy" indicates that the smart contract is placed, or embedded, in a live blockchain environment for public visibility and use.

contract *with* those who use it. *Who*, then, would be the other party "to" the smart contract? *What intention* would the smart contract manifest? The smart contract is just a computer program and cannot be a party. To recall, the very idea behind smart contracts is that they are not controlled by anyone and cannot be stopped. Once written and deployed, smart contracts are immutable and tamperproof – no one, not even their creators, can interfere with their operation. Those who create smart contracts do not become parties "to" their smart contracts – just like manufacturers of vending machines do not become parties to the contracts formed by means of vending machines. The fact that an intention to contract can be manifested by means of computer programs does not mean that such programs become contracts. This simple fact can be explained with reference to the popular misunderstanding concerning the legal character of vending machines, which are often regarded as precursors to smart contracts.[65] The theory seems to be that vending machines are contracts and that smart contracts *are like* vending machines. Consequently, it is assumed that smart contracts can also be regarded as contracts. This theory overlooks the fact that vending machines are not contracts but offers, that is, manifestations of intention to contract with whoever accepts the terms stated in the offer.[66] Such offers are made by the vendor, who expresses his or her intention by displaying the machine and the goods contained therein to the public. Offers can, if accepted, *result in* contracts. Being unilateral acts, offers cannot be contracts. The vending machine can also be regarded as a *mechanism* facilitating both the *formation* and the *performance* of a contract. While its display or its use can be analyzed as a manifestation of intention, the machine itself cannot be a contract.

In sum: computer programs cannot be analyzed in terms of intention and consideration. Even if a smart contract could be regarded as a manifestation of intention to be bound on the terms expressed in its code, it would still constitute a unilateral act. The latter could lead to the formation of a contract. It could not, however, be a contract. In certain circumstances, a smart contract could be described as a tool of performance. Again, this would not make it a contract in the legal sense of the word. It is also worth observing that, when used in a transactional setting, smart contracts are used on the basis or as a result of an underlying agreement. This is indirectly confirmed in the popular statement that smart contracts *embody* or *enforce* contractual terms[67] or, as stated by the UK Law Commission, that they can be used to "perform the obligations of a legally binding contract."[68] Logically, such terms and obligations must derive from a pre-existing agreement that exists independently of the smart contract. Legal obligations do not magically emerge from lines of code deployed on a blockchain. A contrary assumption can be attributed to the frequent conflation of the substance of the agreement with its expression or,

65 Jonathan Rohr, 'Smart Contracts in Traditional Contract Law, or: The Law of the Vending Machine' (2019) 67 Clev St L Rev 67; for a broader discussion see: Mik (n 5) 274.

66 *Thornton v Shoe Lane Parking Ltd* [1971] 2 QB 163.

67 Kevin Werbach, *The Blockchain and the New Architecture of Trust* (MIT Press 2018) 64.

68 UK Law Commission (n 3) 1, 8, 23.

with the inability to distinguish between an agreement in the abstract sense and it physical representation.

Two related misconceptions are worth addressing. Both derive from an uninformed use of legal terminology and illustrate how technical writings amalgamate technical and legal concepts to a point where the resulting theories cannot be used in any structured argument.

"Self-Enforcement?"

The alleged superiority of smart contracts is often associated with the concept of "self-enforcement." It is claimed that in order to eliminate human discretion and opportunism, contracts should be enforced by objective, infallible algorithms.[69] As blockchain-based smart contracts preclude the possibility of modifying their code and interfering with their operation, they provide "execution guarantees" by irretrievably binding both parties to their agreement.[70] "Self-enforcement" is therefore regarded as synonymous with guaranteed performance, the prevention of breach, and with commercial certainty. If performance is guaranteed, there will be no disputes and hence no need for judicial assistance or any other traditional forms of enforcement.

The whole idea of "self-enforcement" is, however, nonsensical. Enforcement relates to the protection of performance by courts, which grant damages or, on very rare occasions, require the contract breaker to perform his or her obligations. In common law systems, the only mechanism compelling the actual performance of an obligation that can be ordered by a court is called specific performance. Orders for specific performance are, however, granted in exceptional circumstances. In other words, courts do not usually ensure or guarantee performance. They only protect it. More importantly, enforceability is tied to the institutional assistance provided by entities that are external to the contract, such as courts, arbitral tribunals, or mediators. As enforcement always involves recourse to an external system, the idea of a contract enforcing *itself* is absurd. Although enforcement concerns the protection of performance, in some contexts self-enforcement seems to be synonymous with performance itself![71] Again, this approach is nonsensical. Contracts or, to be more precise, the contractual obligations deriving therefrom, can only be performed by the parties. Logically, neither the agreement in the abstract, legal sense, nor the physical document can take any actions. Consequently, the idea of a contract performing itself is nonsensical. It can be suspected that the concept of self-enforcement may constitute an unsuccessful attempt at transplanting the technical term "self-execution" into the area of contract law. Self-execution denotes computer programs that autonomously (i.e., without the need for ongoing human

69 Kevin Werbach and Nicholas Cornell, 'Contracts Ex Machina' (2017) 67 Duke LJ 313 at 365.

70 Raymond Cheng and others, 'Ekiden: A Platform for Confidentiality-Preserving, Trustworthy, and Performant Smart Contracts' *in 2019 IEEE European Symposium on Security and Privacy (EuroS&P)* (Sweden 2019) 185–200.

71 Werbach and Cornell (n 69) 332.

input) change their state according to pre-defined rules. In such context, the code operates irrespective of external circumstances and thus guarantees the achievement of some pre-programmed result. In the legal context, such terminology is unnecessary given that contracts cannot "operate by themselves." Additional confusion is introduced by the uninformed use of the legal term *execution*, which is often used interchangeably with self-enforcement. The resulting conceptual and terminological chaos is best illustrated by the statement that smart contracts are "agreements with automatic execution and enforcement that are not reversible by courts."[72] Lastly, although execution concerns the formation of a contract, not its performance, in many contexts it seems to refer to the automated performance of a contract. For example, Raskin states that smart contracts are "agreements wherein execution is automated"[73] and that with smart contract "automation ensures performance, for better or worse, by excising human discretion from contract execution."[74]

"Making Contracts Tamper-Proof"

Consistent with the promise of guaranteeing performance, technical writings emphasize the benefits of the inability to change the code of the smart contract.[75] As the execution of such code cannot be interfered with, the smart contract becomes "tamper-proof" and hence, as the reasoning goes, the agreement embodied therein cannot be changed and its performance cannot be stopped.[76] This has led to suggestions that traditional contracts should be rendered immutable and tamper-proof by "putting them on the blockchain."[77] These suggestions do not necessarily concern smart contracts but traditional contracts or, to be more precise, contractual *documents*. As is often the case with the smart contract narrative, the exact reasoning underlying the proposition that "contracts should be placed on the blockchain" is unclear. Seemingly, the inability to change a contractual document would improve the chances of performance. After all, blockchain enthusiasts fixate on immutability and often assume that the alteration of a contractual document would negatively affect contractual performance. This misunderstanding is academically interesting as it perfectly illustrates the failure to distinguish the expression of the agreement from the actual agreement. It is one thing, after all, to preclude the possibility of changing *executable code*, but it is yet another to preclude the possibility of changing a *contractual document*. Traditional contracts are static documents that memorialize agreements. Smart contracts are computer programs that execute on

72 H Halaburda, Levina and Min (n 1)
73 Raskin (n 49) 309.
74 ibid 306.
75 Wright and Filippi (n 1) 81; C Parisi and D Budorin, 'Smart Contract Security' in K Huang, D Budorin, LJ Tan, W Ma and ZW Zhang (eds), *A Comprehensive Guide for Web3 Security: Future of Business and Finance* (Springer 2023).
76 Christopher D Clack, and others, 'Smart Contract Templates: Foundations, Design Landscape and Research Directions' (2016) ArXiv E-Prints 4.
77 Maik Brinkmann, 'The Realities of Blockchain-Based New Public Governance: An Explorative Analysis of Blockchain Implementations in Europe' (2021) 2 *Digit Gov Res Pract*, 3.

a distributed computing platform. Mapping assumptions and theories from one context to another is bound to create confusion. Making a contractual *document* immutable or tamper-proof is of limited value. Contractual documents are generally not vulnerable to alterations. It is also impractical to alter a paper copy of a contract, as any alterations are immediately visible – unless undertaken by a master forger. Moreover, altering *one* copy of the contract is pointless if the other original copy is retained by the other party. In traditional contracts, most commercial risks derive from the fact that one of the parties may not perform as agreed or become insolvent. The risk of non-performance is unrelated to the contractual document. A perfectly drafted contractual document does not, after all, guarantee that both parties will perform in accordance with the contract. Being cryptographically secured and embedded in a blockchain changes nothing in this regard. One or both parties may simply ignore the contract and deviate from their agreement. Contractual documents describe the parties' respective rights and obligations and provide evidence of agreement. They do not execute, or 'self-enforce," its terms. The obligations are performed by the parties, not "by" the document. Admittedly, in the context of smart contracts, there is a close relationship between code and contractual performance (assuming that the smart contract embodies and executes contractual terms) because the smart contract *is* the mechanism of performance. Consequently, precluding the possibility of altering its code ensures that the smart contract executes as originally coded. This, however, is only of value if the code of the smart contract is technically correct and accurately represents the parties' agreement. If, as described as follows, the smart contract abounds in coding errors and vulnerabilities, then its tamper-proof execution on a blockchain is of no benefit.

6. Guaranteeing Perfect Performance

Leaving the discussion as to whether smart contracts can be contracts in the legal sense, it is more advisable to examine their purported ability to provide unprecedented commercial certainty by guaranteeing performance. After all, this seems to be their core benefit and their main contribution to the decentralized crypto-economy. Crypto-enthusiasts rarely acknowledge, however, that the said certainty can only be achieved if – and only if – the execution of smart contracts can *guarantee* the achievement of some agreed-upon or otherwise specified result. Such guarantee is, however, premised on the ability to write perfect and predictable code. Again, it becomes important to acknowledge that irrespective of their name, smart contracts are computer programs and that computer programs are difficult to write, especially if they are to operate in distributed execution environments, such as blockchains.

Relationship With Blockchains

Smart contracts are ideologically related to blockchains.[78] The close relationship between these two terms has lead to the assumption that smart contracts and

78 see generally: Michael J Casey and Peter Vigna, *The Truth Machine: The Blockchain and the Future of Everything* (St Martin's Press 2018).

blockchains share similar, if not identical, characteristics and that certain attributes of blockchains, such as transparency and immutability, are also beneficial in the context of smart contracts. The technical reality is, however, somewhat different. While smart contracts execute *on* blockchains, they are not *like* blockchains. As indicated, smart contracts are created by human developers and subsequently deployed on blockchains. Blockchains, such as Ethereum or Avalanche, provide a distributed environment for their execution.[79] Given its distributed and decentralized nature, the blockchain environment ensures reliability and resistance to external interference. It is generally overlooked, however, that while blockchains can ensure execution, they cannot ensure the quality of the code being executed. To clarify: smart contracts are *executed* by the individual nodes that form the blockchain and run the consensus algorithm that generates individual blocks. Smart contracts are not, however, *validated* by such an algorithm. Consensus algorithms can only validate (that is, technically confirm) the existence and correct transfer of native assets, such as Bitcoin or Ether, which are also generated by this algorithm as a reward for those who maintain the blockchain.[80] Consensus algorithms cannot determine whether a smart contract is technically correct.[81] In effect, blockchains will execute both good code and bad code.

Quality of Code

Like all other computer programs, smart contracts are susceptible to programming errors and vulnerabilities.[82] Contrary to popular belief, the fact that they operate on blockchains creates additional opportunities for the introduction of such errors and vulnerabilities. The main blockchain supporting smart contracts, Ethereum, is permissionless and therefore open to everyone.[83] There is no need to seek permission to write smart contracts for Ethereum. This means that anyone can create and deploy smart contracts – without any prior skill verification, testing, or quality control. Even malicious and incompetent coders can create smart contracts that, once deployed, will coexist on the blockchain with other smart contracts and will become publicly available for wider use.[84] This fact alone means that even a perfectly written smart contract (assuming, for the sake of argument, that such can

79 Technically, smart contracts do not execute directly on blockchains but on virtual machines, such as the Ethereum Virtual Machine, or EVM. A virtual machine is a self-contained computing environment that emulates the functionality of a physical computer.

80 Buterin (n 6).

81 ibid.

82 The latter are mistakes in the implementation of a system design that result in programs not providing the intended functionality or producing unexpected results. The former enable the malicious misuse of system implementation to achieve effects contrary to its goals (so-called exploits). Vulnerabilities can be caused by but are not synonymous with coding errors.

83 Buterin (n 6).

84 C Schneidewind, Markus Scherer and Matteo Maffei, 'The Good, the Bad and the Ugly: Pitfalls and Best Practices in Automated Sound Static Analysis of Ethereum Smart Contracts' in *Proceedings, Part III, Leveraging Applications of Formal Methods, Verification and Validation: Applications: 9th International Symposium on Leveraging Applications of Formal Methods (IsoLA '20)* (Springer-Verlag 2020) 212.

exist) cannot be protected from unexpected interactions with other smart contracts and from the inadvertent execution of untrusted code.[85] Crypto-enthusiasts rarely mention the downsides of open and decentralized environments, such as the lack of governance and uniform security practices. They also overlook the fact that, in principle, permissionless blockchains constitute hostile execution environments, where competent and professional coders coexist with malicious, fraudulent, or simply incompetent hackers. They also rarely mention that to execute on blockchains, smart contracts must be written in *new* specialized programming languages.[86] Unfortunately, most existing smart contract programming languages[87] have been recently designed to be (relatively) easy to learn to encourage developers to create applications for specific blockchains.[88] It must be remembered that the popularity of a blockchain and thus the price of its native cryptocurrencies generally depends on the number of applications it supports and on the size of its developer community.[89] Promoting a particular smart contract programming language is an indirect way of promoting a particular blockchain. Unfortunately, given the haste with which such languages have been created, they often introduce additional risks because they are often unsuitable for distributed computing environments, unpredictable, and capable of introducing vulnerabilities into the smart contract.[90] Unsurprisingly, the mainstream press abounds in reports of smart contract hacks resulting in massive financial losses.[91]

The Myth of Transparency

It is often claimed that the transparency of the smart contract code contributes to their security and reliability. Transparency often features in stories promoting

85 see generally: Nicholas Kannengießer and others, 'Trade-Offs Between Distributed Ledger Technology Characteristics' (2020) 53 ACM Comput Surv 2.

86 Massimo Bartoletti, and others, 'Verifying Liquidity in of Recursive Bitcoin Contracts' (2022) 81 Log Methods Comput Sci, 1.

87 Most smart contracts are written in a high-level language such as Solidity or Vyper and compiled to the Ethereum Virtual Machine (EVM) bytecode that is stored in blockchain accounts, see generally: Antonopoulos and Wood (n 11) 128–29.

88 In the "cryptoeconomy," blockchains with more functionality are more competitive.

89 The popularity or commercial significance of a smart contract platform is often evaluated based on the number of monthly active developers or by the market value of the assets controlled thereby. Newer blockchains, such as Solana, are likely to boast more monthly commits and a growing influx of new developers; see: Blockchain Development Trends, 2022 Edition, Outlier Ventures.

90 See, for example, the recent exploit of Curve, a stablecoin exchange at the heart of decentralized finance (DeFi) on Ethereum. Curve relies on smart contracts written in the Vyper programming language, and the latter seems to facilitate the re-entrancy attacks, a common bug that allows attackers to trick a smart contracts to release funds. Curve Finance Drained of $50M While CRV Token Sinks 12% in Latest DeFi Exploit (date?) <https://www.coindesk.com/business/2023/07/30/curve-finance-exploit-puts-100m-worth-of-crypto-at-risk/>

91 For examples of financial losses attributable to vulnerable smart contracts, see: Chainalysis, 'The 2022 Crypto Crime Report' 75 <https://go.chainalysis.com/rs/503-FAP-074/images/Crypto-Crime-Report-2022.pdf>

blockchains as technologies fostering the building blocks of Web3: truth, trust, and compliance. In practice, however, the ability to view the code is irrelevant when determining whether a given smart contract will "do" what it is supposed to do or what was *agreed* it would do. Inspecting the code may reveal obvious coding errors but not whether the smart contract will achieve the agreed results or whether it contains security vulnerabilities.[92] The latter may not be immediately apparent. The discovery of programming errors and vulnerabilities generally requires extensive testing and, ideally, formal verification.[93] As indicated, even a perfectly coded smart contract may produce unexpected results due to interactions with other badly coded smart contracts. The transparency of its code changes nothing in this regard. To the contrary, more experienced coders can take advantage of visible vulnerabilities in smart contracts written by their less savvy "colleagues" and, once a given smart contract accumulates control over a significant amount of cryptoassets, exploit such vulnerability to abscond with the assets controlled thereby. In practice then, transparency is only beneficial to experienced and sophisticated coders – not to the average user who may have neither the competence nor the resources to investigate the quality of the smart contract code.

Problems With Immutability

To aggravate matters, once deployed on the blockchain, smart contracts become immutable and their code cannot be modified. As stated on the Ethereum website:

> a smart contract is code that lives on the Ethereum blockchain and runs exactly as programmed. Once smart contracts are deployed on the network you can't change them. . . . This also means you need to design your contracts very carefully and test them thoroughly.[94]

Unlike most computer programs, which can be amended when programming errors are discovered or when users require new functionalities, the code of a smart contract is set in stone. Consequently, smart contracts could be more costly to create than traditional computer programs given that the former require extensive testing, including formal verification as well as advanced programming skills.[95] More

92 Asem Ghaleb and Karthik Pattabiraman, 'How Effective are Smart Contract Analysis Tools? Evaluating Smart Contract Static Analysis Tools Using Bug Injection' in *Proceedings of the 29th ACM SIGSOFT International Symposium on Software Testing and Analysis (ISSTA '20)* (ACM 2020).

93 Joshua A Kroll and others, 'Accountable Algorithms' (2017) 165 U Pa L Rev 633 at 645; Ye Liu and others, 'Towards Automated Verification of Smart Contract Fairness,' in *Proceedings of the 28th ACM Joint European Software Engineering Conference and Symposium on the Foundations of Software Engineering (ESEC/FSE '20)* (ACM 2020).

94 Ethereum website.

95 Grigore Rosu, 'Formal Design, Implementation and Verification of Blockchain Languages' (3rd International Conference on Formal Structures for Computation and Deduction (FSCD 2018) 2018).

importantly, immutability concerns not only the technical aspects of the code but also the substantive rules that are supposed to be executed by the smart contract. To recall, smart contracts are supposed to guarantee the achievement of specified results by precluding changes and deviations from the rules embodied therein. This approach, however, forces the coders to predict and provide for all *future* contingencies and changes in the environment at the time when the smart contract is created. Such changes would include market fluctuations and environmental disasters. The rules encoded in the smart contract must therefore be comprehensive and cover a wide range of events that might affect the commercial viability of the transaction. After all, what would be the point of guaranteeing a specific result if such result is no longer desired or even detrimental given the changed market circumstances? What is the point of a smart contract that contains programming errors that cannot be corrected?

7. Conclusions

The prerequisites of an enforceable agreement remain the same for all contracts, irrespective of the manner in which the parties express their intentions or reach agreement. Just like stating that something is *not* a security because it relies on a blockchain is legally inconsequential,[96] calling something a contract although it is not a contract is legally irrelevant. The legal evaluation of a phenomenon is based on its substance, not on its labelling. If, on the other hand, it is established that the prerequisites of a legally binding agreement are fulfilled, the law will attach the label "contract" to the product of the parties' communications and grant it the resulting protections. To clarify: nothing stands in the way of analyzing smart contracts from a legal perspective. After all, computer programs raise many legal questions when used to generate art, launder money, automate trading, or manipulate user choices. It is one thing, however, to analyze computer programs from a legal perspective *in the context of a particular legal area*; it is yet another to analyze them *as if* they were contracts. Computers programs, including smart contracts, can be used as tools to automate the formation of contracts and the performance of certain contractual obligations. Computers programs cannot, however, be agreements. Absent agreement, it is impossible to speak of a legally enforceable contract.

Stories about smart contracts gloss over conceptual difficulties and technical challenges, including the fact that smart contracts are ridden with programming errors and vulnerabilities, that the immutability of their code its generally detrimental, and that their transparency is of limited use. Legal scholarship must

96 M di Angelo and G. Salzer, 'Tokens, Types, and Standards: Identification and Utilization in Ethereum,' in *2020 IEEE International Conference on Decentralized Applications and Infrastructures (DAPPS)* (IEEE 2020); Y Guseva, "A Conceptual Framework for Digital-Asset Securities: Tokens and Coins as Debt and Equity' (2020) 80 Md L Rev 166.

abandon simplistic stories and become more attuned to the technical attributes of smart contracts as well as to the manner they are used in practice. This might result in a more commonsensical approach to this technological phenomenon, one that is more focused on their function, not on their name.[97] Perpetuating such confusing and nonsensical terms like "self-enforcement" or "tamper-proof immutability" is detrimental to any form of regulation and legal analyses.

97 Notably, Cohney and Hoffman (n 7) avoid this confusion by titling their paper "transactional scripts" and focusing on what smart contracts actually do.

Part B

Reorganising Organisations

4 Law and Regulation for Decentralised Autonomous Organisations (DAOs)

Joseph Lee and Rougang Li

1. Introduction

The decentralised autonomous organisation (DAO) represents an innovative organizational structure rooted in blockchain technology and smart contracts. It enables participants to establish organisation without traditional central authorities, such as company boards, and to automatically conduct organisational activities on the blockchain. DAO enthusiasts assert that they function seamlessly without the need for legal governance, relying solely on blockchain and community-driven management.[1] However, legal scholars propose an alternative perspective by pinpointing the shortcomings of DAOs in terms of self-governance effectiveness and their susceptibility to legal unaccountability.[2] DAOs are not flawless as claimed and necessitate legal governance, a concept being explored through the adoption of legal frameworks, often referred to as "legal wrappers."[3] Nonetheless, just like DAOs themselves, the legal governance of DAOs is still in its early stages.

This chapter aims to enhance the discourse surrounding the legal governance of DAOs by highlighting the mismatch between existing legal frameworks and the distinctive nature of DAOs as a novel organisational model. This chapter aligns with the perspective that DAOs require legal governance, considering the law as a mechanism to illuminate the inherent risks associated with DAO operations. Further, exploring the mismatches can also benefit the discussion of possible forms of legal governance over DAO and Web3, which, as shown in this chapter, is clearly different to the organisations today and possibly require innovative legal governance.[4] Through an examination of the development and evolution of DAOs, this chapter reinforces existing research that sheds light on the imperfections of DAOs,

1 Arvind Narayanan and others, *Bitcoin and Cryptocurrency Technologies: A Comprehensive Introduction* (Princeton UP 2016)

2 Timothy Nielsen, 'Cryptocorporations: A Proposal for Legitimizing Decentralized Autonomous Organizations' (2019) 2019 Utah L Rev 1105.

3 Christopher J Brummer and Rodrigo Seira, 'Legal Wrappers and DAOs' (2022) 6 <or>https://ssrn.com/abstract=4123737>or <http://dx.doi.org/10.2139/ssrn.4123737> accessed 2 March 2023.

4 Roger Brownsword, 'Law's Imperfect Governance: Is the Metaverse the Solution' (2023) 25 Media and Arts L Rev 241.

DOI: 10.4324/9781032618975-7

thus emphasising the necessity of implementing legal governance and exploring better governance. Additionally, by scrutinising current legal wrappers, this chapter emphasises the mismatch and risks inherent in DAOs, substantiating this argument through a comprehensive analysis of DAO dynamics. Theoretical contribution lies in discovering a theory that reflects the conceptual innovation of DAO in creating new organisations.[5] That can provide a facilitation for DAOs, in a similar way to how company law had granted legal personality to corporations in 1860.

To address these matters, this chapter will be structured as follows: Section 2 provides an overview of DAO and Web 3; Section 3 examines the development of DAO; Section 4 discusses theoretical considerations; Section 5 assesses the risks associated with DAO; and finally, Section 6 explores potential legal solutions.

2. What Is a DAO and How Does It Relate to Web3?

2.1 An Introduction of DAOs

Decentralised autonomous organisations (DAOs) are innovative organisational structures that rely on blockchain technology. Despite the absence of a comprehensive legal definition so far,[6] the technological foundations of DAOs consist of blockchain technology, smart contracts, and artificial intelligence.[7] The blockchain combines cryptography with a distributed computer network, allowing participants to construct a decentralised ledger system where transactions can be recorded and verified by every participant.[8] Participants encode their consensus in computer code, to which the network thereafter adheres to. This system claims to eliminate the need for a centralised regulator to facilitate trade and other activities among participants.[9]

The mechanism of automatic execution is often referred to as smart contracts. A smart contract is not accepted as a legal contract; rather, it is a computer programme that automatically executes predefined conditions on the blockchain.[10] Unlike traditional contracts, which rely on trust in the reputation of the involved parties and/or legal enforcement, smart contracts solely depend on the blockchain

5 Kumar Saurabh and others, 'Towards Blockchain Led Decentralized Autonomous Organization (DAO) Business Model Innovations' (2023) 30(2) Benchmarking An Intl J 475.

6 ibid.

7 Wulf A Kaal, 'Decentralized Autonomous Organizations: Internal Governance and External Legal Design' (2021) 5(4) Ann Corp Gov 237.

8 Joseph Lee, *Crypto Finance, Law and Regulation: Governing an Emerging Ecosystem* (Routledge 2022).

9 Edmund Schuster, 'Cloud Crypto Land' [2020] Mod L Rev 989.

10 Kristian Lauslahti and others, 'Smart Contracts – How Will Blockchain Technology Affect Contractual Practices?' ETLA Reports No 680 (9 January 2017) < or <http://dx.doi.org/10.2139/ssrn.3154043>>https://ssrn.com/abstract=3154043> or <http://dx.doi.org/10.2139/ssrn.3154043> accessed 2 March 2023.

system as a guarantee.[11] The blockchain network identifies participants and accurately executes transactions, which then become immutable and tamper-proof. Consequently, the blockchain mechanism itself ensures the execution of smart contracts.

The governance of smart contracts through computer code is a key characteristic of both smart contracts and the DAOs that utilise them. Primavera De Filippi and Aaron Wright analysed the differences between entering into a smart contract and a legal contract.[12] While legal contracts record the consent of parties in natural language, smart contracts translate this consent into computer code.[13] Transactions executed under the terms of a smart contract are carried out according to the conditions specified in the code.

By utilising a smart contract on the blockchain, participants can establish a DAO. Typically, a DAO is initiated by a group of people who present a white paper outlining the organisation's purpose (such as DAO or MakerDAO) and invite participants.[14] This initiating group distributes tokens to participants, who purchase them with cryptocurrencies or other assets.[15] This process, often referred to as an initial coin offering (ICO), enables the DAO to accumulate the necessary funding to pursue its stated activities.[16] Tokens can represent the ownership shares held by participants in the DAO and may confer additional rights, such as voting on DAO management issues, similar to company shareholders. Some tokens serve as proof of ownership of DAO property or services and can be categorised as either security tokens representing joint ownership or ownership-in-common, or utility tokens representing consumption rights.[17]

DAOs have devised various methods to incentivise contributions from individuals through token rewards. These tokens can be traded on the market, and participants are often rewarded based on their contributions to the community.[18] DAOs can also establish parameters to evaluate participant contributions, such

11 Morgan N Temte, 'Blockchain Challenges Traditional Contract Law: Just How Smart Are Smart Contracts' (2019) 19 Wyo L Rev 87.

12 Primavera De Filippi and Aaron Wright Hughes, *Blockchain and the Law the Rule of Code* (Harvard UP 2018) 76.

13 Arati Baliga, *Understanding Blockchain Consensus Models* (Persistent White Paper 2017) <https://web.archive.org/web/20220121100752id_/https://www.persistent.com/wp-content/uploads/2017/04/WP-Understanding-Blockchain-Consensus-Models.pdf?pdf=Understanding-Blockchain-Consensus-Models> accessed 2 March 2023.

14 E.g., 'The Maker Protocol: Maker DAO's Multi-Collateral Dai (MCD) System' <https://makerdao.com/zh-CN/whitepaper/> accessed 2 March 2023.

15 De Filippi and Hughes (n 12) 76.

16 Sabrina Howell, Marina Niessner and David Yermack, 'Initial Coin Offerings: Financing Growth with Cryptocurrency Token Sales' (2020) 33(9) Rev Financ Stud 3925.

17 Scott W Maughan, 'Utility Token Offerings: Can a Security Transform into a Non-Security?' (2019) 2019 BYU L Rev 1113.

18 Xi Zhao and others, 'Task Management in Decentralized Autonomous Organization' (2022) 68(6–7) J Oper Manag 649.

as the number of hours dedicated to DAO affairs or the extent of participation in decisions and votes. The more a participant contributes, the more tokens they receive.

Unlike traditional corporations,[19] which rely on a board of directors and management to achieve their goals, DAOs can operate without such hierarchical structures. Participants simply need to follow the pre-agreed rules governed by computer code. If code upgrades or decisions need to be made, they are subject to a vote by all token holders, who have equal decision-making authority. This absence of hierarchy distinguishes DAOs from traditional companies.

DAOs are not merely electronic corporations on the blockchain but can also function as platforms with broader purposes, such as serving as social community platforms.[20] In contrast to centralised platforms such as Facebook or Twitter, DAO participants retain ownership of their contributions to the community and benefit from them directly, without intermediaries. Envisioning the potential applications of DAOs, Gavin Wood, the founder of Ethereum, has proposed a version of the future internet called Web3.[21]

2.2 DAOs, Web3, and the Future of the Internet

Web3 represents a future vision of the internet where advanced forms of DAOs play a central role in online communities.[22] It diverges from the current Web2 by being composed of decentralised organisations built on blockchain technology.[23] The decentralised structure of Web3 offers greater freedom and personalisation compared to Web2.

The benefits of Web3 can be summarised in three key points. First, Web3 is permissionless, allowing anyone to join the internet without relying on centralised entities such as the tech companies. Users do not have to register on centralised platforms like Facebook or Google. Instead, they can obtain a private key and build their own digital space from scratch. Second, individuals have ownership and control over their data and digital assets. Unlike the current system where centralised platforms control personal data such as photos, videos, or travel and trade records, Web3 allows individuals to take control. Data and virtual assets can be transformed into non-fungible tokens (NFTs),[24] unique tokens that represent the asset. People

19 Nielsen (n 2) 1105.

20 Such as Friends with Benefits DAO, 'About' <https://www.fwb.help/about> accessed 2 March 2023.

21 Jon M Garon, 'Legal Implications of a Ubiquitous Metaverse and a Web3 Future' (2022) 106 Marq L Rev 163.

22 Ethereum, 'Introduction to Web3' (Last update 1 March 2023) <https://ethereum.org/en/web3/> accessed 2 March 2023.

23 Alex Murray and others, 'The Promise of a Decentralized Internet: What Is Web3 and How Can Firms Prepare?' (2023) 66(2) Business Horizons 191.

24 'Non-Fungible Tokens (NFT)' <https://ethereum.org/en/nft/> accessed 2 March 2023.

own the NFTs they create and can dictate how they are used. For example, they can choose to sell their travel records to researchers or travel agencies and define the terms of usage. Third, Web3 facilitates blockchain-native payments, empowering individuals to choose cryptocurrencies as a means of settling transactions. By bypassing fees imposed by intermediaries in traditional banking systems, transaction costs are reduced.[25]

As Web3 operates on the blockchain, DAOs will become the predominant form of organisation, reshaping interactions between individuals and organisations. In Web2, users communicate and share their lives through intermediary platforms like Facebook. In contrast, Web3 enables direct peer-to-peer communication without the need for information intermediaries to transfer images or text. Blockchain-based social groups serve as communities where people can socialise and discuss their shared interests. The relationship between these social groups and their individual members is one of a community of equals rather than that of service providers and users. Compared to centralised companies today, DAOs offer greater convenience and choice to participants.[26]

To make Web3 a reality, further advancements in both technology and blockchain are necessary. While the concept is still in its infancy, the term Web3 has been loosely used to encompass not only blockchain-related developments but also other emerging technologies such as Artificial Intelligence (AI) and the Internet of Things (IoT).[27] In due course, Web3 will have faster transmission speeds and broader population access, enabling a wider range of data exchange facilitated by intelligent networks powered by advanced algorithms.[28] The development of internet infrastructure will also contribute to the growth of DAOs. For instance, broader internet access will enable a larger population to participate in DAOs. Additionally, as the IoT progresses, DAOs will be able to automatically execute transactions involving physical assets, which is currently not possible.

In sum, Web3, as a blockchain-based concept, presents a comprehensive vision for the future of the internet. As the internet's infrastructure evolves, it will further enhance the growth of DAOs. However, the development of DAOs will continue irrespective of the realisation of Web3 since the remaining challenges are primarily organisational or legal rather than technological. Addressing the legal and governance aspects of DAOs is of paramount importance. Doing so not only enhances their development but also helps alleviate frictions between decentralised organisations and traditional centralised legal entities. Moreover, establishing a robust legal and regulatory framework for DAOs can set a precedent for other emerging technologies in the future.

25 See Narayanan and others (n 1) On crypto currencies.
26 Saurabh and others (n 5).
27 Alex Pentland, 'Building a New Economy: Data, AI, and Web3' (2022) 65(12) Commun ACM 27.
28 Murray and others, 'The Promise of a Decentralized Internet' (n 23).

3. The Evolution of DAOs and Different Types and Their Benefits

3.1 Evolution

DAOs have a relatively short history, with the first launch occurring in April 2016 on the Ethereum platform.[29] It raised over 200 million US dollars, setting a crowd-funding record. However, shortly after its initiation, an unidentified attacker exploited a vulnerability, resulting in the loss of approximately 30% of the funds. This incident led to the separation of the system into two components: Ethereum and Ethereum Classic, both operating on the Ethereum network.[30] This divergence took decades to fix, when two blockchains merge again with the fundamental change in the consensus mechanism in 2023.[31]

This event highlighted the initial vulnerabilities and instability of DAOs. However, despite the setback, the enthusiasm for DAOs remained strong, and more DAOs continued to be created. In response, blockchain community programmers have diligently refined the DAO code to enhance usability and security.[32] According to DeepDAOs, the number of new DAOs has experienced rapid growth since 2021, particularly with the emergence of decentralised financial (DeFi) DAOs and DAOs focused on NFTs. The total funds raised by DAOs have now reached $1.6 million.[33]

In the following years, DAOs have expanded in range and complexity of their services.[34] One of the major themes of DAOs related to financial operations in cryptocurrency. These DAOs are referred to as DeFi DAO. These decentralised financial organisations provide a wide range of services from simple lending and borrowing to various financial derivatives without involvement of traditional intermediaries like banks.[35] DeFi DAOs aim to create a more inclusive and efficient financial ecosystem by leveraging blockchain technology and smart contracts.[36]

Another major focus of DAOs is around NFTs. These DAOs focus on the ownership, trading, and management of NFTs, which represent unique digital assets

29 Kyung Taeck Minn, 'Towards Enhanced Oversight of "Self-Governing" Decentralized Autonomous Organizations: Case Study of the DAO and Its Shortcomings' (2019) 9 NYU J Intell Prop & Ent L 139.

30 Quinn DuPont, 'Experiments in Algorithmic Governance: A History and Ethnography of "The DAO," a Failed Decentralized Autonomous Organization' in Malcolm Campbell-Verduyn (ed), *Bitcoin and Beyond* (Routledge 2017) 157.

31 Ethereum, 'The Merge' (2023) <https://ethereum.org/en/roadmap/merge/> accessed 4 August 2023.

32 Joseph Lee and Rachael Ntongho, Chapter 5 in this volume

33 Gail Weinstein and others, 'A Primer on DAOs' (2022) <https://corpgov.law.harvard.edu/2022/09/17/a-primer-on-daos/#1> accessed 2 March 2023.

34 World Economic Forum, 'Decentralized Autonomous Organizations: Beyond the Hype White Paper' (2022) 7 <https://www3.weforum.org/docs/WEF_Decentralized_Autonomous_Organizations_Beyond_the_Hype_2022.pdf> accessed 2 March 2023.

35 Hilary J Allen, 'DeFi: Shadow Banking 2.0?' (2023) 64 Wm & Mary L Rev 919.

36 Christopher J Brummer, 'Disclosure, Dapps and DeFi' (2022) 5 Stan J Blockchain L & Pol'y 137.

such as artwork, virtual real estate, or collectibles.[37] NFT DAOs provide platforms for artists, collectors, and enthusiasts to engage in creating and trading NFTs, fostering new opportunities and markets within the digital art and collectibles space.

Furthermore, DAOs have expanded into other domains, including governance DAOs and social DAOs. Governance DAOs enable participants to collectively make decisions and vote on matters such as protocol upgrades and community proposals. Social DAOs serve as platforms for social interaction, connecting individuals with shared interests and facilitating collaboration and coordination. The benefits of DAOs are multifaceted. First, they promote decentralised decision-making, allowing participants to have a voice and influence in the organisation's direction. This inclusivity fosters a sense of ownership and community involvement. Second, DAOs offer transparency and trust through the use of smart contracts and blockchain technology,[38] ensuring that operations and transactions are visible to all participants. This transparency minimises the risk of fraud or manipulation. Third, DAOs provide economic incentives and rewards for participants' contributions, aligning the interests of individuals with the success and growth of the organisation.[39]

Beside the expansion of domains, the community of DAO participants also adopted improvement on technology and governance strategy. The technological improvement has resulted in an upgrade of major blockchain systems such as Bitcoin and Ethereum. For example, the Bitcoin Taproot update in 2021 improved the privacy protection and trade processing ability of Bitcoin.[40] The Ethereum Merge upgrade successfully converged the Ethereum and Ethereum Classic forks that resulted from the 2016 DAO incident, while simultaneously transitioning from proof-of-work to proof-of-stake.[41] Adopting proof-of-stake significantly contributes to sustainability by reducing energy consumption in mining. The convergence also holds symbolic significance as a remedy for the 2016 DAO failure.

The evolution of DAOs has seen significant advancements since their initial vulnerability. With the refinement of the DAO code, the emergence of various types of DAOs, such as DeFi DAOs and NFT DAOs, has expanded the possibilities and use cases within the blockchain ecosystem. The benefits of DAOs, including decentralised decision-making, transparency, and economic incentives, have fueled their continued growth and adoption. As the DAO landscape continues to evolve, it will undoubtedly shape the future of organisational structures and governance models.

37 Joshua AT Fairfield, 'Tokenized: The Law of Non-Fungible Tokens and Unique Digital Property' (2022) 97 Ind LJ 1261.

38 Temte (n 11).

39 Zhiyong Liu and others, 'User incentive Mechanism in Blockchain-Based Online Community: An Empirical Study of Steemit' (2022) 59(7) Inf Manag 103596.

40 MacKenzie Sigalos, 'Bitcoin's Biggest Upgrade in Four Years Just Happened – Here's What Changes' (2021) <https://www.cnbc.com/2021/11/14/bitcoin-taproot-upgrade-what-it-means-for-investors.html> accessed 4 August 2023.

41 Ethereum (n 31).

3.2 Types of DAOs

Apart from the DeFi DAO, NFT DAO, and Governance DAO mentioned earlier, DAOs are serving diverse and distinct purposes within the blockchain ecosystem. While some types are widely accepted, others are still evolving and have yet to gain widespread recognition.

One well-established type of DAO is the Protocol DAO, which focuses on the governance of a blockchain protocol platform. An example of this is Uniswap, a decentralised exchange service that utilises smart contracts and a blockchain protocol to facilitate cryptocurrency trading.[42] The primary function of Protocol DAOs is to maintain and update the protocol, fostering the growth of cryptocurrencies. While many Protocol DAOs are currently oriented towards DeFi purposes such as lending, borrowing, and mortgages, it is important to note that not all Protocol DAOs fall within the DeFi category.[43]

Ethereum Name Service (ENS) is an example of a Protocol DAO that does not involve DeFi. ENS operates as a decentralised domain name service, allowing users to register human-readable names (such as “myname.eth”) to represent their blockchain addresses.[44] Token holders within the ENS DAO can vote on protocol changes and the allocation of funds. The goal of ENS is to enhance the user experience by replacing complex blockchain addresses with easily remembered names.

Another type of Protocol DAO is the Philanthropy DAO, established to fund public goods.[45] For instance, Big Green DAO promotes and funds environmentally friendly food production and security. Whether a DAO is classified as a philanthropy DAO depends on its purpose and whether that purpose is recognised as philanthropic. For example, UkraineDAO, which raises funds to support Ukraine in its resistance against Russian forces, can be considered a philanthropic DAO if assisting Ukraine is viewed as a philanthropic activity.

When DAOs raise funds with a profit purpose, they fall under the category of Investment DAOs. Investment DAOs can be further subdivided into Grant DAOs and Venture DAOs. Venture DAOs function similarly to venture capital firms, while Grant DAOs focus on funding programmes within specific areas. Aave Grants DAO, for instance, exclusively funds programmes that benefit the Aave ecosystem.

Some Investment DAOs are established for special purposes. Constitution DAO, for instance, aimed at acquiring a copy of the original US Constitution through crowdfunding.[46] However, when this plan failed, Constitution DAO disbanded and

42 Yuen Lo and Francesca Medda, ‘Uniswap and the Rise of the Decentralized Exchange’ (2020) <https://mpra.ub.uni-muenchen.de/103925/> accessed 2 March 2023.

43 Chainalysis Team, ‘Dissecting the DAO: Web3 Ownership Is Surprisingly Concentrated’ (2022) <https://blog.chainalysis.com/reports/web3-daos-2022/> accessed 2 March 2023.

44 ‘ENS Is an Open Source Blockchain-Based Naming Protocol’ (the ENS website) <https://ens.domains/about/> accessed 2 March 2023.

45 World Economic Forum (n 34) 13.

46 Douglas Broom, ‘Explainer: What Is a DAO – and How Did One of Them Almost Succeed in Buying the US Constitution?’ (2021) <https://www.weforum.org/agenda/2021/11/what-is-a-dao-cryptocurrency-group/> accessed 2 March 2023.

refunded the raised funds.[47] Such DAOs are often referred to as Special Purpose Acquisition DAOs (SPADs) or collector DAOs.

Social DAOs, on the other hand, prioritise building decentralised social networks where individuals have direct access to one another without intermediaries. These networks often revolve around specific themes or interests. Develop DAO, for example, serves as a social DAO for Web3 developers, while Friends With Benefits DAO brings together creators and thinkers in the Web3 space for discussions on topics such as traditional market investments, cryptoassets, and NFTs. Friends With Benefits DAO has attracted over 3,000 members and received $10 million in funding.[48] It is worth noting that this selection of DAO types is not exhaustive, and numerous hybrid types cross boundaries. Krausehouse DAO, for instance, serves as a platform for an NBA team, making it both a Collector DAO or SPAC (Special Purpose Acquisition Company) and a social DAO for fans.

Moreover, some DAOs cannot be easily categorised into specific types. LexDAO, for example, focuses on providing legal support for the emerging blockchain and cryptocurrency industry. It operates as a decentralised community comprising lawyers, developers, and blockchain enthusiasts, who are committed to offering accessible and affordable legal assistance to the blockchain community. While LexDAO does not fall strictly into the categories of Social DAO or Service DAO, it is designed to support blockchain-based projects. The classification of LexDAO as a service DAO or a platform DAO may vary depending on the perspective of the classifier.

In summary, DAOs have evolved into complex forms of organisations that span various domains and types. The complexity and variety of DAOs demonstrate the flexibility and effectiveness of the blockchain as an organisational tool. The variety of DAOs poses challenges to the current legal framework, as it cannot be adequately addressed by a single department of law, such as company law. As DAOs are still in their early stages and continue to evolve, the challenges they present will need to be managed through an appropriate legal and regulatory framework to deliver user confidence and for them to scale up.

4. DAO Theory: Exploring the Relationship With Existing Theories

DAOs, as autonomous organisations built on blockchain technology, represent a unique phenomenon. Blockchain enables people to form organisations without geographical limitations or the need for intermediaries. While DAOs offer enhanced organisational effectiveness and a new structure, they also introduce new risks. Given their novelty, management and economic theories have yet to fully

47 Jordan Pearson, 'Constitution DAO Is Shutting Down After Unrelenting Chaos' (2021) <https://www.vice.com/en/article/bvnze5/constitutiondao-is-shutting-down-after-unrelenting-chaos> accessed 2 March 2023.

48 Friends with Benefits DAO (n 20).

encompass the intricacies of DAOs. However, scholars are actively seeking to understand how DAOs align with existing theories.

Carlos Santana and Laura Albareda have examined the literature on DAOs and identified four theories that contribute to our understanding of these organisations: transaction theory, collective action theory, agency theory, and sociomateriality theory.[49] This section will also undergo theoretical analyses to assess the effectiveness and potential issues proposed by scholars.

Transaction theory focuses on the costs associated with the transfer of goods and services, shedding light on the nature of firms and economic activities. It is of great importance in both economics and law. Ronald Coase first came up with the theory in his book *The Nature of the Firm*.[50] Transaction cost is about the efficiency of organisations, as it explains the structure and governance of complex tractions inside organisations. The theory considers environmental uncertainty, bounded rationality, opportunism, and specificity of assets as causes of transaction costs.[51] After decades of development, transaction cost theory has become a predominant economic theory in study management and organisation.[52]

DAOs have the potential to reduce transaction costs in various ways. Blockchain technology enables accurate and swift transfer of cryptoassets by virtue of participants' easy identification and the automatic execution of transactions. According to transaction theory, these advantages mitigate opportunism and environmental uncertainty, resulting in reduced transaction cost.[53] Consequently, DAOs offer greater economic efficiency compared to traditional firms. However, scholars have cautioned that DAOs may not always manifest the expected decentralisation in practice, as hierarchies may emerge from the unequal allocation of cryptoassets.[54] In such cases, transaction costs may not be eliminated, and new costs could be incurred. Sebastien Meunier and Danni Zhao[55] have pointed out that new transaction costs arise from factors such as the inflexibility of smart

49 Carlos Santana and Laura Albareda, 'Blockchain and the Emergence of Decentralized Autonomous Organizations (DAOs): An Integrative Model and Research Agenda' (2022) 182 Technol Forecast Soc Chan 121806.

50 Ronald Harry Coase, *The Nature of the Firm* (Macmillan Education 1995).

51 Zohar Goshen & Richard Squire, 'Principal Costs: A New Theory for Corporate Law and Governance' (2017) 117 Colum L Rev 767

52 Mikko Ketokivi and Joseph T Mahoney, 'Transaction Cost Economics as a Theory of the Firm, Management, and Governance' in *Oxford Research Encyclopedia of Business and Management* (2017) <https://oxfordre.com/business/display/10.1093/acrefore/9780190224851.001.0001/acrefore-9780190224851-e-6> accessed 4 August 2023.

53 Saurabh Ahluwalia and others, 'Blockchain Technology and Startup Financing: A Transaction Cost Economics Perspective' (2020) 151 Technol Forecast Soc Change 119854.

54 JG Allen, 'Bodies Without Organs: Law, Economics, and Decentralised Governance' (2020) 4 Stan J Blockchain L & Pol'y 53, 59.

55 Sebastien Meunier and Danni Zhao, 'Bitcoin, Distributed Ledgers and the Theory of the Firm' (2019) <or <http://dx.doi.org/10.2139/ssrn.3327971>>https://ssrn.com/abstract=3327971>or <http://dx.doi.org/10.2139/ssrn.3327971> accessed 15 March 2024.

contracts, the challenge of finding suitable oracle services, and blockchain security concerns.[56]

Agency theory is also applicable to DAOs, which represent a novel organisational structure with the potential to enhance efficiency. Agency theory analyses the relationship between agents and principals within a corporate framework.[57] It was frequently adopted to analyse company law issues on the relationships between shareholders and company directors and other stakeholders.[58] While the most obvious agency relationship exists between the owners (principals) and company managers (agents) of the company, blockchain and DAOs introduce a new model of a corporation and the accompanying agency dynamics. First, blockchain reduces agency costs by enhancing the efficiency of the voting process. Blockchain technology enables DAOs to conduct cost-effective voting among token holders. Consequently, the transparency and accuracy offered by blockchain technology are also recognised by company law scholars as a potential solution for enhancing shareholder voting within traditional companies.[59] Second, blockchain provides an alternative to the shareholder-management structure of traditional company. In a DAO, where decisions are made by community vote, the owner also serves as the manager. Since the shareholder–manager structure is absent in a DAO, the agency costs typically associated with between shareholder and a company's board is eliminated. DAOs can operate transparently for token holders, reducing the need for supervision costs.[60]

However, this does not lead to the conclusion that agency cost does not exist in DAO structures. For example, the agency cost raised by the lack of expertise in decision-making still exists as token holders are not necessarily expert on the issue to be voted on.[61] Similarly, token-holder voting is especially difficult when fast decisions are required and more frequently.[62] As a result, token-holder voting cannot replace the company board as a decision-making mechanism. Moreover, tokens might become centralised among a small number of holders, resulting in agency costs akin to those observed between majority and minority shareholders.[63]

56 Alex Murray and others, 'Contracting in the Smart Era: The Implications of Blockchain and Decentralized Autonomous Organizations for Contracting and Corporate Governance' (2021) 35(4) Acad Manage Perspect 622 <https://doi.org/10.5465/amp.2018.0066> accessed 2 March 2023.

57 Eugene F Fama and Michael C Jensen, 'Separation of Ownership and Control' (1983) 26(2) J Law Econ 301.

58 Luh Luh Lan and Loizos Heracleous, 'Rethinking Agency Theory: The View from Law' (2010) 35(2) Acad Manag Rev 294.

59 Spencer J Nord, 'Blockchain Plumbing: A Potential Solution for Shareholder Voting' (2019) 21 U Pa J Bus L 706.

60 Wulf A Kaal, 'Blockchain Solutions for Agency Problems in Corporate Governance' in Kashi R Balachandran (eds), *Information for Efficient Decision Making: Big Data, Blockchain and Relevance* (World Scientific 2021) 313.

61 Goshen and Squire (n 51).

62 Chiara Picciau, 'The (Un)Predictable Impact of Technology on Corporate Governance' (2021) 17 Hastings Bus LJ 67.

63 Chainalysis Team (n 43).

As DAOs often have an initiating team to set community discussion and design incentives for participants, new agency problems may arise due to conflict of interest between token holders and the initiating teams. These conflicts can be viewed as agency costs specific to DAOs. New agency costs are also introduced due to the inflexibility of smart contracts, the challenge of finding suitable oracle services, and blockchain security concerns, all of which have also been identified as contributing factors to increased transaction costs.[64]

Another theory relevant to the discussion of DAO is collective action theory. This theory deals with how individuals collaborate and coordinate their efforts to achieve public goals. The process of establishing principles and achieving consensus within a DAO aligns with collective action theory, which pertains to the pooling of resources shared by a community of users. Scholars leverage collective action theory to examine topics such as community governance, automated collective actions, and principle design. Blockchain system could be analysed by collective action with different concepts and more specific theories. For example, Bronwyn E. Howell and Petrus H. Potgieter addressed a DAO as a common-pool system in which participants are faced with limited resources.[65] David Rozas and co-authors analyse the blockchain and community governance tool, particularly in the context of Commons-Based Peer Production communities (CBPP).[66] These analyses indicate the theoretical potential of blockchain in facilitating collective actions while also highlighting the ongoing efforts to refine theories that account for the novel phenomena introduced by the blockchain technology.

Besides the economic and management theories mentioned prior, sociology scholars utilise theoretical tools to analyse blockchain. One of the theories is sociomateriality theory. It emphasises the materiality of an organisation, considering the interaction between social structure and technology utilisation.[67] In the case of DAOs, this theory explores the institutional relationships between participants and between humans and machines. Ongoing discussions aim to determine whether DAOs exhibit superiority over traditional centralised organisations.

In short, DAOs present a novel organisational structure that holds the potential to reduce transaction and agency costs, ultimately leading to more effective organisations and potential competitive advantages. However, DAOs also introduce associated complexities and challenges. Sociomateriality theory suggests that blockchain technology can mitigate agency and transaction costs, but it may also introduce new costs and risks. These risks are significant as they can hinder DAO development and challenge the existing financial market landscape. Additionally,

64 Meunier and Zhao (n 55).

65 Bronwyn Howell and others, 'Governance of Blockchain and Distributed Ledger Technology Projects: A Common-Pool Resource View' (Workshop on the Ostrom Workshop (WOW6) Conference, Indiana University, Bloomington 2019).

66 David Rozas and others, 'When Ostrom Meets Blockchain: Exploring the Potentials of Blockchain for Commons Governance' (2021) 11(1) Sage Open 21582440211002526.

67 Wanda J Orlikowski, 'Sociomaterial Practices: Exploring Technology at Work' (2007) 28(9) Organization Studies 1435.

they pose challenges for regulation, as traditional legal frameworks may struggle to address the unique characteristics of DAOs. Thus, the question remains: How should the law be applied to DAOs?

5. Legal Issues Surrounding DAOs

As a novel form of organisation, DAOs introduce new legal challenges for law-makers and regulators. The decentralised nature of blockchain technology, which underpins DAOs, allows for democratic regulation by token holders following a computer code. While this promotes democracy, it also presents challenges both within and outside the DAO ecosystem. Understanding the risks associated with DAOs is an evolving topic, and this section aims to identify the risks that can be managed by current legal frameworks, even though they were not originally designed to cover DAOs. The analysis is aimed to be the foundation of further discussion on a more effective law governance regime on blockchain and Web3, paving the way for discussions on technology-supported rules and laws.[68]

This chapter will identify three main legal issues associated with DAOs: legal forms, decision-making processes, and token transferability.

5.1 Legal Forms and Wrappers of DAOs

Determining the legal status of a DAO presents a significant challenge. DAOs must interact with other entities in society,[69] leading to two major issues. First, most societal resources are controlled by centralised entities such as companies or governments, and this structure is unlikely to be challenged in the short term. Second, the legal system requires a DAO to possess a legal status to govern the legal relationships between parties within the DAO or network. Without legal form or personality, responsibilities cannot be allocated between DAOs and centralised organisations, hindering collaboration and the expectation of returns. Moreover, a legal wrapper is necessary to protect DAO members within the legal system.[70]

One potential solution is to associate DAOs with existing legal personalities within the current system to provide them with a legal wrapper. However, finding an appropriate wrapper for DAOs is a complex task due to the diverse range of DAO types developed for various purposes, each potentially requiring a unique legal wrapper. Christopher Brummer and Rodrigo Seira have identified a spectrum of legal wrappers under US law that match different types of partnerships and companies, offering suitable matches for most DAO types.[71] For instance, philanthropy DAOs have several options, and Wyoming company law has created a

68 Brownsword (n 4) 249.

69 Aaron Wright, 'The Rise of Decentralized Autonomous Organizations: Opportunities and Challenges' (2021)4(2) Stanf J Blockchain L Pol'y 152.

70 Laila Metjahic, 'Deconstructing the DAO: The Need for Legal Recognition and the Application of Securities Laws to Decentralized Organizations' (2018) 39 Cardozo L Rev 1533.

71 Brummer (n 36) 6.

blockchain-based limited liability company (LLC) specifically for DAOs.[72] While these wrappers may protect a DAO registered in the US, DAOs operating in other jurisdictions may not have such options available.

Although identifying preexisting wrappers helps address the legal problem, there is a risk of mismatch between wrappers and DAO operations. DAOs operate on principles of decentralisation and democratic consensus, whereas traditional companies centralise management power in the boardroom. Much of company law focuses on adjusting the relationship between a company's board and its shareholders, which does not align with the consensus-based DAO structure. Mismatches also arise in terms of liability for token holders, who lack limited liability protection, and in decisions regarding asset distribution on liquidation. Taxation in Web3 also holds significant importance and poses notable challenges.[73] As DAOs continue to evolve, these mismatches may become more pronounced in the future. The specific mismatches will be discussed in the legal solution part.

5.2 Decision-Making in DAOs

Decentralised decision-making is a fundamental characteristic of DAOs as decentralised organisations. In a DAO, governance token holders collectively make decisions through a democratic process. However, this approach can present challenges.

The process of making decentralised decisions must be well-organised to prevent chaos. For instance, a case study on blockchain voting has revealed the potential for a single user to obscure issues and manipulate voting outcomes by submitting bogus proposals.[74] Therefore, although decentralised decision-making offers a powerful and convenient voting system, it does not inherently prevent problems from arising. As a result, DAO participants are engaging in discussions on how to prevent the misuse of delegation power within their communities.[75] This raises additional transaction costs as well as agency cost issues in DAOs, which have not been dealt with in traditional organisations.

To facilitate effective discussions, DAOs may develop their own methods to promote healthy discourse and voting, as well as manage their communities accordingly. Some DAOs opt to establish centralised regulation teams during the organisation's setup. Others explore innovative voting mechanisms such as conviction voting.[76] Additionally, DAOs may control the number of token holders by

72 Wy Stat § 17-31-101 through 17-31-115.

73 Jingyi Wang, Chapter 2 in this volume.

74 Lawrence Mosley and others 'Towards a Systematic Understanding of Blockchain Governance in Proposal Voting: A Dash Case Study' (14 September 2021) < or <http://dx.doi.org/10.2139/ssrn.3416564>>https://ssrn.com/abstract=3416564> or <http://dx.doi.org/10.2139/ssrn.3416564> accessed 2 March 2023.

75 Nounish Discussion, 'Misuse of Delegation and Voting Power' (2022) <https://discourse.nouns.wtf/t/misuse-of-delegation-and-voting-power/3059> accessed 2 March 2023.

76 Jeff Emmett, 'Conviction Voting: A Novel Continuous Decision Making Alternative to Governance' (2019) <https://medium.com/giveth/conviction-voting-a-novel-continuous-decision-making-alternative-to-governance-aa746cfb9475> accessed 2 March 2023.

imposing entrance and engagement standards for new members. Certain Social DAOs, such as Friends With Benefits DAO, and investment DAOs, such as Flamingo DAO, have implemented such restrictions. It has been argued that, by doing so, DAOs can attract participants who genuinely care about the organisation's interests and can foster productive communication, thereby mitigating the risk of short-termism among token holders.

While these approaches aim to address decision-making challenges, there are ongoing studies of additional strategies to enhance the effectiveness of decentralised governance. DAOs may employ mechanisms such as quadratic voting or quadratic funding to ensure fair representation and optimise decision outcomes.[77] The goal is to strike a balance between inclusivity, efficiency, and preventing undue influence within the decision-making process.

5.3 Token Transferability

The issue of transferability relates to how individuals can sell their tokens to realise their value. However, this raises concerns about short-termism and governance instability within DAOs. The problem of short-termism revolves around the incentives of token holders. DAOs raise funds through token issuance, and token holders can profit by selling their tokens on the open market. Consequently, token holders are incentivised to drive up token prices, potentially prioritising short-term gains over the organisation's long-term interests.[78] This mirrors the criticism faced by activist hedge funds benefiting from short-term shareholder activism in the US stock market.[79] Such short-termism can pose a risk to the future development of DAOs.

In response to this issue, the DAO community has proposed the issuance of reputational tokens as a potential solution. Reputational tokens are non-tradable tokens that represent the weighted voting power of participants, similar to golden shares or weighted voting shares. This approach aims to separate benefits from reputation, utilising "coin" and "point" tokens to represent these aspects. Token holders are encouraged to strike a balance between their benefits and reputation within the blockchain community, thereby mitigating the potential adverse effects of short-termism.[80]

Another significant challenge arises when DAOs need to initiate a refund procedure. An example is the Constitution DAO, which aimed to purchase a copy of the US Constitution through an auction. However, the DAO failed to secure the winning bid, leading to the need to refund its token holders. The refund process

77 Yixuan Fan and others, 'Insight into Voting in DAOs: Conceptual Analysis and a Proposal for Evaluation Framework' (2023) 38 IEEE Netw <https://doi.org/10.1109/MNET.137.2200561>

78 Kaal, 'Blockchain Solutions for Agency Problems in Corporate Governance' (n 60) 313.

79 Ed DeHaan, David Larcker and Charles McClure, 'Long-Term Economic Consequences of Hedge Fund Activist Interventions' (2019) 24 Rev of Accounting Studies 536.

80 Jad Esber and Scott Duke Kominers, 'A Novel Framework for Reputation-Based Systems' (2021) <https://future.com/reputation-based-systems/> accessed 2 March 2023.

involved token holders registering on another webpage to receive their refund.[81] Although the community accepted this procedure, it raises legal concerns. While the Constitution DAO's case had a straightforward refund requirement, future DAOs may encounter more complex situations. Insolvency laws have been established to regulate the liquidation of assets, including tokens. However, the simplified refund process of a DAO overlooks many of the risks that cannot be managed through insolvency law. The transparency of the blockchain does not eliminate the potential for risks such as unlawful trading, particularly if a DAO exhibits centralisation or has a management team.

Addressing the legal concerns surrounding token transferability within DAOs requires further exploration and development of appropriate regulatory frameworks. It is therefore important to strike a fair balance between facilitating efficient token transfers and ensuring compliance with existing legal requirements. Regulators and DAO communities should collaborate to establish clear guidelines that safeguard participants and mitigate risks while fostering the growth and innovation of DAOs.

6. Some Legal Solutions?

Steering the legal environment for DAOs can be challenging due to their decentralised and code-based nature. However, existing laws can offer partial solutions and risk mitigation through established legal principles. While there is a mismatch between current laws and DAOs, exploring relevant areas of law such as unincorporated association law, partnership law, company law, and trust law can provide valuable insights and guidance.[82] Better coherence in rules and governance may also be inspired by this exploration.[83]

6.1 Unincorporated Association

Unincorporated associations involve two or more individuals coming together under a common goal, without seeking profits.[84] Philanthropy DAOs and certain social DAOs can potentially organise themselves as unincorporated associations. In this structure, the association does not have a separate legal personality. Instead, its individual members act on behalf of the association when entering into contracts or holding assets.[85] The actions of one member as a representative of the association do not automatically impose liability on other members for the

81 Pearson (n 47).

82 Law Commission, 'Decentralised Autonomous Organisations (DAOs) Call for Evidence' (2022) 26 <https://www.lawcom.gov.uk/project/decentralised-autonomous-organisations-daos/> accessed 2 March 2023.

83 Brownsword (n 4) 251.

84 Nicholas Stewart, Simon Baughen and Natalie Campbell, *The Law of Unincorporated Associations* (OUP 2011) para 2.53.

85 ibid para 2.91.

association's debts. This establishes an agency relationship between the association and its members.

Within an unincorporated association, members are governed by rules that form part of their contractual relationship. In the context of DAOs, these rules are represented by computer code, commonly referred to as "smart contracts." However, it is important to note that smart contracts are not universally recognised as legal contracts.[86] While the computer code can be considered as part of the association's rules, the current legal framework lacks detailed instructions on the status of these rules, which can present challenges in decision-making processes.[87]

The discussion of DAOs and unincorporated associations has seen new developments due to a recent legal case of *Commodity Futures Trading Commission v. Ooki Dao*. The Ooki DAO, previously known as bZx DAO, was founded by Kyle Kistner and Tom Bean. The bZx DAO was registered as bZeroX LLC at the beginning and transferred to a purely DAO in 2021. The major service of Ooki DAO is raising liquidity for DeFi investment. The Commodity Futures Trading Commission (CFTC) imposed a $250,000 fine on bZeroX LLC and its founders

> for illegally offering leveraged and margined retail commodity transactions in digital assets; engaging in activities only registered futures commission merchants (FCM) can perform; and failing to adopt a customer identification program as part of a Bank Secrecy Act compliance program, as required of FCMs.[88]

The Ooki DAO is considered to violate the same law as bZeroX LLC and its founder; therefore, CFTC brought Ooki DAO to the court as an unincorporated association. On 8 June 2023, the U.S. District Court for the Northern District of California supported the CFTC and admitted Ooki DAO as an unincorporated association, which means all people who voted for Ooki DAO will be individually and unlimited liable to Ooki DAO fine and compensation.[89]

The DAO, without requiring additional steps such as registration or formal association, could be classified as an unincorporated association. Under California law, unincorporated associations can be subject to legal action.[90] Consequently, members of the DAO are inherently exposed to unlimited liability for its debts, unless they opt for an alternative legal structure. This potential outcome may carry significant implications for DAO participants and potentially hinder future innovation.

To summarise, forming an unincorporated association does not grant DAOs a legal personality. DAOs organised in this manner are typically nonprofit

86 Eliza Mik, Chapter 3 in this volume.

87 Law Commission (n 82) 26.

88 Commodity Futures Trading Commission, In the Matter of bZeroX, LLC (CFTC Docket No 22–31, 22 September 2022).

89 *Commodity Futures Trading Comm'n v Ooki Dao*, 3:22-cv-05416-WHO (ND Cal, 20 December 2022).

90 Cal Civil Procedure Code § 369.5(a).

organisations, with the main legal risk stemming from the agency relationship between members.[91] Despite these limitations, Philanthropy DAOs and Social DAOs can still benefit from the legal structure of unincorporated associations, as long as members effectively manage associated risks.

While existing laws may not fully align with the unique characteristics of DAOs, exploring legal frameworks such as unincorporated associations can provide some legal solutions and risk management strategies. Further development of laws specific to DAOs is necessary to address their distinct requirements and challenges in decision-making, contractual relationships, and liability. Collaboration among regulators, legal experts, and the DAO community can help establish a comprehensive legal framework that promotes the growth, innovation, and legal compliance of DAOs.

6.2 Partnership

A partnership is defined as a relationship between individuals who engage in a business venture with the intention of making a profit. Unlike an unincorporated association, partnerships have a profit purpose.[92] However, similar to an unincorporated association, a partnership does not possess a separate legal personality.

One challenge of adopting the partnership model for DAOs is transferability. In a general partnership, the departure or inclusion of a member technically dissolves the partnership and establishes a new one.[93] Whether the change constitutes a new partnership may require a court decision.[94] In the context of DAOs, tokens are held and traded, potentially causing the DAO to undergo reorganisation if it is considered a partnership under legal terms. Since token trading is easier on the blockchain than changing partnership members, this exacerbates the transferability problem mentioned earlier. It complicates the liability of partnership members and disrupts the continuity of the DAO, leading to increased transaction costs for token trading and liquidation.

However, certain DAOs may opt to organise on a private blockchain that permits only authorised participants. In such cases, where the number of token holders remains small and stable, it may be reasonable for private DAOs to adopt partnership law as a legal wrapper. Transferability becomes less significant in this scenario, allowing the DAO to interact with third parties under the protection of partnership law.

6.3 Company Law

Applying company law to govern the risks associated with DAOs can be challenging. Traditional corporations are centralised, with power concentrated in the boardroom. DAOs, being decentralised and automated, may not be suitable for

91 *Conservative and Unionist Central Office v Burrell* [1982] 1 WLR 522, 525 by Lawton LJ.
92 Partnership Act 1890, s 1.
93 Law Commission (n 82) 29.
94 ibid 30.

strict application of corporate law. However, company law can still contribute to managing some of the risks as DAOs continue to evolve.

One benefit of adopting company law is enabling interactions between DAOs and other legal entities. Providing a legal personality to a DAO through company law facilitates its engagement with external parties, including tax agencies.[95] Additionally, company law could potentially offer limited liability protection to token holders, although the determination of whether DAO token holders enjoy such protection remains uncertain.[96] Applying company law can clarify the liability of both DAO participants and the organisation's creditors.

Company law also offers a framework for organising DAOs. It provides mechanisms to protect minority stakeholders, such as access to financial documents, the ability to block special resolutions, or the initiation of derivative claims. However, DAOs have not yet established a standard protocol for minority protection. In the absence of such a protocol, applying company law could require DAO participants to discuss and determine the approach they wish to adopt for safeguarding minority rights within the organisation.

Certain company law rules may be irrelevant to DAOs. For instance, DAOs lack a board of directors to make decisions, rendering rules related to directorial power or general shareholder meetings redundant.[97]

In company law, some rules are mandatory, whereas others are default rules that allow for flexibility. This characteristic can guide the operation of DAOs, enabling them to adopt non-critical provisions while adhering to the foundational model and baseline established by legislators. For example, US company law supports private ordering, which grants DAOs some flexibility in applying legal rules.[98]

This flexibility is vital as it accommodates change. As DAOs evolve, the risks and governance requirements will evolve accordingly. Since legal governance aims to manage risks and foster the growth of DAOs, merely applying company law is insufficient. A combination of compulsory and non-compulsory rules can reduce the need for frequent legal changes, strike a balance between conflicting requirements, encourage innovation, and protect market integrity.

6.4 Trust

Trust is another potential legal wrapper for DAOs. A trust is established when a person (the settlor) transfers property to another person (the trustee) to hold for the benefit of a third party (the beneficiary).[99] Similar to incorporated associations and partnerships, a trust does not possess a separate legal personality.

95 Samuel D Brunson, 'Standing on the Shoulders of LLCs: Tax Entity Status and Decentralized Autonomous Organizations' (2023) 57 Ga L Rev 603.

96 Wulf A Kaal, 'A Decentralized Autonomous Organization (DAO) of DAOs' (2021) <https://ssrn.com/abstract=3799320> or <http://dx.doi.org/10.2139/ssrn.3799320> accessed 2 March 2023.

97 Alexandra Sims, 'Blockchain and Decentralised Autonomous Organisations (DAOs): The Evolution of Companies?' (2019) 28 NZULR 423.

98 Wright (n 69).

99 GW Keeton and LA Sheridan, *The Law of Trusts* (Barry Rose Law Publishers Ltd, 12th edn, 1993) 3.

Compared to other legal forms, trust rules primarily focus on asset holding. DAOs can be organised under a trust structure or adopt it as a solution for holding assets. The DAO community can establish a trust by clearly defining the intention, subject matter, and purpose of the trust under general law.[100] Trust is a flexible legal framework for DAOs and does not require every participant to bear unlimited liability. Since the trustees assume liability towards third parties, DAO community members can distribute the risk of liability by carefully selecting their trustees.[101]

Trusts also provide rules governing the fiduciary duty of trustees as agents of the DAO community. Trustees are required to act in the best interests of the trust and its beneficiaries, and they can be held personally liable for breaching that duty. Certain jurisdictions, such as Jersey and Guernsey, may require the appointment of an enforcer to ensure that assets are held in accordance with the trust deed.[102]

While trust structures offer solutions for asset holding, they still rely on trustees as agents to execute transactions. Similar to unincorporated associations, DAOs that adopt a trust structure for asset holding also face the agency cost between the organisation and the individuals controlling the assets. However, the trust structure does not affect the DAO at the organisational level as it does not require specific rules among its members.

In essence, trust is a viable legal mechanism for DAOs to hold and manage assets. It provides specific rules tailored to asset holding while offering flexibility to the DAO community. Trusts can also provide protection to DAOs by allowing for the distribution of liability among trustees and establishing fiduciary duties. The requirement for an enforcer in certain jurisdictions further enhances the protection for DAOs holding assets under a trust structure. However, it is important to note that trust is a limited legal tool as it introduces an agency cost and does not directly address the organisational governance of the DAO.

7. Conclusion

DAOs demonstrate a transformative organisational model facilitated by blockchain technology. As these decentralised autonomous organisations continue to develop, they present a range of technological (cybersecurity), conceptual, and legal challenges that can impact their operational efficiency and integration into the broader economy and society. The selection of appropriate legal wrappers ought to align with the inherent decentralised and autonomous nature of DAOs, taking into account their intended goals and functions. While existing legal frameworks provide a tool for identifying and addressing risks, further exploration and adaptation are necessary to ensure a functioning relationship between DAOs and the legal environment.

100 *Knight v Knight* (1840) 49 ER 58. And Law Commission (n 82) 34.
101 Wright (n 69).
102 Tony Pursall and Matthew Guthrie, *Guernsey Trust Law* (Bloomsbury Publishing 2020).

5 Resource Dependency Theory and Cybersecurity Regulation

Joseph Lee and Rachael Ntongho

1. Introduction

The aim of this chapter is to examine how the law can catalyse companies acquiring their cybersecurity capability by putting in place an effective mechanism for incorporating cybersecurity knowledge on the board, acquiring information from internal and external sources, promoting public accountability, and devising a risk management plan.

In so doing, we use Resource Dependence Theory to construct a paradigm on ways in which corporations can acquire cybersecurity capability to meet regulatory requirements and minimise external pressure from stakeholders.[1] We analyse how cybersecurity as an increasingly important asset in the digital economy can be acquired, as it has suddenly become a competitive commodity. We examine how individual companies should respond in this race to acquire cybersecurity capability and the role the state should play in assisting companies to acquire cybersecurity capabilities through creating effective resource-sharing mechanics and a framework for training market intermediaries such as chartered cybersecurity experts.

To this end, we use RDT to illustrate 1) how states can use law to require companies to acquire this cybersecurity asset, in particular the personnel and organisational aspects; 2) how companies at the organisational levels acquire such capability in response to this state law; and 3) how companies can collaborate and compete in acquiring such cybersecurity assets, such as through information sharing.

2. Constructing Cybersecurity Law and Regulation

The importance of cybersecurity breaches is at the fore of governance policies with growing pressure on the board of directors to incorporate cyberthreats into their risk-management framework.[2] This is strongly advocated by the Financial

1 See Jeffrey Pfeffer and Gerald R Salancik, *The External Control of Organizations: A Resource Dependence Perspective* (Harper & Row 1978).

2 National Cyber Security Centre, 'Common Cyber Attacks: Reducing the Impact' (Cyber Attacks White Paper, January 2016) <https://www.ncsc.gov.uk/guidance/white-papers/common-cyber-attacks-reducing-impact#downloads> accessed 2 February 2024.

DOI: 10.4324/9781032618975-8

Reporting Council that is responsible for drafting the UK Corporate Governance Code, under which companies subject to the Code should explain how they comply with the provisions or explain why they do not comply with them.[3] Such a method increases corporate transparency on their cybersecurity and reply on the markets to enforce cybersecurity norms. International organisations such as the World Economic Forum consider cybersecurity as part of environmental, social, and governance (ESG) issues and recommends that companies should include cybersecurity threats in their ESG reporting framework.[4] This can help companies focus on the long-term sustainable development for the stakeholders rather than short-term profits.

Furthermore, regulations on breaches of information and communication technology (ICT) are getting stricter as states are enacting new regulations on cybersecurity. Initially designed to prevent or mitigate cyberattacks on critical infrastructure, information-sharing policies have evolved to encompass a wider range of applications in addressing various cybersecurity incidents.[5] For instance, in the past two years, the EU has passed at least seven new regulations on cybersecurity. Amongst the new regulations enacted by the EU is the Digital Operational and Resilience Act (DORA) 2022 (EU 2022/2554), which will be enforced from 17 January 2025.[6] The Act applies to financial institutions and third-party providers of ICT services to these institutions. It requires financial institutions to protect against ICT-related risk by notifying relevant authorities of cyberthreats, conducting regular digital operational resilience testing, and sharing information on cyberthreats.[7] In addition, 2023 guidelines for secure AI system development published by the UK National Cyber Security Centre (NCSC)[8] and the US Cyber and Infrastructure Security Agency (CISA)[9] and endorsed by several nations recommend the collection and sharing of information through the creation of information-sharing communities across industries, academia, and government. By sharing information,

3 Financial Reporting Council, 'The UK Corporate Governance Code' (2018) 1 <https://media.frc.org.uk/documents/UK_Corporate_Governance_Code_2018.pdf> accessed 2 February 2024.

4 World Economic Forum, 'Global Cybersecurity Outlook 2024' (11 January 2024) <https://www3.weforum.org/docs/WEF_Global_Cybersecurity_Outlook_2024.pdf?_gl=1*1tpd8bf*_up*MQ..&gclid=EAIaIQobChMIlYPWmMKMhAMVwoGDBx3leABDEAAYASAAEgKrl_D_BwE> accessed 2 February 2024.

5 Jyh-An Lee, 'Hacking into China's Cybersecurity Law' (2018) 53 Wake Forest L Rev 57.

6 Regulation (EU) 2022/2554 of 14 December 2022 on digital operational resilience for the financial sector and amending Regulations (EC) No 1060/2009, (EU) No 648/2012, (EU) No 600/2014, (EU) No 909/2014 and (EU) 2016/1011 [2022] OJ L 333.

7 ibid art 19.

8 National Cyber Security Centre, 'Guidelines for Secure AI System Development' (27 November 2023) <https://www.ncsc.gov.uk/files/Guidelines-for-secure-AI-system-development.pdf> accessed 2 February 2024.

9 Cyber and Infrastructure Security Agency, 'CISA Roadmap for Artificial Intelligence' (November 2023) <https://www.cisa.gov/sites/default/files/2023-11/2023-2024_CISA-Roadmap-for-AI_508c.pdf> accessed 2 February 2024.

companies would easily identify cyberthreats faced by industries and address them swiftly.

The EU Digital Services Act (DSA), which came into force on 16 November 2022, requires companies to report on annual risk assessment measures as of 17 February 2024.[10] The aim of the act is to create a regulatory oversight of online platforms in member states. The act utilises a tiered regulatory approach in order not to burden smaller companies with regulatory bottlenecks. It classifies companies into intermediary services, hosting services, online platforms, and very large platforms. Platforms used by more than 10% of EU citizens are considered as large platforms and have imposed additional measures such as having a code of conduct, external and independent audit, public accountability, and a risk management plan.[11] Intermediary services, hosting services, and smaller online platforms are exempt from these requirements. Thus, companies are expected to acquire cybersecurity expertise to monitor all breaches and rectify them with minimal impact to customers.

In the US, the SEC proposed rule 38a-2 for cybersecurity risk management for investment advisers,[12] registered investment companies, and business development companies requires these companies to review and approve their cybersecurity processes annually by the board.

Cybersecurity is further being considered in a company's overall risk assessment by credit rating agencies.[13] This may impact the ability of companies to access capital from financial institutions as companies with weak cyber risk measures may be perceived as vulnerable, which can lead to financial losses. Furthermore, companies can be fined for cyber breaches. For instance, in November 2020, the Information Commission Office (ICO) fined Ticketmaster UK Limited £1.25 million for failure to protect customers' personal data after 9.4 million customers were exposed to a cyberattack in 2018.[14] British Airways was also fined £20 million when customers' traffic to its websites was diverted to a fraudulent site, and personal data was collected.[15] Firms in Europe can also be fined up to 20 million euros

10 Regulation (EU) 2022/2065 of the European Parliament and of the Council of 19 October 2022 on a Single Market for Digital Services and amending Directive 2000/31/EC (Digital Services Act) [2022] OJ L 277.

11 ibid art 26.

12 Cybersecurity Risk Management for Investment Advisers, Registered Investment Companies, and Business Development Companies, Release Nos 33-11028, IA-5956, IC-34497, 87 Fed Reg 13524 (proposed 9 February 2022) (to be codified at 17 CFR Pts 230, 232, 239, 270, 274, 275, 279).

13 David DiMoffetta, 'Credit Ratings Increasingly Looking at Cybersecurity' *The Washington Post* (21 March 2023) accessed 26 April 2023.

14 Information Commission Office, Penalty Notice, (Case ref:COM0759008, 13 November 2020) <https://ico.org.uk/media/action-weve-taken/2618609/ticketmaster-uk-limited-mpn.pdf> accessed 2 February 2024.

15 Information Commission Office, Penalty Notice, (Case ref:COM0783542, 16 October 2020) <https://ico.org.uk/media/action-weve-taken/2618609/ticketmaster-uk-limited-mpn.pdf> accessed 2 February 2024. (this paper is no longer available on ICO official site, it is still stored in an online archive [https://perma.cc/5NQV-YW9V])

under the EU General Data Protection Regulation 2016 for breaches of data protection rules, which is considered a type of cybersecurity breach.

Although corporations are expected to meet a minimum threshold of cyber risk, how corporations devise their internal and external control mechanisms to meet regulatory requirements and assure stakeholders that they have a robust cybersecurity system is not evident. Cybersecurity is a developing area with untested regulatory paradigms and limited trained personnel.

3. Theoretical Framework

Resource Dependency Theory (RDT) explains the coexistence between resources, information, and external social interactions.[16] The main proposition of the theory suggests that the ability of a corporation to be successful or able to survive is based on how well it can secure vital resources relevant for its survival from external sources.[17]

Several measures are utilised to acquire such resources, such as information sharing and building a network to share common interests and threats.[18] Information from the market through a coordinated approach of knowledge sharing can reduce reliance on external sources, such as external control by experts and regulators, and enable corporations to become more independent.[19] RDT equally contends that firms are constrained and affected by their environment and takes measures to mitigate external resource dependencies by forming interorganisational arrangements.[20] The focus of RDT here is the relationship between the corporation and the other organisations it relies on for its effectiveness and survival. Pfeffer argues that organisations are not autonomous and work in a network of interdependence. If the interdependence leads to uncertainty as to the actions of the other organisations the firm relies upon, it threatens the existence of the organisation. Thus, organisations take actions to minimise the threat to their survival because of the actions of external organisations. What is of most concern to the corporations is that control of their business rests with the company and not with an external organisation. Corporations seek to have influence and control of the market and thus would ensure there are adequate measures in place to minimise external control over the company.

16 Davita Silfen Glasberg and Michael Schwartz, 'Ownership and Control of Corporations' (1983) 9(1) Annu Rev Sociol 311.

17 T Casciaro and MJ Piskorski, 'Power Imbalance, Mutual Dependence, and Constraint Absorption: A Closer Look at Resource Dependence Theory' (2005) 50(2) Adm Sci Q 167–99.

18 Jeffrey Pfeffer, 'A Resource Dependence Perspective on Interorganizational Relations' in Mark Sheldon Mizruchi (ed), *Intercorporate Relations: The Structural Analysis of Business* (CUP 1987) 25.

19 Gerald F Davis and J Adam Cobb, 'Resource Dependence Theory: Past and Future' in Claudia Bird Schoonhoven and Frank Dobbin (eds), *Stanford's Organization Theory Renaissance, 1970–2000*, Research in the Sociology of Organizations, vol 28 (Emerald 2010) 21.

20 Johannes M Drees and Pursey PMAR Heugens, 'Synthesizing and Extending Resource Dependence Theory: A Meta-Analysis' (2013) 39(6) J Manag 1666.

In reframing RDT, Cascairo and Piskorski argue that interdependence in the original theory by Pfeffer consists of two distinct elements, which should be analysed separately. The two distinct elements of interdependence by Casciaro are mutual dependence and power imbalance. In the case of mutual dependence, organisations have an incentive and ability to absorb successful constraints. Thus, as mutual dependence between organisations increases, constraint decreases. On the other hand, in the case of power imbalance, the dependent organisation is motivated to be part of an interdependent network but less able to minimise and absorb constraints. He concluded that power imbalance can act as a hindrance to mutual dependence. This is because, in mutual dependencies, powerful organisations may lose their dominance in the relationship, while weaker organisations would benefit. This may prevent larger, more powerful organisations from entering a dependency relationship with weaker organisations. There is also the issue of benefits in a mutual dependency relationship. If more powerful organisations contribute more into the relationship, there is the likelihood of preventing weaker organisations from being part of the network.[21]

Therefore, an organisation is structured to gain valuable resources and reduce constraints based on the power imbalance and mutual dependencies between that organisation and other external organisations in the market.

4. Resource Dependency as a Mechanism for Regulating Cybersecurity

We apply RDT to cybersecurity by analysing how corporations can best structure the internal and external control mechanism to acquire or increase cybersecurity capability. Internal control consists of mostly the board of directors, shareholders, and employees with expert knowledge on cyber risk.[22] External control mechanisms involve information sharing and interorganisational arrangements between corporations, regulators, and the state. How can corporations interact with external bodies such as the state, regulators, insurance companies, financial institutions, investors, and other companies and organisations in the market to minimise cyberthreats?

The board of directors of corporations is the main organ through which the corporation can gain vital resources. Board members are required to possess the relevant skills and knowledge to build a successful corporation or be able to amass the relevant resources to steer the corporation towards profit maximisation through effective internal and external processes.[23] The UK cybersecurity toolkit for boards published by the NCSC recognises the fact that while boards members need not

21 Edward J Lawler and Jeongkoo Yoon, 'Commitment in Exchange Relations: Test of a Theory of Relational Cohesion' (1996) 61 Am Sociol Rev 89.

22 Lawrence A Gordon and others, 'Cybersecurity, Capital Allocations and Management Control Systems' (2008) 17(2) Eur Account Rev 215.

23 Jeffrey Pfeffer, 'Size and Composition of Corporate Boards of Directors' (1972) 17 Adm Sci Q 218.

have the technical expertise in cybersecurity, they should know enough to be constructive on discussion relating to cybersecurity.[24]

In this sense, the board as a whole is expected to take measures to minimise cyberattacks. This would entail effective mechanisms to identify breaches in internal and external systems of the company that can lead to cybersecurity risk. RDT suggests that directors should not merely supervise and monitor employees or simply hire cybersecurity experts but should possess the relevant skills to be able to understand the cybersecurity needs of their corporation and ask pertinent questions.[25] Thus, while directors are not expected to be cybersecurity experts, they should possess the relevant knowledge to advise and recommend cybersecurity policies to executive directors and assess their implementation.

However, cybersecurity and IT knowledge of board members has been raised as a hindrance to board effectiveness when dealing with cybersecurity issues.[26] In particular, the composition of the board, consisting of older men and women with an average age of 60 years with less appetite for technology compared to their younger directors, is one major concern.[27] Section 174 of the UK Companies Act 2006 requires directors to possess the required skills and knowledge to make informed decisions. They are expected to know the nature of cyberthreat posed to their company and how to address them.[28] Thus, they should have the minimum knowledge about the company's hardware and software and other companies it works with and how the risk can originate and impact their company. The US has recognised the importance of having directors with knowledge of threats posed to their company by passing the Cybersecurity Risk Management, Strategy, Governance, and Incident Disclosure rules. In July 2023, the SEC added regulation S-K Item 407 (J) requiring disclosure about the cybersecurity expertise of the board. The regulation requires the name of any director with cybersecurity expertise and details of the nature of such expertise by public companies. Though less detailed, the 2018 Australian Prudential Standard CPS 234 also requires firms to have named persons in the firm in charge of information security, including cybersecurity attacks in financial services industries. It recommends that firms have clearly defined information security-related roles and responsibilities of the board, senior management, and individuals.

24 National Cyber Security Centre, 'Cyber Security Toolkit for Boards' (30 March 2023) <https://www.ncsc.gov.uk/files/NCSC_Cyber-Security-Board-Toolkit.pdf> accessed 2 February 2024.

25 Catherine M Daily, Dan R Dalton and Albert A Cannella, Jr, 'Corporate Governance: Decades of Dialogue and Data' (2003) 28(3) Acad Manag Rev 371.

26 Caroline C Hartmann and Jimmy Carmenate, 'Academic Research on the Role of Corporate Governance and It Expertise in Addressing Cybersecurity Breaches: Implications for Practice, Policy, and Research' (2021) 15(2) Curr Iss Audit A9; Nigel Phair and Hooman Alavizadeh, 'Cybersecurity Skills of Company Directors – ASX 100' (2011) 15(4) J Risk Manag Financ Inst 429.

27 Oleksandr Talavera, Shuxing Yin and Mao Zhang, 'Age Diversity, Directors' Personal Values, and Bank Performance' (2018) 55 Int Rev Financ Anal 60; Ram Kumar Mishra and Shital Jhunjhunwala, *Diversity and the Effective Corporate Board* (Academic Press 2013).

28 Elif Kiesow Cortez and Martijn Dekker, 'A Corporate Governance Approach to Cybersecurity Risk Disclosure' (2022) 13(3) Eur J Risk Regul 443.

In the past, firms depended on the state to ward off cybersecurity threats, as it was perceived as a social constraint to the overall business environment of a nation. However, with the increase threat of cybersecurity, and the adverse effect to the financial and reputational capital of corporations, firms are seeking different ways of enhancing their cybersecurity measures. The rhetoric of cybersecurity is equally changing, with expectations from the state, customers, credit agencies, and investors that firms should take measures to minimise the impact of cyberthreats to the company and its customers.[29]

Dependence on an insurance policy, which is utilised to water down some of the financial hardship caused by cyberattacks, is facing restrictions as insurance companies have started to limit the type of cyber risk they will insure.[30] For instance, insurance companies are beginning to exclude state-backed cyberattacks from their cyber protection policy.[31] Lloyds of London Ltd, one of the major insurance companies in the UK, has excluded state-sponsored cyberattacks from its cybersecurity insurance policy, which has caused some panic in the financial world.[32] Therefore, taking out an insurance policy on cyber risk as a risk management measure is becoming less effective for certain types of attacks. If insurance companies increase the types of cyberattacks that they will not insure in the future, cyberattacks will be very costly for companies. In the event of reduction in insurance policies as an external measure to reduce the impact of cyberattacks, interdependence among corporations, the state, regulators, and even customers would provide additional safeguards against cyberthreats.

Interdependence between companies becomes increasingly relevant as cyberthreats may be aimed not only at a particular corporation but at a group of corporations or a specific industry. Cybersecurity risk can also be more devastating to some industries than others, for instance, financial services and critical infrastructure. Hence, organisational interdependencies between these corporations can minimise risks to the sector and benefit all companies, especially companies within a network.[33]

A coordinated approach by firms to minimise cyber risk would reduce cyberthreats to all organisations in the network. An interorganisational network of firms is important in warding off cyberthreats, as firms depend on each other for

29 Christine Parker, 'Meta-Regulation: The Regulation of Self-Regulation' in *The Open Corporation: Effective Self-Regulation and Democracy* (CUP 2002) 245.

30 Jan Martin Lemnitzer, 'Why Cybersecurity Insurance Should Be Regulated and Compulsory' (2021) 6(2) J Cyber Pol'y 118.

31 Regarding state-backed cyber-attacks and relevant legal issues, see Jyh-An Lee, 'The Red Storm in Uncharted Waters: China and International Cyber Security' (2014) 82 UMKC L Rev 951, 953–58; Jyh-An Lee, 'Shifting IP Battlegrounds in the U.S.-China Trade War' (2020) 43 Colum JL & Arts 147 161–64.

32 Ian Smith, 'Lloyd's of London Battles Insurers Over "State-Backed" Cyber Attacks' *Financial Times* (31 March 2023) <www.ft.com/content/1e8931ae-461f-47cd-b0b5-aa4931230aa2> accessed 2 February 2024.

33 Annette Hofmannand Hidajet Ramaj, 'Interdependent Risk Networks: The Threat of Cyber Attack' (2011) 11(5–6) Int J Manag Decis Mak 312.

services for their business, either as consumers of a particular service or as a smaller supplier to a larger firm. In the case of technological dependence of one firm on the other, an attack on a smaller and more vulnerable firm impacts the activities of a larger user of that technology. Hackers would typically target smaller, more vulnerable firms in a chain to gain access to larger firms.[34] For instance, hackers gained access to Australian insurer Medibank through an external service provider.[35]

Though RDT argues that power imbalance between companies may prevent cooperation between smaller and larger companies, as smaller companies stand to benefit from the superior resources of larger companies, if companies are in a position of interdependence where there is mutual benefit, both companies are better off. In the case of cybersecurity, if the system of a smaller company supplying IT services to a larger company is compromised, it affects the whole network of firms relying on the IT services of the smaller company. It is therefore in the interest of all firms that are interdependent to form a network of information sharing and cooperation.

However, information sharing with competitors and other companies may be problematic in cybersecurity as there may be conflicts of interest, trade secrets, and confidentiality issues at stake. Firms would be unwilling to disclose cyberthreats to their system for fear of being perceived as not having a robust cybersecurity system. Firms compete for resources and customers and seek to have a powerful position in the market. As a result, the interdependence of firms on cybersecurity threats in terms of information sharing with similar companies or with competitors may be unlikely without trust and integrity from all firms in the network.[36] Randall and Allen identified trust as a major hindrance for effective information sharing between US electric power companies.[37]

Nonetheless, the argument of keeping cybersecurity breaches secret is quashed by the argument of interlocking directorship as an information transmission channel.[38] It is argued that interlocking directors within firms share views, new ideas, and learning processes, and in this way circulate information with other interlocking companies.[39] There is, therefore, the possibility of interlocking directors

34 Tracey Caldwell, 'Securing Small Businesses – the Weakest Link in a Supply Chain?' (2015) 9 Comput Fraud Sec 5–10; Kaylie Gioioso, 'Small Companies, Big Breaches: Why Current Data Protection Laws Fail American Consumers in Cases of Third-Party Hacking' (2016) 10 J Bus Tech L Proxy 1.

35 Juha Saarinen, 'Credentials Theft Behind High-Profile Medibank Hack' *CRN* (23 February 2023) <https://www.crn.com.au/news/credentials-theft-behind-high-profile-medibank-hack-591231> accessed 2 February 2024.

36 Siv Vangen and Chris Huxham, 'Nurturing Collaborative Relations: Building Trust in Interorganizational Collaboration' [2003] J Appl Behav Sci 5.

37 Rick G Randall and Stuart Allen, 'Cybersecurity Professionals' Information Sharing Sources and Networks in the US Electrical Power Industry' (2021) 34 Int J Crit Infr Prot 100454.

38 Ana B Hernández-Lara and Juan P. Gonzales-Bustos, 'The Impact of Interlocking Directorates on Innovation: The Effects of Business and Social Ties' (2019) 57(10) Manag Decis 2799–815.

39 Mark Sheldon Mizruchi, 'What Do Interlocks Do? An Analysis, Critique, and Assessment of Research on Interlocking Directorates' (1996) 22 Annu Rev Sociol 271.

inadvertently sharing cybersecurity information and secrets. It may therefore be beneficial for industries with interlocking directors to formally develop a network of information sharing for cyber risk information to be shared in a consistent manner rather than informally. Interorganisational cooperation between firms would minimise inter-firm opportunism or the fear of information being leaked to a competitor, as research posits that interlocking directorship can be a source of the leak of strategic information.[40] Interlocking directorship can therefore promote cooperation and interdependence between interlocking firms and increase the flow of information on cyber risks.[41]

5. Acquisition of Cybersecurity Capabilities Through Designation of Roles

Designation of roles in corporations has proven effective in other areas of risk management such as auditing in achieving good corporate governance and eliminating the problem of lack of knowledge and awareness. In this section we discuss the different internal and external roles that form the risk management team and in charge of cybersecurity governance. The effectiveness of these three organs would greatly increase the cybersecurity capability of corporations: board of directors, chief cybersecurity officer (CCO), and interorganisational arrangements.

5.1 Role of the Board of Directors and the Risk Committee

Regulation in several countries as discussed earlier suggest that a named person in charge of cybersecurity on the board would minimise the threat of cyberattacks. This is corroborated by research.[42] To meet the SEC requirement of cybersecurity, the named cybersecurity expert should have prior knowledge, skills, or background related to cybersecurity. This can be gained through work experience, certification, or a degree in cybersecurity.

We recommend that this named director, preferably a non-executive director, should also sit on the risk committee or head a cybersecurity risk committee if one exists. Their role is to liaise with the CCO and raise cybersecurity issues to the board and challenge the resources allocated to cybersecurity at the board level. As a member of the risk committee, they would oversee cybersecurity risk in the corporation and direct the chief cybersecurity officer on strategic decisions of the board. These requirements are meant to improve cybersecurity rather than making the individual or board responsible for cybersecurity breaches, as the board is not

40 Exequiel Hernandez, Wm Gerard Sanders and Anja Tuschke, 'Network Defense: Pruning, Grafting, and Closing to Prevent Leakage of Strategic Knowledge to Rivals' (2015) 58(4) Acad Manag Ann 1233.

41 Phillip H Phan, Soo Hoon Lee and Siang Chi Lau, 'The Performance Impact of Interlocking Directorates: The Case of Singapore' [2003] J Manag Iss 338.

42 Sylvie Héroux and Anne Fortin, 'Board of Directors' Attributes and Aspects of Cybersecurity Disclosure' [2022] J Manag Gov 1–46.

required to approve the report of the cybersecurity expert. The cybersecurity expert advises and directs the board based on their expertise and independent assessment of the cybersecurity risk, but it is up to the board to deliberate and decide on the best action to take. The named person, together with the risk committee, should assess the report of the CCO and present it to the board. Furthermore, the company's cybersecurity should also be audited by an independent person and signed off by the risk committee. The named cybersecurity director would bear no liability by being singled out as the expert. Under the US regulation, the named cybersecurity director would bear no greater liability than non-experts. The biggest hindrance to companies is finding the right person with expertise who would be the named person. There are few certified cybersecurity experts to fill these positions, which is why the role of the state and regulators is crucial in ensuring effective training and the acquisition of the necessary experience.

5.2 Role of Chief Cybersecurity Officer (CCO)

Some states require institutions to appoint specific individuals responsible for data security. For instance, the Federal Trade Commission's Standards for Safeguarding Customers' Information, the Safeguard Rules mandates the appointment of a single qualified individual in charge of data security risk in financial institutions.[43] They are usually known as the chief information security officer (CISO). The CISO is responsible for security operations, physical security, and balancing the business and security objectives of the company.[44] They assess and manage risk, control information security, and put in place an effective system and policy to minimise information security risk.[45]

The CISO is different from the chief information officer (CIO), who is responsible for IT governance.[46] The CIO focuses on the product and business development of the company, such as developing the technology-related products or business of the company. The role of the CIO is to put in place an effective IT system that sustains the process and business objectives of the company. These two roles are also different from the chief cybersecurity officer (CCO), who is in charge of identifying breaches, gathering information on cybersecurity threats, being accountable for cybersecurity breaches, and proposing and implementing cybersecurity policies. The role is mainly keeping the company safe from cyberattacks. A similar demarcation is between the chief legal officer, who focuses more on the legal work of the company, rather than the chief compliance officer, who focuses on managing the legal and regulatory risks of the company. Hence, the

43 16 CFR Part 314 Standards for Safeguarding Customer Information 67 FR 36493.

44 Erastus Karanja, 'The Role of the Chief Information Security Officer in the Management of IT Security' (2017) 25(3) Infor Comput Sec 300.

45 TM Catarino, A. Vasconcelos and MM da Silva, *The Role of the Chief Information Security Officer* (IST 2016); Karanja (n 44).

46 Joseph Da Silva and Rikke Bjerg Jensen, '"Cyber Security Is a Dark Art": The CISO as Soothsayer' (2022) 6(CSCW2) Proc ACM Hum Comput Interact 1.

chief cybersecurity officer should not report to the chief information technology officer, who may not be a board member. They should report to the chair of the risk committee and the named cybersecurity expert, who can raise cybersecurity concerns and discuss them with the board. As cybersecurity may be seen as incurring cost rather than generating revenue, there may be a tendency to dispense with it – cutting cost, when it is deemed not necessary or too expensive. It is hence important to ensure that resources are allocated to cybersecurity so that cybersecurity is not compromised when the board increases their risk appetite. The named cybersecurity director can be a more optimal reporting line for the cybersecurity officer, who can raise the issue if the cybersecurity risk is high and the company has overlooked it. While the CEO or other executives could be the reporting line for the purpose of understanding the incidents taking place, the CISO can report to the designated non-executive director in charge of cybersecurity issues. This practice would prevent vested interest on the part of the CISO, who is hired and promoted by the CEO.

If resources permit, these three roles should be assumed by three different individuals to avoid one of the roles being usurped and neglected. In smaller companies with limited resources, who may not be able to appoint different employees in charge of the different roles and must appoint a single person to carry out the duties of these three roles, the three areas should be clearly mapped out and kept separate. The person they report to for each area should be separate. They should report to the CEO on the area covered by the CIO. The reporting line for the duties of the CISO should be the risk/audit committee, while the areas covered by the CCO should be reported to the expert cybersecurity director and the risk committee. Karanja suggests that reporting lines vary with different companies, and there is little consensus amongst companies as to whom the different officers report to.[47] Not having a clear line of reporting hinders good governance and accountability and can compromise the security of the company.

5.3 Interorganisational Arrangements

Interorganisational cooperation can take three forms: information sharing, board interlocking, and larger companies in a network enhancing the capacity of smaller, more vulnerable companies.

Information sharing enables companies to develop cybersecurity capabilities by improving early warning systems, understanding patterns of cyberattacks, and acquiring assets essential for recovery, resolution, and business continuity. However, this necessitates a level of cooperation and resource sharing among companies, which RDT suggests is complex due to competitive dynamics. Large companies may hesitate to share information with smaller ones that could become significant competitors, or with any competitors due to fears of market collusion and the desire to reduce operational costs. To foster a cybersecurity alliance, navigating

47 Karanja (n 44).

competition law and market forces is crucial.[48] The state could facilitate this by providing certain information-sharing services.

Although sharing information can help companies increase their cybersecurity capability, there is a legal and regulatory risk if the companies share their cybersecurity information. First, if the aim is to reduce transaction costs, using it to reduce costs may raise competition law issues, as this may foreclose some companies from obtaining the benefits. Second, information regarding corporate confidential information cannot be shared as it increases the risk of parties breaching the duty of confidentiality and the company's interest. Third, if the information relates to personal data, sharing such information may be in breach of data protection law.

With the shortage of expert cybersecurity directors, interlocking directorship can address this problem through groups of companies agreeing to share information if they have interlocking directors. Sharing of IT knowledge by interlocks has proved to be a source of educational intelligence for directors.[49] Firms have gained valuable knowledge on risks, costs, and performance of IT investments through social networks such as board interlocks.[50] Hence, encouraging firms to build a network of board interlocking to address cybersecurity risks would be beneficial to firms that are mindful of the lack of enough directors with cybersecurity expertise.

As boards are internal to an organisation and mindful of the need for confidentiality to protect their reputation, it is a better channel for sharing information than with regulators.[51] Thus, interlocks can bring in external knowledge gained from sitting on other boards to enhance decision making on cybersecurity for the focal board.

Interlocks from larger companies are equally a source of superior information to smaller companies with limited resources. Since smaller companies in a network are more targeted by hackers, interlocks in larger companies would use their superior knowledge and experience to improve the systems of smaller companies. Larger firms can also provide direct training and support to smaller firms in a network to minimise attacks on all their systems. Thus, firms with part dependency on each other should develop an effective communication, training, and support channel to minimise threats to their respective network. Stakeholders are now advocating for compulsory training on cybersecurity for directors. There should also be mandatory training for new directors on cyberthreats to the company.

48 Matthew Bennett and Philip Collins, 'The Law and Economics of Information Sharing: The Good, the Bad and the Ugly' 6(2) Eur Compet J 311.

49 Zhuo Cheng and others, 'Social Learning in Information Technology Investment: The Role of Board Interlocks' (2021) 67(1) Manag Sci 547.

50 ibid.

51 Kevin Zhu, 'Information Transparency of Business-to-Business Electronic Markets: A Game-Theoretic Analysis' (2004) 50(5) Manag Sci 670.

5.4 Role of the States and Regulatory Authorities in Cybersecurity Resource Acquisition

While corporations require a workforce that can deal with cybersecurity threats and at least a board member with knowledge of cybersecurity, there is a shortage of cybersecurity experts who can fill these positions. The state and regulators must play a role in providing personnel with cybersecurity knowledge who can deal with threats. There is also the legal requirement of cybersecurity personnel with certification. Medibank and Optus hacking in Australia proved that cybersecurity enforcement is the combined responsibility of the state and corporations.[52] Given the scale and importance of the medical industry, the collaboration of the state and these two corporations was essential in minimising the damage of the attack. We discuss three roles the state should play in enabling companies to acquire cybersecurity capabilities: coordination, certification, and regulation.

The state is usually involved when the impact of a cybersecurity breach goes beyond the corporate world and affects users and has a negative impact on the business environment of the state, as in the two examples of Medibank and Optus mentioned earlier. Some kind of voluntary public-private partnership is practiced by western governments to share information and knowledge.[53] The states should provide a framework where firms can cooperate even without oversight.[54] Encouraging a network of firms to form a partnership to address cybersecurity risks is an example. Firms may also be required to report on their cybersecurity framework and expertise. Regulatory reporting has been an effective way of enforcing corporate governance from financial stability to environmental protection. Some of the reports are published for inspection, such as environmental reporting, and some of them are not, such as tax and money laundering cases. Cybersecurity is also a sensitive issue as it relates to a company's defence and sometimes clients' confidential information. Hence, reporting to a designated public authority is often the chosen method, such as reporting to the National Crime Agency in the UK.[55] For financial institutions, they may also need to report to the financial regulators, such as the Financial Conduct Authority (FCA) or the Prudential Regulatory Authority (PRA). If the incidents relate to a data breach, they need to report to the Information Communications Office (ICO).[56]

Certification and training of experts at this early state where the system lacks trained personnel would equally increase the capacity of companies and reduce the need for continuous oversight. Companies should be motivated to use certified

52 Chad Whelan and James Martin, 'Hacking the Hackers': Reflections on State-Implemented Disruption as a "New Model" for Cyber Policing' [2023] Curr Issues Crim Justice 1.

53 Myriam Dunn Cavelty and Florian J Egloff, 'The Politics of Cybersecurity: Balancing Different Roles of the State. (2019) 15(1) St Antony's Int Rev 37.

54 ibid.

55 'Cyber Crime' (National Crime Agency) <https://www.nationalcrimeagency.gov.uk/what-we-do/crime-threats/cyber-crime> accessed 2 February 2024.

56 'Incident Reporting' (Information Communication's Office) <https://ico.org.uk/for-organisations/the-guide-to-nis/incident-reporting/> accessed 2 February 2024.

information system auditors to check their systems. Regulators shape the institutional environment and require firms to acquire cybersecurity capabilities. For instance, in preparation of the US SEC Cyber Security, Risk Management Strategy, Governance and Incident Disclosure Rules, the companies Visa, Nordstrom, Zoom, and Astra Space appointed directors with cybersecurity expertise.[57] According to a report by the *Wall Street Journal*, as of September 2023 just 12% of the S&P 500 has a person with cybersecurity expertise on their board.[58] In the UK, a 2023 report by the UK Department of Science, Innovation and Technology states that 53% of large businesses and 41% of smaller businesses has a director with expertise on their board.[59]

Regulation can also compel firms to work together, either through a network or by requiring firms to work with other network providers such as third parties, cybersecurity vendors, and experts including auditors and certification agents.

6. The Implications for Web3

The players in Web3 are fundamentally relying on digital technologies whether they are corporations, financial institutions, or the new types of business or social organisations. Cybersecurity capability will be critical to their success in the provision of their goods or services on the Web3 space.[60] Although some Web3 infrastructure designed aims to be more independent from centralised stated controls, cybersecurity threats will be a major risk in this space, whether it is centralised Web3 or decentralised Web3.

Our analysis is applicable to Web3 players. It has particular implications on how all Web3 players will compete for cybersecurity resources at the international level, internal market level, and organisational level. Law matters in catalysing an organisation's active behaviours to acquire such cybersecurity capability.[61] Some organisations may only foresee the benefits in Web3 and fail to recognise the threats that cybersecurity poses. Traditional institutions such as listed companies and financial institutions will need to increase their cybersecurity capability if they

57 Jessica Tasman-Jones, 'Cybersecurity Expertise Sets US Boards Apart, as the UK Lags' *FT Professional* <https://professional.ft.com/en-gb/blog/cybersecurity-expertise-sets-us-boards-apart-as-the-uk-lags/> accessed 2 February 2024.

58 James Rundle, 'Boards Still Lack Cybersecurity Expertise' *The Wall Street Journal* <https://www.wsj.com/articles/boards-still-lack-cybersecurity-expertise-70094266> accessed 2 February 2024.

59 'Cyber Security Breaches Survey 2023' <https://www.gov.uk/government/statistics/cyber-security-breaches-survey-2023/cyber-security-breaches-survey-2023> accessed 2 February 2024.

60 Weikang Liu and others, *Web3 Technologies: Challenges and Opportunities* (IEEE 2023) <https://ieeexplore.ieee.org/abstract/document/10273397> and <https://doi.org/10.1109/MNET.2023.3321546> accessed 2 February 2024.

61 Roger Brownsword, 'Law's Imperfect Governance: Is the Metaverse the Solution' (2023) 25 Media Art L Rev 241.

wish to operate in the Web3 space, such as Web3 infrastructure providers, DAOs,[62] and cryptoasset service providers.[63]

The entities operating within Web3, encompassing corporations, financial institutions, and emerging business or social organisations, are fundamentally dependent on digital technologies. Cybersecurity competency is essential for their successful delivery of goods and services within the Web3 environment. Despite some infrastructure in Web3 being designed to operate independently of centralised state control, cybersecurity threats loom large, affecting both centralised and decentralised Web3 systems. Our research indicates that there is intense competition for cybersecurity resources at the international, internal market, and organisational levels. Legislation plays a pivotal role in prompting organisations to actively pursue such cybersecurity capabilities. There is a tendency among some organisations to focus on the potential benefits of Web3, overlooking the significant risks that cybersecurity threats pose. Established entities, such as publicly traded companies and financial institutions, ought to enhance their cybersecurity measures to thrive in the Web3 domain.

7. Conclusion

This chapter examines the application of Resource Dependency Theory (RDT) to assess how laws can mandate companies to develop cybersecurity capabilities in the ever-competitive digital economy. Although UK company law does not explicitly require directors to possess cybersecurity expertise, the Companies Act 2006 implies a need for such knowledge, especially as a company's exposure to cybersecurity risk escalates. The UK's National Cybersecurity Centre has issued cybersecurity guidance for board members, and listed companies face additional obligations, such as information disclosure through regulated channels and conducting risk assessments in accordance with the Corporate Governance Code. It is proposed that the Corporate Governance Code should explicitly mandate roles such as a Chief Cybersecurity Officer and the creation of comprehensive cybersecurity reports subject to audit or risk committee approval and independent verification by external auditors. This approach, long-standing in the financial sector, compels companies to proactively seek cybersecurity capabilities, encompassing infrastructure, hardware, software, and expertise.

Companies might undervalue cybersecurity due to informational asymmetry, short-term perspectives, and a lack of technical knowledge. There is a risk that companies are not fully aware of their current or future exposure to cybersecurity threats, do not recognise cybersecurity as a critical and potentially competitive

62 Joseph Lee and Rougang Li, Chapter 4 in this volume.

63 Joseph Lee, *Crypto Finance, Law and Regulation: Governing an Emerging Ecosystem* (monograph, Routledge 2022) <https://www.routledge.com/Crypto-Finance-Law-and-Regulation-Governing-an-Emerging-Ecosystem/Lee/p/book/9780367086619> accessed 2 February 2024.

resource, and are unaware of how to acquire and develop such capabilities. As cybersecurity resources become scarcer, such as lack of IT experts, and the variety of risks increases, mandating the acquisition and enhancement of cybersecurity capabilities could enhance the competencies of companies, particularly within the UK. The regulatory framework could also generate immediate market demand for cybersecurity resources, potentially making the country a more attractive destination for such resources and accelerating the growth of a digital economy characterised by an increase in digitally dependent businesses.

Part C

Data Governance

6 Data Law in China

Jianzhong Shi

1 Introduction

In the digital era, new technologies such as big data, artificial intelligence, blockchain, cloud computing and internet of things are developing rapidly. Data and its application are of great importance in economic development, social governance and administrative management. In April 2020, data was officially recognized and identified as a kind of production factor in Opinions on Improving the Systems and Mechanisms for Market-Based Allocation of Production Factors, issued by the Central Committee of the Communist Party of China (CPC) and the State Council.[1] On the one hand, data and digital technologies contribute to improving the quality and efficiency of the rule of law. On the other hand, data and its application give rise to a series of new legal problems. The rule of law is an important mark of human civilization and progress. It is the fundamental method of state governance. In January 2021, the CPC issued the Plan for the Construction of the Rule of Law in China (2020–2025),[2] which, for the first time in the form of a five-year plan, makes systematic and phased arrangements on how to promote the rule of law in a comprehensive way. The continuous progress of the rule of law is closely related to the innovation and development of science and technology. Data law is the product of the deep integration of data and the construction of the rule of law, which can respond to the challenges posed by the new digital era and is the inevitable result of state governance in the digital age.

This chapter will be divided into five parts. After the introduction, the status quo of data law in China will be introduced in the second part. Then, the construction of a legal system governing data will be discussed in the third part. In the fourth part, the regulation of digital platforms will be examined and commented upon from the perspective of China's Anti-Monopoly Law. The chapter will end with some conclusions.

1 Opinions on Improving the Systems and Mechanisms for Market-Based Allocation of Production Factors (中共中央国务院关于构建更加完善的要素市场化配置体制机制的意见) 2020.

2 Plan for the Construction of the Rule of Law in China (2020–2025) (法治中国建设规划(2020–2025年)).

DOI: 10.4324/9781032618975-10

2 The Status of Data Law in China

Security is the premise of development. The protection of data security can promote the utilization of data, protect the legitimate rights and interests of individuals and organizations, and safeguard national sovereignty, security and interests in the development.[3] Therefore, security is one of the basic goals pursued by data law. Currently, the data security legal system, which is connected with data utilization, has been established in China. This data security legal system is led by the National Security Law and mainly consists of the Cybersecurity Law (CSL), the Data Security Law (DSL) and the Personal Information Protection Law (PIPL). On this basis, relevant administrative enforcement authorities have initiated a series of investigations of data breaches or violations. In addition, digital technologies have been effectively applied to facilitate the construction of the rule of law in China.

2.1 Main Legislation

With the rapid development of network and information technology, network security has been deeply integrated into every aspect of the economy and society. Cybersecurity can influence national security, social stability and people's well-being, which plays a critical role. Data security is an important part of cybersecurity, related to national security and personal information protection. In the context of the National Security Law, the CSL, the DSL and the PIPL interact with each other and constructed an organic data security legal system.

As a piece of basic legislation for network security in China, the CSL contributes to improving the legal guarantee system, strengthening network supervision and review, and the social network security guarantee capacity has been effectively improved since 2017.[4] The cyberspace security system has been established by the CSL as the core, with other regulations or documents issued by competent authorities, including Regulation on Critical Information Infrastructure Safety Protection,[5] Regulation on Network Information Content Ecological Governance,[6] and Measures on Cybersecurity Review.[7] The CSL is the foundation of the DSL and the PIPL. The DSL aims to regulate data processing activities, guarantee data security, and promote the development and utilization of data to ensure the high-quality development of the digital economy. Compared with the CSL and DSL, the PIPL is a milestone in protecting personal information and privacy in China. It grants basic rights to individuals. The PIPL defines personal information as "all kinds of

3 Joseph Lee and Rachael Ntongho, Chapter 5 in this volume.

4 Daoli Huang, 'The Review and Outlook of the implementation of the CyberSecurity Law for 5 Years' (《网络安全法》实施五年回顾与展望) (2023) 2 Cyberspace Strat Forum 61, 63.

5 Regulation on Critical Information Infrastructure Safety Protection of the People's Republic of China (关键信息基础设施安全保护条例) 2021.

6 Regulation on Network Information Content Ecological Governance of the People's Republic of China (网络信息内容生态治理规定) 2020.

7 Measures on Cybersecurity Review the People's Republic of China (网络安全审查办法) 2022.

information related to identified or identifiable natural persons that are electronically or otherwise recorded, excluding information that has been anonymized".[8] The PIPL confirms the relationship between data and information established by the DSL, that data is the carrier of information and information is the content of data.

As important components of an integrated data security legal system, the CSL, the DSL and the PIPL share some common objectives and have close connections; however, there are also significant differences among the three laws to distinguish them from each other. For example, Article 76 of the CSL explains what network security is, and Article 3 of the DSL defines data security. It can be seen from the two definitions that network security and data security overlap to some extent, but network security focuses not only on the content of data but also on the network facilities.[9] As a result, the network security here incorporates data security, cyberspace security, network facilities security and so on. Moreover, "network data" is adopted in the CSL, which is different from the definition of "data" in the DSL. Article 76 of the CSL articulates that network data refers to all kinds of electronic data collected, stored, transmitted or processed through the network. Article 3 of the DSL regards data as any record of information, either in an electronic form or otherwise. "Network data" in the CSL and "data" in the DSL are defined from different perspectives.

From the perspective of regulating digital economic activities, although there is no special legislation, there are a number of laws related to this, such as the CSL, the DSL, the PIPL, the Anti-Monopoly Law, Anti-Unfair Competition Law, or E-commerce Law. These laws are important parts of the legal system, while different laws have their own objectives and missions and are relatively independent from each other. The loopholes between different legal systems and corresponding authorities, between industry supervision, and between industry supervision and competition supervision may become blind spots out of regulation. They can raise many of the problems in the digital economy.[10] To this extent, the CSL, the DSL and the PIPL are more like behavioral legislation to protect the network security, data security and personal information. However, in order to make effective use of data resources, it is necessary to introduce legislation on data rights. Right is the starting point of behavior, and behavior is the boundary of rights. If the legislation concerning rights lags behind or is absent for a long time, it will have adverse effects on the regulation of behavior or even on the effective use of data. Therefore, it is submitted that when the basic behavioral legislation and framework on data, network and personal information have been established, the focus of the legislation should be placed on the allocation of rights.

8 Personal Information Protection Law of the People's Republic of China (个人信息保护法) (hereinafter referred as the PIPL) art 4.

9 Jyh-An Lee, 'Hacking into China's Cybersecurity Law' (2018) 53(1) Wake For L Rev 57, 70–78.

10 Jianzhong Shi, 'High-Quality Development of Digital Economy Calls for Legislation at National Level' (数字经济高质量发展亟需国家立法) *Economic Daily* (Beijing, 30 September 2021).

2.2 Administrative Enforcement

Based on the established data security legal system, the relevant authorities, such as the Cyberspace Administration of China (CAC), have launched a series of special actions to 'clean up the internet' especially on social media operators, e-commerce platforms, healthcare institutions, financial service providers and educational institutions. In particular, some of these actions concentrated on the rectification of online historical nihilism, the governance of misuse of algorithms, the regulation of traffic fraud and the account operation, the rectification of online entertainment and hot spot ranking chaos, etc.[11] In addition, China's Ministry of Industry and Information Technology has continued to strengthen the rectification of App infringement of users' rights and interests and has initiated many investigations. In 2021, a number of Apps, which collected users' personal information beyond the authorized scope or unnecessary for the provided services, and frequently asked for users' authorization, were warned or punished for their violations.[12] In some circumstances with serious consequences, the Apps concerned were even removed from App stores. In July 2021, the giant Chinese ride-hailing undertaking Didi Global Inc. was investigated by the CAC for its illegal collection of users' personal data, and was finally fined 8.026 billion Yuan in 2022. It is claimed that the processing of data by Didi violated the CSL, the DSL and the PIPL.

2.3 The Role of Digital Technologies in Data Law

To deal with the challenges brought about by the digital era, it is important to construct data law to better serve the digital governance. However, the construction of data law should not only include the improvement of the legal system but also involve the application of digital technologies to support the implementation of the legal system. In China's 14th Five-Year Plan for the Development of the Digital Economy, it is stressed that China should innovate its regulatory model on the basis of new technical means and explore the application of digital technologies such as big data, artificial intelligence and blockchain in the regulatory field.[13] In practice, digital technologies have been effectively applied to facilitate construction of the rule of law in China.

To take China's 'intelligent courts' as an example, during the past five years, digital technologies have been applied broadly in the judiciary of China, and

11 'The Cyberspace Administration of China Launched A Series of Special Actions Called "Clean and Clear"' (国家网信办部署开展"清朗"系列专项行动) *Economic Daily* (9 May 2021) <http://www.gov.cn/xinwen/2021-05/09/content_5605434.htm> accessed 29 April 2023.

12 Announcement on 'Look Back' on Issues such as Overreach for Authority and Excessive Collection of Users' Personal Information by APPs (关于APP超范围索取权限、过度收集用户个人信息等问题"回头看"的通报) (3 November 2021) <https://www.miit.gov.cn/jgsj/xgj/APPqhyhqyzxzzxd/tzgg/art/2021/art_14e43ceb875a4de7846c1df45efbac1f.ht> accessed 29 April 2023.

13 General Office of the State Council, 'China's 14th Five-Year Plan for the Development of the Digital Economy' ("十四五"数字经济发展规划), 12 January 2022.

significant progress has been made to build 'intelligent courts'.[14] With the support of digital intelligent technologies, relevant parties can now access all the legal services via Internet, and legal proceedings are made public within the legal requirements. It is reported that "since the outbreak of COVID-19 in early 2020, nearly 30 million litigation cases have been filed via a nationwide online platform and 5.04 million hearings have been held via video links".[15]

In the governance of digital platform, the first digital supervision system in the platform economy – Zhejiang Fair Online was officially launched at the beginning of 2021. Zhejiang Fair Online adopts different data capture rules and identification models to conduct targeted supervision on five kinds of anti-competitive and unfair practices, such as 'either-or', 'price discrimination based on big data', 'predatory price', 'vertical monopolistic agreements' and 'gun-jumping'.[16]

3 Construction of a Legal System Governing Data

A complete and comprehensive security legal system has taken shape in China, so there is a legal basis for the protection of data security. However, efforts should be made to improve the relevant system to promote the development and utilization of data. For instance, big data exchange centers have been set up in some places, while the volume of data exchange has suffered shrinking. One of the reasons may be the unclear ownership of data, which will also give rise to the confusion over the corresponding obligations and liabilities. Therefore, it is necessary to accelerate the construction of a national institution to build a legal system governing data. In December 2022, the Opinions on Building Basic Systems for Data to Better Give Full Play to the Role of Data Resources (Twenty Data Measures) were issued by the CPC and the State Council,[17] which provides a policy foundation for the construction of data exploitation and utilization system. Given the word limit, this chapter will only discuss the construction of a legal system governing data from two main aspects, namely, the understanding of the concept of data and the allocation of data rights.

14 Xinhua, "Intelligent Courts' Highlight of Chinese Judiciary: SPC' *China Daily* (Beijing, 7 March 2023) <https://www.chinadaily.com.cn/a/202303/07/WS6406f118a31057c47ebb2d7d.html> accessed 29 April 2023.

15 ibid.

16 'China's First Digital Supervision System in the Platform Economy – Zhejiang Fair Online Launched on 26 February'（全国首个平台经济数字化监管系统——"浙江公平在线"2月26日上线）(8 March 2021) <http://www.gov.cn/xinwen/2021-03/08/content_5591516.htm> accessed 29 April 2023.

17 The Opinions on Building Basic Systems for Data to Better Give Full Play to the Role of Data Resources (Twenty Data Measures) (关于构建数据基础制度更好发挥数据要素作用的意见("数据二十条") December 2022.

3.1 Understanding the Concept of Data

A correct understanding of the concept and characteristics of data is the premise to build a legal system governing data.

3.1.1 The Dual Attributes of Data

Data has the dual attributes of being both an information carrier and a factor of production. First, data is the carrier of information, and information makes up the content of data. This has been confirmed in the CSL, the DSL and the PIPL.[18] The carrier of information is not only the most basic function of data, but also the most basic characteristic of data. Second, data has also evolved into an unprecedented emerging factor of production.[19] With the vigorous development and wide application of digital technologies, information can be digitized electronically and processed and transmitted. As a result, data can be integrated into each economic stage, such as production, distribution, circulation, consumption and social service management, which change the mode of production, lifestyle and social governance profoundly. Data is no longer just a carrier of information, but also a key factor of production. To become a factor of production, there is correlation between data.[20] The correlation between data is clearly shown as the correlation between information content. After in-depth mining and analysis, the correlation can be extended between the content and information subject, and between different information subjects.

As the carrier of information, to guarantee data security should take priority; as a new factor of production, how to enhance the value of data and how to develop and use data should take priority. It is necessary to coordinate security and development in the design of a legal system governing data.

3.1.2 The Classification of Data

To understand the concept of data in a multi-dimensional way can facilitate the construction and implementation of a legal system governing data. Understanding the concept is the foundation to build a legal system. Unclear and illogical concepts or definitions will inevitably pose challenges to the system design and bring about practical difficulties. For example, the data-related concepts mentioned in the DSL include not only those defined on the basis of data content, such as government data, data involving personal information and military data, but also those defined on the basis of hierarchy, such as important data and core data. In the PIPL, sensitive personal information and personal information of minors are applied. However, confronted with these related concepts, the relevant laws mentioned here do not stipulate or explain the standard of data classification. What is more, in

18 The Cybersecurity Law of the People's Republic of China (网络安全法) art 76; the Data Security Law (数据安全法) art 3; and the PIPL art 4.

19 Pinar Oruc, Chapter 7 in this volume.

20 It should be noted that the lack of correlation between data is also a correlation.

recent years, more data-related concepts that are not covered by the laws mentioned are created by the legislation and normative documents at the central and local levels, such as public data, social data, corporate data, etc. In this context, the standards to classify data have not observed the principle of identity, and data-related concepts are defined from different dimensions. As a consequence, the ambiguous connotation, confused denotation and poor relationship between concepts increase the difficulty to allocate data rights and obligations in a scientific way.

Given the characteristics of data and the dual attributes as information carrier and production factor, it is more scientific to distinguish data as "concerning" and "control or process".[21] Specifically, "concerning" type of data focuses on the correlation between the subject and the information content carried by the data. The "control or process" type of data focuses on the correlation between the subject and the processing of data. It will make great sense to apply this standard or method uniformly to classify data.

3.2 Allocation of Data Rights

3.2.1 Interests Related to Data

As the carrier of information, once data become a factor of production and enter the market, it will be derived from an information interests carrier to a resource interests carrier. The diversity and complexity of data types, control states and data processing determines the complexity of data rights arrangements. Therefore, to build a legal system governing data, with a data ownership system as the core, the legitimate interests related to data of different data stakeholders should be concentrated on. Considering the value basis and the incremental process of data resources, it is submitted that interests related to data can be divided into interests related to data content and interests related to data processing. Accordingly, data stakeholders should include data content stakeholders and data processing stakeholders.[22] Data content stakeholders can answer the question 'who do the data concern?'; data processing stakeholders can answer the question 'how and by whom are data processed?'. In fact, the allocation of data rights is to recognize and protect the legitimate interests related to data. The protection of the legitimate interests of data stakeholders can not only promote the development and utilization of data but also encourage enhanced consciousness of data security.

3.2.2 Data Rights

The complexity and difficulty to allocate data rights is determined by the complexity of data types and the state of data processing. Interests as the core of the right

21 Jianzhong Shi, 'The Deconstruction of the Concept of Data and the Construction of a Legal System Governing Data – the Connotation and the System of Data Law'(数据概念的解构与数据法律制度的构建——兼论数据法学的学科内涵与体系) (2023) 35 (1) Peking Univ Law J 23, 35.

22 ibid 38–39.

not only determine the starting point of behavior but also determine the boundary of behavior. The purpose of constructing a data rights system is to define the boundary of data processing and clarify the content of the legal relationship caused by data processing. Data rights should be set up by national legislation.

Data has the characteristics of non-competitiveness, replicability, non-exclusiveness and inseparable from digital technology.[23] Hence, the traditional property rights allocation mode is not adapted to data rights allocation. On the one hand, there are inherent conflicts between data and proprietary rights. The rights in rem is not conducive to the development and utilization of data. Even if the data subject is granted with proprietary rights, given the characteristics of data, the subject is not able to exercise the rights exclusively. For example, when surfing the Internet, personal information and data may be 'possessed' by other subjects at the same time due to legal provisions or contractual agreements. If the possession of data which should have been exclusive is violated, it will be either impossible to remedy or the cost of remedy will be high. In this context, the right itself should not be considered as a right by law. On the other hand, access to data is the basis of data rights and is the premise to exercise data rights. The contribution of data to enabling the production and operating activities cannot be separated from digital technologies. Without technical processing, data is limited to the information carrier and will not have the attribute of resource and value. Any processing of data and any exercise of data rights or protection of interests related to data should be based on the access to data.

It is necessary to introduce the paradigm of a legal relationship in the construction of the legal system governing data. It is the basic way to analyze and deal with legal issues concerning data to allocate rights, obligations and liabilities in a scientific way among different subjects of data relationship. The DSL and the PIPL list eight kinds of data processing behaviors, namely, collection, storage, processing, use, transmission, provision, disclosure and deletion. Each processing activity of data can result in the creation, change or elimination of the data social relationship. The allocation of rights, obligations and liabilities should not only deconstruct the data social relationship caused by data processing but also take into account the specific scenarios. In addition, the characteristics and attributes of data and data processing should be respected.

4 Regulation of Digital Platforms

As one of the most critical factors of production in the digital economy, data has a fundamental position with strategic value and competitive significance.[24] Data play an increasingly important role in digital transformation and data-driven innovation. Data processing has a significant impact on market competition in the digital

23 Jyh-An Lee, 'Tripartite Perspective on the Copyright Sharing Economy in China' (2019) 33 Comput Law Secur Rev 434–35.

24 Maurice E Stucke and Allen P Grunes, *Big Data and Competition Policy* (OUP 2016) 36–50; Jyh-An Lee, 'Licensing Open Government Data' (2017) 13(2) Hastings Bus LJ 207, 209–10.

economy. Given the competitive importance of data, undertakings that control data may be reluctant to share data. Data aggregation to a certain extent may lead to anti-competitive problems, such as the foreclosure of data and the abuse of data, which will impede effective competition and damage consumer welfare. Therefore, the regulation of anti-competitive practices in the digital economy constitutes an essential part of data law in China. As a platform economy is the most typical performance of the digital economy, the regulation of digital platforms should be paid more attention.[25]

Though digital platforms play an important role in the development of the digital economy, they also bring significant challenges to competition law. Global competition authorities have paid particular attention to their practices with anti-competitive effects. China, one of the main antitrust jurisdictions around the world, also positively took actions to address these new problems. In this section, the amendment of China's Anti-Monopoly Law and the outcomes of the anti-monopoly enforcement in China will be examined.

4.1 Amendment of the Anti-Monopoly Law

In the past few years, efforts have been made to intensify anti-monopoly supervision, prevent disorderly capital expansion as well as promote regulated, healthy and sustainable development of the platform economy.[26]Against this background, China has revised its Anti-Monopoly Law (AML) in 2022 and released new regulations and guidelines to strengthen the related legal system.

On the one hand, in 2021, the Anti-Monopoly Committee of China's State Council issued Anti-Monopoly Guidelines for the Platform Economy. It sets out principles for assessing anti-competitive conduct involving digital platforms and provides specific guidance on the determination of monopolistic agreements, abuse of dominance and merger control in the platform economy. Besides, the State Administration for Market Regulation (SAMR), known as China's competition authority, published the Guidelines on Implementing the Entity Responsibilities of Internet Platforms (Draft for Comments) and Guidelines on Classification and Grading of Internet Platforms (Draft for Comments). These two draft guidelines aim to better identify the various risks caused by internet platforms with different scales and services. However, there has not been a consensus on the criteria to classify internet platforms, and the two draft guidelines have not been formally in force. In addition, some competition compliance guidelines for internet platform enterprises have been promulgated at the national and provincial levels, such as in Zhejiang and Beijing, to provide clear guidance.

25 Neerav Srivastava and Normann Witzleb, Chapter 8 in this volume; Songyin Bo, Chapter 9 in this volume.

26 Xinhua, 'China Holds Key Economic Meeting to Plan for 2022' *China Daily* (Beijing, 10 December 2021) <https://english.www.gov.cn/news/topnews/202112/10/content_WS61b35be4c6d09c94e48a2100.html> accessed 30 April 2023.

On the other hand, in 2022, the most remarkable milestone was that the amendment to the AML was approved in June and came into effect on 1 August. This is the first amendment to the AML since it was promulgated in 2008. In general, the revised law improves the anti-monopoly enforcement system and increases liabilities as well as clarifies the fundamental principles to tackle violations in the platform economy. For example, the 2022 Anti-Monopoly Law states that operators shall not engage in monopolistic behaviors by abusing data and algorithms, technologies, capital advantages, platform rules, etc.[27] Then, several highlights will be elaborated in detail as follows.

First, 'to encourage innovation' has been incorporated into legislative objectives. Innovation is vital for development of the digital economy. It can create high-quality products and provide new services, which may disrupt the existing competition landscape. However, in order to maintain market position, the tech giants with dominant power may impede the competition from competitors' innovation by merger or exclusionary conduct. Therefore, regarding 'to encourage innovation' as an objective contributes to creating a level playing field for innovation and promotes high-level competition through innovation.[28]

Second, the amendment gives a response to the abuse of dominance in the digital economy. It is more challenging to deal with abuse of dominance in digital markets considering the characteristics of digital platforms, such as the two- or multi-side, strong network effects, etc.[29] New forms of anti-competitive practices like 'self-preferencing' are also difficult to identify.[30] Thus, the amendment emphasizes the principle that an operator with a dominant market position shall not use data, algorithm, technology, platform rules, or otherwise to engage in the abuse of a dominant market position.[31]

Third, the amendment clarifies the notification of transactions below the thresholds of merger control. In digital markets, concentrations involving digital platforms may exclude or restrict competition but escape from mandatory notification due to their low turnovers. To fill this gap, the 2022 AML authorizes the SAMR to require the operators to notify the planned concentration if there is evidence that the concentration may have adverse effects on competition regardless of whether the turnover thresholds are met.[32] It contributes to avoiding false negative risks.

In 2023, the SAMR released four complementary regulations to facilitate the implementation of the 2022 AML and further strengthen the enforcement

27 The Anti-monopoly Law of the People's Republic of China (反垄断法) (hereinafter referred as the 2022 AML) art 9.

28 Jianzhong Shi, 'The Practical Significance and Content Interpretation of the New Anti-Monopoly Law' (新《反垄断法》的现实意义与内容解读) (2022) 4 China L Rev 182–83.

29 OECD, 'Abuse of Dominance in Digital Markets' (8 December 2020) <www.oecd.org/daf/competition/abuse-of-dominance-in-digital-markets-2020.pdf.> accessed 30 April 2023.

30 Shi, 'The Deconstruction of the Concept of Data and the Construction of a Legal System Governing Data (n 22) 187.

31 The 2022 AML art 22.

32 ibid art 26.

framework. The four regulations respectively prohibit monopolistic agreements, abuse of dominance as well as abuse of administrative powers to exclude or restrict competition and also outline the review process for concentrations of undertakings. It is worth noting that the relevant regulations also make responses to the competition problems in the digital economy. The Regulation on Prohibiting Monopolistic Agreements enumerates the ways that operators may use data, algorithms, technology and platform rules to reach horizontal or vertical monopoly agreements, which can facilitate the identification of illegal practices.[33] The Regulation on Prohibiting the Abuse of Dominance concludes the practical experience in anti-monopoly enforcement involving digital platforms. On the one hand, it is articulated that the transaction amount, transaction quantity and the ability to control traffic can be taken into consideration while determining the dominant market position of digital platforms.[34] On the other hand, detailed rules are stated to identify the six kinds of abuses of dominance listed in the 2022 AML, and specific justifications are also elaborated.[35] The Regulation on Merger Review updates the corresponding remedies to deal with competition concerns raised in digital platform transactions. For example, divestitures of data-based intangible assets or related interests are provided as structural remedies. Behavioral remedies incorporate measures like modifying platform rules or algorithms and making commitments of compatibility or not reducing interoperability levels.[36]

4.2 *Outcomes of Anti-Monopoly Enforcement*

In addition to improvement of the legislation, the anti-monopoly enforcement in China has also made achievements. The SAMR has been particularly active during the past few years and has published three key decisions concerning the abuse of dominance by digital platforms in 2021 and 2022. It is worth noting that some characteristics of platforms were considered in these cases.

4.2.1 *The Alibaba Case*

In April 2021, the SAMR imposed a fine of almost 18.23 billion yuan ($2.78 billion, 4% of the domestic turnover in 2019) on Alibaba Group for breaching China's Anti-Monopoly Law.[37] It is claimed that Alibaba Group abused its dominant position in the relevant market to prohibit intra-platform business users from selling or participating in promotion activities on competing platforms. The SAMR followed four steps in this case, which are the definition of the relevant market, the

33 Regulation on Prohibiting Monopolistic Agreements (禁止垄断协议规定) arts 13, 15.
34 Regulation on Prohibiting the Abuse of Dominance (禁止滥用市场支配地位行为规定) art 12.
35 ibid arts 14–19.
36 Regulation on Merger Review (经营者集中审查规定) art 40.
37 *Alibaba*, SAMR Administrative Sanction Decision, GuoShiJianChu [2021] No 28 (国市监处 [2021] 28号).

determination of a dominant position, the identification of the abuse concerned and the analysis and assessment of anti-competitive effects.

The decision concluded that the relevant market is the online retail platform service market within the territory of China. In general, substitutability is the key to define the relevant market, which can be analyzed both from the demand and supply sides. In this case, the SAMR first indicated that the online retail platform service market is a two-sided market, consisting of two groups of operators and consumers within the service platform. The prominent feature is that it has cross-side network effects, which makes the demands of the two-sided users for online retail platform service closely related. Therefore, to define the relevant market in this case, it is necessary to consider the influence of the relationship between the users of the two-sided platform. Demand substitution analysis and supply substitution analysis are carried out respectively from the perspectives of operators and consumers. From the demand side of intra-platform operators, online services have few limitations on time and location, which are quite different from offline services. Online operators spend less costs and can match their products with the demand of consumers more effectively through data analysis. From the demand side of consumers, it is more convenient for consumers to get various goods and personalized services online. From the supply side, it is fairly difficult for a traditional business operator to become a platform operator due to technology barriers. As a result, the SAMR claimed that there is no substitutability between online retail platform services and offline retail commerce services. Alibaba argued that the relevant market should be further restricted into B2C online retail platform services because it has a different business model from C2C online retail platform services. However, the SAMR rebutted that both B2C and C2C provide the same services, such as online business premises, transaction aggregation and information dissemination. It was emphasized that the online retail platform services market constituted a single relevant product market despite different types of transactions like B2C or C2C and different goods being marketed.

The dominant position of Alibaba Group was mainly determined by a market share of more than 50% in 2015–2019 and the high concentration of the relevant market. However, it is discussed that a zero-price model may affect the accuracy of measuring dominant power. To support its conclusions, the SAMR also considered a range of relevant factors in accordance with Article 18 of the 2008 AML (Article 23 of the 2022 AML). With strong financial resources and advanced technologies, Alibaba is powerful to bargain prices and control traffic against counterparties. Meanwhile, it is found that Alibaba had strong network effects, and users were highly locked into the platform, which may result in high switching costs to other competitive platforms.

According to the SAMR's findings, Alibaba Group forced intra-platform business users to sell products exclusively on its platform and forbid them from participating in promotion activities on other platforms through agreements. To strengthen the binding effects of the agreements, Alibaba applied a combination of rewards and punishments. These practices reduced competition between competitive platforms and harmed the interests of consumers by reducing their choices.

Most importantly, these anti-competitive practices hindered the optimal allocation of resources in the relevant market, which impeded innovation.

This case is of great symbolic significance. On the one hand, it considered the characteristics of platforms such as multi-sided markets and network effects while defining the relevant market and determining a dominant position. Anti-competitive practices and their adverse effects are specifically analyzed from both the legal and economic perspectives. These demonstrations are valuable samples for other similar cases. On the other hand, it marked that China's anti-monopoly enforcement on digital platforms has entered a new era and released a clear attitude that China will pay equal attention to the development and regulation in the platform economy.[38]

4.2.2 Meituan Case

Another case was about a food delivery giant Meituan. In October 2021, the SAMR imposed a fine of 3.442 billion yuan ($534 million) on Meituan for abusing its dominant position, which violated the AML.[39]

When defining the relevant market, the SAMR identified that online food delivery platform services within the territory of China can be regarded as a single relevant market. The decision concluded that online services have no substitutability with offline services from both the demand and supply sides. Besides, online platform services have considerable differences from online services provided by intra-platform business users on their own. Meituan is dominant in the relevant market on the basis of its market share exceeding 50% during 2018–2020 and the analysis of the relevant factors in Article 18 of the 2008 AML (Article 23 of the 2023 AML) as well as Article 11 of the Anti-Monopoly Guidelines for the Platform Economy. Consequently, the SAMR found that Meituan restricted intra-platform business users to cooperate only with it by exclusive agreements and technical methods. The illegal practices have excluded competition between rival services, reduced the legitimate interests of intra-platform operators and limited consumer choices. What is more, these anti-competitive practices also have great negative impacts on innovation.

4.2.3 CNKI Case

China National Knowledge Infrastructure (CNKI), an academic database platform service provider, was fined 87.6 million yuan ($12.58 million) for monopolistic

38 Jianzhong Shi, 'Strengthen Anti-Monopoly Supervision to Promote the Development of Platform Economy in the Regulation' (加强反垄断监管 促进平台经济在规范中发展) *Economic Daily* (Beijing, 10 April 2021) <http://www.ce.cn/xwzx/gnsz/gdxw/202104/10/t20210410_36459033.shtml> accessed 30 April 2023.

39 *Meituan*, SAMR Administrative Sanction Decision, GuoShiJianChuFa [2021] No 74 (国市监处罚[2021]74号).

behaviors in 2022.[40] The SAMR concluded that the relevant market, in this case, was the Chinese academic literature online database service market within the territory of China. It was stressed that the Chinese academic literature online database service was totally different from an e-book database service or academic literature online searching service, both from the demand and supply sides. CNKI was found to have been dominant consistently in the relevant market since 2014. This assessment was mainly based on its high market shares exceeding 50% and high entry barriers due to intellectual properties and business licenses. In this case, CNKI abused its dominant position to charge unfairly high prices and required its counterparties to cooperate exclusively with it through exclusive cooperation agreements with a combination of awards and punishments. These illegal behaviors are determined to restrict competition and innovation in the relevant market, raise entry barriers to impede potential competitors and infringe users' legitimate rights and interests.

4.2.4 Merger Control Involving Digital Platforms

In terms of merger control, the SAMR strengthens its investigations on gun-jumping transactions in the platform economy. During 2021, 98 gun-jumping cases involving digital platforms were fined and published to the public, which showed a significant increase in the number of merger control cases.[41] Among these cases, Tencent was involved in 30 investigations and received fines of 15 million yuan in total, and Alibaba was involved in 18 investigations and received fines of 9 million yuan in total.[42]

Furthermore, it was noteworthy that the SAMR blocked the merger between HuYA and DouYu in 2021, which has been the first prohibited transaction between digital platforms.[43] In this case, the new company would have grabbed a market share exceeding 70% in the game livestreaming market after the planned acquisition, which raised big competition concerns. Tencent has sole control of HuYA and joint control of DouYu. If the merger was approved, Tencent would have controlled the union solely, which would further strengthen its dominant position in the downstream game livestreaming market. The SAMR concluded that Tencent would have the ability and motivation to impose vertical foreclosures on both the upstream market of online game operating services and the downstream markets to exclude and restrict competition.

40 *CNKI*, SAMR Administrative Sanction Decision, GuoShiJianChuFa [2022] No 87 (国市监处罚(2022)87号).

41 China's Anti-Monopoly Bureau, 'The Annual Report on Anti-Monopoly Enforcement in China 2021' (中国反垄断执法年度报告(2021)).

42 Michael Gu, 'Spotlight: Merger Review in China' *Lexology* (4 April 2022) <https://www.lexology.com/library/detail.aspx?g=a32809bd-3699-410d-bab1-5c0de78ff6f9> accessed 30 April 2023.

43 Announcement on the Prohibition Decision on the Acquisition of DouYu International Holdings Limited by HUYA Inc (2021) <https://www.samr.gov.cn/xw/zj/202107/P020210710327201713322.pdf> accessed 30 April 2023.

Merger control is an important part of the Anti-Monopoly Law.[44] However, in the digital economy, some data-driven concentrations of undertakings are different from the traditional mergers, which bring difficulties and challenges to the application of the Anti-Monopoly Law. In the concentrations involving startups, whose turnovers are usually very low, the change of market share caused by the concentration is usually small. Such cases cannot meet the notification thresholds stated in the current Anti-Monopoly Law and do not fall within the scope of the merger review. However, given the huge number of users, the amount of data and the volume of deals on the platform, the turnover sometimes can hardly reflect a company's real market power. That is why "killer acquisitions" has become a contentious issue and brought about controversy. The competition authority in German has already involved the transaction value as a supplementary threshold to fill this gap.[45] In China, the amendment of AML and the Regulation on Merger Review to some extent responds to the gap. However, they do not provide a solution to the fundamental problem of bring the data-driven concentration with competition concerns under review. Further improvements to the notification thresholds are expected.

5 Conclusion

Security is the premise of development. Currently, China has established the data security legal system, which is led by the National Security Law and mainly consists of the CSL, the DSL and the PIPL. In this context, the relevant authorities have launched a series of special actions against data breaches or violations to 'clean up the internet'. To deal with the challenges brought about by the digital era, digital technologies have also been effectively applied to facilitate the construction of the rule of law in China, such as the establishment of 'intelligent courts' and the first digital supervision system in the platform economy – Zhejiang Fair Online. However, efforts should also be made to improve the relevant system to promote the development and utilization of data. It is necessary to accelerate the construction of a national institution to build a legal system governing data. A correct understanding of the concept and characteristics of data is the premise of building a legal system governing data. Data has the dual attributes of being both an information carrier and a factor of production. To understand the concept of data in a multi-dimensional way can facilitate the construction and implementation of a legal system governing data. The diversity and complexity of data types, control states and data processing determine the complexity of data rights arrangements. It is submitted that interests related to data can be divided into interests related to data content and interests related to data processing. Accordingly, data stakeholders

44 Jyh-An Lee, 'Unfair Competition and Antitrust Law' in Christopher Heath (ed), *Intellectual Property Law in China* (2nd edn, Wolters Kluwer) 453–54.

45 Guidance on Transaction Value Thresholds for Mandatory Pre-merger Notification (Section 35 (1a) GWB and Section 9 (4) KartG).

should include data content stakeholders and data processing stakeholders. It is necessary to introduce the paradigm of a legal relationship in the construction of the legal system governing data. This is the basic way to allocate rights, obligations and liabilities in a scientific way among different subjects of data relationship.

Given the competitive importance of data, the regulation of anti-competitive practices in the digital economy constitutes an essential part of data law in China. In the past few years, efforts have been made to intensify anti-monopoly supervision, prevent disorderly capital expansion as well as promote regulated, healthy and sustainable development of the platform economy. Against this background, China revised its Anti-Monopoly Law in 2022, and new regulations and guidelines were released to strengthen the related legal system. In addition to the improvement of the legislation, the anti-monopoly enforcement in China has also made achievements, such as the remarkable *Alibaba*, *Meituan* and *CNKI* cases. Though great progress has been made in data law in China, efforts should be made to construct a legal system governing data to promote the development and utilization of data, and detailed complementary guidelines or regulations are in need to facilitate the anti-monopoly enforcement in the digital economy.

7 Copyright Law and the Use of Big Data for Computer Vision

Pinar Oruc

Introduction

Computer vision is a field of artificial intelligence (AI) that focuses on how computers can understand images and videos that has been growing for a while: the first project on computer vision was developed at the Massachusetts Institute of Technology in the 1960s.[1] Despite two periods with slower progress and low investment (known as AI winters),[2] AI is on the rise again, and computer vision is increasingly used nowadays for a wide range of purposes, such as self-driving cars, image detection for medicine and agriculture, or generating new works.

But data is needed to improve computer vision. Not just any data, but it needs to be relevant for the purpose of the project. For example, if a company is developing a computer vision algorithm for their self-driving car, ideally it should recognise traffic lights. To achieve that, this company would need to use many relevant images – traffic lights in all colours, shapes, from all angles. If the only data they have access to are the images of potatoes, then the project would stall until more data is acquired. But even when millions of relevant images and videos already exist, it might not always be straightforward to access and use them.

The availability of training data depends on multiple factors, one of which is copyright law. Copyright is a form of intellectual property right, which provides a limited term of protection to the rightsholder. During that term, the use of their work is subject to authorisation, thus giving the rightsholder the chance to monetise their works. To balance the interests of the rightsholder and the public, copyright law also has defences available for specific circumstances where others' protected works can be used without their authorisation, for purposes such as education and research. If there is no authorisation or defence, there will be the risk of copyright

1 IBM, 'What Is Computer Vision?' <https://www.ibm.com/topics/computer-vision> accessed 23 January 2024.

2 The first wave of AI research between 1956 and 1972 halted due to limitations in computing power, and the second AI wave in the 1980s ended due to the high cost of storage, causing a second AI winter between 1987 and 1993: Tim Winchcomb, 'Ofcom: Use of AI in Online Content Moderation' (2019) 14–15 <www.cambridgeconsultants.com/insights/whitepaper/ofcom-use-ai-online-content-moderation> accessed 23 January 2024.

DOI: 10.4324/9781032618975-11

infringement. There is already a defence specifically for text and data mining, which will be addressed later.

This chapter will discuss the use of computer vision through the specific purpose of content moderation, which is an important concern for digital platforms hosting user-generated content. However, issues and solutions identified here will be partly applicable to other uses of computer vision, such as image generation, and generally applicable to the use of other kinds of training data for purposes such as Natural Language Processing (NLP), which focuses on how computers understand and generate language (text or speech). It is worth keeping an eye on the law, as generative AI will continue to impact and facilitate the decentralised nature of web3 by creating personalised content and making autonomous decisions. Therefore, IP policymakers should ensure that their laws are not discouraging the use and development of AI in their jurisdictions.

This chapter will first introduce the content moderation challenges of platforms, and the second part will introduce the technology behind computer vision. The third part will explain why copyright law is relevant, with a focus on international, EU and UK laws. Finally, in the fourth part, the chapter will delve into a (partial) solution, the copyright defence for data mining, which is different in the given jurisdictions.

1. Digital Platforms and Content Moderation

Digital platforms provide internet users with unprecedented opportunities to share their content without the censorship of the traditional media, such as radio, newspapers, or television. While platforms are able to control and monetise their users' content, it also comes with a heavy responsibility.[3] Platforms containing user-generated content might be inadvertently hosting images and videos, such as child abuse, violent and extreme images, hate speech, or sexual content.[4] In addition, depending on the jurisdiction, platforms might be liable for copyright-protected works being communicated to the public on their platforms by their users. This was recently introduced in the EU with the controversial Article 17 of the Directive 2019/790 on copyright and related rights in the Digital Single Market.[5]

3 Neerav Srivastava and Normann Witzleb, Chapter 8 in this volume.

4 Platforms' responsibility could be based on national or regional instruments on specific types of harmful content. For example, at the EU level, various initiatives put the responsibility on the intermediaries, including the 2011 Directive on Child Abuse, 2017 Directive on Terrorism, 2018 Directive revising AV Media Service Directive (hate speech and violence), also supported by CJEU case law: Giovanni Sartor and Andrea Loreggia, 'The Impact of Algorithms for Online Content Filtering or Moderation – Upload Filters' (2020) Study Commissioned by the European Parliament's Policy Department for Citizens' Rights and Constitutional Affairs.

5 For concerns on art 17, Amy Bishop, 'Article 17 of the Directive on Copyright in the Digital Single Market – Has Anyone Managed to Sufficiently Protect Legitimate Uses?' (2023) 45(6) Eur Intell Prop Rev 354; Thomas Spoerri, 'On Upload-Filters and Other Competitive Advantages for Big Tech Companies under Article 17 of the Directive on Copyright in the Digital Single Market' (2019) 10(2) J Intellect Prop Inf Technol E-Comm 173; João Pedro Quintais and others, 'Safeguarding

This leaves digital platforms in the difficult position of having to filter certain content, while also ensuring that other (safe) content is not erroneously removed. The filtering criteria can be applied before the content is shared with others (pre-moderation), after it is shared and flagged by visitors (post-moderation), or both.[6] While smaller platforms could rely on only human moderators who could intervene and assess, larger platforms need the help of technology to monitor large-scale user-generated content. It is to be noted that the human moderators can be slow and expensive; additionally, their regular exposure to harmful material can lead to negative outcomes for the moderators themselves, so using available technology is a great help. At the same time, relying too much on these non-human filters carries the risk of false positives, where content that is not harmful is removed automatically, therefore limiting the freedom of expression of the users.

Especially at the earlier stages when new content is uploaded to these platforms, several long-standing technologies can be used together with AI or separately. One option is to rely on watermarking, where previously marked digital files are recognised by the computer. Watermarks could be visible or invisible and could carry information about the rightsholder. Another option is hashing, where digital files are run through the same hashing algorithm, where each file gets a unique identifier number. Later on, if any unknown digital files with the same hash is uploaded, the system matches it with the existing one and reacts accordingly, which is commonly used for detecting terrorism and viruses.[7] Another option is to rely on fingerprinting, where instead of assessing the digital characteristics of a file used for hashing, the fingerprints depend on the content of the file and can accurately detect altered images (such as blurred, rescaled, or mirrored).[8] For example, Audible Magic service relies on audio fingerprinting (used by Facebook, Twitch, and TikTok), and Content ID relies on audio and video fingerprinting (used by YouTube).[9] There is also the option of using these technologies together. Finally, to supplement these methods, AI (and its sub-field computer vision) can be used to detect unknown content where no watermarks, hashes or fingerprints can help.

When filtering static images and videos, using computer vision technology would involve processing the user-generated content through a previously trained model, and the computer 'seeing' (through object recognition, image segmentation and categorisation, pattern, and facial recognition) and reacting to the image

---

User Freedoms in Implementing Article 17 of the Copyright in the Digital Single Market Directive: Recommendations From European Academics' (2019) 10(3) J Intellect Prop Inf Technol E-Comm 277; Sebastian Felix Schwemer, 'Article 17 at the Intersection of EU Copyright Law and Platform Regulation' (2020) 3 Nordic Intellect Prop L Rev 400.

6 Winchcomb (n 2) 5.

7 EUIPO, 'Automated Content Recognition: Discussion Paper – Phase 1 "Existing Technologies and Their Impact on IP"' (2020) 7 <https://euipo.europa.eu/tunnel-web/secure/webdav/guest/document_library/observatory/documents/reports/2020_Automated_Content_Recognition/2020_Automated_Content_Recognition_Discussion_Paper_Full_EN.pdf> accessed 23 January 2024.

8 ibid 15.

9 ibid 16–17.

accordingly. Computer vision can also be used jointly with NLP, which allows recognising text within the images/videos or recognising speech within the videos, and filters accordingly. For example, if a user uploads an image on a platform that shows violence, the filters can detect that this image looks like similar images that were used to train the violence-detection algorithm, and be able to automatically recognise this content. But the technology is not perfect yet, so the platforms might choose to initially filter through algorithms, then rely on human moderators where wrongful deletions are flagged.

So in order to use computer vision for content moderation, platforms will have to either develop their algorithm or source it from the other companies providing this as a commercial service, if it is available. This means that they need to acquire the relevant data and feed it into the machine learning process.[10] Therefore, the availability of training data is a key indicator of whether a successful computer vision algorithm can be created.

2. Developing Computer Vision – Need for Data

When developing a new algorithm, or improving an existing one, it is important that the training data used is similar to the ones the computer is aiming to detect. Labelled data are more valuable than unlabelled data, as they need some human oversight to ensure that labels fit the objects in the image. There are already open datasets with labelled images, usually for common objects. One example is ImageNet, which was developed to help with object categorisation.[11] Another database is COCO, which provides images with common objects in context.[12] Another is KITTI (Karlsruhe Institute of Technology and Toyota Technological Institute), which holds hours of different traffic scenarios, and it is used to develop self-driving cars.[13]

Some companies, such as Microsoft, Google, or Meta, already hold large datasets that help them develop their own computer vision algorithms. Their data comes from their users, who willingly uploaded their content to these platforms (subject to terms of service) or through their other projects. As an example of specific projects, the Google Books Project was mostly seen as a positive development for the digitisation of books held in partner libraries, but it also meant a big dataset of scanned pages for Google to mine through and improve its search function. Similarly, these companies may choose to release their labelled datasets or the algorithms developed on these datasets.[14] Recent examples include Azure Open Datasets by Microsoft[15] and FACET by Meta.[16]

10 Jianzhong Shi, Chapter 6 in this volume.

11 ImageNet <www.image-net.org/about.php> accessed 23 January 2024.

12 COCO: Common Objects in Context <https://cocodataset.org> accessed 23 January 2024.

13 The KITTI Vision Benchmark Suite <www.cvlibs.net/datasets/kitti/index.php> accessed 23 January 2024.

14 For example: Open Images Dataset V7 and Extensions <https://storage.googleapis.com/openimages/web/index.html> accessed 23 January 2024.

15 Azure Open Datasets <https://azure.microsoft.com/en-gb/products/open-datasets> accessed 23 January 2024.

16 FACET Dataset <https://ai.meta.com/datasets/facet> accessed 23 January 2024.

But relying on only publicly available databases for common objects would not be useful for (i) digital platforms that are trying to detect less common content and (ii) companies wanting to develop competitive and unique filtering algorithms that the others trained on common data cannot provide – both of these are very likely to fall under commercial use, which would mean copyright will be a bigger obstacle. Most copyright defences are likely to help commercial uses, and this means relying on licensing can be safer when there is a non-commercial element.

Once the data is obtained, parties wanting to develop a new computer vision algorithm will then need to edit this data, such as cropping, resizing, rotating, converting to greyscale, and reducing noise to assist machine learning. This pre-processing stage could therefore potentially have some human involvement to ensure that datasets are up to the task. It is also possible to artificially augment the datasets by introducing AI-generated images into the existing training dataset. We are increasingly seeing the impact of generative adversarial networks on generative AI; by pitting multiple neural networks against each other, they are made to create more realistic data, which can be used to expand the dataset at hand (data augmentation).

If the algorithm is developed through supervised machine learning, then relevant labelled input will be used. First, as mentioned, labelled datasets require humans and can be expensive. Second, it is also important to note that freely found datasets might not be fit for purpose. In most circumstances, they would also reflect any kind of assumptions or biases present in the existing body of material. For example, it was found that *word2vec* trained on Google News corpus reflected the same gender biases present in the news.[17]Another example is the LAION database[18] used to train Stability AI, which includes material scraped from online, where links to illegal material were found in the dataset.[19] Alternatively, if the project relies on unsupervised learning, a large volume of unlabelled input data can be used, and the machine will still learn to recognise the similarities in unlabelled data and categorise them into groups; however, this would still need human oversight to interpret the results.[20] It is also possible to rely on semi-supervised machine learning, where a small set of labelled data and a larger set of unlabelled data are used together to develop AI algorithms.

Once the trained model is in place, it can be used for whatever purpose it was created. If the purpose is content moderation, then the trained model would be able detect similarities and filter user-generated content on the platform based on the

17 Amanda Levendowski, 'How Copyright Law can fix Artificial Intelligence's Implicit Bias Problem' (2018) 93 Wash L Rev 579, 581.

18 Stability AI Was Trained on Laion-400-Million Open Dataset <https://laion.ai/blog/laion-400-open-dataset/> accessed 23 January 2024. Newer version (LAION-5B) is released in 2022, which is 14 times bigger: Romain Beaumont, 'LAION-5B: A New Era of Open Large-Scale Multi-Modal Datasets (*laion.ai*, 31 March 2022) <https://laion.ai/blog/laion-5b/> accessed 10 March 2024.

19 Emilia David, 'AI Image Training Dataset Found to Include Child Sexual Abuse Imagery' (*The Verge*, 20 December 2023) <www.theverge.com/2023/12/20/24009418/generative-ai-image-laion-csam-google-stability-stanford> accessed 23 January 2024.

20 Winchcomb (n 2) 5.

criteria determined by the laws and internal rules of the platform. The algorithm's decisions will be based on the content in images and videos used to train it. Wrong or uncertain decisions can still be flagged for human moderators.

3. Looking at It From Copyright Perspective

While an AI researcher might see this as a process involving multiple stages of data collection, pre-processing, and training, a copyright lawyer would ask different questions, namely: what is being used (data/works), what is being done (copying, editing and training/infringing activities), and can this be achieved (authorisation or defence)?

3.1 What Is Being Used?

The first question is what is being used, or more specifically, how much of this data falls under the scope of copyright law. There is not a complete overlap between the types of data needed by computer scientists and the works that are protected by copyright, but copyright issues will automatically emerge when the training data includes protected material, which is a significant risk. The protected subject matter of copyright can be categorised as authors' works and related subject matter. There is also material that is protected by other rights in some jurisdictions, such as the EU *sui generis* database rights explained later.

At the international level, the Berne Convention determines its scope as literary and artistic works,[21] but leaves the originality and fixation requirements to the member states. Other international instruments that follow also define their scope in the same way as the Berne Convention and focus on protecting expressions over ideas.[22] At the EU level, protected subject matter is clearer for certain types of works in some Directives and CJEU decisions. The UK has a closed list of protected works that consist of (a) original literary, dramatic, musical or artistic works; (b) sound recordings, films or broadcasts; and (c) the typographical arrangement of published editions.[23] In comparison, most of the EU countries rely on originality

21 'Every production in the literary, scientific and artistic domain, whatever may be the mode or form of its expression, such as books, pamphlets and other writings; lectures, addresses, sermons and other works of the same nature; dramatic or dramatico-musical works; choreographic works and entertainments in dumb show; musical compositions with or without words; cinematographic works to which are assimilated works expressed by a process analogous to cinematography; works of drawing, painting, architecture, sculpture, engraving and lithography; photographic works to which are assimilated works expressed by a process analogous to photography; works of applied art; illustrations, maps, plans, sketches and three-dimensional works relative to geography, topography, architecture or science.' Berne Convention for the Protection of Literary and Artistic Works (Berne Convention) art 2.

22 The Agreement on Trade-Related Aspects of Intellectual Property Rights (TRIPS) art 10, WIPO Copyright Treaty (WCT) art 2, with the addition of computer programs, compilations and changes in line with new technologies for digital communication of works.

23 Copyright, Designs and Patents Act 1998 (CDPA 1988) s 1.

criteria to determine what is protectable. Case law shows that originality is interpreted as the work being the 'author's own intellectual creation', which can only be present when the author can make 'free and creative choices' that are not dictated by their technical function.[24]

Other types of data are valuable for research but insignificant for copyright. Facts such as measurements, locations, coordinates, numbers, or financial information would not be protected by copyright due to the subject matter and lack of originality. However, they might be part of a database that is still protected and therefore not easy to obtain or be subject to more stringent contractual terms. Databases are subject to different rules: First, datasets in data analysis and machine learning projects will not necessarily indicate the distinction between protected/unprotected data to the researchers, but such data could be forming a database together. Second, database protection is harmonised to a certain extent in all EU Member States through the Database Directive. The Directive defines a database as 'a collection of independent works, data or other materials arranged in a systematic or methodical way and individually accessible by electronic or other means'.[25] Third, some datasets will struggle with originality and will not meet the threshold of 'author's own intellectual protection' but can still be protected for the investment involved – *sui generis* database right (SGDR).

Copyright-protected databases are 'databases which, by reason of the selection or arrangement of their contents, constitute the author's own intellectual creation'.[26] This does not stop the individual contents from receiving separate copyright protection. For example, if a machine learning project relies on a collection of paintings and the dataset has both the paintings and statistics on these paintings, then both (i) the paintings (artistic work) and (ii) the database will be protected by copyright, provided that database meets the originality criteria. When a database is partially reproduced, the originality of the copied parts should be assessed.

Even if the database is not original, there is also SGDR for the

> maker of a database which shows that there has been qualitatively and/or quantitatively a substantial investment in either the obtaining, verification or presentation of the contents to prevent extraction and/or re-utilization of the

24 Case C-5/08 *Infopaq International A/S v Danske Dagblades Forening* [2009] ECDR 16; Case C-145/10 *Eva-Maria Painer v Standard VerlagsGmbH and Ors* [2012] ECDR (6) 89. It is also harmonised for some works: Directive 2009/24/EC of the European Parliament and of the Council of 23 April 2009 on the legal protection of computer programs (Software Directive) art 1(3) for computer programs; Directive 96/9/EC of the European Parliament and of the Council of 11 March 1996 on the legal protection of databases (Database Directive) art 3(1) for databases; Directive 2006/116/EC of the European Parliament and of the Council of 12 December 2006 on the term of protection of copyright and certain related rights (Term Directive) art 6 for photographs.

25 Database Directive art 1.

26 CDPA s 3A, Database Directive art 3, Case C-444/02 *Fixtures Marketing v OPAP* [2004] ECR I-10, 549.

whole or of a substantial part, evaluated qualitatively and/or quantitatively, of the contents of that database.[27]

The investment is not necessarily measured by a financial threshold.[28] As the rationale is incentivising production of databases, a distinction is made by the courts between the investment in obtaining and the investment in generating the information, the latter not being protected by SGDR.[29] Since they do not require registration for protection, the uncertainty around whether there is substantial investment, and therefore SGDR, might also discourage users of such databases.[30]

As an additional concern, it is necessary to determine the copyright status and (if subject to licenses) licensing terms[31] of the works correctly. Copyright arises without any formality,[32] but it is not indefinite. In most jurisdictions, literary and artistic works are protected for the duration of the author's life and 70 years thereafter.[33] In the UK, computer-generated works, which might be part of a corpus, are protected for 50 years from the calendar year they were made.[34] SGDR lasts for 15 years, unless substantial changes are made to the content of the database.[35] There could also be works with unclear copyright status within the corpus. The use of orphan works[36] and out-of-commerce works[37] are harmonised to a certain extent in the EU; however, it does not allow all types of activities to all stakeholders and requires additional steps. An alternative option to rely on only public domain works can lead to biased results for the machine learning.[38]

27 Database Directive art 7.

28 Database Directive, recital 7 'Whereas the making of databases requires the investment of considerable human, technical and financial resources while such databases can be copied or accessed at a fraction of the cost needed to design them independently'.

29 Case C-46/02 *Fixtures Marketing Ltd v Oy Veikkaus Ab* [2004] ECR I-10, 365; Case C-203/02 *British Horseracing Board v William Hill Organization* [2004] ECR I-10, 415; Case C-338/02 *Fixtures Marketing Ltd v Svenska Spel AB* [2004] ECR I-10,497; Case C-444/02 *Fixtures Marketing v OPAP* [2004] ECR I-10, 549. See also, P.B. Hugenholtz, 'Data Property: Unwelcome Guest in the House of IP' (Paper presented at Trading Data in the Digital Economy: Legal Concepts and Tools, Münster, Germany 2017) <https://www.ivir.nl/publicaties/download/Data_property_Muenster.pdf> accessed 23 January 2024.

30 Rossana Ducato and Alain Strowel, 'Limitations to Text and Data Mining and Consumer Empowerment: Making the Case for a Right to "Machine Legibility"' (2019) 50(6) IIC 649, 655.

31 For the implications of training with different types of licenses, see: Eckart de Castilho and others, 'A Legal Perspective on Training Models for Natural Language Processing' in *Proceedings of the Eleventh International Conference on Language Resources and Evaluation* (LREC 2018).

32 Berne Convention art 5(2).

33 Term Directive art 1.

34 CDPA s 12(7).

35 Database Directive art 10, Database Regulation 1997 reg 30.

36 Directive 2012/28/EU of the European Parliament and of the Council of 25 October 2012 on certain permitted uses of orphan works art 6.

37 Directive (EU) 2019/790 of the European Parliament and of the Council of 17 April 2019 on copyright and related rights in the Digital Single Market and amending Directives 96/9/EC and 2001/29/EC (CDSM Directive) art 8.

38 'Given the friction copyright law causes for accessing certain works, many AI creators turn to easily available, legally low-risk works to serve as training data for AI systems. Data derived from these works are often demonstrably biased.' Levendowski (n 17) 611.

3.2 What Is Being Done?

Once it is established that protected works are being used, what is being done to these works becomes important. Because depending on the activity, it might infringe on the exclusive rights of the copyright holder. If we look at the stages of computer vision, gathering data means copying the works. The reproduction right in the Berne Convention includes all types of copying ('in any manner or form').[39] WIPO Copyright Treaty also states that it 'fully applies in the digital environment' and that storage of a protected work in digital form in an electronic medium counts as reproduction.[40] Both the Information Society Directive[41] and Database Directive require authorisation for 'temporary or permanent reproduction by any means and in any form, in whole or in part'.[42] In the UK, sections 16 and 17 of CDPA 1988 cover the exclusive right to copy the work.[43] Section 17(2) of the CDPA mentions 'reproducing work in any material form', but 'storing the work in any medium by electronic means' is also included. Overall, collecting protected images and videos will count as reproduction in most instances.

There are also pre-processing changes that are made to the collected data before it is ready for training, which requires looking at adaptation right. At the international level, adaptation right partially exists in the Berne Convention,[44] giving the authors of literary and artistic works the exclusive rights to make or authorise adaptations. At the EU level, adaptation right harmonised under the Software Directive and Database Directive,[45] but not for other types of works. In relation to AI, converting to machine-readable language or adding annotation tags can be interpreted as a translation and therefore an adaptation.[46] Furthermore, the changes made on the work could infringe moral rights, if it amounts to 'distortion, mutilation, or other modification of, or other derogatory action'.[47]

If the needed data is protected with SGDR, then it will be infringed when a substantial part is extracted or re-utilised. Extraction means permanent or temporary transfer; re-utilisation means making all or a substantial part of the contents

39 Berne Convention art 9(1).

40 WIPO Copyright Treaty Agreed Statement concerning art 1(4).

41 Directive 2001/29/EC of the European Parliament and of the Council of 22 May 2001 on the harmonisation of certain aspects of copyright and related rights in the information society (InfoSoc Directive).

42 InfoSoc Directive art 2, Database Directive art 5(a).

43 CDPA1988 s 16 (acts restricted by copyright in a work) and s.17 (infringement of copyright by copying).

44 Translation under art 8 and adaptation, alteration and other arrangements under art 12 for literary and artistic works, translations of dramatic and musical works under art 11(2), and communication of translations under art 11ter(2).

45 'Translation, adaptation, arrangement and any other alteration' Database Directive art 5(b).

46 Maurizio Borghi and Stavroula Karapapa, 'Non-Display Uses of Copyright Works: Google Books and Beyond' (2011) 1 QMJIP 21; Thomas Margoni, 'Artificial Intelligence, Machine Learning and EU Copyright Law: Who Owns AI?' (2018) CREATE Working Paper 2018/12; Patrick R Goold, 'Why the U.K. Adaptation Right Is Superior to the U.S. Derivative Work Right' (2014) 92 Neb L Rev 843.

47 Berne Convention art 6bis, CDPA 1988 ss 77–84.

available to the public.[48] The purpose of limiting these uses is protecting the maker of databases and securing their investment,[49] so it also includes indirect extraction and re-utilisation, such as consulting a database and using the results, and does not necessitate physically transferring the database.[50]

3.3 How Can This Be Achieved?

Given that the material is likely to be protected and that these activities are likely to be infringing, parties wanting to use these works will need to find a feasible option to achieve their purpose. The most clear-cut option is to argue that the use of such works should not even be subject to copyright in the first place. Scholars argue that these are not 'used as works' and data mining has no impact on the normal exploitation of the works.[51] This seems to be the most logical option going forward and would be very useful for AI progress if more jurisdictions embraced this approach. Although it is important to keep in mind that it also depends on how much human access and involvement will be needed when the works are being edited prior to training. The second option is to acquire desired datasets, usually by entering into contracts with the parties holding such data, which can be difficult, costly, or not possible. The third option would then be relying on copyright exceptions, especially the text and data mining defence discussed later.

It is important to note here the difficult relationship between contracts and copyright exceptions. Unclear and overly restrictive contractual and technological measures are a significant obstacle to access to training data. The increasing use of 'click-through' contracts leads to the rightsholders extending the scope of control they exercise over their works.[52] Although it is common to have overly restrictive terms in the contracts, this has been partially addressed in the EU, where some copyright exceptions are not overridable by contracts (and such contracts are unenforceable),[53] in order to ensure effective defences that leave some room for the public.

But this creates an uneven outcome for databases that are not subject to copyright: in *Ryanair v PR Aviation*, PR Aviation's price comparison site was screen scraping from Ryanair, while Ryanair terms and conditions explicitly limited the use to non-commercial purposes such as making and changing bookings. Although

48 Database Directive art 7(2)(a) and (b). What counts as substantial will be determined by looking at the volume of data extracted to the volume of the whole data, or if it represents a significant part of the investment viewed quantitively. C-203/02 *BHB v William Hill* [69].

49 Database Directive, recital 48, *BHB v William Hill* [46].

50 Case C304/07 *Directmedia Publishing GmbH v Albert-Ludwigs-Universität Freiburg* [37] [46–47].

51 European Copyright Society, 'General Opinion on the EU Copyright Reform Package' (24 January 2017); Borghi and Karapapa (n 46); Martin Senftleben, 'Compliance of National TDM Rules with International Copyright Law: An Overrated Nonissue?' (2022) 53 IIC 1477.

52 'As the use of electronic resources increases and such contracts become the norm, the 'delicate balance' between owners and users encapsulated in statutory copyright might be sacrificed'. Lionel Bently and others, *Intellectual Property Law* (6th edn, OUP 2022) 362.

53 ibid 253.

they allowed the third parties who had sought a license with them, PR Aviation did not have such a license. Ryanair claimed that their copyright and/or database right was infringed by PR Aviation. After the Dutch courts dismissed Ryanair's claim, the Supreme Court has referred the case to CJEU. The Court was asked if the freedom to use databases, which are not protected by SGDR or copyright, can be limited contractually. The court clarified that the rights established for lawful users are not applicable in non-protectable databases and that such contractual provisions are allowed. It is especially problematic for sole-source databases, where the database owner is the one producing the data.[54] Since the creation of the data does not count as 'obtaining', the investment in the creation of sole-source databases might not amount to SGDR protection. The Ryanair decision means that sole-source databases, whose information cannot be found elsewhere, are more at risk of stricter contract terms.[55] The national court's approach to contractual terms and sole-source databases are also inconsistent.[56]

Given that training data would need works that are protected by copyright, and the activities done with these works do fall under the scope of protection for the rightsholder, there needs to be some kind of balance between the parties wanting to engage in such activities and the authors of protected works.

4. Copyright Defences and Text and Data Mining

At the international level, the Berne Convention has a set of exceptions for the works protected in the Convention, but it also introduces a general limitation for jurisdictions introducing exceptions to the reproduction of works (three-step test, Art.9(2)). The Rome Convention does the same for phonograms and broadcasts. TRIPS, WCT, and WPPT also have the three-step test built into them. At the EU level, there are exceptions in Software, Rental and Related Rights, Database and E-commerce Directives but the instrument that has provided a degree of harmonisation is the InfoSoc Directive, which has taken the 'new electronic environment' into consideration.[57] However, since the Directive leaves the Member States to choose from an exhaustive list of exceptions, it does not achieve full harmonisation – except the only mandatory exception of temporary copying.

4.1 Mandatory Temporary Copying Exception

Under Information Society Directive Article 5(1), implemented in CDPA S. 28A, there is a mandatory exception for certain acts of temporary reproduction, which are transient or incidental, and an integral and essential part of a technological process and whose sole purpose is to enable a transmission in a network between

54 Estelle Derclaye, 'An Economic Analysis of the Contractual Protection of Databases' (2005) 1(2) U Ill JL Tech Pol'y 247.

55 Borghi and Karapapa (n 46).

56 ibid 512–13.

57 InfoSoc Directive, recital 31.

third parties by an intermediary, or lawful use of a work or other subject matter to be made and which have no independent economic significance.

The scope of this exception was further clarified by the CJEU: copies held on screen and in an internet cache for viewing a website (*Public Relations Consultants Association v Newspaper Licensing Agency*), copies held on memory of a satellite decoder and television screen (*FAPL v QC Leisure and Karen Murphy*), and the data capture process (until the printing stage) (*Infopaq*) were all held as temporary acts of reproduction. In *Infopaq*, it was held that being transient should be interpreted

> only if its duration is limited to what is necessary for the proper completion of the technological process in question, it being understood that that process must be automated so that it deletes that act automatically, without human intervention, once its function of enabling the completion of such a process has come to an end.[58]

Such a temporary act can still be an integral and essential part of a technological process when initiated by a human being,[59] which is usually the case with AI training. But the problem with this exception is that training data might have to be held longer than 'temporary' for machine learning purposes.[60] This is especially the case for AI accountability, where it might be needed to assess why the algorithm decides in certain ways.

4.2 EU Text and Data Mining Exception in the CDSM Directive

Under the EU law, CDSM Directive Articles 3 and 4 are relevant for text and data mining. Both are mandatory exceptions for the reproduction of copyright-protected works and SGDR. Article 3 is only for research organisations and cultural heritage institutions, for the purposes of scientific research, and allows the text and data mining of works to which they have lawful access. A few problems exist with this article: (i) the beneficiaries, further clarified in Article 2, are limited, and it puts AI companies and (depending on national implementation) research organisations with commercial partners in an uncertain place;[61] (ii) the lawful access is difficult to determine, especially in automated data collection, but interpreted widely in

58 Case C-5/08 *Infopaq International A/S v Danske Dagblades Forening (Infopaq I)* [64].

59 Case C 302/10*Infopaq International A/S v Danske Dagblades Forening (Infopaq II)* [36].

60 Paul Keller, 'AI, The Commons, and the Limits of Copyright' (Open Future, 22 June 2023) <https://openfuture.eu/blog/ai-the-commons-and-the-limits-of-copyright/> accessed 23 January 2024.

61 The latter is addressed in Recital 11, where research organisations are allowed to carry out research activities involving TDM in public-private partnerships. See also: European Copyright Society, 'Comment of the European Copyright Society Addressing Selected Aspects of the Implementation of Articles 3 to 7 of Directive (EU) 2019/790 on Copyright in the Digital Single Market' (3 May 2022) 14.

Recital 14 to include freely available content;[62] and (iii) Article 3(2) specifically allows storing the copies to verify scientific results, but it is up to Member States to decide who can store[63] and whether externals can access. Article 4, on the other hand, is for a larger set of beneficiaries for the reproduction and extraction of works, as long as the works are lawfully accessible and the rightsholder has not expressly reserved their right in an appropriate manner. Article 4 is a last-minute addition[64] as the proposal version received much criticism about the limited scope.[65] It is also worth keeping an eye on the EU AI ACT, especially because (i) as any potential requirement to disclose training data will in turn make it easier for rightsholders to detect use and opt out, and (ii) the burden of complying on EU copyright law, even for generative algorithms developed outside, put on the EU market.[66]

While the CDSM Directive is mostly a positive development for the EU, the fact that text and data mining require relying on a defence that is mostly for non-commercial use, either subject to certain beneficiaries and/or subject to an opting-out regime, means that the EU is at a more disadvantaged position compared to other jurisdictions with more lenient approaches such as the US or Japan. This also means that due to the law impacting the ability to develop EU-based AI research, digital platforms would have to buy their algorithms from other jurisdictions, subject to the impact of the AI Act. Finally, it is worth noting that the three-step test in the Berne Convention – TRIPS, WCT, and the Information Society Directive Article 5(5)[67] – might be an obstacle for introducing a wider exception in the EU. According to this rule, exceptions and limitations can only be introduced in certain special cases, which do not conflict with the normal exploitation of the

62 See also, Eleonora Rosati, *Copyright in Digital Single Market: Article-by-Article Commentary to the Provisions of Directive 2019/70* (OUP 2019); Thomas Margoni and Martin Kretschmer, 'A Deeper Look into the EU Text and Data Mining Exceptions: Harmonisation, Data Ownership, and the Future of Technology' (2022) 71(8) GRUR Int 685.

63 Recital 15 clarifies that Member States can appoint trusted bodies to store.

64 Pamela Samuelson, 'Regulating Technology Through Copyright Law: A Comparative Perspective' (2020) 42(4) EIPR 214.

65 Christophe Geiger, Giancarlo Frosio and Oleksandr Bulayenko, 'Text and Data Mining in the Proposed Copyright Reform: Making the EU Ready for an Age of Big Data?' 49 IIC 814; European Copyright Society, 'General Opinion' (n 51); Reto Hilty and Heiko Richter, 'Position Statement of the Max Planck Institute for Innovation and Competition on the Proposed Modernisation of European Copyright Rules Part B Exceptions and Limitations (Art 3 – Text and Data Mining)' (2017) Max Planck Institute for Innovation & Competition Research Paper No 17-2.

66 European Parliament legislative resolution of 13 March 2024 on the proposal for a regulation of the European Parliament and of the Council on laying down harmonised rules on Artificial Intelligence (Artificial Intelligence Act) and amending certain Union Legislative Acts (COM(2021) 0206-C9-0146/2021-2021/0106(COD) For full text adopted on 13 March 2024, see: <https://www.europarl.europa.eu/doceo/document/TA-9-2024-0138_EN.html>

67 '. . . shall only be applied in certain special cases which do not conflict with a normal exploitation of the work or other subject-matter and do not unreasonably prejudice the legitimate interests of the rightholder' art 5(5).

work and do not unreasonably prejudice the legitimate interests of the rightsholder, therefore creating a boundary on how open the EU exceptions can be.[68]

4.3 UK Text and Data Mining Defence

The UK has implemented the earliest text and data mining exception in the EU in 2014. Section 29A in CDPA 1988 allows copies made by a person who has lawful access for the purpose of non-commercial computational analysis, accompanied with sufficient acknowledgement. Under the UK exception, contracts to the contrary are unenforceable.

Because the UK left the EU, the CDSM Directive was not implemented, and therefore the UK started seeking the next steps. The UK Intellectual Property Office (IPO) has run a consultation on three specific AI and IP questions between October 2021 and January 2022, namely, on copyright protection for AI-generated works, patent protection for AI inventions, and copyright exceptions for text and data mining. In response to the consultation, the IPO has announced that they will introduce a new copyright and database exception that allows text and data mining for any purpose in order to 'make most of the greater flexibilities following Brexit' and 'help make the UK more competitive as a location for firms doing data mining'.[69] It was also foreseen that under this new exception rightsholders would 'not be able to charge for UK licences for TDM and will not be able to contract or opt-out'.[70]

Considering that these plans were quietly scrapped within a year of citing a huge response and the need to have a deeper conversation with the relevant stakeholders,[71] it looks like the UK will take longer to determine how to progress. In the meantime, the UK does not have the same flexibilities as the EU or that of more lenient jurisdictions introduced next.

4.4 More Lenient Approaches: US and Japan

Compared to the rigid approaches of the EU CDSM exceptions and the UK TDM, some jurisdictions like the US have an open-ended approach to copyright defences: fair-use factors focus on the purpose of use, nature of work, amount and substantiality of the work used, and the effect of the use on a potential market.[72] Given that text and data mining is highly transformative, it is likely to get covered by

68 For a different perspective, see: Senftleben (n 51) 1477.

69 UK Intellectual Property Office, 'Artificial Intelligence and Intellectual Property: Copyright and Patents: Government Response to Consultation' (28 June 2022) <https://www.gov.uk/government/consultations/artificial-intelligence-and-ip-copyright-and-patents/outcome/artificial-intelligence-and-intellectual-property-copyright-and-patents-government-response-to-consultation#text-and-data-mining> accessed 23 January 2024.

70 ibid.

71 HC Deb 1 February 2023, vol 727 cols 152WH–168WH.

72 Section 107 US Copyright Act.

the fair-use provision, as was hinted at in the dispute between the Authors Guild and Google Books regarding the unauthorised copying of protected material.[73] At the same time, ongoing lawsuits against generative AI such as Stability AI, Midjourney, and DeviantArt will be interesting to see how use of copyright-protected works as training data will progress in the United States.[74] Although some claims are already dismissed in this case, an amended lawsuit was filed.[75] Similar cases also exist for text material, such as the recent case filed by *The New York Times* against OpenAI for using articles published by the newspaper.[76]

As even a more lenient approach towards AI, Japan has introduced flexible copyright exceptions in 2018, including Art 30–4 for 'exploitation not for "enjoyment" purposes' that allows exploiting the work when it is 'not for enjoying or causing another person to enjoy the ideas or emptions expressed in such work' that does not unreasonably prejudice the interests of the copyright owner.[77] This approach, in line with the first option introduced in Section 3.3 earlier, gives even greater security to AI developers than fair use, and completely places such uses outside the scope of copyright defences, which will benefit the long-term development of AI in Japan.

5. Conclusion

So far, the use of computer vision in content moderation is still developing and will need more technological progress until it can be solely relied on without any human intervention. One of the most important factors that will determine the success of platforms developing AI content moderation filters (or companies

73 *Authors Guild v Google, Inc* 770 F Supp 2d 666, 679–80 (SDNY 2011); *Authors Guild, Inc v Google, Inc* 05 Civ 8136 (DC), 2013 WL 6017130, 26 (SDNY, 14 November 2013); *Authors Guild v Google, Inc*, No 13–4829 (2d Cir 2015). See also, Rachel Brooke, 'Fair Use Week 2023: Looking Back at Google Books Eight Years Later' (*Authors Alliance*, 24 February 2023) <https://www.authorsalliance.org/2023/02/24/fair-use-week-2023-looking-back-at-google-books-eight-years-later/> accessed 24 January 2024.

74 Adrian Aronsson-Storrier and Oliver Fairhurst, 'Litigation Commenced Against the Developers of AI Image Generation Software' (*IPKat*, 3 February 2023) <https://ipkitten.blogspot.com/2023/02/guest-post-litigation-commenced-against.html> accessed 23 January 2024; Shanti Escalante-de Mattei, 'Judge Appears Likely to Dismiss AI Class Action Lawsuit by Artists' *ARTnews* (21 July 2023) <https://www.artnews.com/art-news/news/ai-class-action-lawsuit-dismissal-hearing-stabilityai-midjourney-deviantart-1234675071/> accessed 23 January 2024.

75 Blake Brittain, 'Artists Take New Shot at Stability, Midjourney in Updated Copyright Lawsuit' *Reuters* (30 November 2023) <https://www.reuters.com/legal/litigation/artists-take-new-shot-stability-midjourney-updated-copyright-lawsuit-2023-11-30/> accessed 24 January 2024.

76 Tom Gerken, 'New York Times Sues Microsoft and OpenAI for "Billions"' *BBC* (27 December 2023) <https://www.bbc.co.uk/news/technology-67826601> accessed 23 January 2024.

77 For more on Japan's exception and its impact, see: Tatsuhiro Ueno, 'The Flexible Copyright Exception for "Non-Enjoyment" Purposes – Recent Amendment in Japan and Its Implication' (2021) 70(2) GRUR Int 145–52; Artha Dermawan, 'Text and Data Mining in the Development of Generative AI Models: What the EU Member States Could Learn from the Japanese "Nonenjoyment" Purposes' [2023] J World Intell Prop 1.

that provide them the trained algorithms) is the availability of training data. While a scientist developing a computer vision algorithm would focus on data collection, pre-processing, and (supervised or unsupervised) training, a copyright lawyer must ask the question about which works are being used, which rights might be infringed, and whether any defences will be applicable. If we look at different approaches to copyright defences, so far the EU is improving with the CDSM Directive, despite some uncertainties and missed opportunities, with the additional complexities in the EU AI Act. The UK introduced their defence earlier and showed a willingness to embrace an even more lenient approach, but that has stalled (for now). Recent cases in the US are currently testing the limits of fair use, but it is still likely to prove more lenient than the EU. Meanwhile, Japan's approach to the non-enjoyment element reduces the copyright uncertainties, and therefore both the US and Japan approaches provide a better chance at developing better AI and better computer vision. So, if overly cautious jurisdictions such as the UK and the EU do not revise their approaches to copyright in text and data mining, they will be at a disadvantage in this fast-developing field.

Part D

Disputes and Liabilities in the Platform Economy

8 What's the Gig? Tort Liability of Platforms for Physical User-to-User Harm

Neerav Srivastava and Normann Witzleb

I. Introduction

This chapter explores the liability of digital platforms in tort for user-to-user harm in circumstances where the platform has facilitated physical interaction between users. Examples of such scenarios include personal injury arising from an Uber ride, an Airbnb stay, or a Tinder date. Uber and Airbnb are part of the 'sharing economy', which comprises companies that 'capture idle resources that are then shared or redistributed by consumers through online platforms'.[1] Uber drivers are also part of the 'gig economy'.[2]

Platform-facilitated interactions are on the rise.[3] Ride-sharing services by the likes of Uber, Didi Chuxing, Ola, and Grab have overtaken taxis. Uber is in over 600 cities[4] and has about 5.4 million drivers.[5] Airbnb has over 7 million lodging listings in over 100,000 cities.[6] Online dating is likewise big business: Tinder made US-$1.79 billion revenue in 2022.[7] It is claimed that about 5 million people in the

1 Fernando Belezas and Ana Dias Daniel, 'Innovation in the Sharing Economy: A Systematic Literature Review and Research Framework' (2023) 122 Technovation 102509.

2 A 'gig' is short-term, project-based, outcome-defined work, rather than full-time employment, that is facilitated by platforms: Julie Mills and Clayton Jan, *Gig Economy: Structure, Measurements & Opportunities* (APSCo Australia, 2018) 5–6.

3 Jianzhong Shi, Chapter 6 in this volume.

4 Until 2023, Uber made very considerable losses to fund its expansion: Richard Watson, 'Uber Makes First Operating Profit After Racking Up $31.5bn of Losses' *The Financial Times* (2 August 2023) <www.ft.com/content/dae2b90e-1ba0-4e8f-aabc-34aae4ca05d7>

5 Rohit Sherwale, '58 Uber Statistics for 2024 (Trending Facts Included)' *Demandsage* (27 December 2023) <www.demandsage.com/uber-statistics/#:~:text=the%20rest%20rides.-,Uber%20drivers,couriers%20work%20with%20Uber%20worldwide>

6 Justin Dawes, 'Airbnb: Record Profit, 1 Million New Listings – Pet-Friendly Filter' *Skift* (1 November 2023).

7 Mansoor Iqbal, 'Tinder Revenue and Usage Statistics (2024)' *Business of Apps* (8 January 2024) <www.businessofapps.com/data/tinder-statistics/>

DOI: 10.4324/9781032618975-13

UK[8] and 3.5 million in Australia[9] have used Tinder. In Hong Kong, it is expected that there will be about 500K users of online dating by 2028.

Therefore, the potential liability of platforms for user-to-user harm is an important issue. First, there is the sheer level of activity. Uber, Airbnb, and Tinder, and other companies offering similar services, are a daily part of urban lives. Second, platforms are supplanting traditional regulated industries, such as taxis, and challenge the enforcement of existing safety standards. When it comes to liability for a worker, gig work represents a sea change. In traditional employment, the employer has deep pockets, is insured, and is vicariously liable for an employee's tort. Platforms, on the other hand, do not appear to be vicariously liable for a gig worker, and gig workers do not have deep pockets. The third point is that platforms do, however, exert various degrees of control over the transactions they facilitate, which should also be relevant to their potential liability. In this new paradigm, the question arising is in what circumstances, if any, should platforms bear responsibility for user-to-user harm.

The chapter specifically considers a platform's potential liability for the wrongful acts of a service provider. Say an Uber passenger is injured by a driver who is regularly intoxicated or fatigued[10] when driving. Or a guest suffers injury due to the negligence of an Airbnb host.[11] Or a Tinder user sexually assaults another user.[12] The chapter will consider whether the platform in question can be liable to a ride-share passenger, a guest, or a dating platform user in these circumstances.

The chapter is structured as follows: Section II explains the new paradigm ('Paradigm') of platform-mediated relationships between service providers and customers. Digital platforms create tripartite relationships in which platforms tend to have superior knowledge and, potentially, control of users. Section III considers the scope for vicarious liability in these circumstances. It concludes that vicarious

8 'Tinder Users by Country 2024' *World Population Review* <https://worldpopulationreview.com/country-rankings/tinder-users-by-country> accessed 26 March 2023.

9 About 15% of Australians, or about 3.5 million Australians, have used online dating. One-third of single Australians have used online dating. 'November 2017: Online Dating' *Relationships Australia* (Web Page, 13 December 2017) <https://www.relationships.org.au/what-we-do/research/online-survey/november-2017-online-dating>. Debbie Rivers, 'Australia Ranked #4 in the World for Dating!' *Dare2Date* (Web Page, 28 January 2020) <https://www.dare2date.com.au/australia-ranked-4-in-the-world-for-dating/>.

10 See also, Jasmine Siu, 'Hong Kong Woman Sues Uber Over 2018 Accident That Left One Dead and Four Injured' *South China Morning Post* (1 March 2021) <www.scmp.com/news/hong-kong/law-and-crime/article/3123617/hong-kong-woman-sues-uber-over-2018-accident-left-one>

11 Dan Grennan, 'Graphic Designer, 43, Who Raped His Airbnb Host and Told Her He Would Leave a "Good Review" After the Attack Is Jailed for Seven Years' *Daily Mail* (18 March 2024) <https://www.dailymail.co.uk/news/article-13209635/Graphic-designer-43-raped-Airbnb-host-told-leave-good-review-attack-jailed-seven-years.html>

12 For a case in which an Uber driver allegedly sexual harassed a passenger, see: *Karlen v Uber Technologies, Inc*, 2023 WL 3570635 No. 3:21-cv-835 (VAB) (D Conn, 19 May 2023).

liability may *not* satisfactorily address this new Paradigm. This is largely because it is uncertain whether platforms are employers of service providers. The main focus is therefore on alternatives to vicarious liability. Section IV considers in what circumstances a platform might be liable for its own negligence. Such *primary* liability can arise, e.g., if a ride-share platform was negligent in allowing a driver to join the service or continue to drive for it. Alternatively, a platform may have breached a non-delegable duty of care, which is addressed in Section V. A non-delegable duty to exercise reasonable care is one that cannot be avoided by delegating performance to an independent contractor. In Section VI, we discuss recent legislative initiatives to protect platform users, and in Section VII we conclude. The jurisdictions covered are Australia, the UK, and Hong Kong, although references will also be made to European and US law where appropriate.

II. The New Paradigm

Digital platforms enable new forms of user-to-user physical transactions between strangers. In the scenarios identified earlier, the transaction does not occur purely online unlike, say, the streaming services provided by Netflix or Spotify.

The platform brings together a service provider and a guest, or in the case of dating apps, two private users, in a tripartite arrangement. The users are strangers and initially liaise through the platform. Because the transactions are mediated by platforms, users are partially dependent on the platform vetting the stranger that they will be in close contact with. Platforms position themselves as neutral arbiters who are simply matching demand and supply. Contractually platforms describe themselves as a 'technological service'[13] or 'online marketplace',[14] and disclaim an employment or agency relationship as well as responsibility for risks arising from the transaction, which purportedly vests with the service provider.

The reality is that platforms have more knowledge and exert more control than a detached and neutral arbiter.[15] The UK Supreme Court has described Uber as exerting a high level of control over drivers.[16] Economically, platforms rely on:[17]

1. *The network effect.*[18] The viability and value of the platform depends on there being a sufficient number of both service providers and consumers. Digital ride-hailing or short-term rental platforms intermediate a 'two-sided network',

13 Uber used to label itself that way. In *Uber BV v Aslam* [2018] EWCA 2748, [2019] RTR 25, the English Court of Appeal described this as a contrivance (at [88]).

14 Airbnb, 'Terms of Service' cl 1 <https://www.airbnb.com.au/terms>

15 Songyin Bo, Chapter 9 in this volume.

16 *Uber BV v Aslam* [2021] UKSC 5, [2021] ICR 657.

17 Neerav Srivastava, 'The Iron Curtain: Controlling Unreasonable Defamation Immunity Clauses' (2020) 50 Hong Kong LJ 685.

18 Justus Haucap and Ulrich Heimeshoff, 'Google, Facebook, Amazon, eBay: Is the Internet Driving Competition or Market Monopolization?' (2014) 11 Int Eco Pol'y 49.

in which more service providers attract more consumers, and more consumers attract more service providers.[19]

2. *Being information brokers*. Through their interactions with users, platforms collect and aggregate relevant knowledge about them, including users' personal characteristics and individual preferences. Platforms share and monetise some of this knowledge when they offer to bring together future digital matches, including through sophisticated recommendation, rating, and ranking systems.
3. *Safety and trust*. Trust is 'a disposition to engage in social exchanges that involve uncertainty and vulnerability, but that are also potentially rewarding'.[20] While an Uber ride or an Airbnb stay is potentially rewarding, it is uncertain how safe strangers, who are in close proximity to one another, will be. Ratings/reviews provide information about how safe and reliable the other user is. A person's past behaviour, as found by peer users, is an indicator of their future behaviour.[21] For example, users will assume that an Airbnb 'Superhost' is safe and trustworthy. By providing rating/reputation systems, platforms have addressed the famous 'lemons problem',[22] that is, that a customer's lack of information about a product or service affects market efficiency and the willingness to enter into an agreement. High ratings from other users generate trust that the service provider is safe.[23] There is also an 'accrued trust' in the platform.[24] The accrued trust is built on factors such as the platform having put in place checks regarding service providers, e.g., minimum average rating requirement, and a secure payment mechanism. Without trust, a guest would be more guarded.[25] In describing its success, Airbnb's CEO, Brian Chesky, stated: 'Trust is the real energy source that drives Airbnb.'[26] An Oxford case study on Airbnb agrees:

   Most of us are taught from an early age not to *trust* strangers, Airbnb . . . has been built to counter this conventional wisdom. Yes, its success is dependent

19 Geoffrey G Parker, Marshall W Van Alstyne and Sangeet P Choudary, *Platform Revolution: How Networked Markets Are Transforming the Economy and How to Make Them Work for You* (WW Norton & Company 2016).

20 Adam Thierer and others, 'How the Internet, the Sharing Economy, and Reputational Feedback Mechanisms Solve the Lemons Problem' (2016) 70 U Mia L Rev 830.

21 Srivastava (n 17) 685.

22 George Akerlof, 'The Market for "Lemons: Quality Uncertainty and the Market Mechanism"' (1970) 84 Q J Econ 488. A 'lemon' is a dud product, for example, a faulty second-hand car. An ignorant car buyer assumes they will be sold a lemon and so is only willing to pay a lemon price. Since the seller is only being offered lemon prices, they start selling only lemon cars.

23 Mareike Möhlmann and Andrea Geissinger, 'Trust in the Sharing Economy: Platform-Mediated Peer Trust' in Nestor M Davidson, Michèle Finck and John J Infranca (eds), *The Cambridge Handbook of the Law of the Sharing Economy* (CUP 2018) 27.

24 Thierer and others (n 20) 830.

25 Srivastava (n 17) 685, 692–93.

26 Airbnb, 'In the Business of Trust' *Newsroom* (6 November 2019) <https://news.airbnb.com/in-the-business-of-trust/>

on the millions of empty spaces . . . but more importantly it's about ordinary people trusting.[27]

In short, a platform profits by creating a network effect, being information brokers, and because guests trust the service.

III. Vicarious Liability

If a party suffered injury due to an act of a worker, then a conventional analysis may ask whether the organisation that engaged the worker is vicariously liable for the act. Vicarious liability is liability for another's wrong 'because of [the first person's] relationship with that individual, and the connection between that relationship and the act or omission in question'.[28] As vicarious liability may arise even if the principal has done nothing wrong, it is a form of strict liability.[29]

A. Employers Vicariously Liable

Vicarious liability arises traditionally when the tortfeasor is an employee of the principal. In contrast, if the tortfeasor is an independent contractor, then the principal is not vicariously liable. In addition to requiring a relationship between wrongdoer and defendant that is sufficient for imposing vicarious liability (stage 1), there must also be a sufficient connection between that relationship and the wrong that causes the harm (stage 2). That connection was traditionally expressed as requiring that the wrong occurred 'in the course of employment'.[30] However, in recent years, common law courts have expanded the scope of vicarious liability. In stage 1, vicarious liability may now also arise in a situation that is akin to employment.[31] For stage 2, the courts now use the broader test of whether there is a 'sufficiently close connection' between the employment and the wrongdoing.[32] Many of the

27 Rachel Botsman and Lauren Capelin, 'Airbnb: Building A Revolutionary Travel Company' (Saïd Business School Case, Saïd Business School, University of Oxford April 2015, updated January 2016) 3.

28 *Cox v Ministry of Justice* [2016] UKSC 10, [2016] AC 660, [15] (Lord Reed, with whom Lord Neuberger, Lady Hale, Lord Dyson and Lord Toulson agreed).

29 Anthony Gray, *Vicarious Liability: Critique and Reform* (Hart Publishing 2018) 103; Paula Giliker, 'Vicarious Liability in the Common Law World: An Introduction' in Paula Giliker (ed), *Vicarious Liability in the Common Law World* (Hart Publishing 2022) 1; Christian Witting, 'Modeling Organisational Vicarious Liability' (2019) 39 Leg Stud 694.

30 On the historical development, see *Mohamud v Morrison Supermarkets plc* [2016] UKSC 11, [2016] AC 677, [18]–[38] (Lord Toulson, with whom Lord Neuberger, Lady Hale, Lord Dyson and Lord Reed agreed).

31 *Various Claimants v Catholic Child Welfare Society* [2012] UKSC 56, [2013] 2 AC 1, [47] (Lord Phillips, with whom Lady Hale, Lord Kerr, Lord Wilson and Lord Carnwath agreed).

32 *Mohamud v Morrison Supermarkets plc* [2016] UKSC 11, [2016] AC 677, [39]–[46]; *Lister v Hesley Hall Ltd* [2001] UKHL 22, [2002] 1 AC 215.

cases that modernised and expanded the law of vicarious liability concerned sexual assault committed by members of religious institutions, and these crimes would be difficult to describe as being committed in the course of employment.[33]

B. Theoretical Underpinnings of Vicarious Liability

The strict liability aspect of vicarious liability means that courts are cautious about extending it. Policy considerations of providing a tort victim with compensation, including access to a defendant with deep pockets, must be balanced with the concern that liability is imposed on a party regardless of personal wrongdoing. There is some difficulty with justifying vicarious liability on the basis of the tort theory of 'corrective justice'. Corrective justice is concerned with *inter se* justice between parties. It requires the wrongdoer to restore losses caused by their wrongdoing[34] and to make the victim whole again. However, vicarious liability is imposed regardless of personal fault. If vicarious liability is imposed although the employer did no wrong, i.e., was not at fault, then vicarious liability appears more difficult (but not impossible)[35] to reconcile with corrective justice. The policy justifications for imposing vicarious liability include that the employer has assumed the risk of harm occurring and so, as they either gain a benefit from the employment or have at least had role in creating the risk, they should bear responsibility if a reasonably incidental risk eventuates.[36] If these policy justifications are seen as in tension with corrective justice, they may be easier to justify with 'distributive justice'. Distributive justice concerns how resources are spread across a just society.[37] In the context of tort law, it is aimed at the proper distribution of risks and opportunities of human activity,[38] as well as the efficient allocation of loss.[39] Vicarious liability of an employer links risk and liability allocation to opportunity, and the loss is distributed to those best able to afford it,[40] i.e., employers. In this sense, 'responsibility for

33 For example, *BXB v Trustees of the Barry Congregation of Jehovah's Witnesses v* [2023] UKSC 15, [2024] AC 567; *Lister v Hesley Hall Ltd, ibid*; *Prince Alfred College Inc v ADC* [2016] HCA 37, (2016) 258 CLR 134; *Bazley v Curry* [1999] 2 SCR 534.

34 Jules L Coleman, 'Tort Law and the Demands of Corrective Justice' (1992) 67 Ind LJ 349.

35 Ernest Weinrib suggested that vicarious liability 'extends [the notion of fault] by imputing the injurious wrong to the employer's organization as a whole' because of the close connection between the faulty actor and their wrongdoing with the employer: Ernest Weinrib, *The Idea of Private Law* (OUP 2012) 186–87.

36 See *Lister v Hesley Hall Ltd* [2001] UKHL 22, [2002] 1 AC 215, [63] (Lord Millett); *Various Claimants v Catholic Child Welfare Society* [2012] UKSC 56, [2013] 2 AC 1, [71] (Lord Phillips, with whom Lady Hale, Lord Kerr, Lord Wilson and Lord Carnwath agreed); see also, PS Atiyah, *Vicarious Liability in the Law of Torts* (Butterworths 1967) 171.

37 Steve Hedley, 'Looking Outward or Looking Inward? Obligations Scholarship in the Early 21st Century' in Andrew Robertson and Hang Wu Tang (eds), *The Goals of Private Law* (Hart Publishing 2009) 193.

38 Marc Loth, 'Corrective and Distributive Justice in Tort Law: On the Restoration of Autonomy and a Minimal Level of Protection of the Victim' (2015) 22 Maastricht J Eur Comp L 788.

39 *Hawkins v Clayton* (1986) 5 NSWLR 109, 138.

40 Loth (n 38) 788, 797.

the risks of our social actions is the downside of the fact that we also profit from the fruits of those actions'.[41] Distributive justice thus also underlies 'enterprise liability theory', which posits that 'characteristic accident costs should be internalized by the enterprise responsible for their infliction and then distributed across the beneficiaries of the enterprise'.[42] Enterprise liability encourages us to think beyond the formalities of the internal corporate structure;[43] whether the primary tortfeasor is an employee or independent contractor is less important.

C. *Platforms Not Employers*

With respect to the Paradigm, it is questionable whether a service provider is an employee[44] of the platform company. Courts have clarified that the description of a worker as an employee in one area of law, such as employment law or tax law, does not predicate their characterisation as such in another area, such as vicarious liability.[45] In the context of unfair dismissal laws, Australian courts have held that a driver is not an employee of Uber.[46] On the other hand, the UK Supreme Court held that Uber drivers are entitled to statutory employee rights, although this is not the same as being an employee, and the question of whether they were employees was expressly left open.[47] Further, it is standard for platform contracts to describe the service provider as an independent contractor. In a case not related to the gig economy, where the workers expressly opted to move from an employment relationship to being independent contractors, the High Court of Australia emphasised that the contractual description of a worker as an independent contractor should be given proper weight,[48] but is not decisive.[49] While the modern law has extended vicarious liability to relationships that have all the essential elements of an employment

41 ibid 798.

42 Gregory C Keating, *Reasonableness and Risk: Right and Responsibility in the Law of Torts* (OUP 2022) 272; see also Neerav Srivastava, Aashish Srivastava and DK Srivastava, 'A Million Winslows: Private Liability of Universities for Ragging in India' (2019) 19 Oxf Univ Commonw LJ 227.

43 Ross Parsons, 'Individual Responsibility Versus Enterprise Liability (1956) 29 Aust Int Law J 714.

44 Australia applies a multi-factorial test: *Kaseris v Rasier Pacific V.O.F* [2017] FWC 6610, (2017) 272 IR 289, 310). On the position in other jurisdictions, see Laura Blandthorn, 'Exploitation in the Gig Economy: Lee Lin Chin Is Having Uber Eats, Why Shouldn't I?' (2019) 1(2) New Econ J <www.neweconomy.org.au/journal/issues/vol1/iss2/exploitation-in-the-gig-economy/>

45 *Barclays Bank plc v Various Claimants* [2020] UKSC 13, [2020] AC 973, [29] (Lady Hale, with whom Lord Reed, Lord Kerr, Lord Hodge and Lord Lloyd-Jones agreed): 'Until these recent developments [of extending vicarious liability to relationships akin to employment], it was largely assumed that a person would be an employee for all purposes – employment law, tax, social security and vicarious liability. Recent developments have broken that link, which may be of benefit to people harmed by the torts of those working in the "gig" economy'.

46 *Kaseris v Rasier Pacific VOF* [2017] FWC 6610 (2017) 272 IR 289; Neerav Srivastava, 'The Spiderman Calculus: Uber's Safe Driver Consumer Guarantee' (2020) 27 Comp & Cons J 134.

47 *Uber BV v Aslam* [2021] UKSC 5 [2021] ICR 657.

48 *ZG Operations v Jamsek* [2022] HCA 2, (2022) 398 ALR 603.

49 *Ferguson v John Dawson & Partners (Contractors) Ltd* [1976] WLR 1213.

relationship without being employment in a legal sense, the UK Supreme Court has affirmed in several decisions that the label 'akin to employment' cannot be used to undermine the traditional position that there is no vicarious liability if the wrongdoer is genuinely a self-employed contractor.[50]

In the context of the relationship between digital platforms and service providers, vicarious liability can therefore only arise if the service provider is an employee. In England, it seems exceptionally,[51] where 'workers may be technically self-employed or agency workers [yet] are effectively part and parcel of the employer's business', it may be fair, just, and reasonable to impose vicarious liability.[52] Although service providers are, to some degree, integrated into the business of the platforms and subject to its rules, they generally carry on business on their own account and are thus more appropriately classified as independent contractors. It remains to be seen whether an English court will find that certain service providers, the most likely candidate probably being rideshare drivers, are in a relationship that is 'sufficiently analogous to employment' such that the ridesharing platform is vicariously liable for a driver's actions.[53]

Despite the residual uncertainty over the correct classification, platforms not being liable for service providers who are independent contractors aligns with corrective justice. When an Airbnb host causes harm, this in itself does not mean that Airbnb has also committed a wrong. A hotel employee is more integrated and subject to more control than an Airbnb host. With a view to distributive justice, a platform collects a commission rather than revenue.[54] In other words, the platform's economic opportunity relates to facilitating the transaction, making it more akin to an agency. Imposing vicarious liability on the platform for the service provider's actions would, arguably, go beyond matching risk to opportunity, although it would serve the compensation aim by providing a tort victim with access to the deep pockets of the platform.

50 *BXB v Trustees of the Barry Congregation of Jehovah's Witnesses* [2023] UKSC 15, [2024] AC 567 [50] (Lord Burrows, with whom Lord Reed, Lord Hodge, Lord Briggs and Lord Stephens agreed), relying on *Barclays Bank plc v Various Claimants* [2020] UKSC 13, [2020] AC 973, [29] (Lady Hale, with whom Lord Reed, Lord Kerr, Lord Hodge and Lord Lloyd-Jones agreed).

51 *Various Claimants v Catholic Child Welfare Society* [2012] UKSC 56, [2013] 2 AC 1 (institute to share with the schools' managers vicarious liability for the abuse committed by the brothers).

52 *Barclays Bank plc v Various Claimants* [2020] UKSC 13, [2020] AC 973, [27] (Lady Hale, with whom Lord Reed, Lord Kerr, Lord Hodge and Lord Lloyd-Jones agreed).

53 For a detailed discussion of whether Uber drivers should be considered employees in the UK, see Margarita Amaxopoulou, Mateja Durovic and Franciszek Lech, 'Regulation of Uber in the UK' in Zaynep Ayata and Işık Önay (eds), *Global Perspectives on Legal Challenges Posed by Ridesharing Companies* (Springer Nature 2021) 101, 121–29. On the US position, see Keith Cunningham-Parmeter, 'Gig-Dependence: Finding the Real Independent Contractors of Platform Work' (2019) 39 N Ill UL Rev 379.

54 Revenue sharing can arise in employment situations.

D. But Platforms Bear Some Responsibility

Tort theory also suggests that platforms should bear responsibility in some circumstances. Under corrective justice, when the platform has been negligent by assigning the task to an incompetent or dangerous service provider, they have committed a wrong and should be liable. Further, the platform's opportunity to make a profit arises from selecting, or facilitating selection, of the service provider as opposed to the actual transaction. Hence, imposing liability *for the selection* would be consistent with distributive justice in that it is matching the economic opportunity of selection to the risk involved.

These positions are reconciled if the platform is held primarily liable for its own wrongdoing in the selection but not, without more, vicariously liable. Therefore, alternatives to vicarious liability should be explored, and that is the focus of the remainder of this chapter.

IV. Primary Liability

A. Independent Contractor

The common law has long recognised the possibility of primary liability arising for negligently selecting an independent contractor that is incompetent. The ensuing damage is the result of a negligent choice of contractor, and the independent contractor's own negligence will not break the chain of causation.[55] In the US, early support for primary liability can be found in two blasting cases.[56] In one case, it was said that a defendant would be liable in negligence not only when knowingly employing incompetent contractors, but also when 'failing to exercise due and reasonable care to select such as were skillful and competent'.[57] The logic of this quote is compelling. Under corrective justice, the employer has committed a wrong. Leading textbooks in other common law jurisdictions likewise accept that primary liability can arise. In Australia, *Fleming's The Law of Torts* states that:

> [t]he employer may incur liability for *personal* negligence in connection with the employment itself; for instance, if the employer carelessly entrusts the work to an incompetent worker; or if the employer, unlike the contractor, knows that there is a risk of harm unless special precautions are taken and fails to give instructions accordingly.[58]

55 Charles W Pierson, 'A Recent Attempt to Limit the Independent Contractor Doctrine' (1898) 8 Yale LJ 63.

56 *Norwalk Gaslight Co v Borough of Norwalk* (1893) 63 Conn 495; *Brannock v Elmore* (1893) 114 Mo 55. See too Pierson (n 55) 63.

57 *Norwalk Gaslight Co v Borough of Norwalk*, ibid.

58 Carolyn Sappideen and others, *Fleming's The Law of Torts* (11th edn, Thomson Reuters 2024) 17–200.

This is similar to the position in England,[59] Texas,[60] and Hong Kong.[61] In *Luen Hing Fat Coating & Finishing Factory Ltd v Waan Chuen Ming*,[62] Bokhary PJ of the Hong Kong Court of Final Appeal held:

> A person is not vicariously liable for his independent contractor's torts. But that only goes to the absence of vicarious liability. A person who engages an independent contractor may be liable for, as it is put in Winfield & Jolowicz on Tort (18th ed., 2010) p. 978, "his own negligence, for example in failing to take care to select a competent contractor". His having engaged an independent contractor does not exclude the possibility of his committing the tort of negligence himself.

In short, even though a person is not vicariously liable for the independent contractor's tort, they might be personally liable for the negligent selection, instruction, or supervision of the contractor.

A statutory expression of primary liability is an occupier's liability for faulty work by an independent contractor in certain situations. In the UK and Hong Kong, the statute provides that an occupier is not liable without more for an independent contractor's work if they acted 'reasonably in entrusting the work to an independent contractor' and had 'taken such steps (if any) as he reasonably ought in order to satisfy himself that the contractor was competent and that the work had been properly done'.[63]

B. Initial Vetting by Platforms

Hence, a failure by a platform to exercise reasonable care in vetting a service provider can result in liability even if they are classified as an independent contractor. For example, if Uber assigns an unlicensed driver to a ride, who then crashes the car, it would be hard for Uber to argue that it bears no responsibility. The driver's subsequent negligent act is a consequence of a negligent choice. In Victoria, Uber being primarily liable would also accord with statute, specifically the *Commercial Passenger Vehicle Industry Act 2017* ('*CPVIA 2017*') that regulates both taxis and ridesharing. Under section 16, a 'booking service provider',[64] which includes

59 Michael Jones and others, *Clerk and Lindsell on Torts* (24th edn, Sweet & Maxwell 2023) 6–66, stating that if the employer 'has negligently selected an incompetent contractor [they will themselves] have committed a tort'.

60 *Freyer v Lyft, Inc*, 639 SW 3d 772 (Tex App 2021).

61 Rick Glofcheski, *Tort Law in Hong Kong* (5th edn, Sweet & Maxwell 2024) 551; Normann Witzleb and Neerav Srivastava (eds), *Tort Law and Practice in Hong Kong* (4th edn, Sweet & Maxwell 2024) 2.039–2.040.

62 (2011) 14 HKCFAR 14 [20] (Ma CJ, Chan and Ribeiro PJJ and Lord Walker of Gestingthorpe NPJ agreeing).

63 *Occupier's Liability Act 1957* (UK) s 2(4)(b); *Occupier's Liability Ordinance* (Hong Kong, Cap 314) s 3(4)(b); the Australian position is similar: eg *Occupiers' Liability Act 1985* (WA), s 6(1).

64 *CPVIA 2017* (Vic), s 7.

Uber, has a shared responsibility of safety with the driver (and others). Under section 24, the duties of a booking service provider include identifying and managing risks, training, supervising, and having systems in place for driver safety. The *CPVIA 2017* does not itself create civil liability[65] but is relevant to a common law obligation.

Circumstances where an Airbnb host is incompetent in managing a property so that it poses risks to a guest are probably less common but may include offering accommodation that is a fire hazard or otherwise unsafe. In principle, the host is an autonomous party who is responsible for their own actions, and there are limits to the level of oversight and control that Airbnb can reasonably be expected to exert. It would not be reasonable to expect a platform for short-term rentals to inspect properties prior to listing. However, if the platform should have been aware of safety hazards through reviews, or listed a host with a known criminal record of violence against guests, the platform might be liable for injury suffered by a guest. In listing the property despite these red flags, the platform has arguably not exercised reasonable care.

The situation of dating apps is distinct in that users are not independent contractors, and indeed no contract between users will be formed, either. The question is whether a platform, such as Tinder, owes users a duty to reasonably screen users before allowing them use of the platform. Dating apps are not specifically regulated, and the risks involved in meeting someone through a dating app are now well-publicised.[66] A survey by Columbia University Journalism Investigations of 1,200 US women who had used dating apps found more than one-third of the women had been sexually assaulted, and for half the sexual assault was rape.[67] Similar figures are contained in a survey by the Australian Institute of Criminology of 10,000 Australians aged 18 to 54 who use dating apps including Hinge, Tinder, or Bumble. There, also one in three participants were found to have experienced in-person sexual violence committed by someone they met through a dating app.[68] One especially distressing case involved the gang rape set up by a Tinder male in Sydney.[69] In the UK, a 'sharp surge in rapes and sexual assaults' has been linked

65 ibid s 21.

66 Abby Vesoulis, 'How Dating Apps Became a Paradise for Predators' *Mother Jones* (September–October 2023) <https://www.motherjones.com/politics/2023/08/how-dating-apps-became-a-paradise-for-predators/>

67 Hillary Flynn, 'Tinder Lets Known Sex Offenders Use the App: It's Not the Only One' *Propublica* (2 December 2019) <www.propublica.org/article/tinder-lets-known-sex-offenders-use-the-app-its-not-the-only-one>

68 Heather Wolbers and others, 'Sexual Harassment, Aggression and Violence Victimisation Among Mobile Dating App and Website Users in Australia' Research Report No 25 (Australian Institute of Criminology 2022).

69 Emma Partridge, 'Woman Gang-Raped by Tinder Date and His Friends' *The Sydney Morning Herald* (8 October 2014) <www.smh.com.au/national/nsw/woman-gangraped-by-tinder-date-and-his-friends-20141008-11353v.html>

to dating apps.[70] The UK National Crimes Agency reported in 2022 that '37% of dating app users have reported someone for inappropriate behaviour, 63% have felt uncomfortable on a date initiated via a dating app and 33% have experienced either harassment or abuse on such dates'.[71] In the US, a Congress sub-committee launched an investigation into dating apps, stating:

> [N]umerous dating apps fail to effectively screen out underage users, creating dangerous and inappropriate situations. This problem is exacerbated by policies that permit, and *in some cases encourage, underage users* to falsely claim that they are 18 years old in order to gain access to these apps . . . many popular *free dating apps permit registered sex offenders* to use them. . . . Protection from sexual predators should not be a luxury confined to paying customers. . . . The United Kingdom has discovered dozens of instances of pedophiles using dating apps to . . . prey on children, *some as young as eight years old*.[72]

In the US and the UK, at least for now,[73] users have the option of conducting a limited check on whether another user has a criminal record.[74] The efficacy of such searches is dependent on what information is publicly available. In Australia and Hong Kong, it does not appear that background checks are available. In Australia, the Government convened a National Roundtable on Online Dating Safety, which involved advocacy groups and major online dating companies. During this process, it applied pressure on the industry to improve its safety record or face stricter legislation.[75] A working group consisting of the companies responsible for popular

70 Jack Hardy, 'Sharp Surge in Rapes and Assaults Linked to Dating Apps' *Daily Telegraph (UK)* (4 January 2023) <www.telegraph.co.uk/news/2023/01/04/sharp-surge-rapes-assaults-linked-dating-apps>

71 National Crime Agency, 'More Under 20s Sexually Assaulted After Meeting Offenders on Dating Sites' *News* (24 February 2022) <www.nationalcrimeagency.gov.uk/news/more-under-20s-sexually-assaulted-after-meeting-offenders-on-dating-sites>

72 US House of Representatives, Committee on Oversight and Accountability, 'Subcommittee Chairman Krishnamoorthi Launches Investigation into User Safety Policies on Dating Apps' (Press Release, 30 January 2020) <oversightdemocrats.house.gov/news/press-releases/subcommittee-chairman-krishnamoorthi-launches-investigation-into-user-safety>; Kenneth Corbin, 'Online Dating Apps Face Scrutiny About Underage Users, Sex Offenders' *Forbes* (31 January 2020) <www.forbes.com/sites/kennethcorbin/2020/01/31/online-dating-apps-face-scrutiny-about-underage-users-sex-offenders/?sh=f375d4b2f9d7>

73 Meera Navlakha, 'Tinder's Background Check Partner Garbo has Ended the Relationship' *Mashable* (21 August 2023) <https://mashable.com/article/garbo-match-group-end-parternship>.

74 Johana Bhuiyan, 'Tinder Now Offers Criminal Background Checks, but There's a Big Problem' *The Guardian* (11 March 2022) <www.theguardian.com/technology/2022/mar/11/tinder-criminal-background-checks-problems>, <https://www.thesun.co.uk/tech/17901551/tinder-allow-users-criminal-background-checks/>

75 Kelly Seal, 'Australian Government Orders Dating Apps to Improve Safety Standards' *Dating Sites Reviews* (5 October 2023) <https://www.datingsitesreviews.com/article.php?story=australian-government-orders-dating-apps-to-improve-safety-standards>.

dating apps Tinder, Hinge, Bumble, Grindr, RSVP, and eHarmony developed a new industry code to improve safety for Australians ('Australian Code').[76] It has been questioned whether a self-regulatory approach is sufficient to reduce toxic behaviour online.[77] Still, it is strongly arguable that the commitments in the Code will now be considered as industry standards. Further, even if the Australian Code is only regulatory in nature, it is likely to inform what constitutes negligence in a private claim by a claimant against a dating platform.

The question of how to determine the existence and content of a duty of care in novel circumstances is complex. Australia, UK, and Hong Kong have their own respective approaches for determining the existence of a duty of care. Australia applies the salient features test,[78] which involves consideration of a number of factors, in determining whether a new duty arises is an incremental step. In the UK, an analogy-based, incremental approach that involves judgement and policy considerations, and is organised by reference to the three-stage test in *Caparo Industries plc v Dickman*,[79] is employed with respect to a *novel duty*.[80] This approach also prevails in Hong Kong. It requires the court to work through the 'labels' of 'foreseeability', 'proximity', and the need to be satisfied that a duty would be 'fair, just, and reasonable', while taking a holistic view and treating these labels as no more than a way of organising one's thinking.[81] Despite these apparent variations in approach, it is clear that the imposition of a duty involves the consideration of finely balanced policy factors: 'differently articulated approaches may sometimes, perhaps not infrequently, yield the same result'.[82] In all three jurisdictions, it is arguable that the likes of Tinder owe users a duty to respond reasonably to complaints and warning signals about online harm. For instance, the Australian Code requires platforms to 'Implement systems to detect potential incidents of online-enabled harm'.[83] It may also be that online dating companies are under a duty to adopt reasonable screening measures before allowing users onto their platforms. Physical or sexual harm during online dates is not only reasonably foreseeable, but it is also arguable that there is sufficient proximity between the platforms and user victims.

76 The Hon Amanda Rishworth MP, Minister for Social Services, 'New Online Dating Industry Code Now in Place' *Media Release* (5 July 2024) <https://ministers.dss.gov.au/media-releases/15161>.

77 Lisa Portolan, 'Love and Theft: Why is Australia's Online Dating App Safety Code only Voluntary?' *The Guardian* (8 July 2024) <https://www.theguardian.com/commentisfree/article/2024/jul/09/australia-online-dating-app-safety-code-voluntary-comment>. The eSafety Commissioner will review the effectiveness of the code in 2025.

78 *Caltex Refineries (Qld) Pty Ltd v Stavar* (2009) 75 NSWLR 649 provides a non-exhaustive list of salient features.

79 [1990] 2 AC 605.

80 *Robinson v Chief Constable of West Yorkshire Police* [2018] UKSC 4 [2018] AC 736.

81 *Luen Hing Fat Coating & Finishing Factory Ltd v Waan Chuen Ming* (2011) 14 HKCFAR 14, [29]–[34].

82 ibid.

83 The Hon Amanda Rishworth MP, Minister for Social Services, 'New Online Dating Industry Code Now in Place' *Media Release* (5 July 2024) <https://ministers.dss.gov.au/media-releases/15161>.

Regarding the factors *against* a duty arising, the starting point is that the sexual assault is committed by an independent third party. In general, negligence law does not impose, without more, liability for failing to act. This is sometimes known as the omission principle, an aspect of which is that, save exceptional circumstances, liability is not imposed on a defendant for failure to prevent the deliberate wrong-doing of a third party.[84] The third party is an autonomous agent responsible for its own actions, and there is only so much a defendant can do. In the UK, in *Smith v Littlewoods Organisation Ltd*,[85] Lord Goff identified four exceptions to the omissions principle, namely: (1) a special relationship between defendant and claimant based on an assumption of responsibility by the defendant; (2) a special relationship between the defendant and the third party based on control by the defendant; (3) the defendant is responsible for a state of danger which may be exploited by a third party; and (4) the defendant is responsible for property that may be used by third party to cause damage. These exceptions probably reflect the common law position generally.[86] Thus, Tinder being liable for harm caused by a user would be an 'exception' to the omissions principle. While Tinder has very limited control over users to prevent harm, it could be argued that flaws in the design of its platform, and particularly in its safety features, may be exploited by bad actors. As was noted in the Australian roundtable, it is not straightforward for a platform to conduct criminal checks on users.

The factors that *support* imposing a duty include that it is foreseeable that harm may result if there is no screening of users. The Australian Code is evidence of foreseeability. Dating apps have been called 'a predator's playground'.[87] The potential harm of sexual assault is serious. There is both contractual and digital proximity between the app and *its* users. An argument that there is an assumption of responsibility by the app needs to overcome the fact that dating apps disclaim liability. For example, the terms and conditions of Tinder and Bumble specifically state that the platforms do not conduct criminal background checks.[88] The contract is relevant for another reason, namely, that premier dating apps sometimes provide higher safety controls as an additional feature. It is tenable that a premier dating app is liable for failing to screen but not a regular one.

An alternative argument in favour of a special relationship may be based on the existence of control. While dating apps lack control to prevent harm once a meeting is arranged, they do control who can use the site. For instance, users could be asked to voluntarily declare that they have not committed any criminal offence before

84 Stelios Tofaris and Sandy Steel, 'Negligence Liability for Omissions and the Police' (2016) 75 Camb LJ 128.

85 [1987] AC 241.

86 DK Srivastava and others, 'A Hazy Shade of Liability: Duty of Care of Universities to Prevent Hazing' (2018) 25 Tort LJ 25, 40.

87 There is 2020 documentary with the title 'Tinder: A Predators' Playground' <topdocumentaryfilms.com/tinder-predators-playground/>

88 Tinder, Terms of Use <policies.tinder.com/terms/intl/en>; Bumble, 'Bumble Terms and Conditions of Use' <bumble.com/en/terms>

joining. For those users who provide such a declaration, the dating app could make clear to other users that they have been self-verified. Self-verification is a limited measure and may provide the app with only limited protection against liability. While criminal checks may be difficult, the point is that dating apps could be taking some steps. Tinder already monitors content through its AI system, and it could remove users who act inappropriately while on Tinder.[89] Further, Tinder can advise users about 'red flags' to watch out for when liaising with other users. Removing users and red flags are examples of what Tinder could be *currently* doing without suggesting that this might be sufficient.

In a recent Pew Research Center Report, six in ten adults in a US survey supported requiring dating apps to conduct background checks before someone can create a profile, although surprisingly there was no majority support for background checks by those who actually used online dating apps.[90] There is a good argument that the common law already requires dating apps to conduct reasonable background checks, where this is legally possible, and should restrict, or warn of, users identified as dangerous by peers. Whether or not a duty arises, there is a need for regulation.[91] It bears repeating that this is a new and risky situation that a large proportion of users are subject to unwanted behaviour, and that apps are – to use US terminology – 'essentially the proximate cause'[92] of any incidents.

C. Ongoing Monitoring

The initial vetting of users is one part of the picture. Ongoing vetting or monitoring is important, too. Just because a driver was vetted by Uber five years ago does not mean that they remain competent, safe, and reliable.

1. Uber

A good claim based on primary liability can be made against Uber. It is arguable that Uber owes passengers a duty of ongoing monitoring for driver safety and competence. Uber makes safety representations to drivers and passengers, and users are reliant on other users to act responsibly. It can also be argued that users are vulnerable, although the vulnerability does not appear to differ dramatically between ride-sharing and ordinary taxis. While Uber has safety programs, it does

89 Ina Fried, 'Tinder Tries to Curb Offensive Messages' *Axios* (20 May 2021) <axios.com/2021/05/20/tinder-offensive-messages>

90 Pew Research Center, 'From Looking for Love to Swiping the Field: Online Dating in the U.S., Research Report' (February 2023) <pewresearch.org/internet/2023/02/02/from-looking-for-love-to-swiping-the-field-online-dating-in-the-u-s/>

91 US lawmakers at federal and state level have become alert to the issue: see, e.g., H.R.8946 – Online Dating Safety Act of 2022, 117th Congress (2021–2022), Utah House (2023) – H.B. 18 Online Dating Safety Amendments.

92 Maureen Horcher, 'World Wide Web of Love, Lies, and Legislation: Why Online Dating Websites Should Screen Members' (2011) 29 J Marshall J Info Tech Privacy L 251, 256.

not conduct daily driver alcohol checks, although it is foreseeable that some Uber drivers might drive under the influence of alcohol. There are many media reports of this happening,[93] and serious harm may result if the drinking leads to a road accident. As for control, it is possible for Uber to regulate drivers by insisting that they use a portable blood/alcohol reader[94] and provide a reading before commencing a shift. However, the issues involved in managing drug and alcohol impairment at work are complex.[95] Testing regimes should be part of a broader preventative strategy that also offers support to workers and has regard to legitimate worker concerns.

Again, an exception to the omissions principle may arise. Further, the imposition of a duty to adopt reasonable safety measures is consistent with legislation, authority, policy, and theory. Under the *CPVIA 2017*, booking service providers owe a duty to provide information, instruction, or supervision to associated drivers. This duty is directed at drivers providing their services safely and includes a requirement to implement systems or processes for (1) the management of driver fatigue, and (2) drug and alcohol testing of drivers.

2. *Airbnb*

Likewise, it is arguable that Airbnb owes a duty of reasonable ongoing monitoring when it comes to hosts. Say an Airbnb host is of good standing when they join the site. Subsequently, a guest complains to Airbnb that the host behaved aggressively. Unlike the Uber scenario, which involved driver negligence, this Airbnb scenario involves an intentional tort by a third party. The host is an independent party, and it is arguable that Airbnb is not responsible for their intentional autonomous actions. Airbnb cannot physically control them.

Nevertheless, if Airbnb continued to allow the host to list on Airbnb, without taking any measures at all, and the host assaulted another guest, then liability *may* arise. Harm in this situation is foreseeable. Like in the Uber scenario, it is arguable that there is reliance by the guest on Airbnb because of safety representations, and Airbnb's ability to exert some control over the danger, for example, by delisting. In the sample scenario, there is also knowledge of the risk. In Australia, *Chordas*

93 For example, Evan Batten and Summer Woolley, 'Uber Bans "Drunk, Drug-Affected, Unlicensed" Sydney Man After He Takes the Wheel of Car' *7news.com.au* (24 February 2020) <7news.com.au/news/nsw/uber-bans-drunk-drug-affected-unlicensed-sydney-man-after-he-takes-the-wheel-of-car-c-713810>; Cheryl Roy, 'Drunk Uber Driver: Who Is Legally Responsible?' *Southern Maryland Chronicle* (25 March 2021) <southernmarylandchronicle.com/2021/03/25/drunk-uber-driver-who-is-legally-responsible/>.

94 Uber is taking good peripheral steps to avoid the dangers of drunk driving. However, they are not specific to a driver. See Rik Williams and Nadia Anderson, 'Creating Designated Riders: A Tale of Two Cities' (*Medium*, 10 January 2018) <medium.com/uber-under-the-hood/creating-designated-riders-a-tale-of-two-cities-c9930588ab14>

95 For more information on current UK approaches and practices, see, e.g., Chartered Institute of Personnel and Development, *Managing Drug and Alcohol Misuse at Work, Report* (Chartered Institute of Personnel and Development 2020).

v Bryant (Wellington)[96] held that a hotel owes a duty to protect the safety of its patrons where it is evident that a patron should be supervised or ejected or another patron warned. *Chordas* is analogous.

3. *Tinder*

With respect to Tinder, subject to the uncertainty of an initial vetting duty arising discussed previously, the same factors support the imposition of a monitoring duty. In addition, with Tinder already using AI to monitor content, and suggesting to people that proposed content might be inappropriate, the reliance and control arguments are stronger. There are calls for Tinder to '[act] on behavior they see on their platform, such as removing someone who is engaging in harassment'.[97] As mentioned, under the Australian Code platforms are now expected to implement systems to detect potential incidents, and this may be relevant to private claims. When there is knowledge of violence, actual or constructive, and a dating app takes no steps such as delisting the user or issuing a warning, then it may very well be liable.

V. Non-Delegable Duties

Non-delegable duties occupy a space that is distinct to vicarious liability and primary liability for the negligent selection of a contractor.[98] In essence, they not only require the duty holders to take personal care themselves, but also to ensure care is taken by others.[99] When a person owes a non-delegable duty, they cannot avoid that responsibility by delegating the performance of a task to an employee or independent contractor.[100] If the independent contractor does not exercise reasonable care, then the person who has engaged them is liable even though they are not the employer.

Non-delegable duties are commonly viewed as a form of strict liability and therefore as exceptional.[101] While the exact circumstances in which non-delegable duties arise continue to be subject to debate, they are well-recognised in employment, hospital, and school settings:

> The classic example is an employer's duty to provide a safe system of work. Being non-delegable, this duty of the employer can be breached not only by employees, but also by an independent contractor.[102] The primary purpose of

96 [1988] FCA 753, (1989) 91 ALR 149.

97 Bhuiyan (n 75).

98 *Woodland v Swimming Teachers Association* [2013] UKSC 66 [2014] AC 537.

99 *Kondis v State Transport Authority (formerly Victorian Railways Board)* (1984) 154 CLR 672.

100 *Bank of East Asia Ltd v Tsien Wui Marble Factory Ltd* (1999) 2 HKCFAR 349.

101 Christian Witting, 'Breach of the Non-Delegable Duty: Defending Limited Strict Liability in Tort' (2006) 29 UNS Wales LJ 33; Jonathan Morgan, 'Liability for Independent Contractors in Contract and Tort: Duties to Ensure That Care Is Taken' (2015) 74 Camb LJ 109.

102 *Kondis v State Transport Authority* (n 97) 672.

> non-delegable duties is to prevent injury to persons. Enterprise liability runs through its veins. They are non-delegable because of their personal character. That personal character is demonstrated by the non-delegable duty owed to patients by hospitals. It does not matter that the doctor, not the hospital, is the expert. . . . As a personal duty, it can even be breached directly by the defendant [, e.g. the main contractor]. *At the very least, there is a distinction between a duty of care in, say, the selection of an independent contractor* [i.e. primary liability] *and the higher duty to ensure that reasonable care is taken by that contractor* [i.e. non-delegable duty].[103]

The distinction between primary liability and a non-delegable duty can be illustrated by the following example: Many doctors are independent contractors, say consultants, and if a hospital appoints a clearly incompetent doctor, then it is *primarily liable.* If a doctor is a competent independent contractor but negligent in a specific instance, then the hospital is not vicariously liable nor primarily liable. It is liable because its non-delegable duty to patients was breached.

The question arises whether, and if so when, a digital platform can owe a non-delegable duty to a user. In the 1983 decision of *Rogers v Night Riders*, the English Court of Appeal held that a proto-Uber service had a non-delegable duty of safety with respect to an unsafe car owned by the independent contractor driver.[104] It was held that a mini-cab service which connected riders and drivers via telephone and radio owed a non-delegable duty to passengers that vehicles were safe. In that case, the driver had negligently maintained the door lock on his cab. The plaintiff-passenger was injured after the door flew open. Eveleigh LJ held that the mini-cab service was liable:

> [W]e are [not] concerned to consider vicarious liability. . . . We are concerned to consider a case of primary duty . . . the defendants could foresee that [the plaintiff] might be injured if the vehicle were defective, and so they owed a duty arising out of this relationship to take care to see that the vehicle was safe. They relied upon the driver to do this. Whether he was a servant or an independent contractor matters not, . . . such a duty cannot be delegated.[105]

Since that time, apex courts have repeatedly considered when non-delegable duties arise.[106] A particularly influential decision is *Woodlands v Swimming Teachers Association*, where a child suffered brain damage during a school swimming lesson due to the alleged negligence of the swimming instructor. The school had contracted out the provision of the swimming lessons.[107] It was held that a school

103 Srivastava, Srivastava and Srivastava (n 42) 227.
104 [1983] RTR 324.
105 *Rogers v Night Riders* [1983] RTR 324, 328.
106 *Kondis v State Transport Authority* (n 97) 672; *Woodland v Swimming Teachers Association* (n 96) 537; *Bank of East Asia Ltd v Tsien Wui Marble Factory Ltd* (n 98) 349.
107 [2013] UKSC 66 [2014] AC 537.

owed a non-delegable duty of care to students with respect to educational functions. Lord Sumption identified five criteria for imposing a non-delegable duty: (1) the claimant is a patient or a child, or for some other reason, especially vulnerable or dependent on the other party; (2) there is an antecedent relationship between the parties placing the claimant in the custody, charge, or care of the defendant, and from which it is possible to impute to the defendant the assumption of a positive duty to protect the claimant; (3) the claimant has no control over how and by whom the defendant chooses to perform those obligations; (4) the defendant has delegated to a third party some integral part of that positive duty; and (5) the third party has been negligent.[108] In addition, it must be fair, just, and reasonable to impose a non-delegable duty.[109]

Regarding criterion (5), Lord Sumption echoed what was held by a majority in the High Court decision of *NSW v Lepore*.[110] *Lepore* concerned the liability of a school for the sexual abuse of a student by a teacher. It was held that a non-delegable duty did not apply to deliberate acts.[111] A different view was expressed by Lord Reed in *Armes v Nottinghamshire County Council*, which also concerned the abuse of children.[112] The children had been placed with foster parents by a local council. The judgment begins with the clarification that the local authority was not negligent in the selection or supervision of the foster parents.[113] It was held that imposing a non-delegable duty on the council to take reasonable care for the safety of children while they are in the care and custody of foster parents would be too broad.[114]

These newer authorities suggest that the mini-cab decision in *Rogers* was a high point of non-delegable duties and may not be decided in the same way today. Using the *Woodlands* criteria, it is questionable whether users are, in the relevant sense, vulnerable or dependent on the platform and in the platform's custody, charge, or care. The answer depends on how Lord Sumption's five criteria are interpreted. A passenger may be regarded as vulnerable in that they are entering a vehicle on the assumption that the driver has been vetted for safety. It is an assumption fortified by Uber's statutory obligations, at least in some Australian jurisdictions, and under its safety representations. There is an antecedent relationship, yet it is doubtful whether it exhibits the hallmarks of other relationships of custody, charge, or care in which the common law has accepted a positive duty to protect the claimant. It may be difficult to argue that, without more, a platform has assumed a positive duty to protect a user from physical harm. However, the possibility of a positive

108 *Woodland v Swimming Teachers Association* (n 96) 537.

109 ibid.

110 (2003) 212 CLR 511.

111 Prue Vines, 'NSW v Lepore; Samin v Queensland; Rich v Queensland – Schools' Responsibility for Teachers' Sexual Assault: Non-Delegable Duty and Vicarious Liability' (2003) 27 Melb Univ L Rev 612.

112 [2017] UKSC 60, [51] (Lord Reed, with whom Lady Hale, Lord Kerr and Lord Clarke agreed).

113 *Armes v Nottinghamshire County Council* [2017] UKSC 60, [2018] AC 355, [1] (Lord Reed, with whom Lady Hale, Lord Kerr and Lord Clarke agreed).

114 The council was held vicariously liable.

duty is reinforced by Uber's statutory obligations under the *CPVIA 2017*. Its shared responsibility provisions are analogous to non-delegable duties, given that section 24(1) provides that a 'booking service provider must, so far as is reasonably practicable, ensure commercial passenger vehicle services provided by an associated driver are provided safely'. Lastly, a passenger has *no* control over how and by whom Uber performs its safety obligations, and the driver is delegated as an integral part of that safety obligations when they are offered, and accept, the ride request.

Since we argue that a non-delegable duty can arise regarding Uber, it should be added that public transportation (taxi, train, and bus, respectively) is also subject to the statutory shared responsibility obligations.[115] Therefore, it is possible that they too are subject to non-delegable duties. There are common features. Moving vehicles pose particular risks, and passengers of public transport are dependent on those who manage them to ensure safety. Taxi companies are booking service providers under the *CPVIA 2017*, while trains and buses have their own legislation. It would be surprising if a bus company was able to avoid liability for driver negligence on the basis that the driver was an independent contractor. A point of difference with Uber is that it might not be accurate to describe a passenger as being in an 'antecedent relationship' with a public transportation company.

It would be harder to argue that Airbnb owes a non-delegable duty to guests to take reasonable care for their safety. A number of Lord Sumption's criteria may not be met: regarding (1), a guest is less vulnerable in that they are not confined within a moving car and, concerning (3), the claimant chooses the property at which they will stay, unlike the allocation that takes place with an Uber driver. Similarly, it is difficult to argue that Tinder owes a non-delegable duty to take reasonable care for the safety of the users. This is because the claimant does have control over whom, and in what circumstances, they meet and, with respect to (4), it is not accurate to describe Tinder as 'delegating' its safety obligations to a prospective partner; instead, it provides a forum for users to meet.

VI. Statutory Reform and EU Approach

The preceding discussion has demonstrated that the new relationships mediated by digital platforms challenge existing liability principles. Although the common law contains flexible standards that can be relied upon to respond to new relationships and the policy concerns they raise, there is considerable uncertainty – as demonstrated herein – how these principles should be interpreted and applied where physical harm is caused in user-to-user situations. In this situation, it may appear desirable to seek recourse to new statutory duties that define the obligations of the parties more directly and specifically than the open-ended standards of the common law. One such attempt is the CPVIA, discussed earlier, which creates shared

115 In the Australian state of Victoria, this is regulated for taxis in s 16 of CPVIA 2017, for trains in s 13 of *Rail Safety Act 2006* (Vic), and for buses in s 9 of *Bus Safety Act 2006* (Vic).

responsibility provisions that are intended to enhance passenger safety. Contravention of these duties, however, constitutes a criminal offence, which means that they have at best indirect effect on the private law rights of passengers who have suffered harm. A different approach has been put forward in the European Union, where the European Law Institute has adopted Model Rules on Online Platforms[116] that are intended to contribute to the ongoing academic discussion on platform liability and to serve as a legislative model to be considered by Union or national legislators. Article 8 of the Model Rules creates a duty to protect users as follows:[117]

Art. 8 Duty to Protect Users

(1) The platform operator has no general duty to monitor the activity of platform users.
(2) A platform operator who, on obtaining credible evidence of:
   a) criminal conduct of a supplier or customer to the detriment of other users;
   b) conduct of a supplier or customer which is likely to cause physical injury, a violation of privacy, infringement of corporeal property, deprivation of liberty or a violation of another similar right to detriment of another platform user, fails to take adequate measures for the protection of the platform users, is liable for damage caused to platform users as a result of this failure.

This provision seeks to cover multiple forms of harm, including that arising from digital communications as well as physical injury. However, Article 8's application appears to be narrower than the common law. Unlike the position under the common law, the duty stipulated is reactive, not proactive. At common law, where there is an assumption of responsibility, a positive duty arises even without evidence of wrongdoing. In line with Article 15(1) of the E-Commerce Directive 2000/31/EC, platform operators have no general duty to monitor the activity of platform users nor any information uploaded to the platform. An obligation to take adequate measures only arises upon the obtaining of credible evidence of misconduct. However, while limiting the monitoring obligation to situations where the platform has positive information about the harm may be appropriate in the context of communication harms, it appears to be problematic not to require proactive steps to address the risk of physical injury between users.

In falling short of current common law obligations for user-to-user harm, Article 8 would appear not to be a desirable way to develop the law in common law jurisdictions, at least as far as physical harm caused in user-to-user transactions is concerned. Although it is thus debatable whether the ELI proposal responds in a sufficiently differentiated manner to the new risks of harm emerging from

116 European Law Institute, 'Model Rules on Online Platforms, Report' (2019) <;>https://www.europeanlawinstitute.eu/fileadmin/user_upload/p_eli/Publications/ELI_Model_Rules_on_Online_Platforms.pdf>; Christoph Busch and others, 'The ELI Model Rules on Online Platforms' (2020) 9 J Euro Cons Mark L 61.

117 European Law Institute (n 114).

platform-mediated relationships, it is a welcome contribution to the emerging need to consider the role that statutory intervention should play in identifying suitable liability rule.

The Online Safety Act 2022 (UK), the Online Safety Act 2021 (Cth), and the EU Digital Services Act[118] contain further attempts to impose duties of care on digital platforms with the aim of creating a safer, more transparent, and more user-friendly online environment. However, these measures are primarily directed at protecting users from harm by illegal or harmful content or services online, rather than the offline harm with which this chapter is concerned.

While statutory intervention can improve consumer protections more quickly and with more certainty than the open-textured standards of the common law, this potential advantage needs to be weighed against the risk of legal fragmentation between jurisdictions, and associated higher compliance costs, if statutory enactments are adopted without international harmonisation.[119]

VI. Conclusion

As a service provider is probably not an employee, it seems that platforms are not vicariously liable for user-to-user harm. Having said that, under general tort principles, a platform should be primarily liable for the negligent selection of a contractor, and it may owe a non-delegable duty in some circumstances. Platforms are not neutral mediators between service providers and customers. They profit by identifying suitable service providers, taking advantage of a network effect, their position as information brokers, and the trust reposed in their service. Primary liability for the negligent selection of an incompetent provider therefore aligns better with tort theory.

Ride-sharing services like Uber might be primarily liable for appointing an incompetent driver. There is also a good argument, based on analogous authority, that Uber owes a non-delegable duty to take reasonable care for the safety of passengers that cannot be avoided by delegating the driving to a third-party driver. Safe driving is integral to the service provided by Uber.

Short-term rental services like Airbnb might be primarily liable for listing a property or host that would have been identified as posing a risk to users if it had exercised reasonable care. Even if a duty to take reasonable care in listing arises, Airbnb may often be able to avoid liability. An exception may occur if the platform fails to act on complaints that the property or host is dangerous. The case for imposing a non-delegable duty on Airbnb to take reasonable care for a guest's

118 Regulation (EU) 2022/2065 of the European Parliament and of the Council of 19 October 2022 on a Single Market for Digital Services and amending Directive 2000/31/EC (Digital Services Act), OJ L 277, 27 October 2022, p 1.

119 Examples of successful international harmonisation include Model Laws promulgated by the United Nations Commission on International Trade Law (UNCITRAL), such as the *Model Law on International Commercial Arbitration* (1985) and the *Model Law on Cross-Border Insolvency* (1997).

safety is also less strong. Guests are less vulnerable than an Uber passenger, not least because it is the guest, rather than the platform, who chooses the host.

For both Uber and Airbnb, we argue that any duty arising is not limited to an initial vetting. Rather, platforms also owe ongoing monitoring obligations. Just because an Uber driver was competent five years ago when they joined does not mean they are safe with respect to the current ride.

Dating apps such as Tinder are perhaps the most novel situation as well as the most concerning. While there is clearly a duty of reasonable care, defining its content is challenging. The principles of liability for the misconduct of independent contractors do not apply directly, given that users are not contractors of the dating app provider. Moreover, in the dating context, the two users are generally on equal footing, rather than one providing a service for reward to another, as with short-term rentals or ride-shares. There is also the uncertainty as to how background checks to protect users from known predators could be conducted. However, when it comes to ongoing monitoring of users, it is easier to argue that proactive steps to protect users are reasonable, as Tinder is already using AI to advise users about inappropriate content.

Heightened user concerns and well-documented examples of user harm in online-mediated encounters are evidence that there is a need for more specific regulation. Specific regulation also informs common law claims. But the example of the European Model Rules on Online Platforms demonstrates the difficulty of formulating liability rules that are properly adapted to the circumstances. When compared with the incremental development of the common law, statutory enactments also bear the risk of legal fragmentation across jurisdictions unless they are internationally harmonised.

9 Envisioning the Future of Online Dispute Resolution From the Case of China

Songyin Bo

Introduction

The proliferation of online dispute resolution (ODR) has closely paralleled the rise of the platform economy, representing a symbiotic evolution of commerce and dispute resolution in the digital age. Digital platforms have developed robust ODR mechanisms as essential components in their infrastructure, adeptly managing an escalating volume of disputes over various online transactions. The adaptation of ODR systems pioneered by private platforms exhibits the most pronounced transformation, characterized by a sequence of dispute resolution innovations, aimed to reconcile cost-effectiveness, business imperatives, and the balance of interests of diverse stakeholders.

Using the recent developments of intellectual property (IP)-related ODR in China as a case study, this chapter explores the intricacies of ODR mechanisms in addressing transaction-related disputes. Such ODR mechanisms emphasize improvements in transparency, expedited resolution efficacy, and the cultivation of user trust, ultimately fostering platform loyalty. This chapter also inspects the trajectory of IP dispute resolution evolution within the ODR paradigm, unveiling a trend towards increasingly malleable approaches in dispute prevention and underlining the harmonization of multi-party interests. Furthermore, this chapter discusses the multifaceted driving forces propelling the development of ODR, entwining considerations of economic efficiency, alleviation of judicial burden, the interpretive challenges posed by ambiguous regulations, and the congruence with national advocacies of diversified dispute resolution (DDR) as well as IP rights protection. Additionally, this chapter contemplates the implications of ODR, acknowledging its pivotal contribution to the refinement of online litigation and arbitration practices and its substantive potential to enrich co-regulation theory. Acknowledging the extant challenges, the chapter articulates prospective advancements to the ODR framework, thus contributing to its continual improvement in the rapidly evolving arena of the platform economy.

The findings in this chapter carry significant implications for the evolution of the Web3 ecosystem. First, as Web3 continues to facilitate an increasing number of interactions and transactions within the platform economy, the likelihood of

DOI: 10.4324/9781032618975-14

disputes between online users will rise. Implementing well-designed ODR mechanisms not only mitigates platforms' potential liability[1] but also enhances the overall sustainability of the Web3 economy. Second, among the various disputes emerging from Web3 platforms, IP-related conflicts have garnered considerable attention in recent years.[2] Third, Web3 envisions users as "not merely as consumers but as active participants and co-creators" of the digital landscape.[3] Similarly, China's ODR development underscores user participation in both dispute resolution and the rule-making process. This aligns with the foundational principles of Web3, fostering an ecosystem characterized by enhanced efficiency, transparency, and democratic ideals. Last but not least, several Web3 platforms have devised unique approaches to address disputes among stakeholders. A substantial portion of this private ordering has drawn inspiration from the past successes of the existing platform economy.[4] Therefore, studying the success of ODR in China's e-commerce platforms can offer a valuable perspective for designing and envisioning similar mechanisms in the Web3 ecosystem.

I. The Evolution of ODR in China: History and Innovations

ODR encapsulates a burgeoning domain in which digital technologies are employed to facilitate the resolution of disputes between parties.[5] It is considered a special subset within the alternative dispute resolution (ADR) spectrum, where it incorporates ADR's foundational principles – offering a less confrontational, structured process for parties to resolve disputes through mediation, arbitration, and negotiation, but executed via virtual environments.[6] This evolution reflects a shift from the physical to the cyber-arena in response to the expansive growth of e-commerce and online interactions, demonstrating a technological adaptation of ADR methods to the realities of the global digital economy.[7]

1 Runhua Wang, Jyh-An Lee and Jingwen Liu, Chapter 1 in this volume.

2 Neerav Srivastava and Normann Witzleb, Chapter 8 in this volume.

3 Pooja Lekhi and Guneet Kaur, *Concepts, Technologies, Challenges, and the Future of Web 3* (IGI Global 2023) 2–3.

4 Runhua Wang, Jyh-An Lee and Jingwen Liu, 'Unwinding NFTs in the Shadow of IP Law' (2024) 61(1) Am Bus Law J (forthcoming).

5 Ethan Katsh and Orna Rabinovich-Einy, *Digital Justice: Technology and the Internet of Disputes* (OUP 2017) 25; UNCITRAL Technical Notes on Online Dispute Resolution (issued by United Nations Commission on International Trade Law 2017) 4 <https://uncitral.un.org/sites/uncitral.un.org/files/media-documents/uncitral/en/v1700382_english_technical_notes_on_odr.pdf> accessed 20 January 2024.

6 Amy J Schmitz and Colin Rule, *The New Handshake: Online Dispute Resolution and the Future of Consumer Protection* (American Bar Association 2019) 3; Amy J Schmitz, 'Addressing the Class Claim Conundrum with Online Dispute Resolution' (2020) 2 J Dis Res 361, 363.

7 ibid.

A. ODR Systems for Transaction-Related Disputes

In the era of the platform economy, predominant digital marketplaces that bring together diverse user groups, such as Amazon and Alibaba, have been at the forefront of pioneering ODR systems. These systems are intricately designed to effectively tackle the challenges posed by the high-volume, low-value, and cross-jurisdictional nature of transactions inherent in the platform economy.[8] By streamlining dispute resolution through algorithmic decision-making and automated processes, ODR systems circumvent the often cumbersome and protracted litigation process, along with its high costs.[9] The streamlined and evolving systems not only enhance the economic efficiency of dispute resolution practices, but also resonate with the broader imperatives of access to justice, as they lower the financial and procedural barriers to redress for platform users.[10]

Taobao, the massive online shopping platform in China owned by Alibaba Group, has been cultivating its online mediation service since the late 2000s. This service is integral to Alibaba's comprehensive customer service and ODR framework.[11] The Taobao online mediation service operates on a digital platform where buyers and sellers can lodge complaints regarding transactions involving unsatisfied service or products, slow delivery, unsuccessful refund, and related issues. When a dispute is filed, the system first encourages the parties to communicate directly and seek an amicable solution. If unsuccessful, the platform offers mediation handled by trained personnel who assess the documentation provided by both parties, including transaction and communication records, to facilitate a resolution.[12] To streamline and expedite the dispute resolution process, Taobao integrates artificial intelligence (AI) and machine learning algorithms into its system to assist in dispute classification and resolution recommendations, enhancing efficiency and scalability.[13] This approach leverages vast data insights to predict dispute outcomes, allowing human mediators to focus on more complex cases that require nuanced judgment.[14] Taobao's online mediation service has successfully handled millions of disputes, resolving the majority without escalating to arbitration or litigation.[15]

8 Michèle Finck, 'Digital Regulation: Designing a Supranational Legal Framework for the Platform Economy' (2017) LSE Legal Studies Working Paper No 15/2017, 21 <https://papers.ssrn.com/sol3/papers.cfm?abstract_id=2990043> accessed 15 January 2024.

9 UNCITRAL Technical Notes on Online Dispute Resolution (n 5) 9.

10 William Davis and Helga Turku, 'Access to Justice and Alternative Dispute Resolution' (2011) 1 J Dis Res 1, 3.

11 Gao Wei, 'The Perils of Making New Media the Philosopher King' (2016) 4(2) Peking Univ LJ 267, 280.

12 Taobao, 'Taobao Service Agreement' <https://terms.alicdn.com/legal-agreement/terms/TD/TD201609301342_19559.html?spm=a2145.7268393.0.0.f9aa5d7cSDR9SE> accessed 20 January 2024.

13 Xin Zhou and others, 'Legal Intelligence for E-Commerce: Multi-Task Learning by Leveraging Multiview Dispute Representation' [2019] SIGIR 315; Alizila, 'How Alibaba Uses Artificial Intelligence to Change the Way We Shop' <https://insideretail.asia/2017/06/07/how-alibaba-uses-artificial-intelligence-to-change-the-way-we-shop/> accessed 20 January 2024.

14 ibid.

15 ibid.

By providing accessible, expedient, and just resolutions to disputes, ODR systems instill confidence and trust in platform users, contributing to a virtuous circle of repeated engagement and platform growth – a manifestation of network effects that drives the platform's expansion.[16] Therefore, following the emphasis of Taobao on ODR service, a trend emerged within the e-commerce ecosystem in China, witnessing all major e-commerce platforms like JD.COM, Pinduoduo, Meituan,[17] and online food delivery platforms like Ele.me emulating this ODR system.[18]

Despite the considerable volume of disputes resolved through online mediation services, a cadre of complex cases would still necessitate the intervention of human mediators, inevitably imposing a substantial demand on labor and lengthening the time to reach settlements.[19] The opacity embedded in the automated resolution or manual review also incentivizes predominant platforms to innovate more efficient and transparent ODR approaches.[20] Taobao, for instance, ushers in an era of deploying crowdsourced arbitration – Alibaba Public Jury, to incorporate diverse perspectives of ordinary platform users as arbiters to enhance efficiency, fairness, and transparency. This service was first launched in 2012 and has constantly evolved.[21] It now permits users with authenticated identities who are in good standing within the Taobao community to enroll as jurors in resolving different types of e-commerce disputes.[22] Upon registration as jurors, users may select particular cases for adjudication within the Alibaba Public Jury section on the Taobao mobile application. Following this selection, they become part of a diverse panel comprising 31 of their peers. In this role, they review the provided case synopsis and cast independent votes on the resolution.[23] The side with the majority votes wins.[24] By tapping into the aggregate expertise of the user community, Taobao manages to resolve a high demand of disputes without the concomitant increase in expert arbitration resources or customer service teams.[25] Furthermore, it can expedite the dispute resolution process as a multitude of users operating simultaneously condenses

16 Junhong Chu and Puneet Manchanda, 'Quantifying Cross and Direct Network Effects in Online Consumer-to-Consumer Platforms' (2016) 35 Mark Sci 870.

17 JD.COM (京东), Pinduoduo (拼多多), and Meituan (美团) are all major e-commerce platforms in China.

18 Ele.me (饿了么) is one of the main online food delivery platforms in China.

19 Gao Wei, 'The Analysis of Dispute Resolution on the Internet: Two Paths and the Problem of Embeddedness' (2014) 26 Peking Univ LJ 1059, 1074.

20 Carrie S Shang and Wenli Guo, 'The Rise of Online Dispute Resolution-Led Justice in China: An Initial Look' [2020] Aus Nat Uni JL Tech 25, 27.

21 'Alibaba Public Jury Official Website' <https://pan.taobao.com/> accessed 25 January 2024.

22 ibid; Alan P Kwan, S Alex Yang and Angela Huyue Zhang, 'Decentralized Governance on Two-Sided Platforms: Crowdsourcing, Learning, and Debiasing' (2020) <https://www.researchgate.net/publication/348838425_Decentralized_Governance_on_TwoSided_Platforms_Crowdsourcing_Learning_and_Debiasing> accessed 25 January 2024 (the jurors mainly resolve disputes over an item's categorization, disagreements over the monetary aspect of the transaction, and general breach of contract disputes).

23 ibid.

24 ibid.

25 ibid.

the timeline. To date, the platform has garnered over 4 million users who serve as jurors, successfully resolving more than 16 million disputes. This is achieved with a significantly shorter processing time compared to Taobao's customer service personnel in reaching a judgment.[26]

This service brings additional advantages as well. Involving the user community in arbitration bestows a democratic dimension to the dispute resolution process, creating an appearance of peer-driven justice. This approach has the potential to enhance the disputants' acceptance of outcomes.[27] Furthermore, user participation fosters community engagement, instills a sense of ownership and investment, and provides assessors with credit upon the successful closure of a case, establishing a hierarchy of rankings based on seniority.[28] Such engagement, rewards, and a sense of achievement deepens the relationship between users and the platform, strengthening user loyalty and potentially fostering a more vibrant marketplace.[29]

Alibaba Group has extended the crowdsourced arbitration paradigm to other entities within its corporate umbrella, including the food delivery service Ele.me and the multi-faceted digital payment platform Alipay.[30] This harmonization of dispute resolution mechanisms creates a consistent and predictable user experience across different platforms. The fluidity of users/assessors within the Alibaba Group's various platforms may predispose them towards participation in similar roles across the conglomerate's diverse platforms, promoting cross-utilization of resources that consolidate user loyalty and enhances Alibaba Group's overall competitiveness.

Lastly, the collective data harvested through crowdsourced arbitration service provides a valuable repository for analytical insights. Platforms can analyze this data to discern dispute patterns, frequent points of contention, and areas ripe for procedural or policy enhancements. This iterative learning informs strategic decisions, allowing for continuous refinement of the user experience. The Alibaba Public Jury, inspired by eBay's Community Court, the pioneering crowdsourced arbitration mechanism in eBay's ODR framework, has achieved larger scale and more profound impact on ODR development compared to its precursor. Initially launched as a pilot initiative in 2008 for handling transaction-related disputes within eBay's Indian sector, the eBay Community Court ceased its operations in

26 ibid.
27 H Jaap Van Den Herik and Daniel Dimov, 'Towards Crowdsourced Online Dispute Resolution' [2011] J Int Comm L Tech <https://www.researchgate.net/publication/228168172> accessed 25 January 2024; Jaap Van Den Herik and Daniel Dimov, 'Can the eBay's Community Review Forum Faily Resolve Disputes?' (2011) <https://www.researchgate.net/publication/228182507_Can_the_eBay's_Community_Review_Forum_Fairly_Resolve_Disputes> accessed 25 January 2024; Wei Gao, 'Let the Collective Intelligence Shine Through' (2018) 6(2) Peking Univ LJ 283.
28 ibid.
29 ibid.
30 'A Crowdsourcing Meeting to Decide Life or Death' (Wenzhai, 2019) <https://epaper.gmw.cn/wzb/html/2019-01/15/nw.D110000wzb_20190115_6-03.htm.> accessed 20 January 2024. (The Ant Insurance (蚂蚁保险) in Alipay adopted the crowdsourcing mechanism to resolve insurance disputes in 2018.)

early 2012.[31] This led to incomplete rules for the juror eligibility and reward system, resulting in limited case volume and a constrained juror base.[32]

In contrast, the Alibaba Public Jury, evolving over a decade, has established detailed criteria for juror registration and a comprehensive rewards system.[33] The scope of adjudication has expanded to encompass IP-related disputes, particularly those involving plagiarism accusations, in addition to transactional conflicts.[34] Notably, jurors also have the opportunity to participate in Taobao's internal rule-making process.[35] Consequently, the Alibaba Public Jury represents the most extensive integration of crowdsourced arbitration into platform-based ODR systems worldwide. Furthermore, it has wielded a more significant influence on the global progression of ODR compared to eBay's Community Court, inspiring various platforms within China and beyond to adopt its methodologies for resolving a broader spectrum of disputes.

B. ODR System for IP Disputes

Within the contemporary milieu of the platform economy, the burgeoning activity centered on content generation and extensive commercial transactions precipitates a highly conducive environment for IP disputes. This phenomenon is exacerbated by the rapid dissemination of digital content, and significant differences in revenue between pirated and legitimately copyrighted materials and between authentic and counterfeit goods. As a result, ODR systems have evolved beyond the mere adjudication of disputes over transactions to encompass the intricate domain of IP disputes, processing notice-and-takedown requests from IP rights owners by various types of platforms.

The notice-and-takedown rule was first codified in the *Digital Millennium Copyright Act* of the United States in the 1990s, mandating prompt platform responses to copyright infringement claims.[36] Compliance with the rule shields platforms

31 Colin Rule and Chittu Nagarajan, 'The Wisdom of Crowds: The eBay Community Court and the Future of Online Dispute Resolution' (2010) <http://colinrule.com/writing/acr2010.pdf> accessed 20 February 2024.

32 Van Den Herik and Dimov (n 27); ibid (By the end of 2010, the Community Court had resolved more than 2,400 cases in India. By then, it had more than 580 jurors, and there were 250 cases pending.)

33 'Alibaba Public Jury Official Website' (n 21) (showing detailed rules about the criteria for juror's eligibility and what rewards – mostly credits could be used on Taobao – could be achieved by deciding each case.)

34 'Alibaba Launches Originals Protection Plan, Big Data Provides Support and also the Crowdsourcing Judgement Mechanism' *TRJCN*.com (2018) <https://news.trjcn.com/detail_194410.html> accessed 31 March 2023.

35 Aliyun, 'Ali Holds Public Hearings to Deal with Meaningless Reviews of Products' <https://developer.aliyun.com/article/621080> accessed 20 February 2024 (For instance, around 40,000 users have participated in a public hearing discussing whether the default delivery time of Taobao should be shortened; and if yes, how many days would be appropriate.)

36 17 U.S.C. § 512 (2006).

from liability upon the expeditious removal of the alleged infringing content, as long as formal criteria are met – hence its delineation as a "safe-harbor" provision.[37] Yet, in China, the expectations levied upon platforms become much higher. With the enactment of the *Tort Law of the People's Republic of China* (Tort Law) in 2009,[38] Chinese e-commerce platforms have been statutorily obligated under Article 36 to take timely "necessary measures" – where the list is inexhaustive but usually includes deletion, blocking, and disconnection – to notice-and-takedown requests.[39] Such requests can be grounded in various claims, including but not limited to those related to copyright, trademark, and patent infringement, as well as allegations of unfair competition. Failure of adherence precipitates liability. This broad application of the notice-and-takedown rule represents an expansion beyond the initial framework established by the *Regulation on the Protection of Rights to Information Network Communication* (Regulation) in 2006,[40] representing the inaugural codification of this rule within China, but exclusively addressing copyright concerns. However, Article 36 of the Tort Law does not delineate the procedural specifics akin to those articulated in Articles 14 to 17 of the Regulation, which prescribes detailed protocols for notifying alleged infringers, processing counter-notices, and the conditions to restore the once-removed links.

Following the promulgation of the Tort Law, a trend emerged among platforms to design and implement sophisticated IP dispute resolution frameworks, which are adept at handling the deluge of IP-related disputes.[41] A typical process entails a requisite registration and authentication of IP rights on the platform, necessitating documentary evidence of such rights. After verification, rights owners can efficiently report perceived infringements through the platform's interface. The platform, in turn, automates the transmission of notices to the alleged infringers, and, contingent on receipt of counter-notices, relays such responses back to the rights owners. Empirical data suggests a very short interregnum is typically afforded for the submission of counter-notices prior to the removal of disputed content.[42] In the absence of a timely counter-notice buttressed by exculpatory evidence, the

37 US Copyright Office, 'The Digital Millennium Copyright Act' <https://www.copyright.gov/dmca/> accessed 20 January 2024.

38 The Tort Law of People's Republic of China (promulgated by Standing Comm Nat'l People's Cong 26 December 2009, effective 1 July 2010, repealed 1 January 2021).

39 ibid art 36.

40 Regulation on the Protection of Rights to Information Network Communication (promulgated by St Council, 10 May 2006, effective 1 July 2006).

41 Alibaba Group, for example, launched the IP Protection Platform (ipp.alibaba.com) to provide IP rights owners with a portal to file and track complaints about IP infringement issues on multiple platforms, including Taobao, Tmall, and 1688.com. Pinduoduo has also launched the IP Protection Portal (ipp.pinduoduo.com) to streamline IP infringement complaints.

42 Songyin Bo, 'The Intellectual Property Dispute Resolution Mechanisms of E-Commerce Platforms in China' (Doctoral thesis, The Chinese University of Hong Kong 2023) (the author collected the public judgments from 2009–2023 where the liabilities of typical e-commerce platforms in China – Alibaba, Pinduoduo, and Weixin were at issue, and this conclusion is based on more than 1000 judgments collected).

platform is generally inclined to remove the flagged content expeditiously.[43] This protocol allows platforms to address the voluminous demands of IP disputes with alacrity – not solely to satisfy legal requirements but also to collect substantive data regarding the nature and frequency of disputes, and further facilitate platforms' substantive intervention in adjudicating complex and far-reaching cases.

With the maturity of the streamlined IP dispute resolution systems and the massive data repository, platforms realize that claims by IP rights owners can occasionally be inauthentic or malicious, intended to disrupt the commercial activities of the accused.[44] Furthermore, even substantiated claims by formal examination do not guarantee actual infringement. In instances where the products are removed under notices that fulfill procedural requirements, yet subsequent judicial determinations negate the existence of infringement, the interim wherein the products remain inaccessible can precipitate substantial financial detriment to both the accused infringing sellers and the platforms involved. In particularly convoluted or crucial cases, they interpret "necessary measures" more broadly than the enumerated measures – deletion, blocking, and disconnection. Instead, they practiced substantive examination of the products implicated before determining the proper measures to be taken, where they often enlisted neutral third-party experts to arbitrate, bringing enhanced scrutiny and impartiality to the resolution process.[45]

Empirical analyses reveal that in response to notices from patent rightsholders, Alibaba Group had enlisted the services of the Zhejiang Intellectual Property Right Research and Service Center (Center) – an entity affiliated with the Zhejiang Intellectual Property Administration (ZIPA) – to undertake assessments of the purported patent infringements for several years.[46] The courts normally adjudged Alibaba's recourse to the Center's expert evaluations as a requisite procedural safeguard. Even in instances where the Center's assessment led to an errant course of action – such as the non-removal of product listings based on the Center's determination of non-infringement,[47] or the delay in removing contentious links pending the Center's review[48] – the courts did not attribute liability to Alibaba. Instead, it was opined that Alibaba's initiative to procure and consider the Center's expertise satisfied its obligation to execute necessary measures. The foundation of the cooperative dynamic between Alibaba and ZIPA, established in 2011, facilitates the provision of expert opinions and patent search services regarding complex complaints

43 ibid.

44 ibid.

45 Ibid.

46 Ibid.

47 *Li Xianjun, Dongguan Wanjiang Simei Metal Products Factory, etc, v Wenzhou Xinda Gold Foil Crafts Co, Ltd etc*, in a Utility Model Patent Infringement Case (Guangzhou Intellectual Property Court 2016); *Yu Zuotao v Shanghai Happy Bird Sports Equipment Co, Ltd, Zhejiang Tmall Network Co, Ltd* in a Patent Infringement Case (Hangzhou Intermediate People's Court 2019).

48 *Yu Zuotao v Shanghai Qizhi Trading Co, Zhejiang Taobao Network Co, Ltd* in a Patent Infringement Case (Hangzhou Intermediate People's Court 2018); *Zhejiang Taobao Network Co, Ltd v Jinan Zuokang Shangmao Co, Ltd* in a Trademark Infringement Case (Jinan Intermediate People's Court 2017).

of invention and utility model patents submitted to Alibaba.[49] Leveraging this collaboration, the Center has assisted Alibaba in determining tens of thousands of alleged infringement cases, as well as in conducting analyses concerning patent stability.[50]

The enactment of the *E-Commerce Law of the People's Republic of China* (E-Commerce Law)[51] marks a significant juncture in delineating detailed criteria and procedures of the notice-and-takedown rule, such as the circulation of notices and counter-notices and the conditions for the revocation of necessary measures initially taken.[52] It extends the procedural ambit to an array of IP rights, thereby addressing the lacunae identified in Article 36 of the Tort Law. Article 42 of the E-Commerce Law stipulates the breadth of necessary measures surpassing those set forth in both the Regulation and the Tort Law. Subsequent case law also indicates a slight shift in judicial assessment regarding platforms' engagement with the Center in resolving patent infringement disputes. In a utility model patent case, the court viewed Alibaba's consultation with the Center as an earnest effort toward a substantive review of infringement notifications.[53] It acknowledged that "this kind of action help[ed] to filter part of the wrong notices, and to reach a balance among right owners, platforms, sellers and public interests to some extent."[54] However, the court further posited that reliance on such consultations did not inherently immunize platforms from liability.[55] Alibaba would be deemed accountable for the expert evaluations supplied by the Center, particularly those that are flawed.[56]

Two critical notions emerge from this ruling. First, the court acknowledges the substantial issue posed by erroneous or malicious notices. As a result, platforms are encouraged to adopt strategies mitigating potential impacts on bona fide sellers, the platform ecosystem, and broader public interests. Second, while consultation with entities such as the Center is commendable, platforms must be prepared to assume responsibility for relying on the guidance received. This underscores the need for a balanced approach between initiative and accountability in such ODR processes.

Pinduoduo, despite its more recent establishment, also initiated a collaboration in 2020 with the Shanghai Intellectual Property Administration (SIPA) to expedite

49 Liu Bin and Chen Qiang, 'Theoretical Analysis and Institutional Design of Intellectual Property Protection Provided by Online Trading Platforms' [2014 Soc Sci Res 16–17.

50 Intellectual Property Development & Research Center of CNIPA, 'China E-Commerce intellectual Property Protection Development Research Report (2021)' (CNIPA, April 2022) <https://www.cnipa-ipdrc.org.cn/article.aspx?id=703> accessed 29 January 2024.

51 The E-Commerce Law of the People's Republic of China (promulgated by Standing Comm Nat'l People's Cong 26 December 2009, effective 1 July 2010).

52 ibid art 42–43.

53 *Cixi Bosheng Plastic Products Co, Ltd v Xie Hui, etc.* in a Utility Model Patent Dispute (Ningbo Intermediate People's Ct 2020) ("Cixi Bosheng Case").

54 ibid.

55 ibid.

56 ibid.

the resolution of patent disputes.[57] Through a streamlined bespoke channel, allegations of patent infringement submitted to Pinduoduo are formalized and conveyed to SIPA, with its experts rendering expedited rulings, usually within two months, significantly more rapidly than traditional civil litigation.[58] Notably, decisions made accordingly bear "the weight of an official authority,"[59] rendering them as authoritative as SIPA's conventional administrative rulings. The collaboration between e-commerce platforms and IP authorities signifies a groundbreaking initiative at the global level by China's e-commerce platforms to counteract the adverse effects of inaccurate and malicious complaints. It also highlights the willingness of IP authorities to support e-commerce platforms in addressing challenges such as the need and inability to adjudicate patent infringement disputes and streamline the ODR process. While both Alibaba and Pinduoduo have sought to harness the expertise of IP authorities in patent disputes, the ramifications of SIPA's and the Center's determinations differ substantially for both patentees and exclusive licensees, and e-commerce platforms. Patentees and their exclusive licensees benefiting from an affirmative administrative ruling by SIPA on the presence of infringement possess a potent instrument in subsequent takedown requests.

These administrative findings obviate the need for repeated substantive analyses in future disputes involving the same parties. In contrast, a conclusion of infringement by the Center does not wield equivalent consequential authority in successive disputes. The implications for the e-commerce platforms are also different. Alibaba, when confronted with litigation for non-removal of contested listings, may assert adherence to the Center's expert position. Nonetheless, should such a position be invalidated by the court, liability may still ensue to Alibaba for soliciting and consequently relying upon the third party's flawed guidance. By comparison, SIPA's decisions – carrying the force of formal administrative rulings – compel compliance, and Pinduoduo is likely to evade culpability upon the demonstration of obedience. Beyond consultations with IP administrations, e-commerce platforms in China also broaden the interpretation of "necessary measures" by securing a deposit and freezing future revenues from sellers alleged to have infringed upon a utility model patent in lieu of removing contested listings.[60] In the Cixi Bosheng case, Alibaba, upon receipt of a counter-notice, stipulated a one million Chinese yuan deposit from the seller and claimed to freeze the storefront's revenues commencing from the onset of the "Double 11" sales event within its Alipay account, conditionally foregoing the removal.[61] From a comparative ODR perspective, this

57 'Shanghai Intellectual Property Administration Signs a Memorandum of Understanding with Pinduoduo, Will Form Deep Collaboration with Pinduoduo in 15 Aspects' (*Sohu*, 26 April 2020) <https://www.sohu.com/a/391269798_120244154> accessed 20 January 2024.

58 Pinduoduo, '2021 Review of Notorious Markets for Counterfeiting and Piracy: Comments Submitted by Pinduoduo' (Pinduoduo 2021) ("2021 Notorious Markets Comments by Pinduoduo") <https://www.regulations.gov/comment/USTR-2021-0013-0074> accessed 20 January 2024.

59 ibid.

60 Cixi Bosheng Case (n 53).

61 ibid.

represents a distinctive approach by China's e-commerce platforms in addressing IP disputes, striving to strike a balance among the interests of diverse stakeholders. The judiciary recognized Alibaba's measures as prudent and rational since conventional actions such as deletions or disconnection were not always suitable to judiciously mediate the rights and interests of all stakeholders involved.[62] The imposed deposit, alongside the freezing of future revenue, was structured to encompass any monetary reliefs arising from the IP infringements.[63] Notably, the sum "exceeded conventional judicial requisites for preserving property rights," ensuring a comprehensive reparation for the patent owners.[64] Meanwhile, this approach preserved the seller's operational continuity, protecting their revenue flow, which was particularly pivotal during significant commercial events like the "Double 11" festival.[65] Alibaba's expeditious response mirrors the effect of court-ordered property preservation, but eliminates the seller's need for a lengthy and complicated legal application process. In fact, the patent owner's lack of subsequent injunctive pursuit over five months – following Alibaba's decision and until the judgment, tacitly indicated his approval of the platform's mediated solution.

In conclusion, platforms have not merely conformed to the notice-and-takedown requirements but have proactively enhanced their role in IP dispute resolution through diversified mediation methodologies. Platforms have underscored their regulatory autonomy by adopting unprecedented measures such as seeking guidance from IP authorities and leveraging financial deposits as collateral against the removal of contested links. Such innovation attempts to form a harmonious equilibrium of interests among the right owners, sellers, platforms, and the public good. Another salutary effect of these proactive initiatives in IP dispute resolution is the aggregation of extensive data, which reveals patterns and frequencies of infringement alongside identifying repeated infringers. This intelligence has catalyzed the "three-strikes" policies that result in service termination for sellers after three substantiated infringement complaints, thus strengthening enforcement mechanisms.[66] Significantly, the analysis of infringement data has also enabled platforms to bolster their ex-ante monitoring and filtration capabilities, proactively identifying and removing hundreds of thousands of listings containing potential infringements, often before any damages are caused.[67] Hence, while dispute resolution efficiency and diversification remain integral, the paradigm has shifted beyond mere reactive solutions. Platforms now increasingly deploy the intelligence gathered through data analytics – and apply advanced computational technologies – to anticipate and

62 ibid.
63 ibid.
64 ibid.
65 ibid.
66 Major e-commerce platforms such as Alibaba, JD.COM, Pinduoduo all adopt the "three-strikes" rule to curb repeated infringers.
67 Alibaba, '2022 Alibaba Annual Report on Intellectual Property Protection' (Alibaba Group 2023) <https://files.alicdn.com/tpsservice/5940733116dc7fd7fadcf72754e4ba1f.pdf?spm=a2o2l.8248579.0.0.361c747buwkEs1&file=5940733116dc7fd7fadcf72754e4ba1f.pdf> accessed 24 January 2024.

forestall disputes at source, transitioning toward a more preventative approach to IP rights protection.

II. The Hallmarks of ODR Evolution in China

The evolution of platform-based ODR systems in China reflects a nuanced interplay between business imperatives and legal requirements. The two elements are not separate but rather form an interactional dynamic, which is particularly evident in the development of IP dispute resolution systems. Platforms established such systems to comply with legal requirements, but the subsequent development predominantly reflects the business concerns, concurrently contributing to the enhancement of existing legislation and codification of new rules. Moreover, the dynamic evolution of legal requirements also catalyzes platforms to continually advance their ODR methodologies, with a pronounced focus on IP dispute resolution and prevention. The reciprocal influence witnessed between legislative developments and the ODR evolution becomes a hallmark of ODR's trajectory in China.

Although platforms initially streamlined their IP dispute resolution platforms to meet the substantial influx of notice-and-takedown requests as required to avoid liability, they have progressively expanded upon the notion of "necessary measures" through a diversity of innovative techniques, beyond those enumerated in the Tort Law and E-Commerce Law.[68] Channeling expert consultation in intricate patent disputes and employing measures such as financial deposits and frozen revenues to obviate link removals are hallmarks of this expanded approach. Such measures have first garnered judicial support and were subsequently echoed by national policy directives. For instance, the *Guiding Opinion on the Trial of Intellectual Property Civil Cases Involving E-Commerce Platforms* (Guiding Opinion 2020) issued by the Supreme People's Court suggests that necessary measures should be based on the principle of reasonable prudence, extending beyond mere deletion, blocking, disconnection, and termination of services.[69] Meanwhile, platforms' engagement with erroneous or malicious notices – increasingly through substantive product reviews – has elucidated the gravity of this concern and the need for legislative attention. Legislative responses, starting from the E-Commerce Law, assign liability to those who send erroneous and damaging notices, with additional punitive damages for malicious action.[70] The Guiding Opinion 2020 of the People's Supreme Court further legitimizes platforms' right to seek redress against complainants sending erroneous and malicious notices and clarifies that such claims are to be concurrently heard with related IP disputes.[71] The platform's empirical

68 Article 36 of the Tort Law enumerates several measures such as deletion, blocking, and disconnection, while those enumerated in Article 42 of the E-Commerce Law are deletion, blocking, disconnection, and termination of service.

69 Guiding Opinion on the Trial of Intellectual Property Civil Cases Involving E-Commerce Platforms (promulgated by the Supreme People's Court, 10 September 2020) art 3.

70 The E-Commerce Law (n 51) art 42, para 3.

71 The Guiding Opinion 2020 (n 69) art 6.

insights, drawn from their business experience, serve to apprise regulatory bodies of emerging requirements, thereby playing an instrumental role in advancing the regulations previously unaddressed.

As e-commerce platforms continue to revamp the ODR frameworks, regulatory authorities reciprocate by entrusting the platforms with increasing responsibilities, especially concerning the prevention of disputes – fueled by confidence in the platforms' capabilities. Initially, platforms were simply suggested by the regulations to suppress repeated infringements and conspicuous infringements of copyrights, especially those affecting renowned creative works and recordings.[72] However, courts have occasionally held platforms liable for not proactively curbing the resurgence of the same infringing links.[73] Therefore, in practice, platforms are obligated to establish, at a minimum, tailored monitoring and filtration systems to thwart repeated infringement occurrences. The People's Supreme Court validated this approach within its Guiding Opinion 2020, essentially upholding practices that leading platforms had already adopted – implementing sophisticated technical measures to intercept links containing terms indicative of counterfeits or knock-offs, alongside the constant proactive removal of the repeated infringing links even without new takedown notices from rights owners.[74] This standard, while reflective of major platform practices, is additionally imparted on smaller platforms, intending to elevate the industry benchmarks. Other courts also escalated the requirement for scrutiny of content associated with well-known trademarks or showing conspicuous signs of infringement.[75] Leveraging the advanced technological prowess of e-commerce platforms, the legal and judicial systems are increasingly raising the expectations for these platforms to utilize their capacities in preventing infringement.

In an effort to facilitate dispute prevention, platforms are increasingly collaborating with rights owners, particularly those holding well-known trademarks. This collaboration allows platforms to gather detailed insights and observe emerging patterns of infringing activities. Consequently, platforms can swiftly identify and remove infringing content, contributing to a more effective prevention of disputes.[76] Platforms are also proactively partnering with law enforcement agencies to facilitate the tracking of entities engaged in the production and distribution of

72 Provisions of the SPC on Several Issues Concerning the Application of Law to Trial of Civil Dispute Cases of Infringement of Information Network Communication Right (promulgated by the Supreme People's Court, 17 December 2012, effective 1 January 2013).

73 *Wang Zhongming v Hangzhou Alibaba Advertisement Co, Ltd* in a Trademark Infringement Case (Guangzhou Intellectual Property Court 2017); *Shenzhen Xuanwei Electronic Co, Ltd, Zhejiang Tmall Network Co Ltd, v Haojun in a Design Patent Infringement Case* (Guangdong High People's Court 2014).

74 The Guiding Opinion 2020 (n 69) art 11.

75 *Guangzhou Junhe Commerce Co, Ltd v Xie Heyue etc* in a Trademark Case (Shanghai Xuhui People's Court, 7 May 2022).

76 For instance, Alibaba establishes the Alibaba Anti-Counterfeit Alliance (AACA), and Pinduoduo establishes Brand Care Program to collaborate with brand owners to prevent counterfeits.

infringing goods beyond the digital sphere.[77] These cooperative ventures represent a comprehensive approach to infringement control, shifting the focus of dispute resolution from mere closure to proactive prevention.[78]

III. The Driving Forces Behind China's ODR Landscape

The foregoing analysis elucidates the reciprocal dynamics between platform-driven ODR development and legislative progress, underscoring the critical interdependence of business incentives and authorities' endorsement in shaping the ODR framework in China. The impetus behind platform initiatives to cultivate ODR systems is relatively clear; however, the rationale for authorities' support of ODR's evolution warrants further examination. The following discussion thus concentrates on the motivations underlying platforms' initiatives and authorities' endorsement of ODR development.

To start with, the necessity to manage the voluminous disputes innate to the platform economy justifies the establishment and evolutionary precedence of indigenous ODR systems over formal regulation. Consequently, when pioneering such systems, platforms enjoyed significant freedom to adapt and refine their ODR processes, resonating with their distinctive operational models and the burgeoning complexities of digital commerce.[79] Alibaba's integration of crowdsourced judgment, which bolstered not only procedural efficiency but also user engagement, epitomizes this trend and has been mirrored by other platforms, including Tencent and specialized mediation entities like Kleros.[80] The IP dispute resolution systems, on the other hand, started from China's unprecedented application of the notice-and-takedown rule across copyright, trademark, and patent infringements,[81] which imposes a unique onus on platforms. This extensive regulatory purview prompts platforms to navigate the intricacies of IP disputes, exacerbated by potentially substantial damages caused by erroneous and malicious notices – issues that are particularly acute concerning trademark and patent infringement notices. In addressing such notices, platforms are challenged to mitigate potential injustices while optimizing cost-effectiveness. Subsequent innovations, born from necessity,

77 Alibaba (n 67) (Alibaba, for example, assisted law enforcement in 2123 cases in 2022, leading to the arrest of 2737 criminal suspects).

78 Kevin Strom, 'Research on the Impact of Technology on Policing Strategy in the 21st Century' Final Report No 251140 (National Criminal Justice Reference Service, May 2016).

79 Chuanman You and Qingxiu Bu, 'Transformative Digital Economy, Responsive Regulatory Innovation and Contingent Network Effects: The Anatomy of E-Commerce Law in China' (2022) 31 Euro Bus L Rev 725, 762.

80 Tencent, '2020 Weixin Copyright Protection Report' (Tencent 2020) <https://ipr.tencent.com/report/content?id=44> (Weixin adopts the crowdsourced judgment mechanism – Collegial Mechanism – to resolve article-spinning disputes since December 2018); Luis Bergolla, Karen Seif and Can Eken, 'Kleros: A Socio-Legal Case Study of Decentralized Justice & Blockchain Arbitration' (2022) 37 Ohio St J Disp Resol (Kleros also offers a decentralized blockchain-based arbitration solution that relies on smart contracts and crowdsourced judgments).

81 The Tort Law (n 38) art 36.

prioritize a balance among the interests of rights owners, sellers, and platforms themselves. Herein, the complexities encountered and addressed by platforms serve as experiential datasets, enabling regulatory bodies to refine existing statutes and fortify China's reputation in IP rights enforcement. Such a partnership delineates a progressive regulatory ethos, one that entwines the empirical heft of platform experiences with the aspirational trajectory of legal standards.

Another reason for regulatory bodies to support the overall expansion of ODR is the acknowledgment of private platforms' pivotal role in the governance of cyberspace[82] and their proficiency in advancing various national policies. These platforms have demonstrated to authorities their adeptness in swiftly addressing digital challenges, emphasizing how, by optimally leveraging the platforms' governance capabilities, the authorities could achieve more substantial outcomes.[83] A case in point is the integration of the platform-developed ODR systems into the broader national strategy of establishing the DDR mechanism since 2014, where non-litigation approaches and the prevention of disputes are highlighted.[84] Platforms have notably contributed to the DDR by alleviating the pressure on limited judicial resources through the resolution of myriad internal disputes via ODR systems. The engagement of a broad user base in platforms' decision-making processes, exemplified by crowdsourced judgment, also aligns with the DDR's multiplicity of adjudicatory approaches.[85] Furthermore, platforms' preventative measures, informed by comprehensive dispute data analytics, correspond with the DDR's proactive stance on preventing conflicts.[86] And authorities can also capitalize on platforms' extensive data collection capabilities to advance their regulatory objectives.

Another illustrative example is the Beijing E-Commerce Cross-Platform Prevention and Management System, established in 2021 by BAMR, mandating over 20 prominent e-commerce platforms to upload IP infringers' information to the system.[87] The predecessor of this system – the Joint Prevention and Management Mechanism – was established in 2020 to mitigate the proliferation of counterfeit

82 See Jack Goldsmith and Tim Wu, *Who Controls the Internet? Illusions of a Borderless World* (OUP 2006) 60; Jean-Christophe Plantin and Others, 'Infrastructure Studies Meet Platform Studies in the Age of Google and Facebook' (2018) 20(1) New Med Soc 893.

83 See Laura Denardis, *The Global War for Internet Governance* (OUP 2014) 78; Nicolas Suzor and Others, 'Evaluating the Legitimacy of Platform Governance: A Review of Research and A Shared Research Agenda' (2018) 80(4) Int Comm Gazette 385.

84 Such goal was brought up in the Fourth Plenary Session of the 18th Central Committee of the CPC in the "Decision of the Central Committee of the CPC on Several Major Issues Concerning Comprehensively Promoting the Rule of Law; see also, Zhiqiong June Wang and Jianfu Chen, *Dispute Resolution in the People's Republic of China* (Brill 2020).

85 ibid.

86 ibid.

87 '21 Major E-Commerce Platforms Joined the Recently Released Cross-Platform Prevention and Management System in Beijing' (*www.cqc.com.cn*, 5 August 2021) <https://www.cqn.com.cn/zj/content/2021-08/05/content_8720699.htm> accessed 20 January 2024.

COVID-19 prevention products.[88] Its contemporary form primarily serves as a nexus for data aggregation, reporting repeated infringers, and promoting data exchange among all platforms involved.[89] Looking ahead, there is potential for augmented applications predicated on data procured through private platforms, which is more streamlined and efficient than direct collection by the system, thereby offering a foundation for future enhancements of functionalities within the system's architecture. In essence, platforms' sovereignty and efficacy within their ecosystems may have enlightened the authorities to leverage their capabilities to reinforce national policies such as DDR and IP protection, and such strategic collaboration may extend into more domains moving forward.

IV. The Implication of China's ODR in Global Dispute Resolution Development

The impact of platform-based ODR extends well beyond facilitating access to justice and reducing the strain on judicial systems but exerts a profound effect on the global landscape of dispute resolution. The evolution and enhancement of ODR systems, particularly those leveraging advanced technological capabilities like data management and blockchain for evidence preservation, could be the cornerstone of the development of online litigation and arbitration. The success of the ODR systems of Taobao facilitated the inception of the three Internet Courts in China.[90] These courts signify a groundbreaking shift by taking the entire judicial process online, setting a precedent for other courts and arbitration institutions to embrace comprehensive digitalization.[91] This digitalization, reflected in the "Smart Court systems," encapsulates a full suite of procedures from case filing to judgment delivery conducted electronically.[92] Leading technologies, such as cloud computing, blockchain, and AI services originally employed by various types of platforms, have not only demonstrated the viability of online legal proceedings but also contributed directly to the Smart Court systems' development. Technology companies owned by Alibaba Group, for example, provided specialized cloud and blockchain services – the "Judicial Cloud" and "Judicial Chain" – for courts in Zhejiang Province.[93] Likewise, Tencent's united judicial cloud platform supplies

88 National IP Administration IP Development Research Center, 'China E-Commerce Intellectual Property Protection Development Research Report (2020)' (2020) <http://cnipa-ipdrc.org.cn/UpLoad/2021-01/2021118163250.pdf> accessed 20 January 2024.

89 '21 Major E-Commerce Platforms Joined the Recently Released Cross-Platform Prevention and Management System in Beijing' (n 87).

90 Shang and Guo (n 20) 29.

91 The Supreme People's Court of the People's Republic of China, *Chinese Courts and Internet Judiciary* (People's Court Press 2019) 63.

92 Opinions of the Supreme People's Court on Deepening the Comprehensive and Supporting Reform of the Judicial System of the People's Courts – Outline of the Fifth Five-Year Reform of the People's Courts (2019–2023) (issued by the SPC, February 2019).

93 Cui Yadong, *Artificial Intelligence and the Modernization of Judiciary* (Shanghai People's Press 2019) 99–100.

a broad range of Chinese courts with cloud computing and storage, and AI services across the country.[94] Similar to litigation, arbitration institutions such as the China International Economic and Trade Arbitration Commission (CIETAC)[95] and the Shanghai Arbitration Commission[96] have refined their frameworks to embrace online processes, which the necessities are amplified during the COVID-19 pandemic through the provision of virtual hearings and digital case management. In essence, the relationship between private platform-generated technologies and the systems of online litigation and arbitration underscores a trend where privately pioneered approaches offer a blueprint for state-endorsed digital legal infrastructures. While in-person interactions within arbitration and court proceedings retain their value post-pandemic, streamlined processes, including electronic filing and judgment delivery, could continue to be useful due to their convenience and efficiency. And such procedural modernization cannot be achieved without the platforms' technological innovations in ODR systems.

The burgeoning sphere of ODR on private digital platforms, particularly concerning IP disputes, also stands as a prominent exemplar within the discourse on co-regulatory models in e-commerce. Co-regulation, a conceptual model entrenched in "New Governance" theory,[97] interrogates the evolving roles of government and multi-stakeholder participation within the expansive global economy.[98] This model showcases a growing awareness toward collaboration of public and private entities, marking a shift from rigid government hierarchies and prescriptive regulations to a network of negotiated norms and eclectic dispute resolution tactics.[99] Encapsulating this shift, co-regulation is delineated as a mechanism "whereby a legislative act entrusts the attainment of the objective defined by the legislative authority to parties which are recognized in the field" – ranging from economic operators to non-governmental organizations.[100] This approach requires private platforms to regulate specific on-platform activities, bolstered by government-prescribed frameworks and oversight procedures,[101] thus circumventing the regulatory vacuum often inherent in self-regulation.[102] In such a collaborative dynamic, the platforms embrace quasi-public functions in the designated aspects, maximizing regulatory

94 ibid.

95 The online case-filing and virtual hearing services are available on its official website: <http://www.cietac.org/>

96 Shanghai Arbitration Commission provides "Smart Arbitration" service where all arbitration processes could be conducted online <https://www.accsh.org/arbviewen/>

97 See De Búrca Graínne and Joanne Scott, 'Introduction: New Governance, Law and Constitutionalism' in Graínne De Búrca and and Joanne Scott (eds), *Law and the New Governance in the EU and US* (Bloomsbury 2006).

98 Julia Black, 'Constructing and Contesting Legitimacy and Accountability in Polycentric Regulatory Regimes' (2008) 2 Reg Govern 137; Julia Black, 'Regulatory Conversations' (2002) 29 JL Soc 163.

99 Lester Salamon, *The Tools of Government: A Guide to the New Governance* (OUP 2001) 1–18.

100 2003 Interinstitutional Agreement on Better Law-Making, OJ C 321, para 18 (2003).

101 Hanneke Van Schooten and Jonathan Verschuuren, *International Governance and Law: State Regulation and Non-State Law* (Edward Elgar Publishing 2008) 2.

102 Finck (n 8); Orla Lynskey, 'Regulation Platform Power' (2017) Les Legal Studies Working Paper No 1/2017 <https://papers.ssrn.com/sol3/papers.cfm?abstract_id=2921021>

efficacy and precision. Co-regulation also emphasizes outcome-oriented regulation, where authorities establish objectives via standards, while platforms are vested with the discretion to formulate and implement suitable strategies for implementation.[103] This paradigm acknowledges the advantages of engaging a diverse assembly of stakeholders in the iterative process of policy formation, norm creation, and oversight, thereby refining contemporary digital governance.

In the Chinese context, the evolution of ODR offers a valuable lens through which to examine co-regulation in action. To start with, the platforms have become active contributors to the rule-making and standard-setting processes. With a long-standing history of innovation in information technology and new business models, Chinese platforms have advanced in consumer trust and IP infringement mechanisms. These include the development of peer-review systems and the adoption of crowdsourced judgment – a tool inviting broad user participation that exemplifies equitable and efficient dispute resolution. Their practices also catalyze legislative and judicial refinements as they keep exploring the appropriate implementation of ambiguous regulations and highlighting to authorities the emerging need for new regulatory measures.

Second, Chinese authorities realize that to achieve a successful co-regulation framework, not only do platforms exercise significant governance functions, but the state also needs to ensure oversight and support to facilitate the fulfillment of platforms' responsibilities. For example, the platforms are required to verify and register sellers' identities, where the verification of individuals' identities is particularly challenging. China, therefore, grants these platforms access to the national ID database to facilitate the verification process and ensure user authenticity. Pinduoduo explains that it "incorporates live facial recognition to verify the identity of individuals and integrated nationwide databases to cross-check the identity," underscoring the collaborative nature of co-regulatory approaches.[104] The synergistic relationships are also reflected by the collaboration between platforms and IP administrations in resolving complex patent disputes, where the benefits are manifold for platforms, disputants, and administrative and judicial authorities. Additionally, in response to the complexities presented by the implementation of the notice-and-takedown rule within the patent domain – specifically concerning the intrinsically unstable utility model and design patent infringements[105] – the National Intellectual Property Administration (NIPA) initiated a pilot program in 2021.[106] This program provided access for Alibaba and JD.COM to the National

103 Finck (n 8).

104 '2021 Notorious Markets Comments by Pinduoduo' (n 58).

105 In the context of Chinese patent law, utility model and design patents are granted based upon a formal examination rather than a substantive one. Therefore, the situation arises when rights are conferred despite the patent owners' awareness of the illegitimacy of their claims – a practice sometimes adopted to disrupt market order and impede competitors' business operations.

106 'The Reply of the National Intellectual Property Office to No 7626 Question from the Fourth Session of the Thirteenth National People's Congress' (National Intellectual Property Administration Official Website, 12 July, 2021) <https://www.cnipa.gov.cn/art/2021/7/15/art_516_165909.html?xxgkhide=1> accessed 20 January 2024.

Patent Evaluation Report (PER) database to aid in effectively navigating these challenges.[107] PERs issued by the NIPA are usually used by utility model and design patent owners to ascertain the validity of their patents.[108] And platforms' direct access to the PER database enables them to both authenticate the PERs presented by rights owners – thereby guarding against falsified PERs – and assess the validity of the patent rights when PERs are not submitted beforehand. This capability enhances platforms' efficiency in addressing notice-and-takedown requests and simultaneously mitigates the incidence of erroneous and malicious complaints, which could feasibly be extended to other prominent platforms in the future.

These practices thus contextualize China's ODR systems as a rich contribution to co-regulation theory and Internet governance. Platforms, vested with increasing regulatory responsibilities due to their technological preeminence, are supported by the authorities through collaborative arrangements ranging from judicial recognition to the provision of database access and professional assistance. In this framework, innovative processes like crowdsourced judgment also address the challenges of limited stakeholder engagement in co-regulation.[109] The proactive measures taken by platforms for dispute prevention are deeply interwoven with collaborative efforts involving multi-stakeholders – ranging from IP administrations to IP rights owners and law enforcement agencies. Although the collaboration between IP authorities and platforms may be unique in China due to the unprecedented implementation of the notice-and-takedown rule concerning patents, the co-regulatory paradigm of China's ODR initiatives still offers valuable insights that transcend national legal specificities. For example, crowdsourced judgment can elevate the transparency, fairness, and efficiency of the dispute resolution process. Furthermore, platforms may assume greater responsibility in authenticating user identities, thereby mitigating fraud and reinforcing the enforcement of resolutions rendered by platform-based ODR systems. Additionally, enhanced cooperation between platforms and law enforcement authorities can be mutually beneficial: platforms can aid in tracing the production and distribution networks of unlawful and counterfeit merchandise, while law enforcement can support platforms in eradicating the presence of illicit sellers within digital marketplaces. Collectively, China's approach to ODR offers global insights into an emerging, efficient model of co-regulation in the field of e-commerce and beyond.

Indeed, platform-based ODR systems in China represent a pioneering approach to leveraging technology within the extrajudicial domain,[110] garnering acclaim internationally.[111] However, as with any nascent framework operating at the

107 ibid.

108 Li Shuo, 'Utility Model Patent Evaluation Report' (National IP Administration, 13 April 2017) <https://www.cnipa.gov.cn/transfer/pub/old/wxfw/zlwxxxggfw/gyjz/gyjzkj/201706/P020170602562910773832.pdf> accessed 25 January 2024.

109 Liu Peng, 'Use the Internet to Regulate Internet: The Rise of the Regulation Power of Third-Party Platforms and the Logics Behind' (2021) 5 Govern Stud 51, 57.

110 Shang and Guo (n 20).

111 For example, Alibaba became the only non-American company that received a U.S. government award – the IPR Center Private Sector Partnership Award from the IPR Center – and the efforts of

intersection of law, technology, and commerce, challenges arise that warrant careful consideration and strategic response. One pressing concern revolves around the substantial authority accorded to private platforms, operating with broad discretion to shape the resolution process. This delegation raises questions about the privacy of users as platforms navigate vast repositories of personal data, illuminating the need for robust privacy protections and oversight to prevent misuse.[112] And ensuring privacy within ODR mechanisms without impeding their effectiveness remains a complex balance to achieve. Second, while crowdsourced judgment has been introduced by several platforms, its application remains constricted to a narrow band of disputes. Consequently, the preponderance of conflicts is still adjudicated via automated systems and traditional customer service – methods that may lack transparency and can sometimes bring into question the equity of outcomes.[113] An expansion of crowdsourced mechanisms to broader dispute types could not only democratize the adjudicatory process but also reinforce the communal fabric of platform governance by empowering a wider user base to contribute to the ODR ecosystem.

Additionally, platforms are encumbered with ever-expanding responsibilities for dispute prevention, including the proactive identification and removal of what are perceived as conspicuous infringements. Expanding such preventive measures places enormous pressure on platforms, to maintain vigilant general monitoring and filtration. It also risks a potential overreach in censorship that could stifle legitimate e-commerce activities. Conversely, platforms were barely held liable by courts for the failure to fulfill dispute prevention liability, and authorities offered minimal incentives or recognition in exchange for the substantial responsibilities shouldered by the platforms.[114] In the future, legislators should exercise prudence when contemplating imposing more duties upon platforms in dispute prevention, by weighing the imperative to fortify IP protections against the potential impact on the vitality of commercial activities, especially for the new entrants to the market. Furthermore, rather than augmenting the burdens on platforms, authorities might consider periodic assessments of platform efficacy in dispute prevention and disclosing the results of such assessments to the public.[115] This approach would stimulate informed choices by consumers, IP rights owners, and sellers, opting for platforms demonstrating superior performance, which would consequently

Pinduoduo in resolving IP disputes have been appraised by the International Anti-Counterfeiting Coalition and Union des Fabricants (Unifab). See 'IPR Center Announces Recipients of 2020 Partnership Awards for Combating Intellectual Property, Trade Fraud Crimes at Inaugural Awards Ceremony' (U.S. Immigration and Customs Enforcement, 19 November 2020) <https://www.ice.gov/news/releases/ipr-center-announces-recipients-2020-partnership-awards-combatingintellectual> accessed 25 January 2024, and '2020 Review of Notorious Markets for Counterfeiting and Piracy: Comments Submitted by Pinduoduo' (USTR, 8 November 2020) <https://www.regulations.gov/comment/USTR-2020-0035-0007> accessed 25 January 2024.

112 'The Perils of Making New Media the Philosopher King' (n 11) 285.

113 ibid.

114 Peng (n 109) 58.

115 ibid.

incentivize platforms to voluntarily bolster IP protection measures.[116] Another concern is pertinent to the notice-and-takedown process, which was initially instituted to ensure the swift enforcement of IP rights, but could potentially be compromised due to the prolonged resolution time if platforms refer disputes to IP authorities for adjudication. Therefore, platforms must select discreetly which disputes necessitate referral to the IP authorities and establish expedited channels with them to resolve the disputes effectively.

Conclusion

The ramifications of ODR systems in China transcend the conventional boundaries of dispute resolution practices. These systems have commendably addressed disputes arising from online transactions, employing crowdsourced judgment to enhance the transparency and efficacy of the resolution processes, and have been instrumental in meeting legal requirements related to IP infringement with notable fairness. In the case of ambiguous or lagging regulations, ODR platforms have moved beyond mere compliance and have been actively engaged in the shaping of regulations through strategic alliances forged with IP authorities and the adoption of creative solutions, which also highlights the platforms' commitment to reconciling the diverse interests of multiple parties involved. However, the progression of ODR systems, particularly in preventive measures, is not without its complexities. It has been an iterative process, shaped in response to the increasing expectations from the judiciary, with the dual objectives of advancing IP rights protection with the assistance of multi-stakeholders and maintaining system efficiency, albeit at the expense of placing high demands on the platforms.

While ODR systems in China have achieved considerable success, challenges persist. Concerns such as privacy issues, lack of transparency in decision-making, the burden on platforms in dispute prevention, and delays in IP authorities' determinations pose hurdles. Addressing these concerns requires a collaborative effort among stakeholders to find innovative solutions. Despite these challenges, the implications of ODR in China are far-reaching. It not only enabled the establishment of online litigation and arbitration systems but also exemplified the effectiveness of a multi-stakeholder approach in achieving co-regulation within the platform economy. The transformative power of technology, combined with the collective commitment of various players, has paved the way for a more efficient and accessible dispute resolution framework, and may further apply across various jurisdictions. As China continues to navigate the intricacies of ODR, it will continue to contribute to global paradigms of dispute resolution, IP protection, and co-regulation within the digital economy.

116 ibid.

Part E

International Law Perspectives

10 Navigating the Cryptosphere

Jurisdictional Uncertainty in Emerging Cross-Border Cryptocurrency Disputes

Abubakri Yekini

I. Introduction

The emergence of cryptocurrencies, blockchain technology and decentralised autonomous organisations (DAOs) has revolutionized global finance and commerce.[1] However, the borderless nature of these innovations also creates complex legal and regulatory challenges. This chapter examines the jurisdictional challenges that arise in the adjudication of cross-border cryptocurrency transactions facilitated through various channels, including peer-to-peer blockchain networks, exchange platforms and DAOs.

Cryptocurrencies represent a disruptive innovation that does not conform to traditional concepts of money or property.[2] Policymakers, legislators and courts across the globe have been grappling with the challenges brought by blockchain technology and Web 3.0 generally.[3] For private international law, which is the branch of law that deals with cross-border issues, legal commentators and judges have been challenged with the propriety of extant legal approaches to issues such as the appropriate jurisdictional grounds for crypto-related transactions, the choice of applicable law and enforcement of judgments against cryptoassets and exchanges.[4] While

1 See, generally, Joseph Lee, *Crypto-Finance, Law and Regulation: Governing an Emerging Ecosystem* (Routledge 2022); Abeba N Turi (ed), *Financial Technologies and DeFi: A Revisit to the Digital Finance Revolution* (Springer 2023); Gino Giambelluca, 'Blockchain: The Regulatory Challenges for Central Banks and Financial Sector' in B Cappiello and G Carullo (eds), *Blockchain, Law and Governance* (Springer 2021).

2 Law Commission, *Digital Assets: Final Report* (Law Com No 412, 2023) 42–55.

3 For a global overview of national legislative and judicial developments, see Permanent Bureau, 'Developments with respect to PIL Implications of the Digital Economy' Prel Doc No 4 Rev of January 2022, HCCH 2022. The text is available at <https://assets.hcch.net/docs/b06c28c5-d183-4d81-a663-f7bdb-8f32dac.pdf> accessed 25 August 2023.

4 ibid; King Fung Tsang, Chapter 11 in this volume; Andrea Bonomi, Matthias Lehmann and Shaheeza Lalani (eds), *Blockchain and Private International Law* (Brill 2023); Andrew Dickinson, 'Cryptocurrencies and the Conflict of Laws' in David Fox and Sarah Green (eds), *Cryptocurrencies in Public and Private Law* (OUP 2019); Giesela Rühl, 'Smart (Legal) Contracts, or: Which (Contract) Law for Smart Contracts?' in B Cappiello and G Carullo (eds), *Blockchain, Law and Governance* (Springer 2021) 159–80; Florence Guillaume, 'Aspects of Private International Law Related to Blockchain Transactions' in Daniel Kraus, Thierry Obrist and Olivier Hari (eds), *Blockchains, Smart Contracts,*

DOI: 10.4324/9781032618975-16

decentralisation and pseudonymity are integral to the development of the crypto industry, these concepts conflict with the core foundations of private international law (territorial connections) and international civil procedure (identity of litigants).

Case law from leading common law jurisdictions such as the United Kingdom and the United States has revealed that due to the cross-border nature of crypto transactions, most disputes often involve foreign elements.[5] This may involve the theft of cryptoassets from hackers who operate from unknown locations across the globe, claims between members of a DAO, claims against software developers or administrators of a DAO, and suits against exchanges for disclosure of wallet holders amongst others. The nature of these disputes indicates that private international law is central to typical crypto-related claims. For instance, when unauthorised cryptocurrency transfers occur, victims tend to sue in their home courts on the basis that the private keys are held in their home state, and thus the property is located in that state. Exchanges are regularly sued abroad on this basis as well. Since the defendants are usually from abroad, there might be needs to enforce judgments, disclosure orders, freezing orders amongst others against exchanges, and unknown persons domiciled abroad respectively.

DAOs have added another layer of complexity with the enabling of collaborative organisations to operate through encoded rules on blockchains without formal legal personality. When disputes emerge within a DAO's decentralised community, or between a DAO and external parties, jurisdictional uncertainty abounds since no defined legal entity or geographic boundaries exist. For regulated exchanges and DAOs with identifiable statutory seats, jurisdiction can be established through traditional connecting factors. Nevertheless, exchanges are faced with lawsuits globally as aggrieved users sue in their home countries, despite the attempts by exchanges to mitigate this risk through dispute resolution clauses.[6] Consumer protection laws often render these choice of court agreements unenforceable.

The thesis of this chapter is that the architecture of blockchain technology appears misaligned with the foundation of private international law, which relies on linking activities and territory. The chapter argues that for the cryptocurrency industry to develop sustainably, both technology and law may require adjustment. While retaining decentralisation, technical solutions enabling transparency and localisation may be desired. This could also assist states in developing an internationally harmonised legal framework that embraces cryptocurrencies' global nature and provides the legal certainty that is required for the development of the crypto industry.

This chapter is divided into five sections. Section II provides a theoretical foundation for the exercise of jurisdiction in private international law and the complexities

Decentralised Autonomous Organisations and the Law (Edward Elgar Publishing 2019) 49–82; Anurag Bana and Ammar Osmanourtashi, 'Blockchain and Private International Law: Implications for Crypto, Payment Systems, Digital Wallets and Jurisdictional Concerns' (2023) 24 Bus L Int'l 121.

5 See the cases discussed in sections III and IV of this chapter.

6 See, for instance, *Payward, Inc and others v Chechetkin* [2023] EWHC 1780 (Comm).

that Web 3.0 introduces. Section III examines emerging national court approaches to crypto jurisdiction and their implications. Section IV considers the challenges of enforcing cross-border crypto-related judgments and orders. Section V concludes the chapter by suggesting both legal and technical solutions to align blockchain architecture with private international law.

II Web 3.0 and Jurisdictional Challenges

A. Jurisdiction of Courts in Cryptoasset Transactions

One of the most settled principles of law is that a state has exclusive jurisdiction over any activities or transactions carried out within its borders.[7] However, beyond the territory of that state, a state's power is always limited.[8] This principle of territorial jurisdiction and limits to extraterritorial jurisdiction traces back to the post-Westphalian European settlement. It was deemed that respecting the sovereignty of states over their internal affairs was the best way to ensure good neighbourliness and prevent the reoccurrence of the devastating Thirty Years' War in Europe.[9] The Treaty of Westphalia, which ended this war, laid the foundation for modern international law.

The foundation of private international law was built on the idea of sovereignty and territoriality. For instance, under the traditional common law rules, a court would only exercise jurisdiction if the defendant is resident or present within the court's jurisdiction at the time the action commences, and the claimant is able to serve the court summons on the defendant.[10] Beyond the territorial connection of the defendant and the forum court, private international law rules also permit a state to exercise jurisdiction over a foreign defendant, but only in limited situations where the activities of the foreign defendant are substantially connected to the territory of that state.[11] To provide legal certainty regarding when a foreign defendant may be sued in a state, private international law scholars from the time of Savigny have identified some legal relations (e.g., contract, tort, family matters, etc.) and strived to establish what may be considered appropriate connections or links between the foreign defendant and the territory of the state (i.e., forum court) to warrant exercising jurisdiction over the conduct of the foreign defendant.[12]

7 *The Lotus Case (France vs Turkey)*, PCIJ, Series A, No 10 (1927).

8 ibid para 45.

9 A Yekini, *The Hague Judgments Convention and Commonwealth Model Law: A Pragmatic Perspective* (Hart Publishing 2021) 24.

10 Trevor C Hartley, 'Basic Principles of Jurisdiction in Private International Law: The European Union, the United States and England' (2022) 71 Int Comp LQ 211, 214.

11 See, for instance, the jurisdictional gateways under English civil procedure rules (Part 6, CPR). See also, Ardavan Arzandeh, '"Gateways" Within the Civil Procedure Rules and the Future of Service-Out Jurisdiction in England' (2019) 15 J Priv Int L 516.

12 Yekini (n 9) 58–59.

It is evident from the discussions in the preceding paragraphs that all of the private international law approaches are territorially defined, and it was never envisioned that any cross-border dispute could be resolved without reference or recourse to the legal system. The justification for territoriality in the 18th and 19th centuries was rooted in the doctrines of justice, fairness and effectiveness. In an era where moving from one territory to another came with great difficulty, it might be considered unfair and unjust to subject a defendant to undue hardship just to answer claims abroad. Therefore, it was generally not permitted to sue non-resident defendants. It would amount to a waste of scarce resources to also sue a defendant over whom the court does not have any control and against whom the court's judgment could not be directly enforced.[13]

With the increase in cross-border activities facilitated by globalisation, technological inventions and improved mass transit systems, it became permissible to assert jurisdiction over foreign defendants regarding their activities within the jurisdiction. This is often referred to as special jurisdiction, as the jurisdictional grounds are limited to the transactions of the foreign defendant in the territory of the forum court. These limited grounds are contained in the long-arm statutes or civil procedure rules in common law jurisdictions,[14] and similar grounds exist in most civil law jurisdictions.[15] Examples of such limited grounds include the place of performance of a contractual obligation, the place where a tort is committed or damage is suffered, and contractual submission to the court's jurisdiction, among others.

The advent of the internet further challenged the foundational approach of private international law altogether. The internet is ubiquitous, and it is difficult to pin activities down to specific territories. Let us consider the case of a UK buyer who bought software from a seller in China via the seller's website. Where is the location of this transaction? Is this a case of a Chinese seller selling their product in the United Kingdom via the internet, or a UK buyer travelling to China via the internet to buy the product in question? Although this question may appear simple, states have not been able to agree on acceptable territorial connections for internet jurisdiction to date.[16] While the challenges of the internet are yet to be resolved, the tech community introduced Web 3.0, adding another layer of complexity to the existing internet jurisdiction conundrum.

B. The Challenges

The rapid growth of cryptocurrencies has sparked a surge in cross-border transactions on exchange platforms and decentralised autonomous organisations. The

13 James Fawcett and Janeen M Carruthers, *Cheshire, North & Fawcett: Private International Law* (14th edn, OUP 2008) 354–55.

14 See Part 6 of the English Civil Procedure Rules.

15 For instance, see art 7, Brussels IA; Adrian Briggs, *The Conflict of Laws* (OUP 2019) 70–75.

16 Pedro De Miguel Asensio, *Conflict of Laws and the Internet* (Edward Elgar 2020) 32–33.

blockchain technology thrives on non-territorial connections, pseudonymity and anonymity, making it possible for users and participants to transact business in a decentralised environment. In addition, the transactions are processed, executed and/or stored simultaneously in several nodes located across the globe. This decentralised and globalised trading platform leads to significant jurisdictional challenges for courts worldwide. As transactions increasingly occur beyond national borders, determining which jurisdiction has the authority to adjudicate disputes becomes more complex.

As of November 2021, the global cryptoassets reached a market capitalisation of over US$2.8 trillion with over 221 million users.[17] On 21 November 2022, *The Guardian* reported the FTX's bankruptcy case in Delaware, USA. The report noted that the platform has about 1 million creditors globally and owed its 50 biggest creditors nearly $3.1bn (£2.6bn).[18] Apart from this high-profile case, an assessment of reported crypto-related disputes in the United Kingdom reveals the nature of the problems arising from transacting business in a decentralised, globalised ecosystem. There have been cases of unauthorized transfers of cryptoassets between exchange platforms,[19] fraudulent misappropriations of cryptoassets by unknown persons,[20] actions against the software developers,[21] operation of fake crypto investment platforms,[22] consumer actions regarding cryptoassets (NFTs) purchased abroad (online) amongst others.[23] The jurisdictional challenges in cross-border or, more accurately, borderless crypto transactions can be summarised as follows: what are the appropriate connections to determine the suitable forum for resolving crypto transaction disputes arising from peer-to-peer blockchain networks, exchange platforms and DAOs?

Concerning DAOs, disputes may arise between miners and developers regarding matters like altering mining algorithms, compensation for work completed or disagreements about protocol upgrades, among others. A dispute may equally arise amongst participants of an open-source online peer-to-peer platform (public blockchain networks) who directly trade cryptoassets globally without intermediaries. Despite the presumed notion that blockchain technology is self-executing and capable of resolving disputes through its built-in codes, this assumption proves

17 Erik Feyen, Yusaku Kawashima and Raunak Mittal, 'Crypto-Assets Activity Around the World Evolution and Macro-Financial Drivers' Policy Research Working Paper 9962 (World Bank Group, March 2022) 7–8.

18 'Crypto Exchange FTX Owes Nearly $3.1bn to 50 Biggest Creditors' *The Guardian* (21 November 2022) <https://www.theguardian.com/technology/2022/nov/21/crypto-exchange-ftx-creditors-cryptocurrency#:~:text=FTX%20and%20its%20affiliates%20filed,of%20alleged%20poor%20record%2Dkeeping.> accessed 29 August 2023.

19 *LMN v Bitflyer Holdings Inc* [2022] EWHC 2954 (Comm).

20 *A A v Persons Unknown* [2020] 1 WLUK 91, a case of the recovery of US $950,000 worth of bitcoin paid as ransom. See also, *D'Aloia v Persons Unknown* [2022] EWHC 1723 (Ch); *Osbourne v Persons Unknown & Ors* [2023] EWHC 340 (KB).

21 *Tulip Trading Ltd v Bitcoin Association for BSV* [2022] 3 WLUK 379.

22 *Jones v Persons Unknown* [2022] EWHC 2543 (Comm).

23 *Soleymani v Nifty Gateway LLC* [2022] EWCA Civ 1297.

to be misguided. Instances where disputes emanate from on-chain activities which necessitate human intervention (e.g., authorising or confirming transactions, or where developers are required to amend codes) render it evident that participants might inevitably seek the courts' intervention to compel specific actions.[24] This becomes pertinent when the supposedly self-executing software or codes fail to secure the performance of the required actions. Where such disputes arise, the real question is therefore which legal system has the appropriate regulatory, adjudicatory and prescriptive jurisdiction over on-chain and off-chain cryptoasset transactions.

The initial obstacle that is encountered in establishing relevant links for asserting jurisdiction over cryptoasset transactions is that most of these transactions are conducted online. This reintroduces the familiar hurdles associated with internet jurisdiction.[25] This is particularly challenging for transactions carried out on non-regulated public blockchain networks and virtual exchange platforms, whose specific locations cannot be determined. The existing internet jurisdiction solutions in various legal systems may not be perfectly suited for crypto transactions, because these transactions are carried out through global decentralised networks simultaneously across different countries.[26] Therefore, pinpointing the transactions to specific countries in order to identify the centre of gravity or closest connection is practically impossible.

For exchanges, the picture is much clearer. This category involves trading activities occurring on exchanges with a tangible physical presence in specific territories or states. In many cases, these exchanges or similar platforms are registered and organised under the laws of a particular state and often operate under regulatory oversight. However, while these platforms are registered in specific countries, their business operations often extend beyond their place of incorporation.[27] Thus, they may potentially be subjected to suits all over the world.

The second major challenge concerning asserting jurisdiction over foreign defendants in crypto transactions arises from the anonymity of the parties carrying out these transactions. Anonymity is an essential attribute of blockchain technology and the transactions conducted through it. This feature provides the participants with the necessary trust and confidence that underpin the technology's continued growth. However, courts typically require the identity of the defendant for several reasons. For instance, in common law countries, the court's jurisdiction is established through the proper service of the writ on the defendant.[28] Moreover, court

24 Rühl (n 4) 3–4; Cemre C. Kadioglu Kumtepe, 'A Brief Introduction to Blockchain Dispute Resolution' (2021) 14 J Marshall LJ 138, 142–43; Amy J Schmitz and Colin Rule, 'Online Dispute Resolution for Smart Contracts' (2019) 2019 J Disp Resol 103–5.

25 See, generally, Tobias Lutzi, *Private International Law Online: Internet Regulation and Civil Liability in the EU* (OUP 2020).

26 Guillaume (n 4) 59.

27 For instance, see the FTX bankruptcy case (n 19), where the exchange has about 1 million creditors globally even though its place of business is Delaware, the United States.

28 Briggs (n 15) 92.

orders are often directed towards and enforced against known legal entities.[29] The anonymous nature of users and participants makes the task of identifying parties for legal service and the enforcement of judgments considerably difficult. Thus, the architecture of blockchain technology and its anonymity inherently conflict with basic tenets of judicial power. Reconciling anonymity and jurisdictional authority remains an ongoing challenge in resolving cryptoassets disputes.

III. Addressing the Jurisdictional Challenges: Some Practical Insights

The jurisdictional hurdles highlighted in the preceding section have started to manifest in national courts across various jurisdictions over the past five years. While the jurisprudence on private international law's response to crypto transactions is still developing, some common and divergent themes are already observable from national responses.

A. DAOs and Other Peer-to-Peer Networks

i. Company Administration/Partnership Disputes

Some scholars have argued that many of the disputes amongst members of unregulated DAOs may be characterised as issues regarding the administration/management of a company/association or contractual disputes between parties.[30] If these characterisations are correct, the usual private international law connecting factors for corporate and contractual disputes can then be applied to determine questions such as the choice of applicable law or jurisdiction.

Theoretically, the relationship among developers or participants within a DAO could be arranged in a manner that aligns with the structure of a company. This alignment could be achieved, for instance, if the DAO's governance rules and operational procedures are embedded within smart contracts on a blockchain. Indeed, the literature indicates that there are governance mechanisms to support decision-making by peers.[31] Nonetheless, in practical terms, DAOs might lack traditional hierarchical organisational structures of companies, such as decision-making bodies like the board of directors or members in general meeting (i.e., shareholders). Despite this, Guillaume and Riva suggest that the absence of a hierarchical

29 On the challenges of suing defendants who are anonymous and cannot be identified, see the recent UK Supreme Court in *Cameron (Respondent) v Liverpool Victoria Insurance Co Ltd (Appellant)* [2019] UKSC 6 [16–18].

30 Dickinson (n 4) 104–5; Florence Guillaume and Sven Riva, 'Blockchain Dispute Resolution for Decentralized Autonomous Organizations: The Rise of Decentralized Autonomous Justice' 17–25 <https://papers.ssrn.com/sol3/papers.cfm?abstract_id=4042704> accessed 30 July 2023.

31 Carlos Santana and Laura Albareda, 'Blockchain and the Emergence of Decentralized Autonomous Organizations (DAOs): An Integrative Model and Research Agenda' (2022) 182 Technol Forecast Soc Change 1; S Wang and others, 'Decentralized Autonomous Organizations: Concept, Model, and Applications' (2019) 6 IEEE Trans Comput Soc Syst 870, 872.

structure and the decentralised nature of decision-making, or existence of only an online decision-making process, should not necessarily disqualify DAOs from being classified as companies provided there is some level of organisation that could be perceived as sufficient to effectively manage the DAO's operations.[32]

Recently, a new trend has emerged where certain states have recognised and registered DAOs as corporate entities under their respective laws, just like conventional companies. These entities are often referred to as DAO LLCs. For instance, in 2021, Wyoming introduced a new legal framework for DAOs.[33] A DAO LLC provides its members with limited liability protections, enabling the DAO to participate in external interactions through contracts while shielding members from potential liabilities. In essence, the DAO is conferred with a legal status or attached to a "legal wrapper" as often described in the literature.[34] Other U.S. states such as Tennessee[35] and Vermont[36] have also recognised DAOs as legal entities that can be established for either profit-oriented or charitable purposes.

The emerging case law also indicates that unregulated DAOs might be more appropriately characterised as partnerships, which often have fewer or even no strict hierarchical organisational requirements. A notable example can be seen in the case of *Christain Sarcuni et al v. bZx DAO*,[37] where the claimants are users of the bZx Protocol, a decentralised platform for cryptocurrency trading and lending operated by the bZx DAO. In November 2021, a hacker exploited a developer's credentials through phishing, resulting in the theft of $55 million in cryptocurrency from the bZx Protocol. The claimants, who are foreign nationals, collectively incurred losses amounting to $1.7 million due to this breach. Consequently, they filed a lawsuit against the bZx DAO and its alleged general partners on the ground of negligence. One of the key legal questions is whether the bZx DAO qualifies as a general partnership under California law, potentially leading to joint and several liability for its partners. The issue further extends to determining if the defendants can be considered general partners of the bZx DAO based on their possession of governance tokens. The court ruled that:

> To plausibly allege the existence of a general partnership, the FAC must plead sufficient facts to demonstrate that the bZx DAO is (1) an association

32 Guillaume and Riva (n 30) 8–9.

33 For a draft of the Bill, see <https://www.wyoleg.gov/2021/Introduced/SF0038.pdf> accessed 29 July 2023.

34 Guillaume (n 4) 4; Simon Moore, 'Towards a Functioning Legal Framework for Emerging DAO Technologies in Australia' (2021) 2 Aus Nat Uni JL Tech 109; Alexandra Sims, 'Blockchain and Decentralised Autonomous Organisations (DAOs): The Evolution of Companies?' (2019) 28 NZ Uni L Rev 423–58.

35 See Ryan McDowell, 'Tennessee Permits Decentralized Autonomous Organization to Organize as LLCs' (Tennessee Bar Association, April 2022) <https://www.tba.org/?pg=Articles&blAction=showEntry&blogEntry=73474> accessed 29 July 2023.

36 For the text of the law, see The Vermont Statutes Online <https://legislature.vermont.gov/statutes/section/11/025/04173>

37 3:22-cv-00618 (SD Cal 2023).

> of two or more persons (2) carrying on as co-owners of (3) a business for profit. See Cal. Corp. Code § 16202 (a). As a starting point, the FAC alleges that the DAO is an "association[] of two or more persons (the tokenholders and investors)." The FAC also alleges that the bZx DAO generates profits through its margin trading and lending products, Fulcrum and Torque. The Leveragebox Defendants don't appear to dispute either allegation. The Court finds that the FAC sufficiently alleges that the DAO is an association of two or more persons and that it operates as a business for profit.[38]

The court, therefore, recognised the bZx DAO as a general partnership that could be sued for negligence and found that token-holders were potentially liable as general partners. This implies that if a forum law is similar to the Californian law, it might be easier to establish that a DAO qualifies, at the barest minimum, as a partnership because they often involve a group of people who come together with the common intention of doing business through the platform offered by the DAO. The existence of partnerships is easier to establish and prove than it is for conventional companies, which are often required to meet some strict registration requirements in most legal systems.[39]

In the case of partnerships, the private international law questions will also depend on whether the partnership is registered or unregistered. For DAOs that meet the criteria to be classified as companies (e.g., DAO LLCs) or registered partnerships according to the laws of the relevant jurisdiction, the private international law rules applicable to registered organisations will be relevant. Thus, for issues concerning the management or administration of DAOs (as companies or registered partnerships), the state where the DAO has its statutory seat (usually the place of incorporation or its registered office) will have exclusive jurisdiction to resolve such matters. This is the law in most states whether common, civil or mixed law jurisdictions.[40] Other contractual and tortious issues (not relating to the administration of the DAO) will be governed by private international rules of contract and tort.

ii. Contractual Disputes

Where a DAO fails to meet the criteria for classification as a company or a registered partnership according to the private international laws of the relevant

38 ibid 7.

39 For instance, see ss 7–16 of Companies Act 2006 (UK). Although, it is debatable whether a DAO that is established for members to transact crypto business without the intention of making profit that can be shared amongst the participants will qualify as a partnership under traditional common law. See the Scottish court decision in *Pitreavie Gold Club v Penman* 1934 SLT 247, where a golf club was considered an unincorporated association rather than a partnership based on the earlier mentioned reason.

40 Art 63 of Brussels IA Regulation has a more flexible solution where the understanding of the domicile of corporations expands beyond the place of incorporation to include the place of central administration, the statutory seat and principal place of business.

jurisdiction, the relationship between the members or participants is, nonetheless, contractual in nature.[41] The relationship is characterised as contractual because it involves obligations freely assumed by the platform's developers and participants. The same applies to all crypto transactions executed through peer-to-peer blockchain networks generally.

Smart contracts do not write themselves. They are often the outcome of prior agreements made by parties, which are then translated into code. As for other participants who join these platforms, they are usually obliged to consent to the rules and regulations that govern these platforms. Smart contracts can lead to unintended consequences and disputes for various reasons. First, mistakes can arise during the translation of a contract into smart contract code, either due to coding errors or misinterpretation of the original terms. Flaws and malfunctions within the code itself might lead to incorrect execution.[42] Second, smart contracts rely on external data sources known as "oracles" to trigger actions.[43] Yet, these oracles might supply inaccurate or outdated information, causing undesired outcomes. Third, even if a smart contract functions as originally programmed, situations can emerge where strict adherence to the coded terms results in outcomes that contradict fundamental principles of fairness, justice, or good faith between parties.[44] When smart contracts behave in ways that are viewed as unacceptable from a contractual perspective, aggrieved parties may seek legal remedies.

The least controversial way to establish jurisdiction is if a smart contract contains a choice of court agreement or an arbitration clause. Courts would usually respect and enforce party autonomy except when there are strong reasons to disregard the parties' choice.[45] In the absence of a choice, the closest connection test applies. Jurisdictional gateways for contracts require a very close connection between the contract and the court. In most common law states, the claimant must demonstrate that the contract was either formed within the jurisdiction or was intended to be performed there.[46] Under the Brussels Ia regulation, the court where the obligation in question is to be performed has jurisdiction.[47] In the United States, for due process reasons, the claimant may also need to establish that the U.S. court has personal jurisdiction over the defendant, and this may be problematic where the defendant's contact with the forum is limited.[48]

41 Dickinson (n 4) 104–5.

42 Amedeo Santosuosso, 'About Smart Contract Dispute Resolution' in B Cappiello and G Carullo (eds), *Blockchain, Law and Governance* (Springer 2021) 208–9.

43 Guillaume and Riva (n 30) 16.

44 ibid.

45 Rühl (n 4) 168–69. On how smart contracts can be subject to jurisdiction agreements, see Paolo Bertoli, 'Smart (Legal) Contracts: Forum and Applicable Law Issues' in B Cappiello and G Carullo (eds), *Blockchain, Law and Governance* (Springer 2021) 188.

46 For England, see Briggs (n 15) 111–12.

47 Art 7(1)(a), Brussels I Regulation.

48 See, generally, Ronald A Brand, 'Due Process, Jurisdiction and a Hague Judgments Convention' (1999) 60 U Pitt L Rev 661.

In cases where negotiations regarding the establishment of a DAO occur in a specific country, it is arguable that the smart contract's formation occurs in that country. Determining the place of performance of obligations is more complicated, given that the execution of the contract typically takes place in a decentralised manner. Consequently, the execution is technically linked to all of the locations where participants or nodes are situated. In such an instance, claimants have three options: initiating legal action in their own place of residence, in the defendant's place of residence or in a third state where any of the nodes is located.

Suing in the defendant's place of residence is generally uncontroversial, as the court within the defendant's residence will normally have jurisdiction over the defendant according to the private international law rules of most states. However, the permissibility of pursuing legal action in the claimant's residence (home court) is controversial, particularly when the foreign defendant has minimal or no contractual links to that jurisdiction. For instance, in *Christain Sarcuni et al v. bZx DAO*,[49] it was held that the trial court lacked jurisdiction over one of the defendants (Tom Beam), a co-founder of the DAO. This was because the plaintiff failed to establish that Beam was a resident of or engaged in any activities within California. The appellate court relied on *Goehring v. Superior Ct. of San Diego County*,[50] where it was held that:

> Jurisdiction over a partnership does not necessarily permit a court to assume jurisdiction over the individual partners. . . . Thus, a California court "has jurisdiction" over only those individual partners who personally established the requisite minimum contacts with California.[51]

The issue is different regarding tortious claims. Most national courts generally permit claimants to commence lawsuits against defendants if the injury is suffered within the forum, even if the wrongful act occurred elsewhere.[52] In the US case of *Kleiman v. Wright*, the claimant who is based in Florida sued Craig Wright, an Australian national residing in London, England, before the US District Court in Florida. The claimant, as personal representative of Dave Kleiman, alleged that Dave and Craig were supposedly partners in developing Bitcoin, and through their collaboration mined over 1 million bitcoins stored in identifiable wallets from 2008 to 2013. The claimant alleges Craig unlawfully seized control of the bitcoins belonging to Dave and W&K Info Defense Research LLC (a company Dave and Craig formed together) and transferred the bitcoins to foreign trusts and companies

49 3:22-cv-00618 (SD Cal 2023).
50 62 Cal App 4th 894 (1998).
51 ibid 904–5.
52 This is the law in most common law jurisdiction. For instance, see the recent UK Supreme Court decision in *FS Cairo (Nile Plaza) LLC v Brownlie [2021] UKSC 45*. In the EU, this used to be law until Brussels Ia, which now requires the claimant to only sue in the place where the harmful effect occurred or may occur. See Art 7(2), Brussels Ia Regulation. On the key differences between English, EU and US laws, see Hartley (n 10) 211, 215–21.

after Dave's death in 2013. The defendant argued, among other things, that the court lacked personal jurisdiction. The court dismissed the motion, finding that the Florida long-arm statute permitted jurisdiction over Craig based on his alleged tortious acts causing injury in Florida against Florida claimants.

In the English case of *Tulip Trading Ltd v Bitcoin Association for BSV and others*,[53] the appellant, Tulip Trading, claimed that its computer systems were hacked, resulting in the theft of Bitcoin private keys and an inability to access digital assets worth over £3 million. The respondents, Bitcoin software developers, were accused by the appellant of having the capability to assist in recovering the assets by transferring them to a new address. Tulip Trading sought an order to compel the developers to restore access. The argument was that the developers owed fiduciary duties to Bitcoin owners by acting as custodians. Initially, the lower court declined jurisdiction over the foreign Bitcoin software developers by refusing permission to serve the claim abroad and concluded that no fiduciary duty was owed by the developers. However, the Court of Appeal reversed this decision, noting that the Bitcoin developers' role entailed authority and control over the network, requiring them to make decisions on behalf of participants. The Court deemed that Bitcoin owners had a valid expectation for developers to act in good faith rather than self-interest.

The implication of these decisions is that the decentralised nature of blockchain technology means disputes arising from DAO activities, whether contractual or tortious, will likely lead claimants to sue in their home countries. The propriety of this emerging trend will be evaluated in the next section of the chapter.

B. Exchange Platforms

A significant volume of global crypto transactions occurs through exchanges, which are trading entities established and organised under the laws of specific countries. These exchanges not only serve as custodians for their users but also function as intermediaries for facilitating the exchange of cryptoassets.[54] Principally, exchanges have encountered cross-border litigation on claims rooted in both contract and tort, with the latter category constituting a larger portion of the overall cases.[55] Exchange platforms typically require users to agree to their terms before accessing their services. Due to the cross-border nature of the activities taking place on these platforms, they often aim to mitigate the potential risk of being subjected to lawsuits in foreign countries by incorporating choice of court agreements in their contracts.[56] However, the effectiveness of this arrangement has come

53 [2023] EWCA Civ 83.

54 UNIDROIT, 'Commentary on the Draft Unidroit Principles on Digital Assets and Private Law', UNIDROIT 2023 – CD (102) 6, 47–48.

55 Most of the reported cases in the United Kingdom, for instance, are connected to unauthorised transfer or theft of cryptoassets. See notes 75–78.

56 See, for instance, 'Appendix 5: Arbitration Agreement' of Coinbase User Agreement <https://www.coinbase.com/legal/user_agreement/united_states> accessed 30 July 2023.

under scrutiny, as foreign users have contested the validity of these clauses in their respective home courts.

This position can be substantiated by referring to two recent English cases. In *Payward, Inc. and others v Chechetkin*,[57] the claimants, representing the Payward group companies, sought to enforce an arbitration award against Chechetkin concerning cryptocurrency trades. Mr. Chechetkin had engaged in cryptocurrency trading through an account with Payward Ltd, a UK-based company, which included an arbitration clause specifying JAMS arbitration in San Francisco under California law. Substantial losses exceeding £600,000 were incurred by Mr. Chechetkin due to margin trading on Payward's platform. Subsequently, he initiated legal proceedings against Payward Ltd in England, based on the UK Financial Services and Markets Act (FSMA). In response, Payward initiated JAMS arbitration and secured an award against Mr. Chechetkin.

The court held that Mr. Chechetkin qualified as a 'consumer' and, as such, was entitled to the protections provided by the Consumer Rights Act 2015. The arbitration clause was considered unjust and unenforceable under the Act, as it imposed significant burdens on Mr. Chechetkin. Thus, the enforcement of the arbitration award was deemed to be contrary to public policy since it would obstruct Mr. Chechetkin's pursuit of his FSMA claim in English courts and deprive him of consumer safeguards. A similar outcome was previously reached by the English Court of Appeal in *Soleymani v Nifty Gateway LLC*.[58] This trend exposes exchange platforms and DAO LLCs to potential lawsuits worldwide, especially when users or investors are natural persons.

For corporate users and investors, consumer protection laws generally do not apply.[59] This category of claimants is bound by jurisdiction clauses, and compelling reasons may be needed for courts to assert jurisdiction in contravention of the agreed-upon venue.[60] If no ex-ante agreement is established between the corporate user or investor and the exchange platform, then it is arguable that exchange platforms can be sued at their registered office or their principal place of business. However, unlike unregulated DAOs, the location of exchanges would likely be deemed the closest connection to any transaction conducted through those exchanges. These platforms constitute the centre of gravity of crypto transactions. In addition, they are custodians, operators, executors or performers of key obligations required for the perfection of crypto transactions.

57 [2023] EWHC 1780 (Comm).

58 [2022] EWCA Civ 1297.

59 The UK Consumer Rights Act 2015, s.2 defines a consumer as "an <u>*individual*</u> acting for purposes that are wholly or mainly outside that individual's trade, business, craft or profession." While it is open to question whether the Consumer Rights Act applies to trading in cryptocurrency, it is debatable whether this qualifies as a sale of goods or service, the inclusion of cryptoassets as a regulated financial service indicates that users may still be regarded as consumers. See s 1G, Financial Services and Markets Act 2000 and s 69 of Financial Services and Markets Act 2023.

60 *Donohue v Armco* [2001] UKHL 64 [para 45]; *Maersk A/S v Mercuria Energy Trading SA* [2021] EWHC 2856 (Comm) [paras 24–27].

Most actions filed against exchanges are tortious claims. These claims may involve an unauthorised transfer of cryptoassets from one exchange to another exchange,[61] from private wallets to an exchange,[62] or from one private wallet to another private wallet on the same blockchain.[63] As mentioned elsewhere in this chapter, most states permit jurisdiction if the event occurred in their state or the injury was suffered in that state. Thus, an exchange platform may be sued in the place where the crypto was stolen (which is usually unknown) or the victim's home (where the injury is usually suffered). Courts have further supported the victim's home court approach based on the proprietary interest of victims in the cryptoassets, which, according to the English court decision in *Ion Science Ltd v Persons Unknown*,[64] is located at the domicile of the owner. In essence, if an owner maintains their private keys in England in any form, the cryptoasset is considered to be situated in England. Consequently, any misappropriation would be deemed to have occurred in England. This approach has consequently led to exchange platforms frequently facing legal action abroad for unauthorized cryptoasset transfers. Examples of such cases include *LMN v Bitflyer Holdings Inc*,[65] *Jones v Persons Unknown*,[66] *D'Aloia v Persons Unknown*,[67] *Danisz v Persons Unknown* and *Huobi Global Ltd*,[68] among others. Comparable precedents can be observed in other jurisdictions as well.[69]

The pseudonymous nature of blockchain technology also presents a further justification for the availability of home courts for claimants. If the owner of a cryptocurrency does not know the identity of the hacker, then it is practically impossible to know their location to determine the appropriate venue to sue. In such circumstances, cryptocurrency owners are left with the alternative of initiating legal proceedings in their own home state or potentially any third state that may bear some connection to the incident. This is why numerous cases pertaining to unauthorised cryptocurrency transfers are brought against persons unknown as highlighted earlier, or "John Doe" as prevalent in the United States.[70]

IV. Enforcing Crypto-Related Judgments

Litigation is a means, not an end. Claimants do not often go to court except when there are serious issues to be tried. In the context of cryptoassets, the goal is to

61 *LMN v Bitflyer Holdings Inc* [2022] EWHC 2954 (Comm).

62 *Jones v Persons Unknown* [2022] EWHC 2543 (Comm).

63 *D'Aloia v Persons Unknown* [2022] EWHC 1723 (Ch).

64 (unreported, 21 December 2020). See also, *Danisz v Persons Unknown and Huobi Global Ltd* [2022] EWHC 280 paras [17–18].

65 *LMN* (n 60).

66 *Jones* (n 61).

67 *D'Aloia* (n 62).

68 *Danisz* (n 63).

69 See *ZG Top Tech Co v Doe*, 2019 WL 917418 (WD Wash Feb. 25, 2019); *Heissenberg v Doe*, 2021 WL 2621100 (SD Fla, 24 June 2021); *Singular DTV GmbH v Doe*, 2021 WL 3668161 (SDNY 16 August 2021).

70 ibid.

trace anonymous defendants and/or recover stolen cryptoassets wherever located. Obtaining judgments might prove futile if they cannot be effectively enforced. Thus, in cross-border litigation and especially crypto-related cases, claimants must make well-informed choices about where to sue, as such decisions can substantially impact the potential enforceability of resulting judgments.

As discussed in section II of this chapter, judgments are issued by the judicial arm of government and are thus considered acts of the state. They do not have extra-territorial effects.[71] In other words, without some form of legal and judicial cooperation, a UK judgment is not enforceable abroad, and foreign judgments and orders are equally not directly enforceable in the United Kingdom.[72]

Currently, the HCCH Judgments Convention of 2019 came into force on 1 September 2023.[73] However, most countries have yet to ratify this convention.[74] Even if the ratification list grows, its applicability to the kinds of judgments issued in crypto-related cases is uncertain.[75] This means that judgment creditors are left with national and regional judgments recognition frameworks. While the space here may not permit reviewing the (in)adequacy of these national frameworks, one can safely conclude that judgment creditors will face significant challenges when trying to enforce crypto-related judgments abroad.[76]

The first obstacle that judgment creditors will face is the propriety of the foreign court's jurisdictional ground (e.g., home state courts). Most states consider a claimant's home court jurisdiction exorbitant, unless that state has a substantial connection to the transaction.[77] In most common law jurisdictions, the concept of foreign court's jurisdiction, or technically international jurisdiction, is even more restrictive. Foreign judgments are recognized only if the judgment debtor was

71 Yekini (n 9) 17.

72 Lord Collins of Mapesbury and others (eds.), *Dicey, Morris and Collins on the Conflict of Laws* (15th edn, Sweet & Maxwell Ltd 2012) 664; Briggs (n 15) 127.

73 HCCH, 'Judgments Convention: Entry into Force and Ratification by Uruguay' <https://www.hcch.net/en/news-archive/details/?varevent=936> accessed 5 September 2023.

74 The EU and Member States (except Denmark), Ukraine and Uruguay are the only State Parties as of 5 September 2023. See HCCH (n 73).

75 Article 5 of the Convention lists harmonised grounds for international jurisdiction. If a foreign court exercises jurisdiction based on the residence of the defendant or the foreign defendant consents to jurisdiction (e.g., unconditional appearance or through choice of court agreements), then any judgment emanating from such proceedings are enforceable under the convention. However, where the foreign defendant didn't submit to jurisdiction, the other reasonable grounds could be contract or tort. It has already been mentioned that determining the place of performance of contractual obligations (Art 5(1)(g)) in a decentralised and global trading platform may be complicated. Meanwhile, tort jurisdiction also under Art 5(1)(j) is limited to 'death, physical injury, *damage to or loss of tangible property*', which may exclude all crypto-related judgments as crypto assets are not tangible property.

76 For some of these challenges, see Yekini (n 9) 2–4.

77 Kevin M Clermont and John RB Palmer, 'Exorbitant Jurisdiction' (2006) 58 Me L Rev 474, 486–95; Ralf Michaels, 'Jurisdiction, Foundations' in Jürgen Basedow and others (eds), *Encyclopedia of Private International Law* (Edward Elgar Publishing 2017) 1049–50. The same is true for most civil law jurisdictions such as China. See, King Fung Tsang, 'Enforcement of Foreign Commercial Judgments in China' (2018) 14 J Priv Int L 262, 264.

resident (or present) in the foreign state or voluntarily agreed to be sued there.[78] Theoretically, the judgments from most of the crypto-related cases cited in this chapter would be unenforceable in most common law states (except Canada[79]) if the foreign defendant or exchange did not participate in the proceedings.

Common law jurisdictions also only recognise money judgments.[80] In crypto-related proceedings, two types of orders or judgments are prominent. The first is interim reliefs such as freezing orders or discovery orders like Bankers Trust orders (to reveal the identity of wallet holders). To illustrate this point, in one of the proceedings in *LMN*, the court ordered exchanges to provide:

> In respect of any customer account(s) which the Target Cryptocurrency was allocated to and/or received on behalf of:
>
> (a) the name the account(s) is held in;
> (b) All 'Know Your Customer' (KYC) information and documents provided in respect of the account(s);
> (c) Any other information and documents held in relation to the account(s) which does (or which the relevant Defendant consider is likely to) identify the holder of the account(s), including email addresses, residential addresses, phone numbers and bank account details, save that any bank account details and/or social security numbers may be partially redacted by the relevant Defendant. . . .[81]

The second type of order is a final judgment that requires the defendant or an exchange to transfer cryptoassets to the judgment creditor, or an order against software developers to execute certain changes to the blockchain protocol (e.g., the relief in Tulip). These two kinds of judgments and orders are not enforceable foreign judgments under traditional common law. Judgment creditors will need to initiate a fresh action abroad and seek fresh orders.[82] It may also depend on how the requested court conceptually treats cryptoassets. Cryptocurrencies represent a unique asset class that blurs the lines between traditional forms of money and property. Therefore, whether a cryptocurrency transfer order directly falls under the category of a "money judgment" or is treated as a distinct remedy may differ across jurisdictions.

78 Briggs (n 15) 133–39.

79 Canada has departed from the traditional common law of international jurisdiction in *Beals v Saldanha* [2003] 3 SCR 416. The courts now adopt a real and substantial connection test. See Tanya J Monestier, 'A "Real and Substantial" Mess: The Law of Jurisdiction in Canada' (2013) 36 Fordham Int LJ 396.

80 By this, we mean that only money judgments can be enforced through an action on judgment debt and summary judgments procedure. See Yekini (n 9) 39; Briggs (n 15) 149.

81 *LMN v Bitflyer Holdings Inc & Ors* [2022] EWHC 2954 [45].

82 Yekini (n 9) 103–4.

It seems that courts may not treat crypto judgments as money judgments since cryptocurrency is not fiat currency. In *Joseph Keen Shing Law v Persons Unknown & Huobi Global Limited*,[83] the English court faced how to best repatriate stolen cryptocurrency from abroad. The court proposed a three-step process: First, there is a need to convert the cryptocurrency to fiat currency. Second, the fiat currency is to be transferred to England and paid to the court funds office. Third, the judgment creditor can then apply for execution against the sums under court rules. It is questionable whether the court would take this approach if the exchange was within its jurisdiction.

The decentralised and fungible nature of many cryptocurrencies, coupled with the seamless movement of funds within exchanges, can present difficulties when seeking to trace and preserve specific assets. In *Piroozzadeh v Persons Unknown and Others*,[84] the claimant obtained a proprietary injunction against Binance concerning 870,818 USD Tether allegedly illegally transferred to Binance by hackers. However, Binance argued it was impossible to comply with the injunction because the Tether had already been transferred to Binance's central pooled funds address and mixed with other assets before the injunction was even served. Mr. Justice Trower agreed with Binance that compliance was practically impossible, and therefore discharged the injunction. Given this constraint, claimants may need to rely more on personal claims against individuals rather than pursuing cryptoassets when ownership is difficult to establish. But even this can be difficult given the pseudonymity of crypto activities. At the litigation stage, allowing the claimant to proceed against unknown persons may be considered pragmatic since the defendant's identity is unknown.[85] It becomes problematic at the enforcement stage, as judgments can only be enforced against identified assets. While some exchanges may cooperate with foreign courts during litigation as in *Law v Persons Unknown & Huobi Global Limited*, others may resist enforcement and thus not comply with disclosure orders.

V. Conclusion

The rapid emergence of cryptocurrencies, blockchain networks and decentralized organisations has disrupted traditional concepts in private international law. As explored in this chapter, the non-territorial and pseudonymous nature of cryptoassets creates significant uncertainties around jurisdiction, applicable law and enforcement for cross-border transactions and activities. However, private international law remains essential to providing legal clarity and stability amidst the global spread of crypto. The growth of cryptoasset transactions on exchange

83 Abu: [2023] 1 WLUK 577.

84 [2023] EWHC 1024 (Ch).

85 On recent cases discussing the challenges of suing or obtaining injuction against persons unknown, see Michelle Caney, 'The Revival of Injunctions Against Persons Unknown' (2022) <https://www.stiveschambers.co.uk/content/uploads/2022/01/THE-REVIVAL-OF-INJUNCTIONS-AGAINST-PERSONS-UNKNOWN.pdf> accessed 5 September 2023.

platforms and non-regulated DAOs poses complex jurisdictional challenges that require creative adaptation of existing procedures, as well as systematic solutions tailored to the architecture of blockchain technology.

At present, there appears to be a fundamental tension between the architectural foundations of blockchain technology and the underpinnings of existing legal frameworks. In order for the cryptocurrency market to continue expanding sustainably, a realignment of technology and law may be necessary. While core tenets of decentralisation and anonymity in blockchain systems should be preserved to support cryptocurrency adoption, targeted technical solutions could potentially be explored to address certain jurisdictional and territoriality challenges. For instance, developing protocols that enable selective transparency and permissioned access to transaction histories in compliance with court orders, without fully compromising the security of cryptocurrency networks, may be desired.

For policymakers and legislators, progressive legal developments are imperative to meet the unique needs of the cryptocurrency industry. National regulatory responses are ill-equipped to address the transnational problems. To address jurisdictional challenges in cryptoasset transactions, international cooperation will be essential. The Hague Conference on Private International Law could serve as a useful platform for the harmonisation of divergent national interests, policies and legislative approaches. Harmonisation of laws can facilitate efficient dispute resolution and enhance legal certainty for the industry. What is needed is a coherent international legal framework that fully acknowledges the borderless character of cryptocurrencies and the complexities of decentralised autonomous organizations (DAOs). Such a tailored framework could provide the flexibility and nuance required to reasonably balance competing national interests and responses.

Pending the ambitious multilateral efforts required for legislative harmonisation, courts must adopt pragmatic approaches when dealing with jurisdictional dilemmas in cryptoasset cases. For instance, most of the grounds for establishing international jurisdiction in common law countries were conceived in an era before instantaneous digital communications and frictionless cross-border commerce. Some of these grounds now merit re-evaluation given that they are ill-suited for the digital world we live in. Beyond re-examining outdated doctrines, enhanced cross-border judicial cooperation is vital in today's interconnected world. Courts should be willing to collaborate to establish mutual recognition of interim reliefs and final judgments rendered in crypto-related proceedings. With ingenious adaptations and international cooperation, private international law can pave the way for cryptoassets to flourish.

11 Rethinking Jurisdiction of Online Defamation

*Dicky King Fung Tsang**

I. Introduction

Courts have been struggling to apply traditional jurisdictional rules, originally designed for printed defamation, to online defamation. The ubiquitous nature of online defamation allows claimants to suffer damage worldwide, though with more substantial damage in some jurisdictions than others. The challenge lies in deciding which countries' courts should have jurisdiction over the defendant. The dilemma for the court is to strike a balance between protecting the claimant and the defendant. It is foreseeable that the jurisdictional issues of online defamation will only increase in the future, especially with the potential for defamation occurrences in the metaverse.[1] This chapter endeavors to examine and rethink this novel jurisdictional issue.[2]

The European Court of Justice (ECJ) attempted to address this dilemma on online defamation in Gtflix Tv, C-251/20.[3] This case represents the latest attempt of the ECJ to elucidate the jurisdictional rules for online defamation within the European Union (EU). Notably, the ECJ affirmed the applicability of the notorious mosaic approach to online defamation. The mosaic approach allows claimants to seek damages in each member state where the defamatory content is accessible, for the injury to their reputation.[4] This article contends that such an approach disproportionately favours the claimant, placing the defendant at an unfair disadvantage. It proposes a more balanced approach, limiting the number of eligible fora. Specifically, the mosaic jurisdiction should only be extended to courts of the member state towards which the defendant directed the defamatory statement, such that this member state is the focal point of the defamatory act. Furthermore, this chapter

* The author would like to thank Han-Wei Liu and Lukas Rass-Masson for the helpful comments and suggestions on the early ideas of this chapter.

1 See Jyh-An Lee and others, 'Legal Implications of Self-Presence in the Metaverse' (2023) 25 Media Arts L Rev 267, 282.

2 For the discussion of jurisdictional issue in cross-border cryptocurrency, another important jurisdictional issue in our metaverse, see Abubakri Yekini, Chapter 10 in this volume.

3 Case C-251/20 *Gtflix Tv v DR* EU:C:2021:1036.

4 Case C-68/93 *Shevill and Others v Presse Alliance* EU:C:1995:61, [1995] ECR I-415, para 30.

DOI: 10.4324/9781032618975-17

argues that the EU should refine this focalization approach by reference to the US experience. The US jurisdiction rules require the defendant to have purposefully directed her conduct towards the forum, thereby limiting to the available fora only to those with a sufficient link to the defamation. Although the US jurisdiction rule on defamation may still be subject to a range of interpretations, the US judicial practices still provide helpful guidance to the EU on developing the proper focalization approach.[5] Particularly, the US approach has been perceived as narrow and more favourable to the defendant. This is imperative as the current EU jurisdictional rule overly favours the claimant, enabling them to claim full damages in the member state of their domicile, in addition to the state where the defamatory statement originated and where the defendant is domiciled.

II. Background of Online Defamation and Jurisdiction

Gtflix Tv is a Czech Republic–based company specialising in the production and distribution of pornographic materials. It also has its centre of interest in the Czech Republic. DR, a person domiciled in Hungary, is a director, producer and distributor of pornographic materials, which are marketed on websites in Hungary.[6] Gtflix TV sued DR in France for disparaging comments made by DR against it in a number of online forums.[7] The choice of France as the forum for this lawsuit, over the more logically connected Czech Republic or Hungary, raises pertinent questions. Both the Czech Republic and Hungary have strong connections to and interests in the dispute. The Czech Republic, as the claimant's base and the probable location of the most significant reputational damage, has a vested interest in protecting its national's reputation. Conversely, Hungary, as the defendant's domicile and the probable origin of the online statements, holds a stake in safeguarding its national's freedom of speech. However, for the reasons to be elaborated as follows, the ECJ affirmed the mosaic approach and thus allowed Gtflix Tv to continue its French proceedings.[8]

The ECJ's affirmation necessitates a deeper understanding of online defamation's unique challenges in private international law. Defamation, inherently a tort, generally falls under private international law rules pertaining to torts. However, each tort is different. One of the key distinctions of defamation lies in its impacts on free speech.[9] With each member state having a different perspective on the balance between free speech and the protection of the claimant's reputation,[10] some member states are bound to have more favourable law that shields defendants from their alleged defamatory statement with its free speech provision. This fuels

5 Case C-251/20 *Gtflix Tv v DR* EU:C:2021:745, Opinion of AG Hogan, para 34.
6 Case C-251/20 *Gtflix Tv v DR* EU:C:2021:1036, para 11.
7 ibid paras 12–13.
8 ibid para 44.
9 Trevor C Hartley, "Libel Tourism' and Conflict of Laws' (2010) 59 Int Comp Law Q 25, 25–26.
10 ibid 26 ("In some countries, the balance tilts in favour of free speech; in others, it tilts in favour of protecting reputation.").

claimants' inclination towards forum shopping to find the most advantageous national law, i.e., the law that has less protection for free speech.

Theoretically, there are two ways to deal with the differences in national laws.[11] The first way is to harmonize the substantive laws, which remains unachieved to date in the EU. The second way is to harmonize the choice of law rules. However, while choice of law rules on tort is generally harmonized under Rome II Regulation,[12] defamation is especially excluded.[13] Thus, there is no answer from these two traditional approaches.

A potential solution to mitigate forum shopping, resulting from this lack of harmonization in choice of law rules, could be the harmonization of jurisdiction rules. For instance, if a claimant perceives Country A's choice of law rules, instead of those of Country B, will yield a more favourable national law for the defamatory suit against the defendant, it will prompt her to initiate the lawsuit there. A harmonized jurisdiction rule between Countries A and B that designates only Country B to have jurisdiction (e.g., for being the country where the defendant is domiciled), will deter forum shopping and reduce the problem caused by the disparities in choice of law rules. This approach aligns with Ehrenzweig's argument advocating for the adoption of lex fori as the general choice of law rule if proper jurisdiction rules are adopted.[14] The degree of mitigation, however, is contingent on the number of jurisdictions available; in the aforementioned scenario, with only Country B having jurisdiction, the potential for forum shopping is eliminated.

In the EU context, many litigations will be subject to the jurisdiction of more than one forum,[15] thus limiting, but not eliminating, forum shopping. The ECJ's adoption of the mosaic approach in this context arguably exacerbates the situation since it renders every EU member state a potential forum.

Since its inception, the Brussels regime has afforded tort victims potentially several forum choices.[16] Presently, under Article 4(1), a defendant may be sued in their

11 See Friedrich K Juenger, 'A Page of History' (1984) 35 Mercer L Rev 419, 459–60, suggesting that multistate problems could only be resolved by three basic methods, the first being the creation of multistate rules of decision, and the second and third both being choice of law rules, though under different approaches.

12 Regulation (EC) No 864/2007 of the European Parliament and of the Council of 11 July 2007 on the law applicable to non-contractual obligations (Rome II) [2007] OJ L 199/40.

13 ibid art 2(g).

14 Albert Armin Ehrenzweig, *A Treatise on the Conflict of Laws* (West Publishing Company 1962) 314–15.

15 Regulation (EU) No 1215/2012 of the European Parliament and of the Council of 12 December 2012 on jurisdiction and the recognition and enforcement of judgments in civil and commercial matters (recast) [2012] OJ L 351/1 art 7. These will include Member State with general jurisdiction, i.e., where the defendant is domiciled, under art 4 of the Brussels Regulation (Recast) and Member State with special jurisdiction under art 7.

16 1968 Brussels Convention on jurisdiction and the enforcement of judgments in civil and commercial matters/* Consolidated version cF 498Y0126(01) */[1972] OJ L 299/32 art 2.

domicile state.[17] This is the fundamental jurisdiction basis and regarded as the general Jurisdiction. Article 7(2) provides for special jurisdiction in tort cases, allowing for "[a] person domiciled in a Member State [to] be sued in another Member State in matters relating to tort, delict or quasi-delict, in the courts for the place where the harmful event occurred or may occur".[18] "The place where the harmful event occurred or may occur" has been interpreted by the ECJ as both the place where the damage occurred and the place of the event giving rise to it.[19] Thus, the current jurisdiction rules offer three potential fora to a tort victim: (i) defendant's domicile, (ii) place where the damage occurred and (iii) place of the event giving rise to it. In typical tort cases, these may coincide. For example, if a French person is hit by a car driven by a German in Germany, then the place of defendant's domicile, place where the damage occurred and place of the event giving rise to it are all Germany. However, defamation is much more complicated. A publication containing the defamatory statement is often circulated to more than one member state within the EU, leading to multiple places of damage. It does not only mean that places (ii) and (iii) will not be identical (two fora instead of one), but also that there are potentially more fora than two due to there being multiple places of damage (i.e., multiple places (ii)).

The landmark *Shevill* case by the ECJ was the first endeavor to address this issue. In that case, the ECJ held that the place of the event giving rise to the damage in the context of defamation is the Member State where the publisher is established. This is because "that is the place where the harmful event originated and from which the libel was issued and put into circulation".[20] In most cases, places (i) (defendant's place of domicile) and (iii) (place of event giving rise to the damage) are identical.[21] Crucially, the ECJ applied the mosaic approach to the place of damage, holding that

> the courts of each Contracting State in which the defamatory publication was distributed and in which the victim claims to have suffered injury to his reputation have jurisdiction to rule on the injury caused in that State to the victim's reputation.[22]

The justification of the court is the sound administration of justice since it regarded that each Member States are "territorially the best placed to assess the libel committed in that State and to determine the extent of the corresponding damage".[23]

17 Regulation (EU) No 1215/2012 of the European Parliament and of the Council of 12 December 2012 on jurisdiction and the recognition and enforcement of judgments in civil and commercial matters (recast) [2012] OJ L 351/1 art 4(1).
18 ibid art 7(2).
19 Case C-21/76 *Bier v Mines de Potasse d Alsace* EU:C:1976:166, [1976] ECR 1735, paras 24–25.
20 Case C-68/93 *Shevill and Others v Presse Alliance* EU:C:1995:61, [1995] ECR I-415, para 24.
21 ibid para 26.
22 ibid para 30.
23 ibid para 31.

This skews the balance in favour of claimants by significantly expanding the range of potential forums, albeit with limited subject matter jurisdiction.

In addressing the complexities of the mosaic approach in EU online defamation cases, the ECJ's stance has led to significant jurisprudential challenges. The court acknowledged a potential difficulty in this approach, but curiously, it was perceived as an issue for the claimant, not the defendant. It viewed the possibility of having to bring the disputes in various fora a problem for the claimant but reasoned that having alternative fora in places (i) and (iii) alleviates the claimant's burden, as these courts can award damages for the entire injury.[24]

However, online defamation introduces further complexities. The public no longer need to buy a newspaper to read the defamatory statement, thanks to the ease of internet access and content distribution.[25] Similarly, anyone having access to the Internet can publish a defamatory statement. Gone are the days when this is the privilege of writers for newspapers and magazines. Perhaps more importantly, publishers, who are often defendants of defamatory suits, no longer have control over who will have access to the content once it is published online:

> the control exerted by a media outlet over distribution of and access to its medium becomes blurred and, on occasions, unattainable. When information content is uploaded to the internet, individuals immediately become – voluntarily or involuntarily – distributors of the information, by means of social networks, electronic communications, links, blogs or any other methods which the internet provides. Even the restriction of content by means of paid access, which is occasionally subject to territorial limitations, faces serious difficulties when it comes to preventing the mass distribution of information. Accordingly, monitoring and measuring the impact of information, or entering it in the accounts, for which there were highly reliable methods in traditional media, becomes a task which is impossible to complete when the information concerned circulates on the internet.[26]

Thus, the ubiquitous nature of online defamation not only increases potential damage locations but also broadens the range of defendants. The question for the ECJ is whether and, if so, how to limit these forum choices under the mosaic approach in online defamation.

In *eDate Advertising v X and Martinez v MGNLimited*,[27] the ECJ upheld the mosaic approach in online defamation cases. While the ECJ recognized the ubiquitous nature of online defamation, its focus was more on the inconveniences to the claimant than the fairness towards the defendant. To facilitate the recovery of the

24 ibid para 32.

25 Cases C-509/09 and C-161/10 *eDate Advertising v X and Martinez v MGNLimited* EU:C:2011:192, Opinion of AG Cruz Villalón, para 44.

26 ibid para 47.

27 Cases C-509/09 and C-161/10 *eDate Advertising v X and Martinez v MGN Ltd* EU:C:2011:685, [2011] ECR I-10269.

entire damages to the claimant's reputation, it created a new ground of jurisdiction by allowing claimants to recover damages suffered in all member states at their centre of interest.[28] It is a very favourable creation to claimants since they can now sue in their home court.[29] This approach raises questions about the necessity of adding yet another forum for the claimants, given the already favourable conditions allowing them to recover full damages in multiple jurisdictions (places (i) (place of domicile) and (iii) (place where the event giving rise to damage occurs)). The ECJ's decision, therefore, seems to excessively favour the claimant, allowing them to pursue existing mosaic lawsuits in addition to suing in the place of their centre of interest.

In short, *eDate* may be seen as lifting off the subject matter jurisdiction of a claimant's home court as a place of damage (place (ii)). Previously, the claimants could only bring a lawsuit at their home jurisdiction to recover the damage for injury suffered there, but not injuries suffered elsewhere. This ruling therefore increased the number of fora that allow the claimants to sue for the entire damages from two to three, adding a place (iv) (the place of claimant's centre of interest). Yet, it continues to allow claimants to pursue the existing mosaic lawsuits if they chooses to do so (places (ii)).

In *Bolagsupplysningen*, the ECJ faced a unique scenario where the claimants sought only the removal of defamatory material.[30] The court held that such remedy in online defamation could only be achieved by suing in the member state where the entire damages may be recovered (i.e., places (i), (iii) and (iv)), considering that it is "a single and indivisible application".[31] The case might be interpreted as hinting at a potential shift in the ECJ's approach towards online defamation, suggesting a move away from the mosaic approach in damages as well,[32] even though the case did not concern damages. Adopting this interpretation, the claimants can only sue the defendant in places (i), (iii) and (iv), thereby concentrating the fora to these three places. For easy reference, this approach is termed the "concentration approach" in this article.[33]

28 ibid para 48.

29 See Trevor C Hartley, 'Jurisdiction in Tort Claims for Non-Physical Harm Under Brussels 2012, Article 7(2)' (2018) 67 Int C LQ 987, 1001. ("It is a new ground of jurisdiction based on policy considerations. The argument is that the claimant should be able to bring a single claim for the totality of their loss wherever occurring, and to do so they should have an option other than that of going to the defendant's country. Despite the attractions of such a rule, however, it has the effect of conferring jurisdiction on what is essentially the claimant's forum. This is generally regarded as undesirable.").

30 *Bolagsupplysningen OU*, Case C-194/16, *Bolagsupplysningen OÜ and Ingrid Ilsjan v Svensk Handel AB* EU:C:2017:766.

31 ibid para 22.

32 Case C-251/20 *Gtflix Tv v DR* EU:C: 2021:745, Opinion of AG Hogan para 44.

33 ibid para 83. ("To consider, as the opponents of the mosaic approach seem to do, that it would be preferable to concentrate all claims for damages in one court, tends to overlook the reality that neither the laws of the Member States relating to defamation, nor even the rules for determining the applicable law, are currently harmonised.").

The *Gtflix TV* case presented an opportunity to clarify the jurisdictional approach for online defamation cases involving damages. In the first instance, the French court declined jurisdiction, asserting that mere accessibility of content was insufficient; the defamatory statements "must also be of interest" to internet users in relevant member state.[34] The court highlighted the fact that the relevant messages only dealt with the recruitment and treatment of actresses in Prague. They were thus not considered as being of interest to France.[35] On appeal to the Lyon Court of Appeal, the first instance judgment was endorsed.[36] The Court of Appeal added that the messages in question were mainly in English and only to a lesser extent in French.[37] There was also no evidence of French internet users being the most frequent visitors to the defendant's websites and online forums.[38]

The Cour de cassation subsequently referred the following question to the ECJ:

> Must Article 7(2) of Regulation No 1215/2012 be interpreted as meaning that a person who, considering that his or her rights have been infringed by the dissemination of disparaging comments on the internet, brings proceedings not only for the dissemination of data and the removal of content but also for compensation for the resulting non-material and economic damage, may claim, before the courts of each Member State in the territory of which content published online is or was accessible, compensation for the damage caused in the territory of the Member State, in accordance with eData or whether, pursuant to Bolagsupplysningen and Iisjan, that person must make that application for compensation before the court with jurisdiction to order rectification of the information and removal of the disparaging comments?

In substance, the French highest court asked the ECJ a critical question: should compensation claims follow the mosaic or concentration approach? However, Advocate General Hogan introduced a third approach,[39] which in this chapter is to be termed the "focalization approach".[40] Under this approach, "the content in question must not simply be accessible by means of the internet, but that instead the publication must also have been specifically *directed towards* the territory of the Member State concerned".[41] In other words, if the claimant only suffered injury in a member state inadvertently since the defendant did not direct the

34 Case C-251/20 *Gtflix Tv v DR* Request for a preliminary ruling, p 8.

35 ibid.

36 ibid 7.

37 ibid.

38 ibid.

39 Case C-251/20 *Gtflix Tv v DR* EU:C: 2021:745, Opinion of AG Hogan paras 87–94. To clarify, AG Hogan was of the opinion that the Mosaic approach should be preserved. The suggestion of the third approach was just in case it is thought that the Mosaic approach should be abolished entirely, see para 86.

40 The term is inspired by the "focalisation criterion", see ibid para 87.

41 ibid para 88 (emphasis added). It must be noted that AG Hogan was certainly not the first in considering adding additional condition to refine the mosaic approach. For example, both the national

statement there, the court of that member state will not have jurisdiction. In effect, this third approach substantially reduces the number of fora available under the original mosaic approach. Claimants can still sue in places (i), (iii) and (iv) under the focalization approach, just that fora available in places (ii) will be cut back. The focalization approach therefore represents a middle ground between the two aforementioned approaches. It is narrower than the mosaic approach because not every member state in which the claimants have suffered some injury to their reputation will have jurisdiction. On the other hand, it is broader than the concentration approach because it still gives some member states jurisdiction so long as they are places where the defendant intentionally directed their statements.

In *Gtflix TV*, the ECJ faced a crossroads: maintain the mosaic approach, abolish it or adopt this new focalization approach, refining the jurisdictional landscape of online defamation within the EU.

III. Gtflix Tv

The ECJ's decision in Gtflix Tv, while clear, was a source of disappointment for those hoping for a departure from the mosaic approach in online defamation compensation cases. The court reaffirmed its stance:

> Article 7(2) . . . must be interpreted as meaning that a person who . . . seeks not only the rectification of the information and the removal of the content placed online concerning him or her but also compensation for the damage resulting from that placement may claim, before the courts of each Member State in which those comments are or were accessible, compensation for the damage suffered in the Member State of the court seised, even though those courts do not have jurisdiction to rule on the application for rectification and removal.[42]

In keeping the mosaic approach, the ECJ made a distinction in jurisdiction based on remedies sought. In essence, places (i), (ii), (iii) and (iv) are available to claimants seeking damages, while only places (i), (iii) and (iv) are available for those seeking the rectification of the information and the removal of the online content. The justification of this distinction is based on its perception that "an application for rectification of information and removal of content[, being] a single and indivisible application,"[43] cannot apply to the compensation cases.

The ECJ also explained why it rejected the focalization approach:

> Article 7(2) thereof does not impose any additional condition as regards the determination of the competent court, such as requiring that the activity

courts in Germany and France asked the ECJ whether jurisdiction under art 7(2) requires the presence of particular connection.

42 Case C-251/20 *Gtflix Tv v DR* EU:C: 2021:745, Opinion of AG Hogan para 44.

43 ibid para 35.

> concerned be 'directed to' the Member State in which the court seised is situated. . . . A limitation, by means of additional conditions . . . could lead, in some cases, to the de facto exclusion of that option, whereas . . . a person who considers that he or she has been injured must always be able to bring proceedings before the courts of the place where the damage occurred.[44]

This interpretation, however, raises questions about consistency and fairness in the application of these rules. If the literal interpretation of the Article 7(2) forms the basis of rejection, then the same argument can be used against distinguishing removal of content as a separate category since Article 7(2) does not refer to any "single and indivisible application" either. Article 7(2) also has no reference to "centre of interest". Similarly, the second part of this quote suggests that the right of the claimant to bring proceedings in the court of the place where the damage occurred should not have any limitation. This too is contradictory to limiting the removal of content cases to particular courts, or imposing subject matter limits to mosaic jurisdiction.

In essence, the ECJ's decision in Gtflix Tv did not embrace the focalization approach, favouring a broader interpretation of jurisdiction in online defamation cases. This approach, while offering protection to claimants, continues to present challenges in balancing the interests of defendants and the practicality of cross-border legal proceedings in the digital age.

Thc ECJ's inconsistent interpretation in online defamation cases is problematic, but a more pressing issue is the practicality of the mosaic approach, allowing proceedings in courts with minimal connection to the claim or defendant. The Gtflix TV case exemplifies this problem. The focal point should be on setting reasonable limitations, rather than allowing unrestricted proceedings. The ECJ might have reservations about the focalization approach, particularly concerning its specificity and how to define whether an activity is 'directed to' a member state.[45] This concern is understandable. Unlike printed publications for which the number of publications circulated into a given country is traceable, doing the same for online publication will be much more challenging, if not impossible.

While the mosaic approach offers certainty in jurisdictional matters, it should not come at the cost of imbalanced interests between claimants and defendants. Its primary flaw lies in providing claimants with excessive forum choices, enabling forum shopping. It is not fair for defendants in an online defamation suit to have to potentially defend themselves in each of the member states. In addition, special jurisdiction should complement, not overshadow, general jurisdiction. If it grants every member state jurisdiction in online defamation, then it undermines the essence of general jurisdiction.

Conversely, the concentration approach, while generally covering the most relevant forums, isn't flawless either. It usually covers the most connected fora,

44 ibid para 41.
45 See (n 40).

including home courts of the defendant (places (i) and (ii)) and the claimant (place (iv)). However, as argued by Advocate General Hogan, there are indeed situations where the "centre of interest" cannot readily be identifiable.[46] One can also imagine that claimants could suffer substantial damage from online defamation beyond their centre of interest and the defendant's place of domicile. In short, there is indeed a need to grant jurisdiction to fora, limited as the cases may be, where a forum (which is neither the defendant nor claimant's home jurisdiction) has a close connection with the online defamation. The focalisation approach, with its promise of reasonable limitations, seems a more balanced solution. The challenge lies in defining under what circumstances the defendant is considered to have directed their defamatory conducts to the forum.

IV. Purposeful Availment Under US Law

While Advocate General Hogan introduced the idea of determining jurisdiction based on whether the defendant 'directed' their statement to the member state, he left the criteria for this direction undefined. For instance, specific details such as the nature of the message, the targeted audience, the language used or Gtflix's business presence in France were not explored.[47] This is not a critique but a recognition that further development of this concept is needed, for which the US legal framework offers valuable insights. This author suggests to look at the American experience for reference given that their jurisdictional rules have been based on this very test.[48] This section summarizes the US approach and explores whether a right test can be transplanted to Article 7(2).

To establish jurisdiction in a state in the United States, the defendant must have "minimum contacts" with the forum state so as to comport with "the traditional notions of fair play and substantial justice".[49] This has been the jurisdictional test of the US since the Supreme Court decided the *International Shoe* case in 1945.[50] However, it has been recognized that this test is still too broad and in need of refinement. As a result, in *World-Wide Volkswagen Corp. v. Woodson*,[51] the Supreme Court further imposed the requirement that the defendant must have *purposefully directed* its conduct to the forum state:

> When a corporation purposefully avails itself of the privilege of conducting activities within the forum State, it has clear notice that it is subject to suit

46 Case C-251/20 *Gtflix Tv v DR* EU:C: 2021:745, Opinion of AG Hogan para 70.

47 ibid paras 87–94. He also did not discuss the difference between this focalization approach and the "interest" condition imposed by the French lower courts. It is submitted that they are similar though not identical. Hogan's approach focuses on the conduct of the defendant, while the French courts appear to focus on the effect of the conduct. In most cases, however, the results should be the same.

48 ibid para 67. The only non-EU jurisdiction AG Hogan cited in his opinion is Australia.

49 *International Shoe Co v Washington* 326 US 310, 316 (1976).

50 ibid.

51 444 US 286 (1980).

> there, and can act to alleviate the risk of burdensome litigation by procuring insurance, passing the expected costs on to customers, or, if the risks are too great, severing its connection with the State.[52]

This is otherwise known as the "purposeful availment" requirement. The requirement closely aligns with Advocate General Hogan's focalization approach.

In connection with defamation, the jurisdiction test was applied by the US Supreme Court in *Calder v. Jones*, a printed defamation case.[53] In that case, it was held that the Florida defendants were subject to the jurisdiction of California for the allegedly defamatory content about a California actress published in a Florida-based magazine.[54] Instead of an elaborated test, the Supreme Court simply listed out a number of relevant factors:

> The allegedly libelous story concerned the California activities of a California resident. It impugned the professionalism of an entertainer whose television career was centered in California. The article was drawn from California sources, and the brunt of the harm, in terms both of respondent's emotional distress and the injury to her professional reputation, was suffered in California. In sum, California is the focal point both of the story and of the harm suffered. Jurisdiction over petitioners is therefore proper in California based on the "effects" of their Florida conduct in California.[55]

Lower courts struggled to derive a consistent formula to this "effect" test to capture the ruling of *Calder*. As one commentator puts it, *Calder* "has mystified courts and commentators alike since 1984".[56] Some courts developed it into a three-pronged test:

> (1) the defendant committed an intentional tort; (2) the plaintiff felt the brunt of the harm in the forum, such that the forum can be said to be the focal point of the harm; and (3) the defendant expressly aimed his tortious conduct at the forum, such that the forum can be said to be the focal point of the tortious activity.[57]

Alternatively, the Fourth Circuit in *Young v. New Haven* articulated a different test:

> We concluded that a State may, consistent with due process, exercise judicial power over a person outside of the State when that person (1) directs

52 ibid 287.
53 465 US 783 (1984).
54 ibid 791.
55 ibid 788–98.
56 Sarah H Ludington, 'Aiming at the Wrong Target: The Audience Targeting Test for Personal Jurisdiction in Internet Defamation Cases' (2012) 73 Ohio St LJ 541, 545.
57 ibid 544.

> electronic activity into the State, (2) with the manifested intent of engaging in business or other interactions within the State, and (3) that activity creates, in a person within the State, a potential cause of action cognizable in the State's courts.[58]

Despite the lack of a consensus formula, upon reviewing the judicial applications of these tests, three things are clear. First, the fact that the plaintiff suffered damage in the forum, without more, is not sufficient.[59] Second, the defamatory message being accessible online in the forum, without more, does not suffice to constitute a purposeful availment.[60] Third, the court must consider whether the forum is the "focal point" of the defamatory conduct.[61] As will be seen as follows, these key observations are informative to the development of the focalization approach for the EU. These points will be illustrated by the *Young* case.

The case stemmed from two Connecticut newspapers that allegedly published on the Internet defamatory comments about a prison warden in Virginia.[62] The issue was whether the defamatory comments were directed at Virginia, the forum state and where the prison warden resided. Applying *Calder* and the aforementioned test, the court held that the defamatory comments were not directed at Virginia.

Going back to the first observation, the fact that the Virginia warden's suffering of damage in Virginia, coupled with the defendants' knowledge of his Virginia base was insufficient for Virginia to assume jurisdiction.[63] The court was in the opinion that "Calder does not sweep that broadly",[64] even though damage suffered by the plaintiff may be a factor.[65] This is succinctly summarized by the court: "although the place that the plaintiff feels the alleged injury is plainly relevant to the jurisdictional inquiry, it must ultimately be accompanied by the defendant's own sufficient minimum contacts with the state if jurisdiction is to be upheld".[66]

Compared with the EU regime, one may argue that the focus on damage to the claimant under Article 7(2) makes the US experience incompatible. However, while the distinction between the US and EU on this point is well known, that US jurisdiction rules requires a link between the defendant and the forum, while the EU jurisdiction rules allow an alternative when there is a link between the claim

58 *Young v New Haven Advocate* 315 F3d 256, 263 (4th Cir 2002).

59 *Walden v Fiore* 571 US 277, 285 (2014) (The "minimum contacts" analysis does not depend on "the defendant's contacts with persons who reside there.").

60 *Young v New Haven Advocate* 315 F 3d 256, 263 (4th Cir 2002).

61 Although the court in *Young* did not incorporate the term "focal point" in the test, as we will see later, the court did consider whether Virginia the forum was the focal point in the application of the test.

62 *Young v New Haven Advocate* 315 F 3d 256, 258 (4th Cir 2002).

63 ibid 262.

64 ibid.

65 ibid.

66 ibid.

and the forum,[67] this difference does not render the US experience irrelevant to the proposed focalization approach to the EU. If the facts of the *Young* case happened in the EU (say, the newspapers are French and the warden is German), there is no question that the warden's centre of interest (Germany) will have jurisdiction as place (iv). However, what we are dealing with here is how to identify proper fora as place (ii), the original Mosaic fora. Thus, the US experience will help us decide whether damage in a third forum, say Austria where the claimant suffered damage, should have jurisdiction. Here, it informs us that mere damage in Austria shall not have jurisdiction.

Turning to the second observation, the Virginia warden also argued that the online articles published by the newspapers were accessible to Virginia.[68] However, the court made it clear that accessibility alone is not sufficient.[69] Instead, "[s]omething more than posting and accessibility is needed".[70] To do otherwise is to give every state jurisdiction.[71] The opposition against accessibility as sufficient basis of jurisdiction contrasts squarely against the Mosaic approach.

If damage to an in-forum plaintiff and mere accessibility are not sufficient jurisdictional bases, then what does it take for jurisdiction to be established? In line with the third observation, the court highlighted that Virginia must be the focal point of the defamation. Here, the court looked at both the outlets and contents of the articles. Both newspapers were local Connecticut papers, which did not solicit or do business in Virginia.[72] The articles were not in Virginia either. This is because "[t]he focus of the articles . . . was the Connecticut prisoner transfer policy and its impact on the transferred prisoners and their families back home in Connecticut".[73] Instead, "[t]he articles reported on and encouraged a public debate in Connecticut about whether the transfer policy was sound or practical for that state and its citizens".[74]

The court fell short in saying that the focal point can only be established by examining the outlets and contents of the defamatory materials. In fact, if one has

67 See Trevor C Hartley, 'Basic Principles of Jurisdiction in Private International Law: The European Union, the United States and England' (2022) 71 Int Comp LQ 211, 213. ("In the EU, links between the facts giving rise to the claim and the forum are regarded as an alternative to links between the defendant and the forum; in the US, on the other hand, there must always be links between the defendant and the forum, even if – where these are not strong enough – they may be supplemented by links between the facts of the claim and the defendant's activities in the forum. The basic idea of the U.S. theory of jurisdiction is that it is wrong – contrary to due process – to subject a defendant to the jurisdiction of the courts of a state unless he has done some voluntary act by which he might reasonably be regarded as submitting himself to that jurisdiction.").

68 *Young v New Haven Advocate* 315 F 3d 256, 261 (4th Cir 2002).

69 ibid 263.

70 ibid.

71 ibid ("Otherwise, a person placing information on the Internet would be subject to personal jurisdiction in every State" (internal citations omitted)).

72 ibid 260.

73 ibid 264.

74 ibid 263–64.

any criticism of the US rules, it lies in its uncertainty, as the courts may look at a number of factors to assess the focal point of the defamatory act. However, one can still identify some commonly considered factors. Beyond outlets and contents, courts also often look at the number of accesses in the forum of the online materials.[75] In addition, if the online message aims at inducing certain actions at the forum, this will also be considered as highly relevant.[76] Finally, as mentioned prior, damage suffered in the forum, while not itself sufficient as the sole basis of jurisdiction, can be a relevant factor as well.[77]

While less definitive than the mosaic approach, this multifaceted analysis aligns with aspects of EU jurisdictional principles. For example, in *edate* AG Cruz Villalón, in his suggestion of adding the "centre of gravity of the dispute" as an additional connecting factor with the competent jurisdiction in online defamation cases, it was suggested to include the nature of the information as an essential element.[78] This shows that a focalization approach modeled along the US experience is viable.

Applying this approach to the Gtflix TV case, it is unlikely that the defamatory statement is directed to France. As mentioned, in the lower court in France, it was found that the defamatory contents did not target the French audience.[79] Thus, the claimant will have to sue in either the Czech Republic (place (i) and (iii)) or Hungary (place iv). This approach thereby limits the total number of fora made available to the claimant and discourages forum shopping. It aligns with the need for a nuanced understanding of jurisdiction in the digital age, emphasizing intentional actions over mere incidental effects.

The comparison with the US approach shows that the EU has been too generous to the claimant. For example, if the defamatory messages made by the defendant in Gtflix TV were directed to the claimant's operations in Hungary, it would not even be possible under the US approach for the claimant to sue in the Czech Republic, its home jurisdiction. With the generous centre of interest rule in place, it is justifiable to limit the focalization approach along the narrower US purposeful availment test.[80] This comparison underscores the EU's leniency towards claimants and suggests adopting a narrower, US-inspired test for jurisdiction in online defamation, balancing claimant protection with defendant rights.

V. Conclusion

The Mosaic approach as affirmed by the ECJ is not ideal. While Gtflix does provide certainty, an important value in choice of law rules,[81] its promotion of forum

75 ibid 260. The court highlighted that one of the newspapers only had eight mail subscribers in Virginia.

76 *Majumdar v Fair*, 567 F Supp 3d 901, 911–13 (ND Ill 2021).

77 ibid 909.

78 Cases C-509/09 and C-161/10 *eDate Advertising v X and Martinez v MGN Ltd* EU:C:2011:192, Opinion of AG Cruz Villalón para 60.

79 See (n 34).

80 Note that the *Young* test is also under criticism for being too narrow, see (n 56) 543.

81 See Hartley (n 21) 987, 1003. ("Where policy considerations are relevant, the most important are the need to have a clear, easily ascertainable rule; the need to have a rule that cannot be manipulated by

shopping, parallel litigations, and potential threat to free speech of other countries leave much to be desired. A better approach is to refine it by giving jurisdiction only to those fora that the defendant intentionally directed its defamatory act at. The inspiration from the US legal framework could offer a more balanced solution to both the claimant and defendant.

---

one of the parties to the disadvantage of the other; and the need to provide for the expeditious resolution of disputes, if possible by giving the same court jurisdiction over all claims arising from the set of facts. In certain specific areas – for example, defamation – clear rules have been established by the CJEU that satisfy these requirements.").

12 Grounding a Right to Internet Access in the Right to an Adequate Standard of Living

Luke D. Graham

I. Introduction

Web3 represents a new foundational layer of the world wide web[1] and is understood as 'applications that run on top of the Internet'.[2] Access to the Internet, that is, 'a global pool of information and services, accessible locally through individual computer stations that are each part of a global system of interconnected computer networks',[3] is a prerequisite for access to Web3. Consequently, Web3 and the benefits thereof are rendered inaccessible and meaningless for those individuals who lack Internet access. Presently, rich discussion exists on the topic of a right to Internet access.[4] It is a topic that has 'slowly gained momentum around the world in recent years',[5] and within this debate, strong arguments have been made that such a right should be recognised.[6]

It is not the central purpose of this chapter to argue for the recognition of a right to Internet access. Rather, this chapter's central purpose is to suggest that *if* a right to Internet access is to be recognised, then it *can* be grounded in Article 11 (1) of the International Covenant on Economic, Social and Cultural Rights (ICESCR).[7] To fulfil this purpose, Section II illustrates the 'need' for a right to Internet access.

1 Dante Disparte, 'What Is Web3 and Why Should We Care' (*World Economic Forum*, 25 May 2022) 5 <https://www.weforum.org/agenda/2022/05/what-is-web3-why-care-future/> accessed 14 April 2023.

2 Margie Cheesman, *Web3 and Communities at Risk: Myths and Problems with Current Experiments* (Minderoo Centre for Technology and Democracy 2022) 11 <https://www.repository.cam.ac.uk/handle/1810/343141> accessed 14 April 2023.

3 Stephen Tully, 'A Human Right to Access the Internet? Problems and Prospects' (2014) 14 Hum Rights L Rev 175–76.

4 Toks Oyedemi, 'Internet Access as Citizen's Right? Citizenship in the Digital Age' (2015) 19 Citizensh Stud 450, 450.

5 Jonathon W Penney, 'Internet Access Rights: A Brief History and Intellectual Origins Contemporary Issues in Cyberlaw' (2011) 38 William Mitchell L Rev 10, 13.

6 See Merten Reglitz, 'The Human Right to Free Internet Access' (2020) 37 J Appl Philos 314; Merten Reglitz, 'The Socio-Economic Argument for the Human Right to Internet Access' [2023] Politics Philos Econ 1.

7 Article 11 (1) International Covenant on Economic, Social and Cultural Rights (ICESCR) (Adopted on 16 December 1966, A/RES/2200) 1966.

DOI: 10.4324/9781032618975-18

As this part makes clear, internet access is increasingly important to the realisation of a range of human rights and to everyday life. In light of the instrumental nature of Internet access, Section III proffers an alternative justification for the recognition of a right to Internet access – one that is grounded within the right to an adequate standard of living, as contained in Article 11 (1) ICESCR. A right to Internet access can be so recognised because it is required to ensure the realisation of a right to an adequate standard of living. At the same time, it is suggested that the right to an adequate standard of living is not fixed or static but is instead capable of responding to – and capturing – technological and societal advancements. This is required to ensure that the right to an adequate standard of living remains meaningful as living standards progress. Grounding a right to Internet access in Article 11 (1) ICESCR is advantageous for two key reasons. First, as illustrated in Section IV, grounding a right to Internet access within the right to an adequate standard of living allows both for the recognition of the role of Internet access in securing the right to an adequate standard of living and an independent right to Internet access. Consequently, such an approach mitigates concerns raised against subsuming a right to Internet access within other rights. Second, as is examined in Section V, anchoring a right to Internet access in Article 11 (1) ICESCR allows the established legal framework of the ICESCR to be applied to delimiting the right. This allows the content (rights and obligations) of a right to Internet access so understood to be tentatively outlined. This can serve to bring legitimacy and clarity to the delineation of a right to Internet access.

II. Justifying a Right to Internet Access

To fulfil the central purpose of this chapter – that is, to suggest that if a right to Internet access is to be recognised, then it can be grounded within the right to an adequate standard of living – the debate surrounding the recognition of a right to Internet access must first be examined. No right to Internet access can be found in the textual provisions of human rights treaties. The lack of a textual provision enshrining a right to Internet access means that there are difficulties in recognising a right to Internet access under international law or within human rights law.[8] Yet, the topic of a right to Internet access has been described as 'an important and timely issue'[9] and has 'gained high-profile international recognition'.[10] As Hert and Kloza observe, there exists 'a growing consensus that the Internet constitutes a value in itself and should therefore receive legal protection. A next step in this development is the plea to give the Internet (or its use) the status of a fundamental right'.[11]

8 Tully (n 3) 175.
9 ibid 195.
10 Penney (n 5) 12.
11 Paul De Hert and Dariusz Kloza, 'Internet (Access) as a New Fundamental Right. Inflating the Current Rights Framework?' (2012) 3 Eur JL Tech <https://ejlt.org/index.php/ejlt/article/view/123> accessed 14 April 2023.

A recurrent theme in the work of those seeking to assert a right to Internet access is the relationship between the Internet and existing human rights.[12] This theme is therefore instrumental in nature.[13] That is, a right to Internet access can be justified because Internet access engenders the realisation of other existing human rights. This evokes the concepts of interrelatedness, interdependence, and indivisibility. These concepts are central to understandings of human rights and recognise the fact that despite their distinctiveness as separate rights, the enjoyment of one right requires the enjoyment of others.[14] It has been argued that this instrumental value of Internet access is both 'practically indispensable'[15] and 'systemic[ally] indispensable'.[16] Both practical and systemic indispensability justify the recognition of a right to Internet access on instrumental grounds.[17] This instrumental nature of Internet access has two strands.[18] Both strands advance 'instrumental' justifications for the recognition of a right to Internet access.

The first of these strands is that the Internet creates 'new dangers and risks' that threaten existing human rights. [19] Consequently, existing human rights are not fit for purpose in the Internet context and as such are incapable of adequately upholding rights.[20] For this reason, there is a need to explicitly protect access to the Internet. Yilma recognises an expectation within the Internet Bill of Rights movement 'that there is – or should be – a human rights framework that better protects human rights on the Internet'.[21] A right to Internet access could provide this framework. The second strand is the inverse of – and is complementary to – the first. As Special Rapporteur on freedom of expression, La Rue recognised that 'the Internet has become an indispensable tool for realizing a range of human rights'. [22] Therefore, a right to Internet access can be recognised as being required to realise other rights.[23]

12 Oyedemi (n 4) 450.

13 Reglitz, 'The Human Right to Free Internet Access' (n 6) 317.

14 See Daniel J Whelan, *Indivisible Human Rights: A History* (U of Pennsylvania P 2010).

15 Reglitz, 'The Socio-Economic Argument for the Human Right to Internet Access' (n 6) 5. Here the term 'practically indispensable' is used to describe something that is 'sufficiently useful to deserve the status of a right in the strongest sense if it is in practice necessary or indispensable (i.e. "practically indispensable") for the realisation or enjoyment of an uncontroversial anchor right'.

16 ibid. Here the term systemically indispensable is used to describe something that is 'highly useful for a range of other rights'.

17 ibid 20.

18 'The protection and promotion of other well-established human rights'. See Reglitz, 'The Human Right to Free Internet Access' (n 6) 316.

19 Reglitz, 'The Socio-Economic Argument for the Human Right to Internet Access' (n 6) 22.

20 Kinfe Micheal Yilma, 'Bill of Rights for the 21st Century: Some Lessons from the Internet Bill of Rights Movement' (2022) 26 Int J Hum Rights 701, 5.

21 ibid.

22 Frank La Rue, 'Special Rapporteur on the Promotion and Protection of the Right to Freedom of Opinion and Expression, Report of the Special Rapporteur on Key Trends and Challenges to the Right of All Individuals to Seek, Receive and Impart Information and Ideas of All Kinds Through the Internet' (Human Rights Council 2011) UN Doc A/HRC/17/27 [85]; La Rue's work on this issue has been widely cited by those advancing arguments for a right to Internet access. See, Penney (n 5) 12; Hert and Kloza (n 11); Oyedemi (n 4) 450.

23 Reglitz, 'The Human Right to Free Internet Access' (n 6) 314.

Much of the focus on the role of the Internet in realising other human rights has been on civil and political rights.[24] In particular, the right to freedom of expression has been in sharp focus.[25] Reglitz has argued that a right to Internet access

> is already uniquely effective for the realisation of important political human rights (free speech, free association, and information); and . . . [i]f it would be governed appropriately, it would be extremely effective in protecting other basic human rights (i.e. life, liberty, and freedom from torture).[26]

This demonstrates the relationship that exists between the realisation of these civil and political rights and access to the Internet. More recently, there has been some focus on the role of a right to Internet access for the realisation of economic, social and cultural rights,[27] and this role is especially important in some contexts where 'Web3 technologies and applications have gained traction as solutions to the most intractable problems like humanitarian disaster, forced migration, socio-economic exclusion, and financial crises'.[28] For example, Szoszkiewicz has explored the right to benefit from scientific progress and its applications in Article 15 (1) (b) ICESCR. Not only this but the United Nations Committee on Economic, Social and Cultural Rights (CESCR) has engaged with the relationship between Internet access and the ICESCR. Specifically, the CESCR's work has largely focused on two areas: the right to education and cultural rights.[29] Beyond this, Hert and Kloza have recognised that a 'certain level of the protection of the Internet . . . could most probably also be derived from other rights' and that the right to an adequate standard of living can play a role in this regard.[30]

III. Grounding a Right to Internet Access Within the Right to an Adequate Standard of Living

Grounding a right to Internet access within this existing right is preferable than seeking to establish a new independent right and serves to bolster claims that such

24 Colin Crawford, 'Cyberplace: Defining a Right to Internet Access Through Public Accommodation Law' (2003) 76 Temple L Rev 225; Michael L Best, 'Can the Internet Be a Human Right?' (2004) 4 Hum Rights Hum Welf 23; Penney (n 5); Hert and Kloza (n 11); Tully (n 3); Oyedemi (n 4); Łukasz Szoszkiewicz, 'Internet Access as a New Human Right? State of the Art on the Threshold of 2020' [2018] Adam Mickiewicz Uni L Review 49; Prabhash K Dutta, 'Internet Access a Fundamental Right, Supreme Court Makes It Official: Article 19 Explained' *India Today* (2020); Reglitz, 'The Human Right to Free Internet Access' (n 6); Orit Fischman-Afori, 'Taking Global Administrative Law One Step Ahead: Online Giants and the Digital Democratic Sphere' (2022) 20 Int J Const L 1006; Yilma (n 20).

25 Dutta (n 24).

26 Reglitz, 'The Human Right to Free Internet Access' (n 6) 314–15.

27 Reglitz, 'The Socio-Economic Argument for the Human Right to Internet Access' (n 6) 20. These examples include the right to social security (p 10), the right to education (p 12), the right to health (p 13), the right to housing (p 13) and he right to work (p 14).

28 Cheesman (n 2) 5.

29 Szoszkiewicz (n 24) 56.

30 Hert and Kloza (n 11).

a right ought to be recognised.[31] This is because grounding a right to Internet access within established norms and practices may bring greater legitimacy. In the context of an Internet Bill of Rights, Yilma has explored the advantages of building on such established foundations and suggested that '[t]he central advantage of such an approach is that it brings some level of legitimacy to the instrument'.[32] This legitimacy offers to reduce resistance to the recognition of a right to Internet access.[33]

Article 11 (1) of the ICESCR recognises 'the right of everyone to an *adequate standard of living* for himself and his family, *including* adequate food, clothing and housing, and to the *continuous improvement of living conditions*'.[34] Notably for the purposes of this chapter, the textual provisions of Article 11 (1) do not include a right to Internet access. This is understandable given that, at the time of drafting of the ICESCR, these technologies did not exist. However, the fact that such technologies are not explicitly listed within the provision does not prevent Article 11 (1) ICESCR as being interpreted to include a right to Internet access, and a number of high-profile rights have been interpreted to derive from Article 11 (1).[35] Broader interpretation of Article 11 (1) ICESCR is possible with the right being understood as going beyond the necessities listed in Article 11 (1). As such, that which is required to secure an adequate standard of living goes beyond the textual provisions. The issue of contention is in determining exactly how far. As Eide recognises, the extent to which the right to an adequate standard of living goes beyond the textual provisions of Article 11 (1) ICESCR is subject to a range of context-specific considerations and cannot, therefore, 'be stated in general terms'.[36]

Internet access is required to enjoy adequate standards of living, and the text of Article 11 (1) also contains a right to the continuous improvement of living conditions. The right to continuous improvement of living conditions has been largely ignored in scholarship.[37] Whilst a recent edited collection has sought to redress this neglect,[38] 'much remains to be done in order to fully flesh out what such a right might mean'.[39] A previous exploration of the relationship between poverty and the

31 Szoszkiewicz (n 24) 57.

32 Yilma (n 20) 4.

33 ibid.

34 Article 11 (1) ICESCR. *My emphasis.*

35 The right to adequate water and the right to adequate sanitation are accepted in human rights orthodoxy as deriving from Article 11 (1) of the ICESCR. See Luke D Graham, *International Human Rights Law and Destitution: An Economic, Social and Cultural Rights Perspective* (Routledge 2022) 65–71.

36 Asbjorn Eide, 'Adequate Standard of Living' in Daniel Moeckli and others (eds), *International Human Rights Law* (3rd edn, OUP 2018) 187.

37 Jessie Hohmann and Beth Goldblatt, 'Introduction: Situating the Right to Continuous Improvement of Living Conditions and Considering Its Interpretations and Applications' in Jessie Hohmann and Beth Goldblatt (eds), *The Right to the Continuous Improvement of Living Conditions: Responding to Complex Global Challenges* (Hart Publishing 2021) 1–18, 4.

38 Jessie Hohmann and Beth Goldblatt (eds), *The Right to the Continuous Improvement of Living Conditions: Responding to Complex Global Challenges* (Hart Publishing 2021).

39 Jessie Hohmann, 'Sources for a Nascent Interpretation of the Right to Continuous Improvement of Living Conditions: The Travaux Préparatoires and the Work of the CESCR' in Jessie Hohmann and

right to continuous improvement of living conditions has argued that the resources/goods required to realise the right to an adequate standard of living and the right to continuous improvement of living conditions should advance in line with societal and technological advancements.[40] As a response to poverty, as understood by the CESCR, the right to continuous improvement of living conditions may be understood as a right to the continuous improvement of 'the resources, capabilities, choices, security and power necessary for the enjoyment of an adequate standard of living and other civil, cultural, economic, political and social rights'. [41] This right allows the meaning of adequate standards of living to develop in line with societal and technological developments. Consequently, the right to an adequate standard of living can be understood to include a right to Internet access. Thus, the existing provisions of the ICESCR may be understood to support a right to Internet access, and the right to continuous improvement of living conditions can legitimise claims that the right to an adequate standard of living should be interpreted to include other necessities for life.

IV. An Independent Right to Internet Access as Deriving From the Right to an Adequate Standard of Living

Concerns have been raised against grounding a right to Internet access within other rights. Reglitz fears that 'if access to the Internet as a right is merely subsumed under, or only seen as an instantiation of, a particular other right, a person can lose their right to access the Internet if that grounding right is legitimately curtailed'.[42] An advantage of understanding a right to Internet access as deriving from Article 11 (1) of the ICESCR is that this would understand the right to Internet access both

Beth Goldblatt (eds), *The Right to the Continuous Improvement of Living Conditions: Responding to Complex Global Challenges* (Hart Publishing 2021) 19–40, 40.

40 Luke D Graham, 'The Right to the Continuous Improvement of Living Conditions as a Response to Poverty' in Jessie Hohmann and Beth Goldblatt (eds), *The Right to the Continuous Improvement of Living Conditions: Responding to Complex Global Challenges* (Hart Publishing 2021) 65–85, 77; see, in particular, 'Thus, in the future, if the rights forming the subject matter of the right to continuous improvement of living conditions are "fully" realised, three possible outcomes exist. The first of these outcomes is that the right to continuous improvement of living conditions becomes superfluous and that any claim to further improvement is eliminated. The second outcome is that the full realisation of the rights related to living standards we envision today in no way relate to the standards of living required of the future. This would require continuing improvement. *The third outcome is that the right to continuous improvement of living conditions enters a state of hibernation only to awaken when societal and human rights advances (such as new standards of well-being, new resources and goods, and new rights to these advancements) occur. The second and third of these outcomes are preferred as they account for relativist understandings of living conditions, suggesting that there is no limit to the continuity of improvement within the right to continuous improvement of living conditions.*' Emphasis added.

41 Committee on Economic and Social Rights CESCR, 'Substantive Issues Arising in The Implementation of The International Covenant on Economic, Social and Cultural Rights: Poverty and the International Covenant on Economic, Social and Cultural Rights' (2001) UN Doc E/C 12/2001/10' [8].

42 Reglitz, 'The Socio-Economic Argument for the Human Right to Internet Access' (n 6) 21.

as part of a greater whole (the right to an adequate standard of living) and as an independent right.[43]

Previous attempts have been made to suggest that Article 11 (1) recognises only 'a right to an adequate standard of living' but not rights to the constituent parts of this provision.[44] These 'simply not tenable' suggestions were dismissed by Alston who,[45] acting in his capacity of Chairperson of the CESCR, indicated that the right to the overall package of adequate standard of living rights entails a right to the constituent parts.[46] Alston's reasoning is as follows. The practice of UN Bodies in combination with a failure to object to such practice supports the independent nature of the rights contained within Article 11 (1).[47] This first ground, made in the context of the right to housing in which there is a long history of clear and consistent practice, is less applicable to a right to Internet access specifically. This is because despite recognising the 'positive obligation of States to "facilitate" access to the Internet under the right to freedom of opinion and expression', the UN Bodies have fallen short of directly recognising a right to Internet access.[48] Rather, they have selectively focused on 'protecting existing offline rights online'.[49] Nevertheless, this reasoning can be applied to the practice of UN Bodies in treating Article 11 (1) rights as independent rights. Thus, rejecting the independent nature of the rights contained within Article 11 (1) 'would directly contradict innumerable resolutions adopted by every United Nations body from the General Assembly and the Economic and Social Council to the Commission on Human Rights and many others'.[50] More so, such an interpretation is logically required.[51] It is therefore well settled that Article 11 (1) contains both (i) a composite right and (ii) rights to its constituent parts.[52] Framed in this way, anchoring a right to Internet access within the right to an adequate standard of living addresses the concerns raised by Reglitz.[53]

43 Elsewhere I have examined how Article 11 (1) has been interpreted to contain independent rights. Luke D Graham, 'Reasserting the Right to Adequate Clothing in International Human Rights Law' (2024) 24 Hum Rights L Rev 1.

44 See Philip Alston, 'Letter Addressed by the Chairperson to the Committee on Economic, Social and Cultural Rights to Mr. Wally N'Dow, Assistant Secretary-General, United Nations Centre for Human Settlements (Habitat)' UN Doc E/C.12/1995/18, Annex VII' (1995) These arguments were made in the context of the right to housing. However, this chapter expands this reasoning to the constituent parts of Article 11 (1) more broadly.

45 ibid 8.

46 ibid 10.

47 ibid.

48 Yilma (n 20) 5.

49 Reglitz, 'The Human Right to Free Internet Access' (n 6) 314.

50 Alston (n 44) 9.

51 ibid 10.

52 Graham, *International Human Rights Law and Destitution* (n 35) 54–55.

53 See (n 42).

V. Rights and Obligations Stemming From an Article 11 (1) Derived Right to Internet Access

Alongside addressing Reglitz's concerns, grounding a right to Internet access within the framework of Article 11 (1) ICESCR offers a route to delimiting the scope of the right. Whilst '[t]he question [of] what a human right to Internet access entails is a crucial one',[54] '[t]here is no shared understanding on how such a right can or ought to be defined'.[55] Consequently, it is not clear what rights claims and corresponding obligations stem from a right to Internet access.

Whilst presuming that a right to Internet access entails 'the right to connect to the Internet without any kind of state interference with that right of access',[56] Penney recognises 'this simple explanation masks more complex issues', such as whether a right to Internet access goes beyond this negative understanding to include positive obligations.[57] The distinction between positive and negative obligations is, however, not so clear-cut, with Wibye recognising that '[a]ll human rights require for their fulfilment both acts and forbearances, and so the need for active measures will necessarily feature even in cases that hinge on negative duties'.[58] For example, Reglitz suggests that '[n]egatively, public authorities should protect Internet access from arbitrary interferences by states and private companies'.[59] This is not purely a negative obligation. The state can refrain from interfering (a negative act), but Reglitz's suggestion here that the state should also protect from arbitrary interferences from private actors is a positive one.[60] As such, considered through the lens of the justifications of a right to Internet access, it is clear that negative obligations alone are not enough to ensure this right.[61] Positive obligations are also required. Such positive obligations may include 'expanding Internet infrastructure, ensuring its affordability, and the importance of building digital literacy in the society, particularly in the most disadvantaged and marginalized groups'.[62] Similarly, Reglitz has argued that 'public authorities should provide Internet access free of charge (in whatever form) for those who are unable to afford it and (as mentioned earlier) basic digital skills training for all citizens'.[63] What is clear from the existing literature, and from these observations, is that a right to adequate Internet access is not an absolute right. This means that a right to adequate Internet access can lawfully

54 Reglitz, 'The Socio-Economic Argument for the Human Right to Internet Access' (n 6) 1.
55 Tully (n 3) 186.
56 Penney (n 5) 15.
57 ibid.
58 Johan Vorland Wibye, 'Beyond Acts and Omissions – Distinguishing Positive and Negative Duties at the European Court of Human Rights' (2022) 23 Hum Rights Rev 479, 499.
59 Reglitz, 'The Socio-Economic Argument for the Human Right to Internet Access' (n 6) 21.
60 Below the tripartite typology of obligations in which the obligation to 'protect' from third party interference is examined. See (n 68–73).
61 See s II.
62 Szoszkiewicz (n 24) 59.
63 Reglitz, 'The Socio-Economic Argument for the Human Right to Internet Access' (n 6) 21.

be interfered with. It would therefore be a qualified right,[64] one subject to lawful interferences.[65] This may result in full or partial restriction to Internet access.

Even despite these initial offerings, there is a lack of clarity concerning the scope of the obligations, which may be said to stem from a right to Internet access. Anchoring a right to Internet access within the right to an adequate standard of living addresses this by allowing the legal framework of Article 11 (1) to be applied. This is because the independent rights that form a part of the right to an adequate standard of living each have their own legal content and entail legal obligations for states.[66] Grounding a right to Internet access within the right to an adequate standard of living offers a sensible route to delimiting the content of such a right, one that recognises 'the essential importance of international co-operation based on free consent' and as such may legitimise calls for international assistance and co-operation in realising the right to adequate Internet access.[67]

Whilst it is beyond the scope of this chapter to fully flesh out what obligations may or may not be said to stem from a right to Internet access so understood, this chapter places a right to Internet access within the context of the right to an adequate standard of living to tentatively sketch out the scope of this right. In doing so, this chapter places a right to Internet access within the framework of Article 11 (1) ICESCR and ICESCR provisions more broadly. To be expressly clear, a right to Internet access as grounded in a right to an adequate standard of living must be understood as a right to adequate Internet access. This concept of adequacy acts as a crucial qualifier in delimiting the right. Thus, it is not a right to unlimited, unfettered Internet access.

The tripartite typology of obligations recognise 'that all human rights impose three types of obligations upon States parties: the obligations to respect, to protect, and to fulfil'.[68] This tripartite typology has been repeatedly affirmed in the context of the ICESCR by the UN. CESCR.[69] The tripartite typology captures both positive

64 Tully (n 3) 193.

65 ibid 193–94.

66 Jessie Hohmann, 'Protecting the Right to Housing in England: A Context of Crisis' (*Just Fair*, 2015) 17–18 <https://www.qmul.ac.uk/law/media/law/docs/news/154442.pdf> accessed 7 February 2020.

67 Article 11 (1) ICESCR contains the obligation to 'take appropriate steps to ensure the realization of this right, recognizing to this effect the essential importance of international co-operation based on free consent'.

68 Luke D Graham, 'The Right to Clothing and Personal Protective Equipment in the Context of COVID-19' (2022) 26 Int J Hum Rights 30, 41.

69 See Committee on Economic and Social Rights CESCR, 'General Comment No 12: The Right to Adequate Food (art 11)' (1999) UN Doc E/C.12/1999/5 [15]; Committee on Economic and Social Rights CESCR, 'General Comment No 13: The Right to Education (art 13 of the Covenant)' (1999) UN Doc E/C12/1999/10 [46]; Committee on Economic and Social Rights CESCR, 'General Comment No 14: The Right to the Highest Attainable Standard of Health (Article 12 of the International Covenant on Economic, Social and Cultural Rights' (2000) UNDoc E/C12/2000/4 [33]; Committee on Economic and Social Rights CESCR, 'General Comment No 15: The Right to Water (arts 11 and 12 of the International Covenant on Economic, Social and Cultural Rights)' (2002) UNDoc E/C12/2002/11 [20]; Committee on Economic and Social Rights CESCR, 'General Comment No 17: The Right of Everyone to Benefit from the Protection of the Moral and Material Interests Resulting

and negative obligations and '[e]ach element of the tripartite typology of obligations has a generally applicable nucleus.'[70] The obligation to respect may be understood as an obligation to refrain from interfering with the enjoyment of a right.[71] The obligation to protect may be understood as an obligation to take measures that prevent individuals or enterprises from interfering with the enjoyment of a right.[72] The obligation to fulfil may be understood as an obligation to take positive steps intended to further the enjoyment of a right.[73] As is clear, the obligations that have already been proposed to stem from a right to Internet access neatly fit within this typology.

Greater clarity is provided through considering a right to Internet access within the general obligations of the ICESCR. This is especially with respect to whether a right to Internet access grounded in Article 11 (1) of the ICESCR would create immediate or progressive obligations. ICESCR Article 2(1) of the ICESCR states that:

> Each State Party to the present Covenant undertakes to take steps, individually and through international assistance and co-operation, especially economic and technical, to the maximum of its available resources, with a view to achieving progressively the full realization of the rights recognized in the present Covenant by all appropriate means, including particularly the adoption of legislative measures.

This progressive realisation clause is central to understandings of the nature of obligations stemming from the ICESCR. Progressive realisation and maximum available resources provide for varying levels of obligations between contexts.[74] Consequently, most obligations under the ICESCR are not immediate in nature.

---

from Any Scientific, Literary or Artistic Production of Which He or She Is the Author (art 15, para 1 (C), Of the Covenant)' (2005) UNDoc E/C12/GC/1 [28]; Committee on Economic and Social Rights CESCR, 'General Comment No 18: The Right to Work' (2006) UN Doc E/C12/GC/18 [22]; Committee on Economic and Social Rights CESCR, 'General Comment No 19: The Right to Social Security (art 9)' (2007) UN Doc E/C.12/GC/19 [43]; Committee on Economic and Social Rights CESCR, 'General Comment No 21: Right of Everyone to Take Part in Cultural Life (art 15, para 1(a), of the International Covenant on Economic, Social and Cultural Rights)' (2009) UN Doc E/C12/GC/21 [48]; Committee on Economic and Social Rights CESCR, 'General Comment No 24: State Obligations Under the International Covenant on Economic, Social and Cultural Rights in the Context of Business Activities' (2017) UN Doc E/C12/GC/24 [10]–[11].

70 Graham, 'The Right to Clothing and Personal Protective Equipment in the Context of COVID-19' (n 68) 41.

71 See Sigrun I Skogly, *Beyond National Borders: States' Human Rights Obligations in International Cooperation* (Intersentia 2006) 68–69.

72 See Magdalena Sepúlveda Carmona, 'The Obligations of "International Assistance and Cooperation" Under the International Covenant on Economic, Social and Cultural Rights: A Possible Entry Point to a Human Rights Based Approach to Millennium Development Goal 8' (2009) 13 Int J Hum Rights 86, 90.

73 See ibid.

74 Committee on Economic and Social Rights CESCR, 'General Comment No 3: The Nature of States Parties' Obligations' (United Nations 1990) UN Doc E/1991/23 [9]; see also, Philip Alston and Ryan

However, immediate obligations stem from the concept of the minimum core obligation. The CESCR has read the minimum core obligation into Article 2 (1) ICESCR.[75] This is an obligation of every state party to realise, 'as a matter of priority', the 'minimum essential levels of each of the rights' enshrined in the ICESCR.[76] The minimum core obligation is immediate in nature and consequently, failure to achieve the realisation of the minimum core obligation constitutes a prima facie breach of the State's obligations in that it is a violation of the 'corresponding core rights'.[77] That is, unless a state is able to demonstrate the 'defence' of an inability to realise the minimum core obligation because of a lack of available resources. To rely on this 'defence' the state must demonstrate that it has made every effort to prioritise its resources to fulfil this obligation.[78] Thus, a right to Internet access grounded in the right to an adequate standard of living would create mainly progressive obligations with some minimum core obligations that would be immediate in nature. Although the General Comments of the CESCR have provided some guidance as to the minimum core obligations of specific rights, some difficulty in determining the extent of the minimum core obligation still exists.[79]

If a right to Internet access is to be grounded within Article 11 (1) ICESCR, future work will be required to determine a minimum core of a right to Internet access. However, at this stage, it is appropriate to indicate that such a minimum core would plausibly contain several key elements. The first of these is that Internet access is enjoyed in-line with the principles of equality and non-discrimination. These principles underpin the entire ambit of human rights law. Article 2 (2) ICESCR contains an undertaking 'to guarantee that the rights enunciated in the present Covenant will be exercised without discrimination of any kind'.[80] Beyond equality and non-discrimination, it is plausible to suggest that any failure to respect, protect, or fulfil a right to Internet access must be non-arbitrary and as such subject to a requirement of lawful process. This is a procedural obligation and one that extends beyond merely withdrawing access to the Internet. It could include having a lawful

Goodman, *International Human Rights* (OUP 2013) 316; see also, Graham, *International Human Rights Law and Destitution* (n 35) 45.

75 David Bilchitz, 'Towards A Reasonable Approach to The Minimum Core: Laying the Foundations for Future Socioeconomic Rights Jurisprudence' (2003) 19 S Afr Hum Rights 1, 12; see also, Lillian Chenwi, 'Unpacking "Progressive Realisation", Its Relation to Resources, Minimum Core and Reasonableness, and Some Methodological Considerations for Assessing Compliance' (2013) 46 De Jure 742, 754.

76 CESCR, 'General Comment No 3: The Nature of States Parties' Obligations' (n 74) [10]; see also, Robert E Robertson, 'Measuring State Compliance with the Obligation to Devote the "Maximum Available Resources" to Realizing Economic, Social, and Cultural Rights' (1994) 16 Hum Rights Q 692.

77 Amrei Müller, 'Limitations to and Derogations from Economic, Social and Cultural Rights' (2009) 9 Hum Rights L Rev 557, 581.

78 CESCR, 'General Comment No 3: The Nature of States Parties' Obligations' (n 74) [10].

79 Magdalena Sepulveda, *The Nature of the Obligations under the International Covenant on Economic, Social and Cultural Rights* (Intersentia 2003) 367; Sandra Liebenberg, *Socio-Economic Rights. Adjudication under a Transformative Constitution* (Juta 2010) 150.

80 art 2 (2) ICESCR.

process in place for, *inter alia*, monitoring, censorship, and invading privacy to give some examples. It is feasible, also, that a context-specific minimum can be determined concerning both quantity and quality (i.e., speed) of Internet access. It is beyond the scope of this chapter to propose such a minimum. However, it should be tied to the instrumental nature of Internet access in any given context. It follows that a society in which more Internet access is required to realise other rights may have a higher immediate obligation for the right to Internet access.

In General Comments addressing other economic, social, and cultural rights, the CESCR has clarified States Parties' obligations under the ICESCR.[81] Although the CESCR's interpretation of these obligations has developed throughout its life course, it is evident from the CESCR's most recent General Comments addressing obligations stemming from Article 11 that ESCRs have a normative content that includes a core content and a wider scope of the right.[82] As such, the minimum core obligation only forms a part of the broader normative content of economic, social, and cultural rights. The broader normative framework has, in the context of other Article 11 (1) ICESCR rights, been understood to include several elements. These elements determine the adequacy of rights realisation and '[i]n determining adequacy, the CESCR has referred to such factors as availability, quality, accessibility (both physical and economic) and cultural acceptability (AAAQ-framework)'.[83] Availability means that 'the substance of the right is available for use and/or consumption'.[84] This would mean that the infrastructure required to access the Internet is available for use. The state would have obligations to ensure the availability of this infrastructure and would have freedom as to how best to achieve this. For example, through state investment, public-private partnerships, or private companies. Beyond availability, 'accessibility relates to physical access'.[85] Thus, if the infrastructure is available, states will have obligations to ensure that individuals are able to physically access that infrastructure. For example, by reducing barriers to physical access and also through ensuring that infrastructure is designed to allow physical access. Affordability also forms a part of (economic) accessibility, and the state must ensure that cost does not act as a barrier to accessing adequate Internet access. Acceptability relates to social participation and is of particular relevance to

81 Graham, 'The Right to Clothing and Personal Protective Equipment in the Context of COVID-19' (n 68) 35.

82 See Committee on Economic and Social Rights (CESCR), 'General Comment No 14: The Right to the Highest Attainable Standard of Health (art 12 of the International Covenant on Economic, Social and Cultural Rights)' UNDoc E/C12/2000/4 (2000); CESCR, 'General Comment No 15: The Right to Water (arts 11 and 12 of the International Covenant on Economic, Social and Cultural Rights)' UN Doc E/C12/2002/11 (2002).

83 Graham, 'The Right to Clothing and Personal Protective Equipment in the Context of COVID-19' (n 68) 36; ee footnote 58, CESCR, 'General Comment No 15: The Right to Water (arts 11 and 12 of the International Covenant on Economic, Social and Cultural Rights)' (n 69) 15; see footnote 12 CESCR, 'General Comment No. 12: The Right to Adequate Food (Art.11)' (n 69) 12.

84 Graham, 'The Right to Clothing and Personal Protective Equipment in the Context of COVID-19' (n 68) 36.

85 ibid 37.

ensuring that when Internet access is available and acceptable, that is in a way that is responsive to the needs of particular groups. Quality could be broadly interpreted in the context of adequate Internet access. It could perhaps relate to the amount of data to which individuals ought to be entitled, or to the speed of Internet access. As is clear, the AAAQ framework is but that – a framework – but it may serve as a useful starting point for further delineating a right to adequate Internet access.

VI. Conclusion

It has been suggested that '[n]ew technological advances, for instance, can lead to new rights'.[86]

This chapter argues that the right to an adequate standard of living is capable of capturing these advancements. Thus, a right to Internet access should be recognised as an economic, social and cultural right grounded in Article 11 (1) of the ICESCR. This leads to the recognition of an independent right, one that can employ the economic and social rights framework to provide greater clarity in understanding its scope. This chapter has therefore advanced an alternative justification for – and approach to – recognising a right to *adequate* Internet access. Such Internet access is a prerequisite for interaction with Web3 and the many advantages (and disadvantages) that flow from this technology. However, it is also instrumental in the realisation of a range of human rights, and as Reglitz observes:

> [t]he acknowledgment of a human right to Internet access would have considerable theoretical and practical significance. Theoretically, it would present a clear case of how momentous technological innovations require us to reconsider our human rights. Practically, a human right to Internet access would change the support and protection people could demand from public authorities concerning their opportunities to use the Internet.[87]

Not only may this serve to 'rectify deficient Internet access and ensure greater equality for deprived groups', but this may also 'propel the political willingness of States into a legally binding commitment' by bringing to bear the 'unquestioned moral authority of human rights discourse'.[88]

86 Reglitz, 'The Socio-Economic Argument for the Human Right to Internet Access' (n 6) 8.
87 ibid 2.
88 Tully (n 3) 189.

Index

Note: Page numbers in *italics* indicate figures, **bold** indicate tables in the text, and references following "n" refer notes.

FSC
www.fsc.org
MIX
Papier | Fördert
gute Waldnutzung
FSC® C083411

Kolibri 360 GmbH
Ferdinand-Jühlke-Straße 7
99095 Erfurt, Deutschland
produktsicherheit@kolibri360.de